HAPPIER PEOPLE
HEALTHIER PLANET

HAPPIER PEOPLE
HEALTHIER PLANET

TERESA BELTON

SilverWood

Published in 2014 by SilverWood Books

SilverWood Books Ltd
30 Queen Charlotte Street, Bristol, BS1 4HJ
www.silverwoodbooks.co.uk

ISBN 978-1-78132-260-4 (paperback)
ISBN 978-1-78132-261-1 (ebook)

British Library Cataloguing in Publication Data
A CIP catalogue record for this book is available from
the British Library

Set in Bembo by SilverWood Books
Printed on responsibly sourced paper

In praise of the qualities of kindness and compassion, independent thinking and unusual insight, creativity, integrity, courage and determination; characteristics possessed by both my parents, Betty and Henry, to whom I am forever grateful. Such human attributes are the foundations on which a better world can be built.

Contents

Acknowledgements

Many colleagues, friends and strangers have played a part in the construction of this book. Firstly, I am enormously grateful to all those people, most of whom I have never met, who took up the challenge of contributing to the Modest Consumers study which lies at its heart. I owe a particular debt to those whom I interviewed in addition to their completing a searching questionnaire; I greatly enjoyed my conversations with them and learnt a lot.

My warm gratitude goes too to the readers of draft chapters, particularly for the generous time and careful thought devoted to critiquing several chapters each by Alex Haxeltine, Kath Kite and Ellie Phillips. I have also appreciated the comments of Caroline Brown, Alan Cottey, Anne Dismorr, Kathleen Lane, Darren Love, Jo Mack, Anna Magyar, Mark McNay, Ken Moss, Chris Roberts, Barbara Walker, Jackie Watson and Sharon Weekley.

As I have found myself exploring beyond my own sphere of knowledge I have been really grateful to Neil Adger, Patrick Bateson, David Baulcombe and Philip Corr for their willing sharing of their expertise.

I have also much valued the books kindly given to me by Michael Bassey and Patrick Bateson, and lent by David Baulcombe, Caroline Brown, Peter Clarke, Mick Collins, Rich Faulding, Terry Haydn, Diana Stephenson and Barbara Zamorski, in the piecing together of my thinking; as well as the suggestions for further reading made by David Ball, Richard House, Tim Kasser and Rupert Read. I thank them all.

I also appreciate the support of Nigel Norris in his enthusiasm for the original idea for this book and our discussions about the primary research it involved; of Chris Walton, Pauline Chinnery, Sarah Rockliff and Mark Scott in telling me about their experiences of out-door initiatives with children; of Brenda Crowe in generously allowing me to publish some lines from personal correspondence, and of Libby Allen for her kind typing of questionnaires. My warm thanks go too, of course, to my family, Pete, Mother, James, Thomas and Ben, for all their thoughts, practical help and patience.

Preface

Riding the Tandem of Personal Wellbeing and Environmental Sustainability

The beautiful, awe-inspiring, intricate biophysical world that is home to human beings and countless other species is becoming more degraded day by day. Due to the excessive demands that humans make on the environment for the provision of more than we actually need, the Earth's capacity to furnish our essential requirements for water, food, land and raw materials is measurably declining. And yet, for the many of us whose basic needs are fully met, all the other stuff we have and all the ever-increasing convenience and comfort, the luxury even, has not increased the sum of our happiness. The norm of our society, and of many others, is to desire the acquisition of new possessions and the enjoyment of more ease throughout our lives, and to expect to meet any perceived need or want in return for money. But, if anything, people are less satisfied now than they were before the culture of consumption took hold; it has conditioned most of us to want more, however much we already have.

Happier People Healthier Planet sets out to draw disparate aspects of human experience together into a coherent whole. Unusual in the breadth of its sweep, it explores the many ways in which the two issues of the cultivation of personal wellbeing and the shrinking of unsustainable material expectations can be understood as bound together. The book is intended to be a thoughtful and thought-provoking exploration of how the minutely personal can ultimately have global ramifications, and of what we need to do as individuals and society to promote flourishing. Developing such understandings will help us to shape both more fulfilled individual lives and a rosier collective future.

Because the pleasures and satisfactions attained by accumulating wealth and buying things, as our economic system pushes us to do, are neither deep nor long-lasting, I decided to seek a better sense of the sources of true wellbeing by investigating the lives and perspectives of some of those people who find happiness in relatively low-consumption lifestyles in Britain. These tell a very different story from that of advertisers and business leaders. The insights offered by these modest consumers animate the discussions of the book with the vitality of lived experience and a fascinating variety of personal views. They throw down a gauntlet, while offering a hand; quietly or spiritedly they reveal some rewarding and damage-free ways of seeing and being.

1

Line Drawing: A Sketch of the Contemporary Landscape

While the potential of green technology to improve the condition of the global environment is huge, technology alone cannot achieve nearly enough to sustain life as we know it; and its potential to enhance wellbeing is strictly limited. We therefore have to look at how we can change ourselves and our culture in order to build more promising prospects for ourselves and our world.

I will advance four simple propositions:

1. Consumption patterns in the developed world, and to which many in the developing world aspire, are doing irreversible damage to the global climate and other aspects of the environment, yet they are entirely unnecessary for leading a happy and satisfying life. This is hardly a novel idea but one which I shall explore in new ways.
2. Individuals who find their own lives satisfying and who feel a sense of close personal relationship with the natural world are likely to behave in ways that are less ecologically harmful than others.
3. To be able to enjoy to the full the many sources of real wellbeing, we need certain skills and qualities; these require cultivation.
4. We also need to develop those emotional capacities which will help us to respond as constructively as possible to inevitable shifts in the parameters of life resulting from the ecological impacts of past and present consumption; and individuals with high levels of wellbeing will be more able to adapt successfully to changing conditions.

It is not material wealth but non-material assets, such as strong relationships, active engagement, and thriving communities, that enrich our personal and social wellbeing. Thus the two issues of the Earth's declining hospitality resulting from over-consumption, and the unhappiness to be found in today's Britain, a relatively rich country, can be seen to be related to each other in a number of respects. The need for an earnest reappraisal of everyday life in order to address these issues could not be more urgent. But I do not set out a blue print of measures to this end. Rather, I explore the territory of fundamental human experience, showing how different facets of it can be seen to be interrelated, and how one kind of change thus has the potential to influence another. Much of the discussion is informed and illustrated by the findings of the study I conducted in order to investigate the views and experience of individuals who live lives of relatively modest material consumption which they find satisfying, and is thus rooted in real life. But first of all I will sketch some of the notable features of the wide-ranging landscape which the book sets out to address. The view may seem bleak to begin with but encouraging signs emerge. Although many of the details are particular to Britain, the general picture is by no means exclusive to the UK and many of the observations are far more widely applicable.

First Perspective: Our Culture of Consumption

So much stuff

Our social environment is awash with goods; every newspaper and magazine, every television, computer and cinema screen, and most postal deliveries, present us with messages egging us on to buy, buy, buy. As fashions change and technologies develop many of us like to purchase the latest goods, if we have the money – and maybe even if we don't. But although this pattern seems quite normal it is a relatively recent development. Well within the lifetime of many people living today it was common to have just one Sunday best outfit, worn with pride; families were delighted if they were able to sit together round a small television in the living room; and it was not uncommon for there to be only an outside toilet. But over the last fifty years the picture of material consumption has changed radically. Today we have so many clothes that it is reckoned that the average person wears only twenty per cent of their wardrobe eighty per cent of the time, so most of their clothes remain rarely worn.[1] The extreme profligacy that exists in some quarters regarding apparel is illustrated by the new breed of men, contemporary 'dandies' who, it has been reported, think nothing of spending around £1,000 a month on clothes.[2] Most homes have a television in the kitchen and/or bedrooms as well as a large one in the living room; multiple bathrooms and toilets per house, and en suite facilities, are commonplace. Expectations have changed out of all recognition in a few decades. This is not surprising in light of the doubling of average income in the UK between 1970 and 2010.[3]

Buying beyond our means

From the late 1960's until the early 2000's business boomed. More shops and mail-order catalogues opened than ever before, shopping hours were extended to allow Sunday trading and twenty-four hour opening of supermarkets, and the internet and credit cards made it possible to buy almost anything at almost any time. Shopping, it was said, became the nation's favourite pastime. The evidence of its popularity is manifest in the levels of debt due to personal consumption reached before the credit crisis erupted in 2008 and the unprecedented cuts to public expenditure began in 2011: according to Credit Action, a national money education charity, there were more credit cards in the UK in 2005 (74.6 million) than people (about 60 million). Consumerism became part of life at an increasingly young age, and the Personal Finance Education Group revealed that over half of England's teenagers had been or were in debt by the time they were 17; 90% of this age group worried about their money and spending but tended to think of overdrafts and credit cards as easy ways to spend more than they earned, or to buy things they couldn't normally afford.[4]

At the end of June 2007 debt per household (excluding mortgages) averaged £8,841; and 24.5m transactions, worth £1.4bn, were being spent on plastic cards every day.[5] It is salutary to contrast this picture with that of the tribal peoples who still choose to live outside mainstream society, whose ancestral lands are integral to their lives, providing their livelihoods and sustaining their ways of life in an immediate and far less destructive relationship with the natural world.[6] However, the great majority of human beings have not lived in this way for a long time. For most, the opportunity to increase wealth and comfort, if it has come, has not been turned down. There are few whose desire for and expectation of goods and ease does not go substantially further than their basic needs.

A long-lived characteristic

Human beings have always been enthusiastic consumers. The pursuit of wealth and all that it makes possible has motivated people throughout history. Archaeological finds show that humans have had a love of artefacts from when they were first able to fashion them. The last two or three generations in the West have simply led the way in taking these impulses to an

15

extreme; now the growing middle classes in other countries, most notably the BRIC countries, Brazil, Russia, India and China, are following suit. At one time it was only the wealthy who could enjoy consumption much beyond basic requirements but the coming of mass production, combined with increased affluence across the board in the West, has enabled the great majority in industrial economies to do so. Consumerism has certainly meant the pursuit of comfort and liberation from drudgery.[7] But more than that, consumption "gradually freed itself from being functionally tied to 'needs' and necessities to assume its own distinctive character and purpose – propelled, above all else, by its own *pleasurability*".[8] So pleasurable is it, indeed, that it means that you might choose to 'shop till you drop'.

Expectations

According to a 28-year-old journalist, one of a generation who find it very difficult to save the money to buy their own home, her peers' habit of cavalier expenditure, buying digital cameras, expensive clothes, iPods, holidays, and meals out whenever they feel like it, is a significant cause of their supposed poverty. "I have never really practised the necessary self-imposed deprivation to redress the situation", she confesses; and it's a problem she has in common with many of her contemporaries. "Young adults", in her view, "do not know what it is to be careful with money. We lack discipline and have no real sense of priority. We are obsessed with self-indulgence".[9]

The urge to consume is indeed felt early in life. According to research published in 2007 by the Future Foundation which specialises in identifying global consumer trends, "Children and tweens are now a new epicentre of the marketing world. Their taste drives market trends, their opinions and preferences structure brand strategies".[10] The report asserted that, "Today's European tweens are like no generation before them. As a demographic group they move and live in a milieu where they are exposed to more consumerism than any generation... Today's youngest are already seen as a 'market' in their own right with significant consumer influence."[11] It points out that increasingly sophisticated merchandise is being pitched at much younger children with far more advertising. Such is the desire among susceptible children for certain highly advertised toys that the parents who feel impelled to satisfy that demand are prepared to enter into fisticuffs with other parents in order to get their hands on particular items. One such toy was the Sesame Street puppet TMX Elmo which appeared in 1996; ten years later when a second version was launched and pushed as the next

'Christmas must-have', more than five hundred a day left the shelves of the Hamleys West End toy store.[12]

But toyshops seem rather quaint compared with the interactive online possibilities which are now accessible all over the world. One of the fastest growing virtual worlds has been Mattel's *BarbieGirls*™,[13] launched in April 2007. The site attracted one million registrations in the first twenty-eight days, and had accumulated more than thirteen million by the end of 2008.[14] Once registered, girls created an avatar, selecting facial features and clothes for her from a menu, and interior decorations, furnishing and accessories for the home in which the character socialized with other characters. Purchases were made in 'B Bucks', earned by playing games, watching films and advertisements, and winning style-ranking contests. Particularly desirable purchases required the payment of a monthly subscription by credit card. Thus consumption as a means to display taste and style was central to girls' identity generation throughout the site. The parent who paid for it, moreover, endorsed the idea that material consumption is of itself a source of pleasure, as well as the idea that purchasing power is required to produce individual identity.[15] While this site is no longer live, so many little girls have become self-focused and aware of appearance, that 'pamper birthday parties' offering young children manicures, make-up and hairstyling have become commonplace in the UK, and the first, luxurious, child-only beauty salon was set up in response to demand from mothers for daughters as young as six.[16] The view is not so different at the other end of the age spectrum, however, for figures suggest that the number of people in the UK trying to improve their image increased six-fold between 1998 and 2004, and that many of the estimated 25,000 surgical procedures performed in that time could be attributed to baby boomers, those people born in the years following World War II.[17] But in other ways, the consumption pattern bought with the silver pound is beginning to look different from that of younger people as, having accumulated plenty of material possessions, the older generation who can afford it are tending to choose instead to purchase experiences, particularly travel to distant destinations for adventure or education.[18]

The widening gulf in spending capacity

Since the financial world started to unravel in 2007-8 things have begun to look rather different. Consumer credit is no longer so easy to come by. The enticement of many by banks into unrepayable levels of debt brought about a banking crisis which resulted in recession, under-unemployment and huge reductions in government welfare spending; it has left significant numbers of people with less money, or none at all to spend on non-essentials. At the same time, however, the rich have somehow got richer. The ever widening gulf between the richest and the poorest in Britain is graphically illustrated by two articles in a single edition of *The Observer* newspaper in 2012. The first describes the rapid rise of concierge companies servicing the demands of the vastly rich, largely émigrés from Russia, India, China and continental Europe who have come to live in London and, after payment of a monthly retainer of £5,000, are able to purchase services such as the overnight sourcing of $20millions' worth of diamond jewellery for a breakfast proposal of marriage, or the instant arrangement of the kind of shopping expedition that effortlessly nets four women a haul of £250,000 worth of clothes, shoes and accessories.[19] The other article gives figures released by the National Society for the Prevention of Cruelty to Children which showed that reports of child neglect received by their helpline had increased by 30% in a year, numbering 12,000. Among other emergency situations, callers to the helpline described children going hungry and begging neighbours for food.[20] In fact, so many people are now at times unable to feed themselves or their families that in 2011 the government directed jobcentres to issue certain benefit claimants with food vouchers which could be exchanged for basic foodstuffs at charity-run food banks. 61,000 emergency food boxes had already been handed out in 2010 by the Trussell Trust, a Christian charity particularly active in this field, and demand continued to soar in many parts of the country: Coventry food bank, for one, it was reported, fed 171 people in April 2011 and almost 800 people three months later, and there were also substantial jumps in demand in other places, like Bournemouth and Norwich.[21] In February 2013 the Resolution Foundation, an economics think-tank, published a report whose analysis showed that inequality grew sharply in the previous fifteen years. During that time the top 1% of earners increased their share of the national income by 7%, to 10% of all income, while the share of the poorest 50% of earners went down by 1% from 19% to 18% of the national pie.[22]

Changing times?

The obscene extremes of wealth and poverty glimpsed here are a shameful indictment of the political economy pursued in Britain by successive governments, and the injustice of economic inequality is a major, urgent issue. But this book is not about individuals' relative income, nor about the gross inequalities of wealth and power between the developed and the developing world. Rather, it is about the material consumption choices made by those who are financially able to make them – and in Britain that means many, maybe most, of us. There are plenty of people in Britain who still do have disposable income, and many of these would like more than they have got. Rare indeed is the person, even amongst high earners, who turns down a pay rise or a bonus on the grounds that he or she already has enough; and the dream of winning the lottery is not the province of the poor alone. There is something very compelling about money and consumption to most human beings. The economic structure we have depends on us buying; it exploits our inclination to do so, and stokes cupidity at every turn. Thus wanting things, acquiring things, possessing things, has become the deeply embedded rule. Consumption-soaked living has not yet evolved with the economic downturn into willingly reduced expectations all round. For the most part, our society's sights and aspirations are trained on a vision of a return to things as they were before the financial crisis, to a climate of constant economic growth and unfettered consumption.

While certain companies have gone out of business since the financial crisis took hold, the range of goods to be found in shops, catalogues and on the internet looks little different from what was on sale before, and the desire of many people for acquisition continues unabated. On Boxing Day 2009, scenes of 'absolute bedlam' were reported across the country as queues at shopping centres began to form in the early hours of the morning, followed by brisk sales of full-price and sale items alike.[23] Christmas in Britain, originally an important time of Christian observance and traditionally a period of family festivities and respite from the hurly-burly of the world, is now chiefly characterised by frantic consumption. The buying of consumer goods to give as presents is largely regarded as *de rigueur* (hence the tradition of 'Christmas shopping'), yet we are collectively in possession of so many already that significant numbers of such gifts are rejected by the recipients: by 28th December 2009 six hundred unwanted items, including iPods, Nintendo DSs, perfume and hair straighteners, had been listed on the classified sales website Gumtree.[24] But a casual attitude to belongings is not confined to the Christmas season: hundreds of radios and an average of two thousand tents are apparently abandoned at the Reading and Leeds music festivals every summer.[25] These contradictory patterns suggest the existence of a paradoxical attitude towards consumer goods which both desires them and regards them as expendable. Perhaps the appetite for what we haven't got is more powerful than the satisfaction of having it.

Unthinking consumption

Because the hegemonic ideology of economic growth requires the constant buying and selling of newly manufactured products, ever changing demands must be created. This is also in keeping with humans' common fondness for fashion and novelty. Thus many homes and personal possessions are subject to regular 'upgrading', and innumerable fatuous items are marketed, such as wheelie bin 'make-over kits' and decorative electric hob covers; toast 'tattoos' which stamp 'Smile' and 'Good Morning' into bread before toasting; plug-in 'air-fresheners' to mask stale odours with chemical fragrances; and battery-driven, digital skipping ropes that save the exerciser the trouble of counting their skips. There seems no end to the absurd goods that are produced – and that find a market. There's the wellington boot-shaped bag for clean storage of muddy boots, (when languishing plastic bags abound); the motorised ice cream cone that saves you turning your wrist as you lick; the plane seat cover designed to "transform a tired, overused airline seat into a cosy, happy place"; the USB chameleon which plugs into your computer and rolls its eyes and sticks out its tongue at you; and sterling silver lids for Marmite jars and ketchup bottles.[26]

Consumption has been defined as all that is consumed, and consumerism as consumption which meets something other than real needs or that meets needs in an unnecessarily superfluous fashion.[27] Leaving aside the far from simple business of distinguishing between 'real' and 'unreal' needs, (given the complexities of human psychology, in terms, for instance, of the need to belong and the need for social status), it is clear that a great deal of our consumption is unnecessary. Here are some examples of conventional, unthinking, avoidable consumption. First take the everyday; large quantities of aluminium foil and cling film are routinely used to cover food for storage or transport when a plate or a clean tea towel would do just as well. Some occasions, such as Hallowe'en, arise just once a year; between 2001 and 2009 UK spending on Hallowe'en goods – fancy dress, decorations, toys and games – rose from £12million to £235million;[28] yet much more fun is to be had out of making your own. Hopefully only once in a lifetime, and at a more socially momentous level, the standard wedding is likely to involve a wedding dress that may be worn but once, flowers that are almost certainly imported (either in a juggernaut from Holland where they have been grown in hothouses or by air from Colombia or Kenya),[29] and perhaps the transporting of tens or scores of guests from the marriage location to a wedding reception venue some distance away. Celebrations might begin with stag and hen parties in continental destinations or luxury hotels and end with an intercontinental honeymoon. And then there are the wedding presents, perhaps chosen from a store's wedding gift list. It may not be long before the first pregnancy is the occasion of a 'baby shower' of brand new baby goods, demanding yet more special shopping.

Discourses of consumption

Everyday discourse and images are shot through with thoughts of consumption. Here are a few random examples I have come across: a government student finance advice publication which shows a picture on the front of an attractive young woman with a text underneath which reads, "This is Taj, 18. Taj likes shopping, Maximo Park, spending time with her friends and chatting on Facebook...", and a flier for Cornwall's No.1 Family Fun Destination, the Cornish Gold and Treasure Park holiday retail village. A mobile phone network has offered me a £40 M&S voucher as an enticement to sign up to a broadband connection with them. My supermarket 'loyalty' card offers me points that can be redeemed against goods and services sold by other companies, from cut-price retailers to airlines. On 11th April 2007 the *Daily Mail's* front page claimed under the headline, 'Disrupt School and Win an Ipod!' that government advice to schools for dealing with indiscipline was to reward the good behaviour of disruptive pupils with prizes of highly desirable consumer goods.[30] Even donating money to charity is often rendered more enticing by raffles whose prizes hold out the temptation of a new car, television, exotic holiday or store voucher. Towns and cities are measured in terms of their popularity with shoppers or 'retail footprint'.[31]

There are regular shopping columns to be found in the press, for instance those in *The Observer Magazine* under such headings as *Life and style*, *Most wanted*, *The wish list*, *The lust list: things we fancy this week* and *What I bought this week*, all of which are advertising masquerading as journalism, subtly propagating the notion that the buying of things of the kind they feature is a routine practice. Media discourse can give every impression that the acquisition of consumer goods is not only acceptable but necessary. One article, for instance, titled *The Ten Best In-flight Essentials* featured, among other things, frankincense hydrating facial mist and 24-hour manuka oil and shea butter 'skin saviour'.[32] None of the listed items was in the least essential. Indeed, how many flights themselves are unavoidable?

Second Perspective: Heating up and Eating up the Earth

A question of essentials

Water, unlike most other items marketed as 'essential', is something that one really cannot do without. Yet tap water – which would feel like pure luxury to the millions of people in the world who have to manage without clean, running water – isn't good or convenient enough anymore for the many who buy bottled water. However, there is an invisible cost to bottled water. The oil required to make the plastic to meet the demand for bottled water in the US amounts to 1.5 million barrels per annum, and the process of manufacturing a 1 litre plastic bottle itself takes three litres of water.[33]

It is in this breakdown of process that we can see the terms in which we must now view material consumption. It shines an X-ray onto the definitions above of consumption as, 'all that is consumed' and consumerism as the meeting of needs in an unnecessarily superfluous fashion, highlighting the now blurred distinction between the two concepts. The analysis of the environmental cost of bottled water alerts us to the hidden reality within any given product, of the raw materials and energy expended in the production, packaging, distribution, retailing and use of that 'all' of consumption. We do now really have to understand that absolutely everything which is bought – other than anything that is second hand, or hand made out of renewable, biodegradable materials and transported by foot or bicycle – entails some depletion of resources, and the production of waste which will one day find its way into the earth, waters or air around us.

As well as the goods that are bought and sold, this 'all' of consumption encompasses the energy involved in almost any process, be it transport, the warming and cooling of buildings, screening of a film, sending of an email, heating of a patio, use of gym equipment, processing of food and drink, laminating of paper… and on and on. We need to change the criteria by which we judge our consumption. No longer should the first consideration in evaluating the affordability or desirability of a particular product or activity be its price tag or the pleasure, functionality or social status it would bestow, but the extent of the toll it takes on the environment. Bottled water, is an apparently humble manifestation of consumerism compared with wardrobes full of unworn clothes, widescreen televisions, multiple handbags, continental weekend breaks, unused power tools, and all the innumerable other forms which are a familiar part of the fabric of contemporary Western life. Yet it embodies in one simple product the causes of several aspects of the environmental catastrophe which faces us unless we change our ways fast. Let's take a brief look at them.

Climate change

A pressing danger is the change in the global climate being brought about the emitting into the atmosphere of carbon dioxide, methane (which is twenty-one times as powerful as $CO_{2)}$, and other so-called greenhouse gases which trap the sun's heat and prevent it from escaping the Earth's atmosphere. Once in the atmosphere, greenhouse gases continue to be active pollutants.[34] Between 1992 and 2004 UK CO_2 emissions grew by 48% due to increased consumption.[35] By 2010 human activities, wherever they occurred in the world, had deposited the equivalent of about half a trillion tonnes of carbon dioxide in the atmosphere, with annual emissions continuing to rise. In 2011 81.4% of the world's energy was generated by the burning of oil, coal and gas;[36] and economic growth between 1970 and 2010 was a far more powerful driver of greenhouse gas emissions that the large increase in world population over the same period.[37] This means that we are currently putting one million years' worth of sequestered carbon into the atmosphere each year.[38] Photosynthesis by plants absorbs carbon dioxide, so large-scale deforestation compounds the problem. Scientific data analysis has now clearly established that there has been an upward and accelerating trend in temperatures over the last fifty years, and in the year to April 2010 a record high was reached, the year being the hottest in a temperature record dating back to 1850.[39]

In September 2012 US the National Snow and Ice Data Center announced that Arctic sea ice had melted to the lowest summer minimum extent on record. Scientists were taken aback by the speed at which the ice was shrinking: "We are now in uncharted territory", said NSIDC Director Mark Serreze. "While we've long known that as the planet warms up, changes would be seen first and be most pronounced in the Arctic, few of us were prepared for how rapidly the changes would actually occur."[40] In addition to the increase in temperatures to date since pre-industrial times, an additional 0.5°C to 1.0°C is inevitable due to the delayed effect of past emissions, and projections calculate a further increase of 1.2°C – 6.4°C by 2100.[41] A total increase of a maximum of 2°C has been adopted by more than 100 countries as the limit below which it may still be possible to contain impacts.[42]

On 11th January 2013 the US National Climate Assessment draft report was published,[43] projecting an average temperature rise for America of between 2°C and 10°C. Climate change was already affecting the American people, it warned; human health, water supply, agriculture, transportation, energy and many other aspects of life had already been affected and would continue to be. The report pointed out that, "As climate change and its impacts are becoming more prevalent Americans face choices. As a result of past emissions of heat-trapping gases, some amount of additional climate change, and related impacts, is now unavoidable... However, beyond the next few decades, the amount of climate change will still largely be determined by choices society makes about emissions."[44]

It seems that we have a window of only a few years to determine by our actions whether the rise in global temperature remains relatively limited or whether it rises catastrophically for life on Earth.[45] Sea-level rise is already starting to displace people from their costal homes in Bangladesh, a trend that will increase, causing Bangladesh's finance minister to call on Britain and other wealthy countries to agree to accept millions of displaced people, who might number up to 20 million in the next 40 years.[46] In the view of the UK government's Foresight Committee, environmental pressures of all kinds, including floods, storms, heat waves and droughts, will add to the existing powerful economic, political and social drivers of migration, and their impact will continue to grow.[47] James Lovelock, the ecologist who proposed the Gaia theory of the planet, which conceptualises the Earth and all its inhabitants as a self-regulating super organism, has predicted that the climate of Britain will be less badly affected by global warming than that of many other places, but that this will make it a desirable destination for future climate refugees, so swelling our population enormously.[48]

But in Britain, too, the pattern of weather and seasons is now increasingly unpredictable, and serious flooding is becoming noticeably more frequent. The kind of severe flood that befell Cockermouth in Cumbria on 19th November 2009, causing hundreds to flee their homes and a police officer to be swept to his death as he went to someone's aid, had been regarded until that point as a rare occurrence, but climate projections now show that extreme weather events will become more frequent as the century progresses.[49] Indeed, there have already been several periods of serious flooding in parts of Britain since Cockermouth, notably during the winter of 2013-14 when storms lashed Wales and the south and south-west of England for weeks on end, inundating houses and farmland in the Somerset Levels and causing the Thames to burst its banks as it flowed east through Berkshire and Surrey. Affected inhabitants in several counties were forced to evacuate their flooded homes; and Cornwall's rail connection with the rest of the country was severed as the land beneath it was washed away. The Environment Agency have identified that over five million people in England and Wales live or work in buildings which are susceptible to flooding from rivers or sea level rise.[50]

One area of the UK which is particularly vulnerable is the flat land of East Anglia, much of which lies below sea level, notably the extensive fertile agricultural area of fenland in Norfolk, which produces cereals, sugar beet, oilseed rape and potatoes.[51] This region also includes many and varied sites of nature conservation, some of them internationally important habitats.[52] Thus homes, food production, livelihoods and biodiversity all have an uncertain future in East Anglia. How, then, might life in the UK in general change as global warming has an increasing impact? In his book *Turned Out Nice: How the British Isles will Change as the World Heats Up*, Marek Kohn has attempted to make projections from standard models of climate change to imagine life in Britain at the end of the twenty-first century if the world continues to pursue the same economic path seeking constant economic growth. According to his reckoning, if we don't change course, the UK will be hit, at least initially, more by the indirect impacts of an increasing temperature than its direct effects, because the cooling currents of the North Atlantic insulate the British Isles from 'what the climate is really like'.[53]

Although we will have heat waves and floods, there will be no climatic effects in the British Isles to compare with the kinds of shocks that will hit Spain, half of which could become semi-desert, Kohn says, where heat waves will become ten or twenty times more intense than they are now. In Africa and southern Asia the impact will be greater still. The consequence for the UK will be a vast influx of migrants, thus "climate change will not just be a physical process. It will influence people's relationships with each other... and rearrange human communities as well as plant and animal communities".[54] People in the relatively affluent and comparatively much less affected British Isles will have to decide how they are going to treat the many millions of people driven out of the south by uninhabitable conditions. Hard as this could be in itself, it is likely to have to be undertaken against a whole world background of failed food crops, failed businesses, constant uncertainty and the chronic stress these conditions induce, and in the sometimes exceptionally warm conditions which give rise to more aggressive behaviour.[55]

Water shortage

While flooding is a grave consequence of climate change at times, another serious effect of the rising temperature is reduced rainfall at other times and higher levels of evaporation, causing drought. Currently 3,400 litres of water per person per day are taken from rivers, lakes and groundwater reserves to go into the food and goods produced and consumed in England and Wales.[56] Over-extraction is already a problem in southern England. On the basis of this factor, as well as the plans to build three million new homes by 2020 and the impact of climate change, the Environment Agency has calculated that average river flows in England and Wales could reduce by as much as 50-80% by 2050.[57] But it is not only our own local water supply that is relevant to consumption in Britain, for water is used in all sorts of products imported from all over the world. Every foodstuff and other product requires water in its production; the term for the volume of fresh water used to produce the product, is virtual water. For example, it has been calculated that to produced 1 Kg of beef takes 15,500 litres of water, 1 Kg of pork takes 4,800 litres, 1 Kg of rice takes 3,400 litres, a T-shirt takes 2,700 litres and a single sheet of A4 paper takes 10 litres.[58] Finding ways to reduce our industrial and personal demand for water is thus an urgent need.

Peak oil

While life itself is impossible without water, industrial production as we know it is impossible without oil. Not only is oil the fossil fuel from which one-third of the world's energy is generated, and which powers most cars and lorries and all planes and ships,[59] but there are few goods whose production does not depend on oil as a raw material. Its transformed presence is ubiquitous and unavoidable. Look around almost any home and in the kitchen you will find a washing up bowl, brush, rubber gloves, sandwich bags and storage boxes, milk bottles and other food packaging (including that mineral water bottle!) made of plastic. In the bathroom the bath, shower and lavatory seat are likely to be of plastic, as are the toothbrushes, combs and bottles of household chemicals, and pharmaceuticals and cosmetics will also contain oil. In the living room the television and the computer, and the CD and DVD collections are all of plastic, as are most children's toys; and in the bedroom it is a fair bet that clothes, shoes and bedding contain quite a proportion of oil among their constituents. It is likely that the flooring, paint and insulation of the house also have a high mineral oil content. And then there is the plastic card with which these things were probably paid for.

Oil is so versatile in product manufacture that we have been using it in ever greater quantities and have come to consume more in total every year than is now being discovered.[60] It is generally agreed by those who study the field, including geologists and executives in the oil industry, that oil production will inevitably begin to decline from a point of maximum production, though exactly when 'Peak Oil' will occur is still a matter of debate.[61] Estimates have varied from 2007 or earlier to 2023 or later.[62] The most significant immediate effect is likely to be a long period of economic decline because the infrastructure of industrialised countries, including production, transportation and settlement patterns, has been built up on the assumption of an unlimited supply of cheap oil.[63] Due to its lessening abundance and because most of the easy to find and easy to produce oil has been found and produced, remaining oil is bound to rise in price.[64]

So even if we could miraculously decarbonise the world's energy supplies overnight, we would still not be able to continue to consume as though there's no tomorrow, as an important feedstock of many products will have run out or become prohibitively expensive. The progressive exhaustion of the Earth's resources, including oil, fish stocks, tropical forests and the extinction of several major animal species, is an issue that has received much less attention than climate change or the continuing economic crisis but may, according to some, be even harder to resolve.[65] The area of life which would be hardest hit by a shortage of oil would be transportation, particularly planes, diesel trains, ships and the road vehicles which cannot be run on other forms of fuel.[66] Biofuels which are plant materials converted into liquid fuel, are no real alternative because their energy density is lower than that of petrol, the energy produced is nearly equalled by the energy required to produce it, and the land that would be needed to grow biofuel crops is needed for food crops.[67] The long and the short of it is that within the foreseeable future the dwindling of oil stocks will limit choices and impose major changes on the way we live. Whether we like it or not, we will have to get used to different ways of living.

Diminishing minerals

The finite nature of oil is also true of other minerals. While an important difference between oil and other minerals is that oil cannot be recycled and metals generally can, this is not always possible: copper is often locked in long-term use in wires and pipes, as iron can be locked into steel girders.[68] Phosphorus, reserves of which are expected to be used up in 50 to 100 years, is a vital and irreplaceable ingredient in fertiliser, and is difficult to recycle due to its being dispersed in the environment with use.[69] Researchers who constructed a prediction of the world's mineral reserves, conclude that it remains to be seen whether they will be sufficient to meet the expected demand of the 21st century, and warn that in any case mineral extraction requires a great deal of energy.[70] According to the European Environment Agency, resource use in Europe is increasing. It increased by 9.1% per person in the EU-27 between 2000 and 2007, reaching some 17 tonnes per person annually. Of the 8.2 billion tonnes of materials used in the EU in 2007, minerals and metals accounted for more than half, while fossil fuels and biomass were approximately a quarter each.[71]

Although we have not yet reached the point at which minerals are in seriously short supply, we do from time to time have little foretastes of the upheaval to our established way of living that even brief shortages immediately induce. The blockade of oil refineries by road hauliers in September 2000 resulted in the closure of thousands of petrol stations, meaning the cancellation of operations in hospitals, the threat of school closures, reduced supplies to supermarkets, and the loss to businesses of £250million a day.[72]

A different kind of disruption has been caused by the theft of copper signalling cable across the rail network as copper prices have soared, costing Network Rail up to £10m in 2008 in repairs, train delays and extra security. Rail chiefs and transport police have come to see cable theft as their greatest challenge after terrorism. The cost is not only financial, for the delays to trains, amounting to 2,000 hours in three months, were already eight times higher on the line between Rugby and London Euston between January and August 2008 than during the whole of the previous year.[73] The sudden disappearance of cable means a great deal of inconvenience, uncertainty and anxiety for train travellers.

Waste

Once that bottle of water has been drunk, the bottle may be recycled, sent to landfill or exported, but the world will never be rid of it for even the small proportion of plastic waste that is incinerated becomes toxic particulate matter.[74] If, instead, plastic items are dumped, they degrade into small particles in the environment which are ingested by wildlife and contaminate the food chain. When Rebecca Hosking, working as a camerawoman for the BBC Natural History Unit, went to Kamilo Beach in Hawaii, she found not golden sand but multi-colours stretching as far as the eye could see, the beach knee-deep in plastic cups, keyboards, DVDs, cutlery, toys, TVs, drinks bottles, shoes, plugs and much else. Beneath this detritus, rather than sand, were trillions of plastic fragments. On another Hawaiian island Hosking found a beach covered in dead and dying albatross chicks which had been fed plastic bags, cigarette lighters, toys and so on which their parents had mistaken for brightly coloured squid.[75] Bisphenol A, or BPA, one of the commonest chemicals in the world, is used to toughen plastic. It is used massively by the food industry to line various types of food containers, and has been found in the bloodstream of more than 90% of people. BPA is an endocrine disruptor and there is some concern about its effects on the brain and behaviour in foetuses, infants and children.[76] The Chem Trust has suggested that there is some connection, too, between the absorption of phthalates, chemicals which make plastics bendy and rubbery, and the development of obesity and type 2 diabetes.[77] The effects of waste, whatever the material concerned, are not usually straightforward, nor simple to remedy.

Planetary boundaries

Every aspect of consumption, from production, through transport, packaging, storage and retail to waste disposal, impacts on the physical environment on which we depend, and has now reached such a scale that it is undermining the viability of many life-forms. A team of twenty-eight international scientists have attempted to identify and quantify the limits of this damage which must not be transgressed if unacceptable environmental change is to be avoided. They term them 'planetary boundaries' and summarised their position in an article in *Nature* in September 2009.[78] The article set out how the Earth's environment was unusually stable during the past 10,000 years, with temperatures, fresh water availability and biogeochemical flows all remaining within a relatively narrow range, its regulatory capacity able to maintain these conditions in the event of naturally occurring environmental change, but now human activities, chiefly the intensive burning of fossil fuels and industrialised agriculture, have reached a scale that could have consequences that are "detrimental or even catastrophic for large parts of the world".[79]

The nine boundaries which the scientists identified were:

- climate change
- biodiversity loss
- interference with the nitrogen and phosphorus cycles

- stratospheric ozone depletion
- ocean acidification
- global fresh water use
- change in land use
- chemical pollution
- atmospheric aerosol loading

Their analysis suggests that the first three of these have already transgressed their thresholds, and that humanity may soon be approaching limits for global fresh water use, change in land use, ocean acidification and interference with the global phosphorus cycle. Amongst the boundaries proposed is that the concentration of carbon dioxide in the atmosphere should be no higher than 350 parts per million; this compares with 280 in pre-industrial times and 387 in 2009, a level which risks irreversible climatic effects such as the loss of major ice sheets.[80] As for bio-diversity loss, there have always been some natural extinctions, but today's rate of loss is 100-1,000 times the 'background' rate, bringing the prospect of 30% of all mammal, bird and amphibian species being threatened with extinction during this century; this needs to reduce to ten times the natural rate in order to preserve ecosystems. The Earth systems described do not act in isolation but interact in a delicate balance. Thus, the article points out, significant land-use changes in the Amazon could influence water resources as far away as Tibet. All the boundaries need to be addressed in concert. The signs of massive change may seem to point to unavoidable cataclysm, yet the article concludes hopefully, "The evidence so far suggests that, as long as the thresholds are not crossed, humanity has the freedom to pursue long-term social and economic development."[81]

Population
While the surface area of the Earth is limited, the human population of the world is not. It was reckoned that 31st October 2011 saw the birth of the baby who brought the world population to 7 billion. Babatunde Osotimehin, the UN Population Fund's Executive Director, remarked that the population of the world had almost tripled in his lifetime;[82] the UNPF's report forecast that the number is likely to swell to about 9 billion by 2050.[83] While the ballooning world population clearly means that there are far greater numbers of bodies to feed, shelter, warm, cool, wash and clothe than ever before, the average global birth rate has plateaued. But the consumption that has brought us to the critical ecological situation in which

we find ourselves is the overconsumption of the minority, the rich Western and Northern peoples. These people are now being joined by many in the East and South who, for the moment at least, are rapidly increasing in affluence and whose material aspirations are no different.

Curbing emissions

People in the UK are on average each responsible for about 10 tonnes of greenhouse gas emissions every year. This means that the average per capita UK figure needs to reduce to about 2 tonnes per year by 2050 if the British government's target for UK emissions to drop by 80% is to be met.[84] In order to achieve this level of reduction it will be necessary both to stop using fossil fuels in the generation of energy and the fuelling of transport and to take significant individual actions. The biggest changes will need to be made by the wealthiest, whose lifestyles do the most damage.[85] However, changes will need to be made by everyone; there are few who do not participate in a culture in which travel (whether for work or pleasure), the ubiquitous availability of goods for sale (which makes the very idea of a 'Buy Nothing Day' a challenge), and the notion of disposability, are the norm. Technological innovation is critical to reducing carbon emissions and other environmental damage, but personal lifestyle choices are no less important.

In his book *How to Live a Low-Carbon Life: The individual's guide to tackling climate change*,[86] Chris Goodall draws on many sources of data to explains in some detail the cost in greenhouse gases of everyday behaviours and choices. Goodall sets out how space heating accounts for much the highest direct carbon emissions generated by the running of a home, while the food supply chain is by far the most important source of indirect emissions. Food-related greenhouse gas emissions arise particularly from the cultivation of cows and sheep which produce methane, the use of nitrogenous fertilisers, the processing and packaging of food, and the rotting of waste food in landfill, which together are the biggest contributors to the approximately 2.1 tonnes of food-related carbon emissions per head per year. Next comes clothing. On average every year we apparently each purchase fifty items of clothing, weighing a total of 20kg; they are responsible for approximately 910kg (or the equivalent) of CO_2 in the growing and harvesting of wool and cotton, processing of natural and manmade fibres, and cutting and sewing of garments About 30 million mobile phones are sold annually in the UK, each one costing about 25kg in CO_2 (though the running cost in energy is negligible). Data from Apple suggest that making a laptop computer involves emissions of about one-quarter of a tonne, and double the amount for a desktop.[87]

Our use of paper is also significant, for Goodall points out that the making of wood pulp and paper is one of the most important sources of greenhouse gas emissions in the world, and that making virgin paper also takes huge amounts of water and produces large quantities of chemical effluent. The impact of making recycled paper is much less. According to his calculations, the average annual household purchase of 25kg of newspapers and 15kg of magazines produces 365kg of carbon emissions per head, and if it goes into landfill rather than being recycled it will generate methane in addition.

But perhaps flying is the biggest culprit of all when it comes to personal carbon emissions. The decision to stop flying, asserts Goodall, dwarfs all other actions the individual can take to reduce their own responsibility for climate change. This seems evident when one considers that the one tonne of carbon which is produced by a return flight from London to Vienna or Madrid is the same per capita level of emissions produced by travelling 10,000 miles by train, 10,714 miles in a small car with two other people, or 12,500 by long-distance coach.[88] However, it has also been calculated that if the embodied carbon involved in the construction and maintenance of roads and railways is added to the consumption of fuel used simply to propel the vehicle, the total life-cycle emissions per passenger-mile of travel by train, car, coach and bus can be even greater than that of flying through the air, particularly on new roads and railway lines. The uncomfortable fact is that, until truly damage-free technology is devised, no form of transport is without significant negative impact on the environment – except bike, horse and our own feet.[89]

In 2006 the UK had the fourth highest per capita carbon footprint in Europe,[90] and households are responsible for more than three-quarters of the UK's carbon emissions.[91] A group of eminent scientists, economists and others in the field all agree that, "To transition to a more sustainable future will require simultaneously redesigning the economic system, a technological revolution, and, *above all, behavioural change*"[92] (italics added). There is no getting away from the fact that the way you and I live involves a significant degree of climate-changing behaviour, behaviour which we can and must modify. The human race is effectively in a race with the planet. If we do not learn to radically reduce our material consumption, the depleted, degraded Earth will impose its own drastic limits on what is possible. Material resources will shrink while a significantly changed climate will inflict many forms of suffering. It is our responsibility to leave the Earth in a state in which all of today's children can live out their lives in a habitat that meets basic human needs. Those who come after them will have the same need. As a campaigner for future generations has put it, "Just because we can't hear the cries of anguish of our descendants yet to come, doesn't mean that they don't count." [93] It is now incumbent on each of us to work on cultivating a mind-set that asks, "Do I (or we, or does he or she) really need it?" whenever taking any action that involves material consumption. Whether booking a flight or getting into a car, deciding to add an en suite bathroom to a bedroom or considering a new outfit, upgrading personal technology or even turning on a light or a hot tap, we need to confront our use of the world's finite supplies and the waste materials produced. There is no getting away from it, such a challenge to the daily expectations, assumptions and unthinking habits that are the norm in our consumption-saturated culture will be tough. It should, however, become easier if we also keep asking ourselves, "What really makes me happy? What gives me lasting satisfaction? When do I feel a sense of fulfilment or contentment?" – and listen carefully for the answers.

Third Perspective: Illbeing in Britain Today

What is wealth?

Does all our consumption actually make us feel satisfied, fulfilled or contented? The evidence is that it does not. Although we really know at heart that money doesn't make us happy, the consumption habits and material aspirations which characterise British society and many others suggest that the notion that money and what it can buy makes us feel good, has a tight grip over the majority of human beings. Rather to the contrary, however, there is plentiful research that shows that people who are overtly materialistic, who value wealth, appearance and social status above other aspects of life such as community and self-acceptance, rate their wellbeing lower than those who are not particularly materialistic.[94] The belief that having more money than is required to ensure a reasonable, modest life makes us happy, is given the lie by statistics that show that for most types of people in the West, measured happiness has not increased since 1950; in the UK happiness has flat-lined despite massive increases in income for all income groups; the story is similar in Japan.[95]

What the Happy Planet Index tells us

An intriguing international perspective on the relationship between wealth and wellbeing emerges from the new economics foundation's Happy Planet Index. This is based on the understanding that a successful society is one that can support a good life for its people which does not cost the Earth. The HPI scores the success of 143 countries, representing 99% of the world population, by bringing together measures of life expectancy, life satisfaction and ecological footprint to produce a single, integrated score, and some telling results have surfaced. In the 2009 Index, Costa Rica, with a life-expectancy of 78.5, an average life satisfaction score of 8.5 and footprint of 2.3gha,[i][96] scored the highest overall mark, with 76.1 out of 100, followed by the Dominican Republic and Jamaica. Rich, developed nations fell in the middle, the UK coming 74th out of 143 with an integrated score of 43.3. The USA, together with Luxemburg (whose per capita rate of consumption is as though there were nearly five planets to live off) and the United Arab Emirates, had the largest ecological footprints, yet Costa Ricans live slightly longer than Americans, report much higher levels of life satisfaction (in fact the highest in the world), and have an ecological footprint of less than a quarter of the size of America's. It only goes to show that 'it is possible to have a good life without costing the Earth'.[97] The earlier Happy Planet Index which dealt only with European countries[98] presented a similar picture. Sweden's mean life satisfaction score of 7.8 was higher than the UK's 7.2, yet Sweden's carbon footprint of 1.60 was less than half the 3.32 of the UK, while Luxembourg's life satisfaction score of 7.7 was bought at the cost of a carbon footprint of 6.8, more than four times higher than Sweden's. True wealth is a matter of wellbeing, not of money.

So how is an absence of wellbeing apparent? There are numerous signs of significant levels of what might be called 'illbeing' in our society. Here are some of them:

Intoxication

A journalist shadowing ambulance crews in the run up to Christmas 2011 hinted at several aspects of alcohol abuse in a piece worth quoting at length:

> At nearly 2am last Friday the young woman lying on a bench outside the bar in London's West End is so drunk she has passed out. She is in no state to notice, much less care, that her short skirt has ridden up – and she does not appear to be wearing knickers – or indeed that her Gucci handbag and credit cards are there for the taking.
>
> Not a pretty or dignified sight, but more dangerous and disturbing

---

i   Gha, or global hectare, was the measure of environmental footprint used. In 2005 the 'fair share' of the world's then bio-capacity in relation to its population at the time was 2.1 gha per person.

is that the girl is easy prey for a passing attacker. Paramedic Brian Hayes shakes his head: "Look at the state of her. These young women just don't realise what risks they're taking when they go out and get smashed. They're so vulnerable."

Christmas is the busiest time of the year for the crew of what the medics like to call the London Ambulance Service's 'booze bus'. Tonight is no exception. The 30-year-old woman helped by Hayes turns out to work for an international bank. He checks her pulse, asks her to open her eyes and tries to get her into the ambulance. But she is unable even to stand.

Back in the ambulance, his colleague John Morgan has taken four more calls in as many minutes to scoop up Christmas revellers who have overdone the seasonal spirit. Antonia Gissing, the third member of the crew, is dealing with a trainee lawyer wearing silver cuff links who has vomited over himself and the booze bus. As she wipes his face and nose, he mutters insults. Almost paralysed with drink and slumped in the chair, he slowly, deliberately, curls his hand and waves his middle finger abusively in her face. "Fuck you, I pay your wages," he slurs before vomiting again.

"I've been spat on, punched, kicked, bitten, slapped... you name it," says Gissing. "It was frightening at first, but it happens at least once every shift and I'm used to it now. You can usually read the situation and guess when it's going to happen, but not always. The other night I gave a tissue to a girl who was crying and she bit my hand."

Morgan shows the gap where he lost three teeth after a drunk butted him a few weeks ago. Then the mobile rings again and we are off, lights flashing, sirens blaring; another street, another drunk.

The cost of treating each drunk is estimated at around £220 a time; the total cost to the NHS of treating alcohol-related injury and illness is thought to be about £3bn a year.[99]

Alcohol abuse became a significant feature of life in Britain during the boom years: in the last three decades mortality from alcoholic liver disease rose by over 450%, with 4,580 deaths in 2007.[100] Non-prescription drugs are also a problem. The figures produced by the European Monitoring Centre for Drugs and Drug Addiction for 2010 showed that Britons took more cocaine in that year than any of their fellow Europeans.[101] In fact the Office of National Statistics records for 2007 and 2008 showed that drug deaths from heroin and morphine were increasing year on year, with an increase between 2006 and 2007 of 16% with 2,640 deaths.[102]

Social ill health

A study by the Young Foundation carried out at around the same time into 'unmet needs',[103] those needs which can legitimately claim social support to help people avoid unnecessary harm and suffering, provides a snapshot of a significant absence of wellbeing in Britain – before the era of economic 'austerity' set in. One of the study's surveys indicated that about one in five people would experience a mental health problem at some stage of their lives, 15% suffering severe depression. On many mental health measures Britain compared poorly with other countries and the rates of self-harm, for example, were the highest in Europe. Absence of mental illness does not equal good psychological health, however, and the study found that in 2007-8 as many as ten million people experienced poor psychological wellbeing, the worst affected group being lone parents of dependent children. 14% of the whole sample reported a severe lack of social support, and one million people felt they had no-one to talk to and that no-one appreciated them. In the same period it was estimated that there were 2,164,000 instances of violent victimisation and there were 327,466 problematic drug users. People living alone are particularly susceptible to poor wellbeing, lack of a sense of self-worth and of control. The numbers of single people have doubled since 1971 and they now make up 12% of households. The elderly are another particularly vulnerable group. According to the Young Foundation study, nearly half of people over 75 regard television as their main form of company; over half a million spent Christmas Day 2006 alone; and just over a million older people in England always or often feel lonely. While the figures in the study show that the poorer you are the greater the likelihood that you will suffer aspects of 'illbeing', unmet psychological needs are not exclusively the province of the inadequately paid, as shown by the miserable binge drinkers described above.

On a societal level there has been a general erosion of trust: in 1959 56% of people felt that most people could be trusted but by 1998 that proportion had fallen to 30%.[104] Fragmenting families eat away at the cohesiveness of communities.[105] It is now common for notices to be posted in public places, be they railway stations, buses or hospital waiting rooms, warning that aggression towards staff will not be tolerated. They point to something amiss in our society, a malaise which has a very complex relationship with the distribution and spending of wealth. Poverty certainly plays a role but the issue is not so much about the effects of poverty *per se* as the effects of gross economic inequality. There is a great fund of evidence, as shown in Richard Wilkinson and Kate Pickett's book *The Spirit Level*,[106] that indicates that the wider the gap between the richest and poorest in a society, the greater the problems that society will experience, such as addiction, violence, poor educational performance, teenage pregnancy and obesity. Today's social unease became apparent in the outbreak of rioting and looting in the summer of 2011 which spread from London to England's 'cathedral cities and market towns' in the words of seasoned social and economic commentators Henry Porter and Will Hutton. Their analysis was:

> ...our society produced students, apprentices, school workers, middle-aged men with steady jobs, mothers, fathers and kids as young as 11 who all joined organised gangs to loot and burn down their neighbourhoods.[107]

It is possible that the looting which was a prominent feature of the disturbances was a symptom of a discomfort that many people experience in contemporary life, for studies have shown that some people use materialism as a coping mechanism when they lack self-belief, feel a lack of control over their lives, or have a sense of normlessness, ie, that society provides no clear guidelines for behaviour.[108] It may be, then, that some degree of the success of consumerism can be accounted for by attempts by individuals to bring meaning to their lives by buying things.

Unhappy children
A particular spotlight has been shone on the wellbeing of children in recent years. The publication in 2007 of a report by UNICEF[109] on the wellbeing of children in rich countries, which ranked UK children as having the lowest overall wellbeing among twenty-one industrialised nations, caused something of a stir here. The comprehensive assessment was carried out under six headings: material wellbeing; health and safety; education; peer and family relationships; behaviours and risks; and subjective sense of wellbeing. The UK came at or very near the bottom of the ranking in every dimension apart from health and safety. This exception to the poor ranking is ironic in light of the fact that about eighty-five children aged 0 – 17 die every year in England as a result of maltreatment or violence.[110] An indication of the emotional distress suffered among the young is also apparent in figures reported by the University of Oxford Centre for Suicide Research. The approximately 5,000 suicides per year in the UK and the estimated 170,000 cases of deliberate self-harm presenting in hospitals annually, involve large numbers of young people, many in their teens.[111]

Hospital admissions in the early years of the twenty-first century due to instances of self-harming by young people rose by 68% in a decade,[112] and an internal report produced by NHS England in 2014 provides evidence that, against a background of spending cuts to services, swingeing in some areas, the number of young people needing treatment for complex mental health conditions is rising.[113]

One feature of life in Britain, which is both a sign and a cause of unhappiness, is the common occurrence of poor family relationships. Family stability has been in continuous decline since the early 1970s and Britain has one of the highest divorce rates in Europe.[114] Conflict between parents has been associated with an array of adjustment issues for children, including poor peer relationships, behaviour problems, depression, poor self-esteem, and lowered educational outcomes.[115] While dysfunctional, fractured or fatherless families, whether parents are married or not, are more often found amongst the most disadvantaged groups, the increasing incidence of family breakdown is profoundly affecting people across the socio-economic spectrum.[116] One-third of 16-year-olds now live separately from their father.[117] Apart from the personal loss of a father's attention for the young person, this can have wider repercussions for society in that 70% of young offenders come from lone parent families. Dysfunction entails a breakdown of nurture so that an increasing number of families are unable to meet certain core needs of their young, including secure attachment, protection, realistic limits and self-control, freedom to express valid emotions, a sense of identity, and spontaneity and play.[118] Sometimes neither parent is able to provide good enough parenting, and every year 8,000 children enter the care system for a period.[119] Given the level of family breakdown it is, perhaps, not surprising that an estimated 140,000 unhappy children run away from home each year.[120] The issue of early attachment and its effects is one to which we will return.

The UNICEF researchers found no obvious relationship between child wellbeing and GDP per capita, and the Czech Republic achieved a higher overall rank than much wealthier countries such as France, Austria, and the US. UNICEF followed up their study with another one which compared child wellbeing in the UK, Spain and Sweden. The researchers found that, "The message from all the children who participated in the research was simple, clear and unanimous: their wellbeing centres on time with a happy family whose interactions are consistent and secure; having friends; and having plenty of things to do, especially outdoors."[121] However, the perspective of parents was less united. While family time seemed to be part of the fabric of everyday life in Spain and Sweden, parents in the UK said they struggled to find time to spend with their children, or to help them participate in sporting or creative activities. In all the countries consumer goods played a role in children's lives, and status technology and clothing brands did tend to create or reinforce divisions between the more and the less affluent, but the pressure to consume appeared much weaker in Sweden and Spain and the children and parents were much more able to withstand it. UK parents found it harder to resist the commercial pressures around them and their children.

Fourth Perspective: Reconstructing Economics

The roots of alternative thinking

The ubiquitous pressures to buy things that parents, children and independent adults experience are the direct result of our economic system which demands incessant growth. The way to remedy the ailing economy, we are constantly told, is to produce, buy and sell more. Since the 1950s, economic growth has been taken to be a continuous process that would persist forever.[122] The dogma of economic growth has, indeed, become indistinguishable from a religion, its critics considered heretics.[123] At the end of 2013 the BBC's economics editor, Robert Peston, was saying, "The big question of our time is can the west return to anything like the kind of growth rates it enjoyed before the 2007/8 crash on a sustainable basis or do we face many more years of low growth?"[124]

But other ideas of economics have been articulated for a long time. Their roots go as far back as the writings of John Ruskin in the second half of the nineteenth century, and different visions have been developed by various others, such as E.F. Schumacher, author of *Small is Beautiful: Economics as though people mattered*, who has been dubbed the 'father of the new economics'.[125] He shares that honour, perhaps, with American economist Herman Daly who argued from the early 1970s for 'steady state economics'. Within this framework, there is a constant stock of physical wealth (capital, goods) and of people (population), and the rate of replacement matches the rate of loss. This minimises waste and pollution, and operates within ecological limits.[126] Developing his thinking, Daly pointed out that only the stock of artefacts and human bodies need be kept constant; technology, information, wisdom, goodness, genetic characteristics, distribution of wealth and income, product mix, and so on do not. While growth refers to an increase in stock and throughput, development refers to an increase in service or efficiency with constant throughput.[127] In formulating the steady state concept, Daly was drawing on the writing of John Stuart Mill, who wrote in 1857 with astonishing prescience:

> I know not why it should be a matter of congratulation that persons who are already richer than anyone needs to be, should have doubled their means of consuming things which give little or no pleasure except as representative of wealth... Nor is there much satisfaction in contemplating the world with nothing left to the spontaneous activity of nature; with every rood of land brought into cultivation... If the earth must lose that great portion of its pleasantness which owes to things that the unlimited increase of wealth and population would extirpate from it, for the mere purpose of enabling it to support a larger, but not a happier or a better population. I sincerely hope, for the sake of posterity, that they will be content to be stationary, long before necessity compels them to it. It is scarcely necessary to remark that a stationary condition of capital and population implies no stationary condition of human improvement.[128]

And now we have concrete confirmation of Mill's wisdom. In the words of a contemporary professor of Economics, Andrew Oswald, "[T]oday there is much statistical and lab evidence in favour of a heresy: once a country has filled its larder there is no point in that nation becoming richer" because greater wealth does not result in greater happiness but does result in global warming.[129] In the 21st century new economic models are being formulated in response to the two growing recognitions that economic growth does not deliver personal wellbeing, and that it is the ecological predicament in which we find ourselves, not the economic one, that is the ultimate challenge.[130]

Here is a flavour of some of the emergent thinking...

A different approach to manufacturing

Circular economy is a concept which is gaining traction. In the face of resource depletion and volatile prices, it embodies a shift away from the linear take-make-dispose model towards "an economy in which today's goods are tomorrow's resources, forming a virtuous cycle that fosters prosperity in a world of finite resources",[131] in which businesses explore ways to reuse products or their components and restore some of their material, energy and labour costs, rather than dependence on virgin raw materials, based on a whole system approach. Initial research suggests that there is the potential for annual net material cost savings of up to US$380 billion during the transition phase and of up to US$630 billion in an advanced scenario, in only a subset of EU manufacturing sectors.[132]

A different form of capitalism

A prevailing view holds that capitalism is here to stay but must be reshaped. Political economist and journalist Will Hutton considers that, "The quest is on for better ways of making capitalism work both for itself, and for workers, consumers and citizens."[133] Jonathon Porritt, the long-time environmental campaigner, is a commentator who has written passionately on the matter.[134] He too believes that capitalism is so deeply entrenched in the world's political thinking and business structures that it cannot be overturned. He therefore proposes that capitalism must be embraced as the only overarching system capable of achieving some reconciliation between ecological sustainability and the pursuit of prosperity and personal wellbeing. The way to apply the concept of sustainability to profitability is through regulation, he maintains. A somewhat different slant is given to the question by economists Dieter Helm and Cameron Hepburn who point out that that the rapid rate of extinctions and collapse of eco-systems on the one hand and of the failure of economic policy on the other provide an enormous impetus for policy improvement.[135] Their prescription is to incorporate a valuation of natural capital and biodiversity, alongside conventional capital, into the core calculations of economics.

Both these approaches take environmental concerns as the primary drivers of the need for a transformation of capitalism. Others put more emphasis on individual wellbeing. Classical economic theory has, after all, always assumed that income is a suitable proxy for personal wellbeing. But in the light of understanding built in recent decades that individuals also value non-material good such as social relationships, competence and self-determination, and that higher incomes simply raise the bar on material expectations, the findings of happiness research have been seen to have the potential to revolutionise economics.[136] Tim Jackson, Professor of Sustainable Development at the University of Surrey, takes account of both agendas, and talks in terms of prosperity.[137] Prosperity is for Jackson an expression which carries the sense of things going well for us, but also the notion of things continuing well in the future. For this to be possible within the ecological limits of the planet demands a different kind of macro-economics in which people can flourish without more stuff, he says. From a global perspective the limits of economic activity determined by the planet's ecology and equitable distribution among the world's population, need to be coded directly into the organisation and working principles of the economy. In the UK, he suggests, this would mean sharing out the available work more fairly, a structural transition to service-based activities, and investment in ecological assets. It would also involve the development of community-based social enterprises for food production, transport, education, recreation and so on, and the better stewardship of buildings and agricultural land. "The task", says Jackson, "is to create real capabilities for people to flourish in less materialistic ways... In particular, we need to revitalise the notion of public goods. To renew our sense of public space, of public institutions, of common purpose".[138]

Andrew Simms and David Boyle of the new economics foundation,[139] also focusing on Britain, share the view that a shorter working week is an important part of a new economic structure, offering more equitable distribution of work and more time for workers to spend with their friends and families, and engage in activities both satisfying and enabling of lower consumption, with money for buying replaced by time to make, grow and mend. They advocate a citizen's wage for all, possibly combined with personal tradable carbon entitlements; massively reducing house prices by capping mortgages; a holistic education system which produces rounded and motivated people; restricting advertising; and a health system which is refocused on promoting health.

A bigger picture

Far more radical and universal thinking, however, comes from Ross Jackson, a Canadian-born expert in international finance and operations research, with extensive experience in business and non-government organisations (NGOs), who lives in Denmark and is chairman of the Danish-based Gaia Trust. In his 2012 book *Occupy World Street: a global roadmap for radical economic and political* reform,[140] Jackson sets out an alternative economic system for the whole world. Describing the current global structure as, "dysfunctional, undemocratic, corrupt and exploitative of the environment, the developing countries and even the citizens of the wealthiest nations",[141] it is time, Jackson says, "to reinvent ourselves as a sustainable and far more desirable civilisation based on a new world view of universal values." To make that vision a reality requires that we "design a new kind of economics and a new kind of politics that will revolutionise every aspect of our lives".[142] Only a fundamental revamping of our global economic and political structures will get to the root of the problem of environmental destruction and gross inequalities, and provide workable solutions that address real human and environmental needs. Action is required at all levels, he says, from day-to-day behaviour patterns of individual citizens to the way we organise our international relations at the highest level.

There are two fundamental flaws in modern economics in Jackson's view. The first, echoing Helm and Hepburn, is that the environment is treated as a subset of economics when the economic system should actually be allocating resources according to the physical restrictions of ecological space. Secondly, the growth model is based on the availability of labour and capital and does not take proper account of the input of energy. The failing with this model, says Jackson, is that economic growth actually seems to follow net energy use very closely. He calls the new economics he envisages Gaian economics. It will be "something quite different from any historical precedent, being based on ecological economics, with wide-ranging freedom of the private sector to innovate and develop efficient technologies, but within a framework that is protective of the environment and the social wellbeing of all world citizens."[143]

Ecological economics distinguishes, as did Daly, between growth, which is physical and therefore ultimately limited, and development, for example in quality of life, which has no such limits. Jackson faces us with the stark choice between staying in collective denial of the facts or starting to take ecological sustainability seriously and changing our high-consuming lifestyles. The goal he has in mind is "to achieve a more modest ecological impact in a happier society under the full control of its citizens".[144] Political reform will need to go hand-in-hand with economic reform, and he has thought out in considerable detail the new international institutions and structures, from local currencies to a Gaian Council of proven, wise, incorruptible elders who would have the power to veto legislation in order to protect the planet and its peoples.

Reasons for Hope

The possibility of human intervention
The picture I have sketched of the state of the Earth and the unhappy plight of a significant proportion of the population of Britain, a relatively rich country, may sound pretty desperate, and the theoretical ideas for economic reform impossibly idealistic, but there are many reasons to hope that things can change for the better. The key lies, somewhat paradoxically

43

perhaps, in the declaration of the Intergovernmental Panel on Climate Change, in their Fifth Assessment published in September 2013 and adopted by a hundred and ten governments, that there is at least a 95% probability that most warming that has occurred since 1950 has been due to human influences. If climate change was attributable principally to natural causes humanity would have no possibility of effective intervention; but as it is, there is scope and hope for us to slow and limit the process to some extent by changing our ways. There are many routes by which human endeavour and ingenuity can alter our interaction with and impact on the biophysical environment – and indeed enhance every other aspect of human wellbeing too.

There is still time

On the macro-scale, scientists believe that the majority of 'planetary boundaries' have not yet been crossed.[145] It is still possible to stop and reverse the loss of biodiversity and degradation of ecosystem services by concerted planning based on adequate data, a well-managed protected areas network, and a proper valuing of the role of natural capital in economic development. An integrated approach would set up a virtuous circle.[146] In addition, empirical evidence shows that, rather than being costly, switching from oil and coal to efficient use and a variety of renewable energy supplies is profitable.[147] This is in keeping with the conclusions of the United Nations–sponsored Millennium Ecosystems Assessment[148] which investigated the consequences for human life of the unprecedentedly rapid and intense changes wrought on ecosystems by human activity in the fifty years up to 2001. While they found substantial and irreversible loss in the diversity of life on Earth and damage to the 'ecosystem services' on which we rely for food, fresh water, raw materials, regulation of climate and waste, and supporting services like soil formation and photosynthesis, which they predicted could grow much worse in the coming century, they suggested nevertheless that the adoption of significant changes to policies, institutions and practices could still ameliorate some of the damage. "Many options exist", they concluded, "to conserve or enhance specific ecosystem services in ways that reduce negative trade-offs or that provide positive synergies with other ecosystem services".[149] On the micro level, the fact that the lion's share of the UK's carbon emissions are produced by households indicates the extent of the potential power of each individual to make their own small dent in global warming. Chris Goodall believes that quite small changes in lifestyle are able to take the individual a long way towards the

2 tonne target. Thus the curbing of flying, a form of consumption which is undoubtedly a means to an often genuinely life-enhancing end, is the only area of life in which reducing our carbon emissions need involve sacrifice.

Encouraging moves and inspiring exemplars

There is now ample evidence that the adoption of circular economy principles by certain businesses has started to make inroads on the traditional, linear economy model, moving it beyond the proof of concept stage;[150] and the businesses are thriving. So pressing is the need for change of this kind perceived to be in China that promoting a circular economy was identified in its eleventh five-year plan for economic and social development, enacted in 2006.[151] The European Commission, too, has decided, as part of its Strategy for Europe 2020, to move to a more restorative economic system.[152] In other parts of the world, imaginative grass roots actions are showing what can be done to improve life without environmental damage – and even with ecological benefit. An inspiring example comes from Africa, where the training of illiterate rural grandmothers as solar engineers resulted, in six months and at modest cost, in the bringing of solar electricity to 15,000 houses in 100 villages all over the continent.[153] Other examples come from the application of non-chemical, permaculture principles to small-scale agricultural projects in unpromising terrains. Permaculture has been demonstrated to be capable of remarkable productivity, such as the enormous diversity of plants grown by an Austrian farmer, Sepp Holzer, working with nature rather than in competition with it, in a high-altitude mountainous environment with an average temperature of 4°C. Another example is the rapid production of fruit, including dates, pomegranate, mulberry and figs, in the parched, salty soil of the Jordanian desert, by permaculture teacher, Geoff Lawton.[154] Such schemes show that the seemingly impossible is possible, given the will and imagination.

Shifting paradigms

From a more holistic perspective, there appears to be a paradigm shift in personal values going on. As Ross Jackson[155] explains, Thomas Kuhn, the outstanding twentieth century philosopher of science, who originated the concept of the paradigm shift, observed that this phenomenon occurs when the old paradigm is no longer satisfactorily dealing with problems, and adjustments need to be made. Jackson believes that we are now in the middle of a transition period, moving towards a new, not yet fully defined world view which he calls the Gaian paradigm. It is only a matter of time, he suggests, until a tipping point is reached when the minority who see the Earth as a living organism, whose animal, vegetable and mineral elements are all intimately connected and interdependent, become the majority. The basis for his belief in a changing paradigm is that there has been an explosion in non-governmental organisations (NGOs) since World War II, gaining both popular support and political influence in matters such as human rights, the environment, poverty and social reform; and since 1960 there has also been an enormous increase in the proportion of individuals who hold values in keeping with the new paradigm. In 2008 it was reckoned that as many as 35% of the populations of Europe, the US and Japan held such values, representing an unusually large value shift in a very short time. Such people have been dubbed the 'Cultural Creatives';[156] they are characterised by their valuing of the environment and community, their reflectiveness and open-mindedness, their propensity to read more and to watch less television than others, their preference for the real and authentic and their rejection of consumerism, status display and social inequality.

Along related lines, a report published in 2010 by WWF and endorsed by four other major charities,[157] points out that to produce responses commensurate with the scale of the bigger-than-self problems we face, requires the strengthening of existing common values that have been long held but insufficiently esteemed. Such values include empathy towards those who are facing the effects of humanitarian and environmental crisis, concern for future generations, and recognition that human prosperity resides in relationships, both with one another and with the natural world. Everyone, whether individual citizens or actors in business, civil society organisations or government, says the report, can help to advance these values and seek to diminish the primacy of many damaging values which are prominent in Western industrialised society.

There have also been signs of a new economics in action for decades, in the rise of local food, ethical investment, fair trade, downshifting and ethical businesses.[158] In fact, it seems, Buddhism is entering the boardroom! Clare Melford, CEO of International Business Leaders Forum, a global coalition of companies whose aim is to use their core business as a force for good in the world, believes that the tenets of Buddhism, i.e. accepting and acting in accordance with the interconnectedness of everything on the planet; the need to master our impulses and desires; and that a middle way between extremes is best, represent a new way forward for successful and responsible business. In a talk at the Royal Society for the Encouragement of Arts, Manufacture and Commerce, Melford gave as examples of these principles in practice a UK clothing retailer who had adopted an advertising strategy of marketing under the banner, 'Do not buy our clothes', challenging shoppers to consider the implications of their desire for something new by encouraging them instead to repair, reuse and recycle their clothes, and by a DIY retailer who was radically changing its business model by encouraging consumers to move away from buying equipment like power drills and lawnmowers which are only used from time to time, and adopt shared ownership instead, in a street-by-street pilot scheme.[159]

There are real grass-roots signs, too, of slowly changing attitudes towards stuff: other emerging forms of collaborative consumption are car clubs, clothes swaps and garden-sharing. As far as personal ownership goes, the 100 Thing Challenge, thrown down by American environmental activist Dave Bruno, asks people to manage life with no more than a hundred belongings; there's international Buy Nothing Day when we are exhorted to 'unshop, unspend and unwind';[160] there is the flourishing trade in second hand goods via charity shops; and there's Freecycle/Freegle, the internet-based scheme which enables people to pass on unwanted goods to someone living locally without money changing hands.

A better understanding of wellbeing

The burgeoning field of wellbeing research offers us a good understanding that the sources of real human fulfilment are to be found in non-material aspects of life. It confirms what we largely already know deep down but tend not to heed, that lasting happiness and satisfaction derive not from money and material acquisition, but from good relationships, active engagement in life, a feeling of belonging combined with one of self-determination, and a sense of meaning or purpose. Setting out with our plastic cards or cash in the belief that happiness can be bought over the counter or with the click of a mouse, usually leads us in the end into a cul-de-sac or up a path to dissatisfaction. This futility is now being taken to another level by the increasing recognition that most of what we buy is also, one way or another, wrecking the planet.

*　　*　　*

The core argument of this book is that proactively constructing our day-to-day lives, both individually and as a society, around those factors which generate real wellbeing will have two prized effects, indeed the most valuable outcomes possible. Shaping individual and collective life in this way will simultaneously make us happier and reduce our environmental toll. The Happy Planet Index provides the invaluable insight that it is possible to devise ways of living that create happy people with minimum cost to the environment. In the first HPI, published in 2006,[161] the nation with the highest overall score was Vanuatu. Vanuatu is described as an archipelago in the Western Pacific, made up of eighty islands, inhabited harmoniously by a population of immense cultural diversity, with an economy based largely on small-scale agriculture, where people are satisfied with very little and life is about community, family and goodwill to other people.[162]

A further contention of this book is that we need to prepare ourselves to deal successfully with what is to come. Even if we permanently overturn our material demands tomorrow, the physical and social world would still be sure to change in ways predictable and unpredictable in the coming decades; we would therefore be wise to fortify ourselves psychologically for living well with these changes. We need to develop our capacities to make the most of the opportunities for experiencing wellbeing that will exist under new, shifting conditions. Scientists talk about physical and social adaptation to climate change; we must think too about individual, psychological adaptation. So, given that the very same capacities that nourish wellbeing are those which foster resilience and flexibility, bringing about a change of personal and political priorities in order to concentrate on the true foundations of wellbeing in the present would also serve as a critical investment for the future. Whatever the scenario in which we, our children, grandchildren and other fellow human beings will be living, all will wish, as ever, to be able to gain as much enjoyment from life as possible. Let us embrace the future, moving proactively towards it, our hearts open and our minds prepared, encompassing some kind of wholeness.

2

Investigating Happily Modest Consumers

The Road Here

All of what follows in this book is set within the all-pervasive context of the consumer culture in which we are steeped. While levels of poverty are rising horribly in Britain, southern Europe and North America, so that increasing numbers of people can no longer feel secure in their ability to provide for their own and their children's most basic needs, let alone have money left over to spend in ways they choose, the fundamental character of our political economy has not changed. Indeed, it is ever more trained on privatisation, commodification and the maximisation of private profit, which in turn depends on creating consumer demand. Thus advertising and marketing are constantly deployed to persuade us, by one means or another, to keep buying. While a growing number of people are questioning the personal benefit and environmental prudence of such an economic model, there is no doubt that casual material acquisition remains the general order of the day in Britain and elsewhere, dreams of money and spending are enjoyed by many, and material expectations are understandably rising rapidly elsewhere in the world.

Despite the widespread recognition that contemporary society is characterised by a culture of consumption, and despite the fact that a much more modest yet satisfactory lifestyle for the great majority is still within living memory, it would be a mistake to think that the drive towards consumerism is a recent development. In order to gain a better appreciation of today's scene it is helpful to have some awareness of how its shape has developed. The first writings on consumption date from the sixteenth century and criticise material abundance, regarding novelty as the harbinger of social unrest and disintegration.[163] How far-sighted this was in light of such incidents as the unholy scrum that broke out during the opening of a new IKEA store in North London in February 2005, causing injuries to customers and the temporary closure of the shop.[164]

The eighteenth century economist Adam Smith realised that production and consumption were the drivers of modern market-led society, yet also believed that the development of a passion for accumulating frivolous objects would convey the false assumption that wealth would bring happiness. This, too, has been borne out by a great deal of recent research that shows that increased prosperity has not brought a commensurate increase in wellbeing in its train.[165] However, the immense and unprecedented rise in production brought about by the industrial revolution was matched by a paradigm leap in consumption, and from the middle of the eighteenth century the production of new inventions did introduce a level of comfort into everyday life for many, providing a happy medium between bare necessity and indulgent luxury. The second half of the eighteenth century was, for the affluent, the time of Adam houses, furniture by Chippendale, Hepplewhite and Sheraton, and porcelain made in Chelsea, Worcester and Derby. Formal gardens, orangeries, menageries and silverware, among other things, appeared on the domestic scene. Novelty was greatly sought after and each social stratum strove to emulate the one above it, assisted by the advertisements that filled newspapers.[166]

Until the late seventeenth century shops for retail had been little more than anterooms to warehouses, with large signboards outside indicating what was on sale within. Shops themselves then developed and built up a trade in luxury goods, becoming popular places for members of high society to meet and pass time. This led to great attention being paid to shop interiors which came to be fitted in rare woods, marble, brass, glass and mirrors. Around the middle of the eighteenth century the shop window developed from an ordinary window to a display space. A century later, technology developed in such a way as to allow shop windows to be constructed out of a single large pane of glass. The transformation of the shop as a display space, and one that could remain open in the evening, was made possible by the invention of artificial light – first gas lamps, and then electric light.[167] And so the department store was born, first in America, then in Britain. Such opulent and abundantly supplied emporia proved seductive. To some, the temptation of the goods on display proved so irresistible that shop-lifting became a real problem. To these individuals the impulse to acquire was stronger than any actual need for the stolen items or the wish to own them, for it was found that they were often given away or hoarded rather

50

than put to use by the thief. In fact, shoplifting became such a drain on the profits of American department stores that a whole new industry grew up around the need for secure store fittings and display cases. In 1891 the Norwich Nickel and Brass Works in Connecticut published an eighty-page illustrated catalogue of fixtures, counters and mirrors, and by 1910 most department store displays were fully under or behind glass.[168]

So the first expansion in production of consumables concerned household articles of an aesthetic kind. After the invention of the sewing machine in 1851, mass production of clothes became possible, initiating the development of the fashion industry.[169] During the second half of the nineteenth century and into the early decades of the twentieth, major changes in domestic technology came about, ushering in new purchases of a more utilitarian kind. Municipal provision of gas, water, electricity and sewerage services became established; indoor plumbing, better lighting, better stoves for cooking, and early central heating all appeared; and new household appliances were invented: the fridge, vacuum cleaner and washing machine. These developments combined to make housework much easier, more effective and less time-consuming, and reduced the need for servants. There was a general move by middle class families out of cities into new suburbs, where they bought houses that then needed to be decorated, furnished and equipped.[170] The shift in the late nineteenth century and early twentieth to the consumer society was common to Britain, France and the United States, much the most developed countries in terms of industrialisation and their exploitation of cheap raw materials imported from their colonies.[171]

A major change to everyday purchasing in the mid-twentieth century was the advent of the supermarket, a single retail outlet for all manner of food stuffs, sold ready weighed and packaged to enable the self-service of customers with the help of a shopping trolley and check-outs where purchases could be paid for all together. The hypermarket followed, with its much expanded range of merchandise, allowing alcoholic drinks, pharmaceuticals, clothes, kitchen equipment, and electrical items all to be displayed and sold under one roof. In the twenty-first century, opening hours have also expanded, for some to a full twenty-four hours a day, so that trade now continues even in the early hours of the morning when it would formerly have been inconceivable to go shopping.

Another development was the spreading of the shopping mall across the Atlantic from the United States to Europe. Now huge areas, on several floors, were devoted entirely to the buying and selling of a vast range of

51

consumer goods. While the high street or town square where people had shopped in earlier times had been interspersed with buildings with many civic functions, such as the library, town hall, post office and police station, the mall became a matrix of entertainment, and encouraged shopping as recreation. The specifications for Manchester's 135-acre Metro Centre, opened in 1986, for instance, included in addition to its 360 stores and shops, more than fifty cafes, restaurants and fast food outlets, a £20 million indoor amusement park, a twenty-eight lane bowling alley, a multi-screen cinema, a themed 'Mediterranean village', a 'Roman forum' and an 'Antique Village'. In 1991 it attracted twenty-six million visitors.[172] Shopping, albeit much of it 'window shopping', was said to have become the most popular family leisure activity in Britain.

Invisible money

The physical means of trading have expanded in such ways that much can now be bought without the buyer ever encountering the seller. A great deal of today's purchasing is done remotely in virtual space online, made possible by the use of credit cards. There has been a marked change in the way that buying on credit is perceived, from the once ill-advised 'never-never', to be avoided as the slippery slope into debt, to the now socially accepted exhortation to buy now pay later. Although disposable income in 2005 was nearly two-and-a-half times the level it was in 1971, levels of debt had begun to soar. Collectively we were living well beyond our already not inconsiderable means. In March 2007, when consumer society was at its zenith, just before the beginning of the financial crash, it was reported that Britain's personal debt was increasing by £1million every four minutes.[173] In the year to May 2007, the Citizens Advice Bureau had dealt with 1.4 million debt problems, and in January 2007 they were approached for help with 15% more debt problems than in the January of the previous year. This lavish scale of consumption was made possible only through the availability of credit, by the use of plastic cards, overdrafts and personal loans.

Introducing the Modest Consumers Study

There is now an urgent need to reach sustainable levels of material consumption. Yet the idea that we as individuals have seriously to lower our accustomed expectations of acquisition, comfort, convenience, and the often pleasurable habits of shopping, is not an immediately appealing prospect for many people. Without the financial necessity to do so, it may even seem to be the surrender of entitlement. In sharp contrast with this attitude, however, there have in recent years been some admirable attempts by individuals in Britain to try ways of living that severely limited their consumption. The most radical of these was undertaken by Mark Boyle, who wanted to find out if it was possible to live for a year without spending any money at all. He found himself a caravan free of charge and parked it on an organic farm in return for three days' voluntary labour a week. To eat, he foraged for wild food, grew vegetables and made use of food disposed of by shops and restaurants.[174] A second explorer of seriously reduced consumption has been Katharine Hibbert. Her cash-free life also involved the use of unwanted food and other necessities, but was urban and depended on living in a succession of squats.[175] The lengths to which this man and this woman found they had to go in order to construct an essentials-only existence, and the very abnormal shapes of their lives during this time, shows just how saturating consumer society is. A somewhat less drastic yet still telling experiment was carried out by Samantha Weinberg, the mother of two young children who, on 1st January 2008 embarked on a year of buying nothing except what was strictly necessary. She went through a phase of having to resist habit and temptation, learnt to be ingenious in meeting needs in other ways, and, she reported, finished the year with a much weakened buying impulse.[176]

The buying, selling and use of 'stuff', and our dependence on energy, is so taken for granted in personal, domestic, institutional, cultural and public life that we rarely look beyond the site of our own consumption to gain a proper awareness of the depletion and contamination it wreaks on the natural substances necessary for human and other life. Despite the stark disparity between what Boyle and Hibbert have demonstrated is possible, and 'normal' consumption in Britain, their extreme approaches to everyday existence would be both unattractive and impracticable for the majority of people. Their food-foraging activities, moreover, would also ultimately be unsustainable: reliance on commercial waste is dependent on the immoral and environmentally damaging profligacy of the current over-production, packaging and unequal distribution of food; and the harvesting of wild food, if much more widely engaged in, would disrupt local eco-systems by depriving wild creatures of sustenance, while not in any case stretching to meet mass need.

There are, however, significant numbers of people who simply choose to be materially more modest than the norm, who resist or reject the shopping practices and expectations that the majority live by, though maybe not always to the degree tried by Weinberg. I wondered what could be learnt from those who positively enjoy quietly routine modesty rather than deliberately experimental frugality. How could their habits and perspectives help to develop understanding of what enables or encourages people to pursue enjoyable lives in which material consumption plays little part, and its avoidance is not their primary focus? I decided to explore this territory, for it is people who actively prefer to live modestly but more conventionally than Boyle and Hibbert who might be able to shed some practical light on the dual subjects of reducing consumption and increasing wellbeing in a way that might be applicable on a societal scale.

Before going any further it is important to emphasise that material 'modesty' is a relative term – as, indeed, is poverty. While the numbers experiencing serious financial hardship in the UK have been growing significantly since the banking crisis of 2008 and the subsequent savage public spending cuts of the Coalition government, the UK is still a rich society, relatively speaking. It has a national health service and an education system, both still more or less free at the point of use, and universally available clean running water; it collectively discards mountains of perfectly edible food, wearable clothes and innumerable other good and materials. There are many parts of the world where all this is far from true. Absolute personal poverty is thankfully a rarity here in comparison with great tracts of the world. This is not to sweep UK poverty aside; indeed, the fact that real material privation exists at all in Britain is a shocking indictment of the political values of this country which endorse a grotesque degree of financial inequality – in contrast to the much greater equality found, say, in Scandinavia. But that is not the subject of this book. The focus here is rather on those many people *who are in a position to make free choices* in how they wish to live and what they consume.

To find out more about those who resist or reject typical levels of material consumption, I looked for adults who could answer yes to these two questions: Do you live a life of modest material consumption? Are you happy with your lifestyle? I did not define material modesty because I was interested to discover how people might perceive it and identify themselves in this respect. In order to gather a diversity of experience and views, it was important to find men and women of all ages from the general population, rather than approaching a particular political, religious, cultural, interest or other social grouping. Having first carried out a small pilot study with people I knew, others they passed on to me, and some who volunteered themselves, I therefore placed advertisements in *The Big Issue*, the general interest magazine sold in the street nation-wide by homeless and vulnerably housed people, asking for recruits to a questionnaire study. I felt that it could safely be assumed that purchasers of the *The Big Issue* had compassion and perhaps a certain amount of disposable income in common, but maybe little else. The advertisements drew quite a number of direct responses; a number of participants came in addition through word of mouth; and other recruitment attempts brought some more.

Who were the modest consumers?

The questionnaire asked respondents to indicate the ways in which they were modest consumers of goods and energy. Then it asked open-ended questions about what they valued and what they felt had influenced their current way of living. Of the total of ninety-four people who completed the questionnaire, sixty-five were women and twenty-nine were men, and they ranged in age from 18 to 83, the greatest proportion being in their 30s. Fifty said they were modest in their material consumption due to a combination of choice and financial constraints, while forty-two claimed to have taken this route purely out of choice. Only one was originally constrained entirely by economic circumstances – but, as we shall see in the next chapter, had grown to love her life of reduced consumption. A good half of the respondents worked in or had retired from a range of professional jobs; the others included manual workers, students, secretarial staff and grass roots charity workers. They encompassed single people living alone, people with partners, seventeen parents with children up to 18 (six with under 5's, and eleven with school-age children), and individuals sharing accommodation with housemates. Their homes were of many types, including modern houses on private developments, two-up-two-downs, larger Victorian terraced houses, current and former council houses and flats, housing co-operative homes, a hut in a field, cottages, 1930's semis, and a narrow boat. The two-pronged question in the advertisement about being happy living a materially modest lifestyle led me to men and women living all sorts of different existences, and doing so for a whole range of reasons.

Informative as the responses on the questionnaire were, I was keen, too, to talk to some of the people who completed it, to learn more about their own positions. So in a second phase of this Modest Consumers study, as I called it, I interviewed thirty-seven of the participants in order to gain further insights. My aim was to explore the perceptions, feelings, histories and practices of individuals who considered that they could describe their lifestyles as happily materially modest. My intention was not to make judgements on or comparisons between them. Rather, I wished to develop some sense of the underpinnings of a positive preference for material modesty, and to find inspiration from the ways and choices of those who pursed it. This understanding, and the inspiration provided by these modest consumers could then be shared with others.

What does relative material modesty look like?

The questionnaires revealed that, predictably, the modest consumers included many active re-users, repairers and recyclers. It was common amongst them to buy furniture and other household items second-hand. Indeed, charity shops and the challenge and possibilities they present were extremely popular, and many people relied on these for all or most of their clothes. They generally cooked from scratch, and some made their own clothes, gifts and cards. A number avoided supermarkets, preferring to use local shops, and some made a point of using ethical sources of goods. They included a number who were happy to go without things that many people regard as necessary or even essential – a few did without a washing machine or a mobile phone, both of which most of us now feel are indispensable. Several had no television. Thirty-four had no car, while others owned a small or economical one, or restricted their driving. Altogether, their transport needs were largely met by cycling, walking and public transport. Many had limited the flying they were prepared to do or had given it up altogether in order to cut down their environmental impact. It was not uncommon amongst the modest consumers to holiday only or largely in the British Isles, and many enjoyed camping, caravanning, youth hostelling, self-catering and staying with friends and family. Several said they made a point of reducing their energy use, particularly by wearing extra jumpers before turning up the heating. This little habit is more significant than it may sound, for heating accounts for as much as two-thirds of total British household energy consumption.[177]

In describing certain common patterns of consumption, I don't want to give the impression that the modest consumers were a homogeneous collection of people – this was far from the case. For one thing, their judgements regarding what counts as a modest level of consumption diverged considerably. These encompassed no electricity or internal running water at one extreme, to sending sheets away to be ironed at the other; no flying at all and camping holidays in the UK, to a week's holiday in New York; growing fruit and vegetables and shopping at farmers' markets and small local independent stores, to buying food at Marks &Spencer, or Waitrose. Some conversations revealed, too, that an individual's consumption can be inconsistent across different categories, for instance a purely functional approach to clothes-buying but the purchasing of a more sophisticated computer than necessary, or living peripatetically with minimal possessions yet flying quite frequently.

Of course it was not possible to measure the CO_2 emissions of these individuals. It seems likely, though, that few would have achieved the extremely low but sustainable total level of 2 tonnes each year,[178] but possible that some approached the 4 tonnes per annum level suggested as a more achievable target by one source of advice and encouragement.[179] Without actual measurement, it does, however, seem probable that all were responsible for less (and often significantly less) than the current British annual average, as well as for less use of raw materials and less waste to be disposed of. Portrayals of many these modest consumers and glimpses of the thinking and ways of living of others are sprinkled through the following chapters. While it is clear that some of their lives were unusual, many showed that avoiding conventional consumption patterns or expectations need not push you into the fringes of society; it doesn't have to make you peculiar.

From talking to some of the modest consumers it became apparent that there are two distinct approaches to assessing one's own level of consumption. One is absolute; the other relative, judged either in comparison with other people or with one's own former habits. The majority of the contributors to the study clearly assessed their own consumption in comparison, implicitly or explicitly, according to their knowledge of the ways of other people, either others in the same social bracket as themselves, or the very poor in the developing world.

Money is not the same as material consumption
Another clarification. The point here is not about how much money these people had at their disposal; there were some amongst the modest consumers who were plainly financially very comfortable, while others had little to their name. Nor was the inquiry about how much money people spent, but rather a question of what they valued, how they perceived life and why. While it is certainly true in general that the more money people have the more they spend, spending does not necessarily translate into environmentally harmful consumption. After all, a fortune lavished on buying antiques, commissioning works of art, tree-planting or charitable donations will do negligible harm or none at all, and may indeed do good, while a fraction of that sum, if spent on clothes, shoes,

DVDs, home decorating, gadgets, novelty items, cheap flights, or many of the other popular objects of expenditure, will have a measurable, damaging environmental impact. It is, then, sadly necessary to underline at this time of rapidly increasing poverty in the UK that the lifestyles of modest material consumption we are concerned with here are those which are actively welcomed and enjoyed.

Differences and similarities

As I have said, I found great variety amongst the individuals to whom I applied the label modest consumer – or rather, who identified themselves as such. On the basis of this small sample it seems that freely chosen modest material consumption is not the special province of a particular age or level of income or education. And though some of the people I spoke to would certainly stand out in some way if one met them in a crowd, most would unobtrusively blend in. Some of those who lived with a partner found that their attitude to material consumption was shared with him or her, but this was by no means always the case. While certain lives were fundamentally shaped by a desire for frugality, most of their ways of living simply incorporated limited consumption into more conventional shapes. For some individuals, their modest consumption was a private matter, but others felt it their responsibility to try and influence those with whom they came into contact.

What this whole chance collection of people had in common was that they were all proactive in living. Not one of them waited for life to happen to them; rather, each one went to meet it and forged their ways of doing things according to their personal wishes and principles. Their activities included many live interests, as we shall see in Chapter 4. It seems that a high proportion of these interests and skills had their origin in childhood. New activities and concerns most often developed as a result of personal experience or the infectious enthusiasm of others, and sometimes resulted from reading. Tellingly, several remarked that the material conditions of their childhood, which would be considered deprived today, had never felt impoverished, so much the norm were they in their communities at the time. And notably, no matter how deeply committed these people were to minimising their current consumption, the women and men I spoke to were unanimous in their refusal to jeopardise their relationships with close family members because of differing values.

Now it's time to stop talking about the modest consumers in the abstract, and in the next chapter I will begin to introduce them and their stories.

3

Lives That Tell Stories of
Happy Modest Consumption

The modest consumers divided between those who had long lived materially modest lives and those whose lifestyles had altered with time. Some individuals had been materially undemanding all their lives; some had made a radical change to their way of living, while others, though never great spenders, had consciously pared down their material expectations further. This chapter relates the thoughts and experiences offered to me by five of those who had continued the modest material tenor of their childhood into independent adulthood, while putting their own stamp on their contemporary lives, and five whose ways of living had changed notably.

Lifelong Material Modesty

EMMA

Emma, born in 1961, was a single parent with twin boys and two daughters aged between eighteen and twenty-five. She worked three days a week at a job which she combined with other freelance work. Several years earlier she had had a high powered career but found the pressures of it very difficult to square with having children and wanting to be part of the community and having more meaning in the place where she lived. She decided to give it up; it simply meant, "If we had less money we had less money". "Our modest consumption is tied up with modest income," Emma told me, "but I don't think I would live very differently if I earned double what I do earn except that I would probably run a car." Later, however, she reconsidered this possibility:

> "I wonder if life would be easier with a car; but on the other hand
> if you don't have a car you have a lot of space, and you don't do that

running about that you do if you're ferrying children backwards and forwards, etc., etc. If you're driving somewhere, you leave work, you get in the car and you're home, quick, quick, quick. Whereas when I leave work I've got a two-mile walk; OK I may be tired but the actual walk clears my head. When I was writing I used to write in my head."

Apart from walking, Emma's family's modest consumption looked like this:

"We buy second hand, revamp, refurbish, I like making things. I tend to buy good quality second hand or antique rather than new because you tend to get better quality; I use sales, I use fabric, I knit, make things, buy old china in odd bits but the colours sort of match rather than sets; we have a sharing system with a friend who's got an allotment, we've had organic box schemes, I shop locally, use the Co-op and the credit union. For holidays we go to Quaker camp and visit family. It's lack of money more than anything else that we don't go away, but I wouldn't do what other people do and go without good food or beautiful books and go to Kenya for two weeks."

Emma was a reflective person, who brought some unusual angles to bear in explaining her chosen lifestyle:

"It strikes me that the kind of exchange between friends (vegetables, jams and preserves, sewing and mending, passing things on like children's clothes, lifts) happens between women who are at home or working part-time. So, have things changed very much from the dim and distant days when Marx and Engels identified the development of labour away from the home as a primary site of oppression and alienation? As a woman I never much fancied the alienated workplace, as a feminist I don't much fancy it for men either.

It also strikes me that many of the things I value I value as much for aesthetic reasons as for sustainable ones. I prefer wholefoods and home-cooked foods. I cook and I am concerned about the relationship between health and food. I knit and sew because I love to do both and I enjoy making things for people. I don't like the pressures of the mass produced, maybe because I'm awkward and don't see why all kitchens have to be made of chipboard. I like old fabrics, old wood. I like the look and feel of milk and chalk paints over the look and feel of acrylic-based ones. I prefer Victorian houses to modern ones."

The knitting and sewing that Emma so enjoyed began when she was very young, taught by her mother and grandmother in an attempt to get her to sit still. Her mother, like Emma, had also been a keen cook. Indeed, Emma carried with her much of what she imbibed from her parents. So what was her childhood home like?

"Materially we were not well off, culturally and emotionally we were. My dad worked but my mum didn't. We had the kind of house where the door was always open and you could always have something to eat – my mum would always make a cake if one of us brought somebody round. If some trade unionist from Chile had turned up my dad would bring him round to sleep on the sofa, that sort of thing. He was a builder.

"Neither of my parents had any formal education but they were incredibly well educated. They always read. My dad was in the army and he seemed to have learnt a language wherever he went. They both travelled, and my mum was a musician, so they didn't have a narrow working class outlook. Both of them had not been able to go to grammar school because of poverty in the 30's so they were very concerned that there would be books and music and we would have the chances we wanted. They weren't very typical working class, no they *were* typical of a kind of working class that has disappeared because it was self-taught, it was trade union-motivated, Labour Party-motivated, they would go to WEA classes, language classes, all those things that don't seem to be there anymore."

It remained important to Emma to have an open door, not to shut her eyes to the world and to other people just because she was alright herself. She felt it was important to be committed to education and social justice. Doing your duty, what you know is morally right in your own conscience, she believed, while perhaps not easy, changes you in unexpected ways because it takes you outside your own limitations. "I have been thinking about the issue of values," she told me:

"I was brought up not to consume: my parents came from Christian and Socialist perspectives, my mother especially was strongly influenced by the Catholic traditions of social responsibility. We talked about global markets, environmental damage, the over-use of chemicals, years before these were fashionable issues. My father was a craftsman who valued the old over the new. My mother's philosophy was 'people before things'."

The only regrets that Emma had with regard to her modest lifestyle were that she had not been able to visit Venice and that she sometimes found herself thinking that she could not afford £50 for a book. Otherwise, she felt very blessed and rated her satisfaction with her life at 8 out of 10. What might increase her satisfaction would be to realise her hopes to write. Books were of enormous importance to her, and she believed they were the other main influence on her, after her parents:

"I mean if you were a reading teenager in the 70's you could read a lot of things in the public library. I mean I read Simone de Beauvoir, I read Germaine Greer from the library, I read Kate Figes, I read my way through intellectual feminism in my teens, I read my way through political theory, I read Rawles, I read all sorts of stuff because it was in the library, and although we didn't have the money to buy those books I could borrow them from the library. Oh and the school library had Rachel Carson, *Silent Spring*; I remember now I took it out and took it home and my mother read it and I remember we talked about it, about environmental things."

Musing about modest living, Emma said:

"A very good bit of advice I was given by somebody who was left as a single parent in the 60's with no money was always keep yourself a luxury: she said, 'you can do without foreign holidays but if you feel miserable without butter on your toast buy butter!'"

She concluded:

"The things that make you happy in life are not the things that necessarily you can buy with money, and I would fully accept that I went to university, and was able to buy a house, I have environmental advantages, and I don't have to live on the kind of council estate a friend of mine in Manchester is trying to get off. Not having money is a nuisance, but it's a superficial answer to problems."

§

CHRIS
Learning to be in the present was important to Chris. He was 57 and lived in a small Victorian terraced house in Norwich. He had grown up in

Brentford, London, which he described as a cohesive, fairly working class area at the time. His father was a teacher, a not particularly well paid job in those days, so the family's lifestyle was 'basic'. Chris had written that he had chosen to live modestly because, *The general misgivings about material goods – or rather – the illusion that they can make people happy – is something I had had for a long time; and so, as I have become more simplified, I think I have become more content/happy in myself.*[ii]

I asked him to tell me about how his life had unfolded:

C I grew up with a relatively simple lifestyle, and then later on when I went to university I was quite rebellious in a way, in that I wasn't interested in what, apparently, a lot of my peers were interested in, which was a lot of material stuff, a career and all the rest, I didn't really feel sort of drawn to that. It wasn't particularly ideological, it was more that I didn't really feel that this was going to be anything fulfilling.

T That was a conscious feeling, was it?

C Yes, that was a conscious feeling, and I think it was affected by my sort of spiritual sense; that's a difficult word for some people, but I remember having had it since being a child, I've always had a sense of something other than myself going on, other than the material world going on, so that helps if you have that. I find it quite difficult to hear people talking about not having any sense of anything bigger than themselves really.

T Have you any idea where that sense came from? Was it something that was in your family?

C Yes, it was originally a religious upbringing in the traditional sense of the word. I think that's where it originated, so I sort of imbibed this in the family. They were regular church-goers, and I found myself quite steeped in it really, and didn't realise till I was 13, 14, 15, that this was a bit odd really, that it wasn't normal compared to my peers at school. I was interested in the more mystical realm, I suppose. I was drawn in by the sort of ritual. And then being, as I was, a child of the 60's, I started reading about eastern religions and so on, and realised that this mystical tradition was universal. So I was a bit of a puritan student, I remember being quite austere with myself and quite disciplined on what was then my student grant.

---

ii Where quoting directly from questionnaires, the participants' responses appear in this typeface.

In his twenties Chris was still living in London and was an almost incessant activist of one kind or another, mostly in the development field. He was in a group that ran a coffee campaign, a forerunner of fair trade. He was also involved in anti-apartheid activities, the World Development Movement and such like. "It was the heyday of activism. I loved it, it was my time of adrenaline. I could get drained by it as well but on the whole it was what made me tick." Then, when Chris was first married, he did a course in Theology which, looking back, seemed to be a 'marker' because, in the course of the training, he met a Franciscan priest called Eric Doyle who became his mentor and a hero figure. Doyle probably 'sowed the seeds', Chris thought, because he made a link in his theology between activism and spirituality, and because caring for the earth and animals is at the heart of Franciscanism.

While his children were small and Chris was working full-time in the fairly stressful role of a social worker with The Children's Society, his activism went into abeyance for several years, a period that he found frustrating. In 1999, several years after the end of his marriage, he decided to go part-time with work: "It was a quality of life decision. Essentially I wanted more time to do what I was then counting as the 'other work', so some of the campaigning work I was then involved with, which was Oxfam at the time, more time with friends, more leisure time, and to an extent with the children, who were then in their teens." Modifying his consumption following his reduced income was much easier than he had expected because he hadn't been a great consumer before. The financial adjustment he made was to stop paying into a pension fund.

Chris often went for bike rides in green spaces with friends. Being outside in a natural environment was very important to him, and he felt it brought him back to himself. His experience was that, "It touches on the spiritual realm. For me it can be where you can get these little glimpses that there are these much deeper things going on. There's a sense of history and ancientness, that things have been around for a while. I mean if I'm walking around in a wood there might be trees that are three or four hundred years old, that's something bigger than ourselves, there's something bigger than me."

In contrast to cycling, flying, Chris reckoned, was the most environmentally damaging thing the individual could do: "To go up in a standard kind of wide bodied jet that travels across Europe and over to the States is like going up in a power station essentially, it's the same level of energy consumption. It's also using up future energy supplies." This was the one sacrifice that Chris found had resulted from his modest living, particularly because he had longstanding friendships in America. But he knew of the effects of climate change on the developing countries for which he had so keenly put a lot of voluntary energy into development education, so the end of travel to the States was something he felt he had to 'manage'.

In recent years, both Chris's spiritual slant and his activism had taken new directions. He had developed an interest in dance, movement and the arts, and belonged to an 'authentic movement' group. He explained:

> "That's essentially a movement meditation group, very loosely. Authentic movement has got its roots in Jungian psychotherapy, but it's not used as a therapy, it's entirely impulsive through each individual movement which comes from reading body sensation and internal body impulse. The art of it is to learn to witness yourself as you move, which is not easy, it's a real discipline to learn. It's about understanding different aspects of yourself in the present... It's completely about the non-material and that group of people, it's like a little oasis, a way of checking ourselves and the world really, and it's a way of grounding ourselves. Being present is what a lot of it's about. And it teaches me to be more present in the rest of my activities."

Recently Chris had put a lot of energy into the Transition Town Network. [The Transition movement is something I shall return to later]. He was part of the core group of five people who, eighteen months earlier, had decided to get this nation-wide community initiative going locally. For him Transition was the way forward and the means to involve more and more people in what needed to be done in local communities to address the twin challenges of climate change and peak oil. "For me", he said:

> "It is bringing together the two strands I was talking about, the activist strand and the more reflective and artistic sort of strand, they're constantly being brought together within the Transition movement, because we need to be able to maintain what we do and we need to be able to support each other, and that's an area where I think sometimes the more pure activists amongst us have fallen down, we haven't understood that. We haven't understood that we need to attend to our own personal sustainability; you get burnt out if you don't."

§

MARY

Mary, a Yorkshirewoman of 62, lived in a small ex-council flat on a low-rise estate in a pleasant outer London borough. Since retiring three years before, her life had been occupied with gardening on her allotment, swimming, walking, reading, painting, and playing with her grandchildren. She worked voluntarily in a primary school one morning a week, helped to set up an annual art exhibition locally and was involved in organising artist exchanges between her local area and its French twin town. She rated her overall satisfaction with her life high, at 9 out of 10. Earlier, she had turned her hand to various jobs, as a library assistant, psychiatric social worker, teacher, barmaid, charity administrator and secretary. Now she earned some money by teaching English to young French students to whom she also gave hospitality, for three weeks at a time during the summer.

For most of her life Mary had lived with limited means. Her father had been unable to work owing to ill-health and died when she was twelve; her mother was untrained and only able to find poorly paid office work. Yet Mary did not feel materially hard done by. She told me, "We certainly didn't get everything we wanted for the asking, but we were always well fed, we had holidays – we had an auntie with a caravan at the seaside. It certainly didn't feel deprived. I mean our social ideas were to visit the relatives, but that's what everybody did then". Her mother knitted all her woollen clothes, even a swimming costume that was taken apart when outgrown so that it could be re-knitted in a bigger size.

Divorced when her son was very young, Mary's adult life continued to be financially constrained. Now she was more comfortably off but chose to continue with her modest lifestyle, travelling by bike or public transport rather than buying a car, staying with friends or family or in a B&B for holidays, shopping at the local market, cooking from scratch, using Freecycle to find items she needed, such as a high chair for her grandchild. Why? "Because too many people in the world have insufficient for the rest of us to waste resources, and waste clutters up the environment". This was a recent rationale because, "It's sort of trendy now to de-clutter and downsize, but I never upsized so that was never an issue for me! I've always thought some things were wasteful and I've never been able to go along with it, the café culture and Starbucks coffee, for instance. I mean, if I had millions I still wouldn't do that, pop into Starbucks as people do", and she cited a man she had met who lived on the tenth floor and did not keep coffee in his flat because he simply went down ten storeys and round the corner to Starbucks every time he wanted a cup. "If we weren't so wasteful of resources, and if there was the political will, if people put their minds to it, then everybody could have clean water and something to eat every day."

Acquisition of possessions was of no interest to Mary and she was also keenly aware of the circumstances in which some consumer goods are produced:

> "I mean jewellery, on the whole I don't like the way that it's mined, the production, I don't like the way that people are exploited to get it, I don't like the way people's lives are endangered to go and mine silver and gold, I don't want to buy it, I don't want to be part of that. I've seen those photos of the silver mines, and it's like a big quarry, and there were ladders higher than this [four-storey] building, homemade things with bits of wood, and it was all wet and slippery, and the guys had to go up and down these and it just looked horrendous. I think they shouldn't have to live like that. And the gold mines in South Africa as well, just unspeakable."

Although Mary felt so strongly about such matters, she kept her views to herself:

> "I wouldn't normally comment unless I was asked. I mean if I was looking in a jeweller's window with a friend I wouldn't be saying, 'you're not going to be buying gold are you, think about it', because it's not for me to comment, it's just for me to decide about my own behaviour really. Some things I do try and communicate, if I think that there might be the sort of result that I'm after, but it's difficult. I mean I'm in a fair-trade financial set-up and I tell people about that, thinking that if they've got some spare money they might want to but, no, I don't bang on about, 'I think this is wrong and that is wrong'."

There had been a time when Mary:

> "…had more cash than I knew what to do with and I found it quite difficult to spend it really because I couldn't see a sensible thing to do with it. One of the things I could have done, for instance, was buy a little place in France, as many of the people round here do, but the last thing I want is a little place in France! You know, the trips back and forth, having to go because the neighbours complain about the state of the garden, they worry about the security, I mean I've got a perfectly

sensible little place here that's fine, and if I go to France I'll stay in a hotel for a couple of nights or with a friend. So I've never really been acquisitive even given some opportunity."

Working on her allotment was one of the aspects of Mary's life that brought her most satisfaction. She had been doing it for about thirty years, starting when she had a 'stroppy adolescent', and finding it a relief to have somewhere to go and do something physical and work her exasperation out of her system. It was also very sociable, and now she considered it as being her green gym, as well as a source of free food. Her allotment neighbours were particularly caring, and, as her son and his family now lived some distance away, Mary found that her friends made all the difference to her life. Some of her oldest and closest friends were still the other single parents she had met as a young mother and who had provided mutual support; they still gave each other companionship and laughter. Community was important for Mary and she recognised that this does not just happen, it depends on people doing things to create it.

Now that she was retired and in control of her time, Mary particularly enjoyed her life. Her plan was to earn money in the summer with her language teaching so that in the winter she could go somewhere she hadn't been before to "try and do something useful with the locals", such as helping children at a school in India with their English and working in a centre in Swaziland which looked after children orphaned by Aids: "How brilliant is that!"

§

NAOMI

Naomi, who was 35, had chosen to prioritise interesting and useful work; she was not interested in money, she said, and had a social and environmental conscience. What was important to her was achievement and getting recognition for what she achieved. She lived in a large northern city, where she missed hearing birdsong and seeing gentle landscapes which had a peaceful effect on her mind. Her home was a small flat in a new-build housing co-op and, after eight years there, she still hadn't got round to putting up the bathroom mirror or shower rail, and the flat was only half-decorated. She was working as a community development worker and volunteered with an asylum seekers group, and was considering doing a PhD. She realised that everything would be different if she had family: "I'd need money and it would be obvious what I'd spend it on. I wouldn't want to bring kids up in penury! I wouldn't want them to want for things, but I wouldn't want them to take stuff for granted."

Naomi derived particular pleasure and satisfaction from being outdoors: hiking in the country, swimming in the sea, and seeing beautiful sunsets; from dancing and singing, live music and theatre; and from getting involved in actions or campaigns with great people. She felt sure she had developed her interests during childhood. Although her parents had had a comfortable income, they were never materialistic. She had had a lot of clothes but they came from jumble sales, and much of the furniture at home was second hand. The one thing in which she and her brothers were indulged was books: "If I told my dad I'd finished the book I was reading there would often be another one in my place on the breakfast table, which was really nice". Naomi's father was an influence on her love of theatre too. She remembered as 'magical' the time she went to see a performance of *My Fair Lady* that he had directed at the FE college where he taught, and being swept away by the atmosphere, going out late and dressing up; it resulted in her getting involved for several years in the theatre group in the next door village.

It was her mother taking her on CND marches that started Naomi on her campaigning activities. She had enjoyed the demonstrations outside military bases, singing protest songs, seeing boys with long hair and girls with long dresses, finding it romantic and wanting to be a hippie herself. Back at primary school, having heard the issues discussed at home, she could not understand why other children would not think that it was a good thing to go on a CND march, and believed now that this the experience had "built my identity a bit".

Naomi's love of nature began with her family's camping holidays and beach trips and her own solo explorations around her village. She felt that exposure to things at a young age was hugely important, and referred to the director of the Black Environment Network she had recently heard saying that they took people from inner city communities out on walks in the countryside and involved them in conservation work because people who have never had gardens have not had the chance to develop a relationship with nature or to love it, and, "if you love something you want to protect it and you have to experience it".

§

ANTHONY

A retired scientist of 70, Anthony had lived modestly all his life. "It always seemed natural," he said, "even genetic!" Spending money did not give him a sense of self-worth, he said, and he felt that trying not to consume too much relieved one of money worries and made life more pleasant.

Anthony's attention was turned in the direction of making the world a better place, and he belonged to several organisations concerned with peace, the environment and social justice.

Anthony's approach to life was characterised by a well-informed and analytical thoughtfulness, down to the details of everyday food shopping:

"I'm not vegetarian. It's said that going vegetarian is one of the most important things you can do but I do have a very small amount of meat and fish, in terms of footprint. In addition, with fish, I'm quite concerned about endangered species and fish stocks, so I go quite a bit by what the Marine Stewardship Council say is OK; it's quite limiting, though I don't say I never have things on the list. I never waste food. It does take time and thought. I was widowed about seven years ago and after that was solely responsible for the shopping and looking after everything and I amazed myself by getting quite interested in shopping. Before, I'd tried to avoid it but, because I was actually interested in walking lightly on the earth, I developed a different attitude; when I really had to do it I realised that we can't be self-sufficient, everyone depends on other people for textiles, food, virtually everything, and I got to appreciate that commerce is a good thing, so that on the one hand I'm a critic of the worship of business and perpetual economic growth, but on the other hand fair exchange is good, and people helping each other, and economies of scale and production, and transfer of skills, and all these things are a really important part of a reasonable life. So I shop trying to balance things out. To be local, organic and fair trade all the time would give you a really hard time, so my principle is that if I can perhaps have one of those, that's alright."

One way in which Anthony had consciously reduced his consumption was in relation to newspapers. Now he bought just one paper a week, the *Guardian Weekly*, weighing ounces in comparison with the pounds of papers he thought most people buy. Having let go of the need to buy more newspapers, he was no longer burdened with the pressure to read them. Personal possessions were of no interest to him, indeed he had found that the simpler he made life, the happier he was. He wasn't sure whether this was because his conscience became clearer in the process or whether it was just that there was less 'stuff' to keep track of and maintain. He felt that he was naturally "something of a socialist or collective person" who would ideally have liked to live communally, and who much preferred using the library to having his own large collection of books. Indeed, his personal preference shaded into a political perspective, as I discovered from his political analysis, particularly of capitalism and economic growth:

"I've got quite interested in recent years in where the need for economic growth comes from. My take on it is that a lot of it has to do with the system of interest on capital, it isn't just the values from the big people, the CEOs of the banks, and it isn't just institutions solely, it isn't government solely, it's ordinary people like you and me. I mean if we have £100 in a savings account we want it to be £105 next year, if it's £103 we're disappointed. It may be that my economics is very naïve but it does seem to me that this translates into economic growth. I think perhaps the problem is that in earlier times it was a scarcity economy, it was a real struggle to get enough and to produce enough but now, for at least half a century, we've had a post-scarcity economy and so the problem is not that it's difficult to make enough stuff to keep us clothed and fed, etc, but it's too easy to make this stuff and the momentum to make all this stuff still exists."

Environmental activism had recently extended Anthony's political thinking from a socialist standpoint to encompass an admiration for the potential of anarchism:

"I've long had an interest in anarchism but in recent years it's become quite a bit deeper… Yes, so politics, in the sense of the polis, how people live together, how they resolve their conflicts, is interesting to me. Going back to the first climate camp in 2006, I learned about it shortly before it first happened, and I was really turned on by finding out about it and thought this is something I want to be part of. And so I went, and learned a lot from people there and then I went to most of the monthly planning meetings, and it was the radically democratic way in which the people who are involved in this operated, and it's part of their ethos and it's written into the terms of reference of what Camp for Climate Action is. Sometimes people think anarchism is not organised, but in fact what I discovered is that the people involved in the Camp for Climate Action were highly organised and there wasn't a leader. I was incredulous, it seems a logical contradiction but it isn't. And the weekend gatherings for planning the forthcoming camps were astonishingly efficient. Something remarkable was achieved, and they don't do it with money. That's the other interesting thing, the budget in each case was very small, and the cost of the weekends was very low, and they were very relaxed about money, because some people who went really have no money, and so they said if you can only pay 10p pay 10p. There would typically be between fifteen and about a hundred people at these weekend meetings, and things would be discussed in great detail, with great passion, in a completely democratic way, and very efficiently and quickly; people were required to be very concise and never to interrupt, and to have hand signals. You have facilitators who are very skilled and trained. I remain very impressed by all that."

So impressed was Anthony, in fact, that he felt that the interesting experiences and people associated with climate camp were in some ways more exotic than going abroad and having a holiday in an international hotel.

As the son of tenant farmers on a West Country hill farm, Anthony had grown up in a very frugal environment. His parents had saved all the money they could in order to be able to buy their own farm, so their life was not deprived but very simple: "and one accepted it. There were more important things. So the simple way of living didn't give me a problem and never has, in fact it's stayed with me." But Anthony's self-confessed "intellectual take" on things undoubtedly also had some impact on his consumption. Always with his nose in a book, apparently, ideas were what had given him particular enjoyment and satisfaction all his life.

Anthony rated his satisfaction with his life at 9 out of 10, deriving particular enjoyment from anything with intellectual content. Part of the reason for his high level of life satisfaction was his deliberate decision on the death of his wife to adapt to his new situation and be positive. Thus, for instance, he never complained about bad weather. Even he, however, had been surprised to discover how high he rated his satisfaction with his life, particularly in view of his concern at the state of the world and the prospect of climate change, a phenomenon which he believed was more likely to have been underestimated than exaggerated. Mulling over the surprise he had given himself with such a high spontaneous life satisfaction rating, he explained, "The 9 out of 10 relates to how I see myself in the world as it now is, having a favoured existence, considering the many ways things could be worse for me. However, if I consider the many ways in which human society and the state of the world could be better I would rate things as 9 out of 100."

The feeling that the prospects for a long, good life for his grandchildren were really quite slight could feel completely overwhelming, and yet he felt that his own life now was good: "It doesn't seem to stack up". Anthony could only understand this apparent paradox by reference to two factors, a less than happy childhood, due to his intellectualism not having been understood by his father who often criticised and rarely praised, and the receding of his earlier fear about the arms race and possible nuclear annihilation.

> "I really did feel bad about that, and did feel, you know, what's the point of going on? And we haven't got a future and we don't know what's going to happen, and we're going to die in a really awful way. I worked through that somehow, and I like the saying 'what doesn't kill you strengthens you', and both that and my bereavement, I think if you *can* respond positively to things; I mean of course I'm not indifferent to what happens to my grandchildren. But I also don't expect to change the world single-handedly, that's the other thing. When you're younger you think you're going to put some energy in and watch the results. I don't mind doing a little bit that I think is right, and I like to see results, it doesn't seem to worry me if the results come after I'm gone."

Forging New Ways of Living

SARAH

Sarah was in her mid-thirties and had children of 18 months and 5 years. They lived in the north-west of England, near to where she had grown up. Of her income she said, "I'd say our average annual income, including benefits, is about £9,000. It certainly feels like we have plenty of money and are very lucky relative to the vast majority of families in the world."

Of her lifestyle she wrote on her questionnaire:

> *Although I have a 7.5 ton truck, this is a camper van/ traveller live-in, and we don't use it at all while we're in the city. We cycle, walk or catch the bus/train. We generally have a policy of buying everything second-hand, and we've also encouraged our families to give second hand presents to us and our children. For example, when the hoover broke (it used to be my grandma's so was quite old) I preferred to pay £65 to repair it, than buy a new one for the same money, which in any case, probably wasn't as good quality as the original one. We don't have a telly, but do enjoy reading the paper, listening to Radio 4, and music.*

All our food is bought from a co-op which sells whole-foods and animal- & sugar-free things, with top-ups from the nearer but more expensive health food shop. In that sense, food is different – we choose to spend a lot of money on very good food. This is because of wishing to have a lower impact, support independent shops, support organic, help the environment, not contribute to the dominance of supermarkets, and also because we think it's better for our long term health. In terms of energy consumption, we don't drive unless essential and wouldn't dream of taking a short-haul flight, and have a 'put on an extra jumper' mentality about keeping the house warm. Though we do use the heating and won't live in a freezing house! I use old fashioned washable terry nappies for my daughter, and soak and rinse by hand rather than have the washer on every day.

We have a very low income, relative to national averages. In fact my children would probably be described as being in child poverty. Yet they have the best food, a houseful of great toys and books, frequent visits to the countryside, etc, etc. We actually have lots of spare money and are saving rapidly, but that's because we have really low expenditure. If we need something, we can generally buy it without thinking about the cost. Lucky to live in a council home, where rent is cheap, which makes a big difference.

Sarah's stated reasons for living the way she did were that she didn't want to buy plastic rubbish that would last two days yet remain twenty thousand years in landfill; or cheap clothes that were made in sweatshops; or cheap food, both because of the use of pesticides and because of the suffering of farmers. She was also aware that over-consumption in the west is responsible for environmental degradation and for poverty and suffering in the third world.

Sarah's lifestyle was entirely politically inspired, and contrasted considerably with her upbringing. She explained in some detail how it had come about. First of all:

"Until I was 12 I lived in a terraced house which was quite a comfortable house. My dad was an electrician and my mum was a nursery nurse and then a dental assistant, so what you might call upper working class or lower middle class. They were very, very conventional in outlook and I guess like proper working class they had things very hard in the past and so material goods were an important aspect of their rise in status. My dad started working for himself, and when they built themselves up a bit they started to have more material wealth and we moved to a new house, from the bottom of the hill to the top, which was a 1930's semi-detached with a big garden in a much more salubrious area. The house we lived in and the décor was always absolutely spotless, nothing out of place, no dirt, it seemed as though nobody lived there. We also bought a better car, and my parents started going on foreign holidays. Also spending on clothes was very, very important; still is, my parents like to look good."

But Sarah did not regard her parents' values as immodest, or their spending extravagant: "I was taught to respect the value of money, never get into debt, don't buy anything you can't afford. My parents dislike excessive and conspicuous consumption. But they do buy stuff, and value their self-worth to some degree by their ability to buy nice things. Just not excessively."

Sarah had shared her parents' outlook while she was still at home:

"I guess I inherited my parents' value systems to a very large degree, but I went to a university which put a lot of emphasis on questioning and discussion, and I guess I was compelled to abandon much of that value system at university. What I'm basically saying is I went from being working class to being fairly middle class, and so with that comes a much more liberal attitude through the constant discussions and challenges from university friends."

Some of those discussions arose out of the frequent visits Sarah made to the theatre while a student; exposure to new perspectives resulted in her becoming more politically aware, within a conventional framework, she said. After the discussions came the first-hand political influence; the nuances of the dramatic change that her life underwent emerge from her detailed account:

"I also had a boyfriend at university whose parents were quite far left, and he was much, much more politically aware than I was and we had lots of discussions, and it was with him that I went on the first Criminal Justice Bill demonstrations. I changed course at the end of my second year, so I did my final year in Politics which again was something which raised political issues, and then I guess it could have all just stopped there, I could have been a middle class liberal quite happily all my life were it not that I and this boyfriend went to a road protest. To cut a long story short, I gave up my job in order to become a protester, and at the time I felt it was almost like a year out from my career, to kind of explore that culture. But I guess the bypass was never just about the bypass, it was about the whole political system, about challenging the status quo, and I became aware of a whole political network of resistance, met people at that time who are still my closest friends, and I guess never looked back. It took me a while before I realised I wasn't going back. I knew I was never going back once I realised that the Newbury bypass was just one episode in a long history of direct action, that there were people out there who were in the trees and then went back to other types of political action in their own communities that I had previously known nothing about. Meeting all those people in this kind of national network and realising that there was a whole supportive subculture of people for whom the things I'd previously held important, career, money, status, success in certain terms, those things didn't matter, and I realised that I actually could abandon all those things and I would be alright. Having been taught that money was very, very important in life, all my life, I think it was quite a big step to abandon that sense that you must have money. I mean I was the first in my family to go to university so it was a massive step to abandon all that, it did come kind of gradually that I don't need to have a career, and then you don't need much money at all to have a happy life. And it was so much more fun, ultimately! I think I'm definitely happier, freer; I think there is a sense of liberation in not being attached to money or to realising that you can have a not penny in the world and you'd still be able to look after yourself. I learned lots of basic survival skills like how to build a basic shelter, skipping for food, hitchhiking, etc, etc. It was just liberating to realise that you can survive on very, very little in this country. The people that I met were really interesting. People travel the globe looking for different cultural experiences when in fact there's a whole different culture, a sub-culture that exists on our own doorstep."

Sarah's stance on the world was somewhat different in its explicitly political motivation from that of other modest consumers who were concerned about overseas poverty and climate change:

"I wouldn't have said I was particularly green or environmentally focused when I got involved in the environmental direct action protests. In fact, the reason I got involved was that they were trying to change the status quo. They were the most visible resistance in this country at that time and I already felt that the system and the law in this country was wrong from the point of view of social justice. It links up with my parents, you know they're conservative with a small c but very, very much Labour voting people, and my grandparents they always vote Labour. It just so happened that the environmental focus at the time were the most exciting, offered me a way in to this alternative lifestyle that I felt was a vision of a fairer society, and the fact that it focussed on the bypass was incidental in a way. Obviously the environment is very much linked in with capitalism, destroying the environment, you can't separate the two. I've been arrested very many times while campaigning for environmental and ecological causes, but I'm not particularly involved in climate change campaigning now, I'm more interested in struggling against the arms trade or British involvement in wars."

Having young children had not made it any more difficult to live a low consumption lifestyle because they were still perfectly happy to have entirely hand-me-down clothes and toys bought at car boot sales. Sarah realised, though, that there might come a time when she would send her children to school and when the external world of consumption would impinge on them. Apart from not being able to fly to warm places, she herself encountered two difficulties as a result of her self-imposed material modesty. One was practical, having to go shopping by bus because she was unable to transport two children and the shopping by bike. "It would be so much easier to put them in the car and drive. It's my stubborn determination not to be a hypocrite, the same as not buying our council flat. It's a desire not to be a hypocrite as much as not be polluting," she said. The other was the difficulty in getting her parents to understand her position:

"They've never understood and they still don't, and I've almost got to the point of giving up trying to get them to understand. It's come to a head because I've got children and I don't want my parents to buy loads of stuff for the children, whereas my mum gains intense pleasure from purchasing things for them, and she's very, very good with them in that she does an awful lot of childcare, and she thinks it's a God-given right to literally spoil her grandchildren with stuff that they don't need basically. We did write to all our family and say we don't want any Christmas presents this year and my partner's side of the family were very understanding but my side of the family almost completely ignored the letter."

Sarah believed that change in the world would come from the bottom up not the top down, and that supportive community is the fabric of a good society. Thus she spent much time and energy on local activity, involved in the community garden, the tenants association, organising weekly communal vegan meals, and would have done more if she had not been home educating her children. What gave her particular satisfaction was finding genuine happiness in living a worthwhile life. So how did she define worthwhile?

"I can define more what it's not. Not financial security or the kind of things that my parents aspire towards or what they would wish for me, in terms of having a large house, a comfortable lifestyle, that sort of thing, having a career in something which is pointless. I guess what I mean is, first of all do no harm, try and live life treading on the Earth as lightly as you can, and that's challenging in itself because a lot of our lifestyle in the west is intrinsically damaging to somebody somewhere; and then the second part would be actively trying to improve things."

Sarah recognised that some of her satisfaction with her life derived from the fact that she was a happy sort of person, and some from knowing that she was trying to do the right thing. But she did not want to feel smug: "I'm not so full of myself that I think that I'm going to have a lasting impact on the world as a legacy I leave behind; I enjoy life, and the way I live my life is extremely enjoyable."

§

SUSAN

Susan was the only modest consumer to say that her modest lifestyle was solely a matter of financial constraints. For her there was no element of choice. Five years earlier, at the age of 47, she had had to give up her job as a secretary after developing rheumatoid arthritis. She had therefore had to get used to living without earnings, as well as with greatly reduced mobility and energy. And yet she now rated her satisfaction with her life at 9 out of 10.

Contributing to Susan's acceptance of her situation was her realisation that, "I had everything I wanted to start off with; if I was 18, 19, 20, and I'd found myself in this position it might have been harder. I don't feel it was such a hardship, I had a roof over my head and all the rest of it. I had all the basic material things so I don't really think I'm badly off." She was, moreover, used to having little money at her disposal. Although well-off for a period when living with her former husband and two young children in Kuwait, she had spent much of her adult life bringing up her boys on her own. She had planned, once her sons left home, to pursue a different career and earn more money "and do all sorts of things", but her illness had put an end to this idea a year before she would have been able to put it into effect. Her modest living included looking for clothes in sales, cheap stores or charity shops, shopping around for bargains and discounts for household items, buying surplus produce sold by local people, and having largely home-based or nearby entertainment. Susan did not find this difficult; she loved gardening and was happy just to go for a walk with a pair of binoculars and a wildlife book. It had, however, taken her a long time to come to terms with her reduced mobility and income, their main, joint impact being to cut her off from physical contact with people who lived a considerable train-ride or car journey away. Travel was now not possible without booking into hotels to deal with the fatigue it brought on, but she could not afford to do this.

The change in Susan's life had turned out not to be all negative, however: "The most wonderful thing is having more time," she told me. Now, she said, she had time to be reflective, to learn to enjoy her own company, time to be creative, to listen to the radio, for instance. Her situation had also given her the opportunity to get to know her home area and its many attractions, and so many were there within a 20-mile radius of where she lived that she felt no need to go away on holiday:

> "We've got the river, there's an awful lot of antique fairs; even if I don't
> buy the things, I like going to antique fairs, craft fairs, arts, the Suffolk
> Crafts Society. I used to live in central London and I thought that all
> the life and soul and activity was there but there is a lot going on here.
> There are arts festivals, there's a little cinema just down the road. And
> of course there's the library, there's so much that's free that occupies
> time. There's a really good community spirit here in Woodbridge,
> which I've learnt since I've been here; a lot of voluntary work, there's a
> more caring and community feel than I've ever experienced anywhere

else; that costs nothing except someone's time. I've discovered that since I've been at home. There's something going on almost every day in the community centre, it's not swanky or flash or expensive".

It was all these experiences and possibilities close at hand that contributed to Susan's satisfaction with her life. She also derived much pleasure from her own art, craft and sewing activities. Now with a new partner, she had enjoyed spending a great deal of time planning and researching the doing-up of their house, room by room, searching for bargains in furniture and furnishings on the internet, going to antique and bric-a-brac fairs and auctions to try and find necessary bits and pieces, increasing her knowledge of makers and marks. Given more money, Susan would have liked to be able to "collect a few really nice pieces of either art or jewellery, just to look at something really beautiful, find out how it was made and admire it." She liked having projects to work on, indoors and out, "it gives me more pleasure to do something like that, like in the garden, than to own the latest model of car." In fact, experience had taught Susan to be wary of placing too much value on personal possessions, when her home in Kuwait was looted of its entire contents when Iraq invaded the country in 1990 while she and her family were on home leave: "As soon as I could, I tried to replace like with like, but I could never afford to do it and I did buy a lot of junk just to fill things up, but over time I've realised they didn't replace what I lost so I'm quite happy to discard things. You don't need them."

Susan's partner had similar interests and, in his big workshop, made things for the house and worked on his sailing boat. Susan no longer went sailing, but she did enjoy nature. "Wildlife in my garden is a joy all year round", she said. "Having more time and no money and living in the countryside: brilliant, absolutely wonderful for me, watching the birds on the feeder and things like that. Honestly, it gives me so much pleasure to watch them, and we've got hedgehogs and a little pond, it's wonderful. It's much deeper and more satisfying to watch something that happens over a period of time, naturally, than going into the shop and what you buy and get bored with in five minutes."

In fact, the germs of Susan's interests were first evident in her childhood, and she was aware of her early days as an important influence on what she enjoyed and valued now, for she wrote, *As children we were brought up in central London but we also had a house in Essex which was surrounded by fields to run free in and that we stayed in for holidays. Those early experiences taught me to value sophisticated pastimes like art and theatre, and education and, although we played in Regent's Park, the countryside brought me in touch with my natural surroundings and the value of community.* She had seen her mother sewing, knitting and cooking, never wasting anything, and her father, who worked at two London museums, had been a great handyman, "So", she said, "I have never been a stranger to doing things for myself, but the knowledge that my dad did it to save money taught me that not only was making things yourself pleasurable and creative, it also saved money."

Despite Susan's natural disinclination towards material things, and greater affinity with nature and creativity, it was a big adjustment for her to have to give up her former life as a result of her chronic condition, believing at the time that, "it was the buzz of going to work and managing everything that was keeping me alive and lively." However, she had now come to see things differently, in a way that perhaps made life more comfortable:

> "When I was working I really used to like clothes and looking nice and make-up and all that kind of thing, and now I'm beginning to think how small I am in the world, whereas perhaps when I was working I used to think I was a bit more important than I was, and it really doesn't matter that you are so small, there are so many things going on outside there that are much more important than the individual. It's a good thing to realise that you aren't all-important, that the world can go on well with you and without you."

§

ANGELA

Angela, 33, was in a transition process away from conventional life. She had originally lived economically as a student on a very limited income, learning to look for bargains, but found, along with her husband of eight years, that she got used to it and actively enjoyed living this way. Their constant efforts to save money included shopping at the supermarket at 8.00 pm so as to be able to pick up reduced items. But they weren't just keen on saving money for its own sake, they were both fully aware of their environmental impact and took deliberate steps to reduce it. For example, they washed their car only once a year, and Angela walked or took her motorbike where possible in preference to driving; they only went out in the evenings to places they could get to on foot, grew vegetables on an allotment, avoided goods with excess packaging, rarely shopped for clothes (thus needing only a small wardrobe each), and had few possessions.

Angela lived in a small, unobtrusive house on a busy main road, the front door opening straight into the living room. It was a deliberate choice on the couple's part not to buy a bigger house or to look in a smarter area because this house was sufficient for their needs.

Until four months before, Angela had worked in the City of London as an insurance underwriter. Her husband still worked there, for an insurance broker. She explained:

> "Since we've been married our whole plan has been that we would retire as early as possible so that we could set up a small-holding and live more self-sufficiently. I've been collecting information over the years on energy saving devices and eco-friendly ways of generating electricity, solar, wind, geo-thermal, things that we can't necessarily do here but so that when the time comes I'll be able to say this is the best thing and I know who to go."

They were attracted to self-sufficiency because:

> "The idea for us at the moment is trying to get ourselves off the grid a little bit, trying not to be so reliant on all the services, generally trying to sort of control our lives a little bit more, because you do find that you think you look after yourself and you are independent but you are actually controlled by quite a lot of factors, especially the energy industry. You look through your finances and see how the banks are into everything you do, and insurance companies need to know everything about you, and you start to think, gosh, everyone knows everything about me and I'd quite like to be away from that a little bit. So the idea of not paying into supermarkets, and growing your own stuff appeals. But also to generate my own electricity and get to the point where I'll be generating enough to get back onto the grid and get paid for it – make them pay me for a change, that's wonderful! Whether it'll come to that I don't know."

This was not the way Angela had been brought up. "My parents were, and still are, very keen on material things, keen to have me dressed nicely. I was a child of the 80's so I had things like tape recorders and walkmans, so I did lead a very materialism-oriented lifestyle when I was younger, but this changed once I'd left home." As they had got older, her parents had acquired more electrical appliances, things they had always done without before. "They like their comforts and they say 'we can afford it, we might as well have it, we're not going to rough it'."

Mild-mannered though she seemed, Angela said she could be 'militant' in discussions about lifestyle if she felt people could take it. "So I'll say to Mum sometimes, 'That's ridiculous, you don't need that on all night, why do you do that?' For instance she'll put two plates and knives and forks in the dishwasher to wash and I'll say, 'That's ridiculous. You've got water, soap, wash it by hand, you used to do it all your life', and my mum and dad go, 'We're old, we just like all this now we can afford it and we'll do it no matter what you say'." But she did not push her views if she thought it might jeopardise a friendship. Despite certain differences of opinion, Angela recognised that her parents had been a strong positive influence on the way she lived: "Yes they have always been there for me. We haven't always agreed on everything, as you don't, but they've never let me down, and I've tried never to let them down. And having a good set of parents does give you confidence. I see that in comparison to people who haven't had such good parental support, or the parental relationship has broken down."

Angela had grown up in rural Lancashire and north east England and was used to being around animals and mixing with farming people. Her husband came from the Ukraine and had spent his summers on a farm with no services:

"He's travelled extensively, studying international business and finance, economics, management and language in a number of countries, before getting a job. He's come full circle really because at one point they were living in Siberia, in a house in the forest, and then moved back to Kiev, where his father's family had a farm. So he's done all that, had a wild life in cities, and he's continuing to work in the City which he enjoys, but he intends, the same as me, to return to the earth, so to speak, to start to cultivate and do a small job here and there to make some money, but just live for ourselves. We find that the simpler you make your life the happier you are, the less worries you have. Having so many things to think about all the time can make you quite stressed. You don't need that, we just need to come home and eat our dinner and sit down and talk, and he'll read a book and I'll do some knitting or something, it's so comfortable."

Angela had left her job in the City because she found that it really wasn't the right thing for her, being a "hands-on, outdoorsy sort of person", and because she had found the nature of it stressful. Sometimes having to take money from people unnecessarily in her eyes, just for the benefit of the company, was soul-destroying. She was now thoroughly enjoying the combination of being a housewife, doing a part-time horticultural course, doing craft activities and helping friends with their gardens. She was not new to horticulture as her parents had taught her to grow vegetables when she was young. Now she derived particular pleasure from being able to help others, in contrast to her former work. "To have the opportunity to go out and help people is definitely much better. It makes you feel better. It's not just for my own self-gratification, it makes you feel a calmer person too, or it does for me, I feel I'm doing something useful with my time." During her ten years in London she was extremely stressed all the time. Since she had left her job, her satisfaction with her life had risen from 4½ to 8 out of 10. In addition, she didn't have the stress of her house being full of extremely expensive equipment and of a burglar alarm:

> "I see that with my parents, they have this Fort Knox thing going on at their house. They hardly like to go out because they're so worried. I say, 'if you didn't have all this kit you wouldn't worry so much'. And they don't live in a bad area. They worry terribly about things, possessions, constantly. So I think it reduces a lot of stress, only having basic things. Also just not demanding too much, constantly trying to get away from the mindset, this constant need and want, that's fuelled by the media in a lot of cases, celebrity culture. If you can get yourself out of the idea of 'I want this, I want this, I want this', and think, 'I don't actually need that', and just relax about everything and think, 'what do I really need to live?'"

In the same way that Angela and her husband made only modest demands of their home and belongings, so they found pleasure in simple entertainment and social life. Rather than dressing up and spending a lot of money on a meal and wine in a restaurant, "our idea of fun is going down the pub, having a couple of beers and playing Jenga. It's a really silly thing. Some of my friends thought it was a bit odd and came down with us and played and we had a really, really cheerful night, and you don't have to worry about dressing up and you can just relax. Some of the people I know in London have to have something to stimulate them every weekend, be it a theatre trip, a concert, going on the London Eye. I've always wanted to do something relaxing, perhaps a bit playful."

§

Ed

Ed, a 26 year-old American, came from wealthy origins, and he was surely the modest consumer who had made the biggest change to his lifestyle. This is how he described his materially abundant childhood and youth:

"I grew up in what by most standards would be considered a wealthy family. My father is an American doctor, owns his own practice, has his own surgical centre as well as a radiation treatment facility. As I grew up he acquired more and more wealth, to the point when I was about 10 years old he bought his first airplane and since then about every 2 years he's always gotten a new one, a bigger one, a faster one with a different engine. It started with a propeller and then it moved up to turbo prop, but now it's a jet. So when I became a teenager he would fly every weekend, and at least once a month I would go with him and we would fly to the mountains for breakfast, or whatever, and every holiday would be away from our state. We lived in a big house, we all had cars, so when I was 16 it was accepted that I would have a car, as is the case for my little brother and sister who are teenagers now. We bought new clothes every year; whenever the new academic year would start we'd go and get a bunch of new clothes, and then when the season changed to summertime we'd get a bunch of clothes. I had an allowance, but I also worked because I figured I needed to do something to kill the time. So I would drive my car to school and school would be about a mile-and-a-half away, and I would drive to lunch, even though it would take five or ten minutes to walk. There wasn't anything unusual about what I did. My peers bought a lot more clothes, but in comparison to my friends I think they would have said I had a far more consuming lifestyle, particularly when it came to electronics or anything else. I also used to eat lots of meat, lots of everything, fast food, processed food, things that would satisfy me at that particular point in time."

The house where Ed had lived had a basement with two bedrooms, a living area, an office and a darkroom; the ground floor consisted of a dining room, a living room, a den where the television was, a kitchen, another dining room for more informal dinners, a washer-drier room; and on the first floor there were another four bedrooms. Outside was a garage for three vehicles, and at the back there was a half-acre of land with an outdoor Jacuzzi.

All this was a far cry from how Ed lived now, as he described it on his questionnaire:

In general I view products that meet my environmental and social requirements as being the only option available. For instance, I do not compare the cost of a Tesco chicken with the cost of my local free range organic chicken farm supplier that is located 5 miles from my house and has her chickens at the local farmers market. It is simply the only option if I wish to consume chicken, which I do only on occasion. I rarely spend my money on material goods, instead focusing on events and experiences that provide greater social satisfaction. So the average life of our material goods are as follows: Ecoballs for washing machine (5 years+), clothes (5 years+), computers (5-6 years), television (15 years+). I do not buy out of season fruit/veg, or eat beef – actually rarely eat meat and will always go with the fair trade/local/organic option if available. However, my principal question that will always be asked first is, do I need this? Equipment purchases must exceed the environmental qualifications of existing ones.

I do not fly for a personal holiday, however I do fly when there is a significant family event/emergency. Any overseas air trip would need to be for a period of at least 3 months and only ground transport would be used once I got to the general area. I cycle to work and around town and do not own a car or motor bike. I will only live in a location where I am able to travel this way.

What had changed Ed's approach to life so radically turned out to be not some revelatory life-experience but academic learning, acquired almost by chance. He could trace the sequence of events that had led him to adopt his changed lifestyle. He had taken a degree in Communication, and in the American university system, he explained, students chose their major emphasis of study, and then had to take other modules, including science courses. Ed picked Geology as he liked walking. He enjoyed the course, found he could add a secondary emphasis in Geology, and so took a module on environmental issues and geosciences. In a country where, in his view, the media are appalling in conveying messages about the environment or other global issues, it was this course that had had a major impact on his thinking:

"We just started going through the different aspects that made me think we're just being a bit stupid in how we were choosing to live as a society. And one of the most useful exercises was to supply the world with energy in 20 years' time, and our professor had a table with all the known reserves and the current consumption rates, and then he would show you how long they would last with certain fuel mixes. It was fun just to go through; every country, you would have an assignment of what their fuel mix is going to be, and what the consumption rates are going to be, and there weren't many ways that you could work it! Then we'd sit there and he'd be, 'OK, so how are you going to improve efficiency?', and it wasn't like we were sitting there going, 'we're going to need all these new technologies or develop these new technologies', it was for the most part, 'you know, if we make sure that every building that we build faces south-west because that's where the sun is going to be most of the time, and then you can put this wall here for winter insulation, but in summer you've got sunlight', it was just kind of basic things that people could do immediately, and that's when I started to go home and initiate making it."

Further experiences built on this foundation of Ed's new-found interest in sustainable living. He followed the elective undergraduate course with a Masters in Environmental Management, and then went to live and work voluntarily in a rural community in Uganda for a while. Here he saw people with very little in the way of material goods living apparently happily:

"When you attended to things like food security and access to medical care, there wasn't this constant state of depression. When you spoke to them they didn't speak about money or other stuff, they would just be interested in you and your family, or sharing jokes or dancing, so you would have these things that conceptually you would say put them at a lower stage of development, but in terms of happiness, I think that surveys say that most people in Africa are happier than most people in the Western world, and you just kind of see that in practice. Happiness was just part of living; but here it has to be earned."

This gave Ed a whole new perspective:

"When I got back from there I never really settled back into the procurement-type issues that I had beforehand, it was just sort of it doesn't really matter, and also seeing how far I can go and how much you can do, I just started seeing a bit more about people my age who would have a house or whatever and would complain about not having enough money so they could never go out. And I thought it was much more interesting for me to go out than to own a house".

While he was in Africa Ed met his wife, a British volunteer in Uganda, who cared about the same issues. She was Katarina, an environmentally-concerned young woman whom we will meet in a later chapter. Living with Katarina further supported the changes in lifestyle that Ed was undertaking. Now established in England, he worked as a sustainability consultant, investigating for multinational companies the environmental footprints of their products. He also volunteered for the British Red Cross as an emergency responder and chaired the Overseas Projects Team of an international development charity.

Despite the difference between Ed's former lifestyle and his current one he was sure that there was nothing he missed about the old one. Indeed, amongst the experiences that had helped to reshape his way of living was seeing people who had a lot materially who were unhappy and seeing people who did not own 'the latest everything' be happy. He elaborated on this with respect to his family and friends:

> "My father's been married three times, and I think that says a lot – I've described his lifestyle. Is he happy with it? I think it's all very fragile, and when it falls apart his whole life does, and he seems to get his way out of it by spending more to fill the void. So that's one thing, but my entire family on that side has a great deal, and every time I see them, all they do is complain about things, whatever it may be. I think it would be a rare occasion when I would spend a conversation of more than five minutes with any member of my family without money coming up."

There seemed to be a direct connection in Ed's observations between a deficit in emotional fulfilment and over-consumption of material goods, a profligacy which he found exasperating:

> "I mean when I go back to visit occasionally it really kind of sickens me, it depresses me. I kind of get excited about being away from that, because when I'm out there it's not just that people are living like that. I assume, especially with my friends and family, they're intelligent people, who have me in their lives telling them things about how we

need to be changing our lifestyles, yet they are not only failing to make those changes, but they are actually increasing their harm. So my dad, for instance, built a new house a couple of years ago, he actually has two now. You know, his attempt to be green was saying, 'Oh yes we'll put solar cells on, oh no that's too expensive.' That was a few years ago, and then he got divorced and he remarried and they just moved into a new house, and the new house is unbelievable; there's a waterfall that's just constantly running, from 8 in the morning till 10 at night, every single day, with the lights on, though nobody's in the house."

Despite the huge gulf in outlooks and values that had opened up between Ed and his father, their relationship remained cordial.

"I tell him every year, we've had conversations about it for the past three years, but he just doesn't understand. It's one of those things. Up until I was 18, 19, you just assimilate to your parents' views, and it was after I left home, at that point, when we had discussions, because he would talk to me about politics, that I started disagreeing with him and when that started to happen there was just an acceptance that, as an individual, he respects my opinion thinking differently from him, he doesn't tell me that I'm stupid or anything else. Even though he disagrees, he'll try and find common ground between the two of us, he does say, 'You and I we both care about the environment'. He does turn off the light every time he leaves the room, but then he has this waterfall running all the time. He does think we should be using renewable energy but he also thinks he has a right to use as much energy as he wants. We agree to disagree – is it worth fracturing family relationships for it?"

Ed felt that he'd gained in several important ways as a result of his new, modest lifestyle. The first was feeling healthier and more productive, which he put down either to his improved diet or to cycling everywhere. The second was that he now had more memorable experiences. Unlike people he knew who invested a lot of money in their houses and therefore wanted to stay at home to enjoy them, Ed often spent money on going out to the theatre, cinema or concerts, and enjoyed walking and discussions with friends. But one of the biggest benefits, he felt, was developing a sense of community, building familiarity with regulars at the farmer's market in a way that would be impossible with supermarket shopping, and meeting like-minded people who were interested in sharing, not acquisition.

§

SITA

Born in 1926, Sita was the oldest of the modest consumers. She was also the only Asian participant in the study. She was one of six daughters of an indigenous employee of the Imperial British Government, and she explained to me that:

> "Imperial administrators were not allowed to have any private income or to indulge in private business and trade. That stopped them being open to a plethora of temptations. But to make up for it they were paid very handsome salaries. My father's salary was enormous, and of course he was expected to have a standard of living which conformed with his status, which was overridingly important. We lived well, with eight servants living in. It was a rented property but there were 2½ acres of ground, and there were two cows in the outhouses and all the milk we drank was produced by those two cows tended by our servants. I think it was a kind of generally understood principle and philosophy that there was a certain standard of living which was in conformity with human dignity and so on. One lived accordingly and there was no need to have excess and extravagance and ostentation."

Coming from a different culture, I was somewhat puzzled by the idea that such a standard of living did not involve extravagance or excess, and put it to Sita that there seemed to be a paradox here. Her explanation put an unfamiliar slant on the matter of wealth and its use:

> "Yes, because opulence, but not excess, was necessary for a dignified human life. The servants were part of your extended family, and lived under the same roof and ate the same food and it was very much a feudal kind of life, very much a homestead with two cows and a fowl yard and one's own supply of coconut. Also you wore the best clothes, not for the sake of being ostentatious but because it was aesthetically more satisfying and acceptable to wear clothing which was becoming and well made and would last, than to wear something of lesser quality just in order to save up money and put it in the bank. I would like to explain further: services and goods used provided someone else with a living. Money in the bank was often invested unethically and benefited only vested interests."

So in Sita's formative experience an important distinction was made between generous but thoughtful expenditure and the flaunting of wealth. The kind of consumption that she considered excessive now was the owning of a thousand pairs of sneakers by someone whom she'd heard about on the radio.

In 1957 Sita left for England and took up teaching English, History, Economics and Sociology in secondary schools. She continued to dress well, always buying designer garments, "the minimum amount of clothing which cost the maximum amount of money!" clothes of such good quality that that they never wore out and could be passed on to her niece when, much later, she no longer wanted to wear them. This, she said, was a way in which she had always lived modestly, a habit she had learnt from her parents. She was, though, a little ambivalent about the modesty of her lifestyle. At first Sita stated that she had had a modest lifestyle in some ways all her life, and in its present form since she stopped working. But on talking things over she mused:

> "Well it seems to be a little bit misguiding for me to say all my life as I've been working since I left university and always had money in my pocket and I'm afraid I had the philosophy of spending the money I had and living as fully as possible. In that sense I was not living modestly but as much as my means enabled me to. But in another sense I was really living modestly because of a very traumatic childhood: I had to learn to have a lot of iron self-discipline and always exercised that. I was always very abstemious in my diet and never touched any alcohol until I stopped working. Then I started drinking a little bit of wine and I rationed it daily. So my health has always been very good."

The trauma of which Sita spoke had been the result of her parents' divorce when she was 6 years old. Her mother, to whom she was extremely attached, had moved to England, her father remarried, and her stepmother caned her regularly because, Sita thought, it was the belief in those days that to spare the rod was to spoil the child.

Once in England, Sita continued to spend considerable sums, such as on visits to London theatres "night after night". But perhaps her greatest expenditure was on travel:

> "I travelled as much as I could, not indulging in prestigious travel, but as the opportunity arose. For 8 years I worked in Africa. I was recruited here in London and the contract was such that after the first 2 years they paid for you every year to come back for the summer holiday

to London. Each time I did that, I took a different route and stopped in a different place. I stayed in the best hotels because I had money and I was working and earning it. I stayed in the Palace Hotel in Marrakesh, and it was the only place in which I felt a bit scared, the bedroom was so large! The washbasin was so large you could have bathed a baby in it! As I said before, using services and goods was a way of paying towards someone else's wage packet; that's how I saw it."

The reason for Sita's greater modesty in living these days was that it was "appropriate for my age"; she no longer had the stamina and energy for long haul flights, late nights and irregular meals. The theatre she attended was now the local fringe theatre, and celebrations took the form of meals at home with friends. Instead of exotic locations, she swam at the local public baths, and recreation was found with the University of the Third Age. She no longer flew at all, indeed never left London any more except to visit family in Sussex, whom she reached by public transport. Although her greatly reduced travel was not due to environmental considerations, Sita was aware of environmental issues and did actively support some campaigns:

"I'm glad that I don't fly because I'm very concerned about all the carbon emissions. I'm a supporter of Greenpeace and I write letters and send them money for their various projects: the hunting of whales in the Pacific and lumbering in Canada. They had given the lumbering rights to a firm, I remember, and it was the only sanctuary of the white spirit bear, I hear. Hundreds and thousands of us wrote letters, and as a result the company voluntarily withdrew, it was fantastic. I've been on that historic boat, the Rainbow Warrior, when it was in dock here in Docklands."

Sita was also a member of the Woodland Trust, admiring the work they do in buying land and converting it to native woodland, and providing places for children to enjoy natural surroundings. She remembered the large grounds in which she had grown up, mostly planted with coconut.

Sita's increasing modesty had meant that she had given away as presents almost all her personal possessions of jewellery, porcelain, crystal, and silverware, beautiful things she had bought herself. Neither did her possessions include a washing machine or any kitchen gadgets other than a kettle. I thought this must mean that she washed clothes by hand or went to the launderette, but no, again the early lessons learnt came into play: "I don't do those two things, I do what my mother used to do, I have a laundry service. They collect the washing and bring it back all ironed. Just think of ironing all those sheets at the age of 83! No, I'd much rather give part of my income to a laundry service than use it for doing something else."

As well as early lessons about appropriate expenditure, Sita had also learned to appreciate beauty and culture, and these continued to give her great pleasure. Her love of beauty she felt she owed to the introduction from an early age to a beautiful environment and objects: "They were around me all the time and I just absorbed them through the pores of my skin; that's why I think it's very important that children should have beautiful surroundings." In particular, there was a strong paternal influence. "My father," she explained:

"was very much an aesthete, he was very artistic. He was very good at painting; I remember he did a pastel drawing of some chrysanthemums and even as a child of 8 or 9 I was transfixed looking at that. And then I remember him gathering us all round him and reading poetry. One of the poems he used to read was Edgar Allen Poe's *The Raven*: 'Quoth the raven never more'; and every Sunday he used to play the piano and we had to stand round it with my stepmother and sing hymns. And the furnishings, and the arrangement of furniture, the décor, the colours of the walls, all of these things were carefully thought out. And in our bedrooms every so often my father would change the arrangement of the furniture; he used to consult with us as to where each piece should go and so on, and I became aware of these things and developed preferences and decided opinions."

The capacity to appreciate the simple beauty of the natural world and the built environment, was still of great importance to Sita. As we talked on the phone she looked out of the window, revelling in the view:

"We are having a beautiful day in London today; the oak tree is turning golden, and the cherry tree has lost its leaves but round the bole of the tree there's a carpet of lovely peach and cream and yellow leaves. Every day I go out there and pick up a few leaves of various kinds and bring them home, sycamore and oak from the street. They only last a day and then I go and pick up new ones. They're *entrancingly* beautiful, and the sky's entrancing, it's so beautiful, and the street and the houses, old Georgian houses. I've never tired of looking at the houses and the architectural styles and so on."

A recently developed form of enjoyment for Sita, however, was food:

> "Because you know as children, one of the things my stepmother did was to force feed us, and I and all my sisters completely lost all interest in food. Every time you retched, the cane came down on your back. It was regimental, we had to eat x number of crumpets every morning, a raw egg had to be swallowed every morning. Lunch and dinner we would eat on our own before they did, and she would suddenly swoop down to find out if anyone hadn't had all of the various curries that were on the table."

At last, Sita had learnt how to enjoy food, and took particular delight in simply cooked dishes made of ingredients of the best quality. She had a box of organic vegetables and fruit delivered fortnightly:

> "So for the first time I'm eating vegetables which I never ever ate because I didn't know how to prepare things like kale and Swiss chard. I said to somebody, 'What on earth do you do with celeriac?' It is delicious! I give Abel & Cole a month's order as well and they bring me things like organic beef, which is so tasty, and organic lamb steaks, and all their fish comes from the sea in Devon and Cornwall, and the vegetables come from the home counties; I get some lovely sheep's cheese which comes from Sussex, and I get goat's cheese from Abergavenny, and salmon pate from Inveror – straight from the places where they are made. And the taste of that food! I've stopped eating in cafes and restaurants now because the food at home is so much better!"

At an earlier stage of her life in London, Sita had lived in a flat in a block which she was delighted to discover was run as a community: "It fitted in with my own feeling of egalitarianism because of my childhood experience. I was always on the side of the underdog because I had been one myself. I always vote for the Labour Party, I was always a friend of the destitute, the dispossessed." When the block was bought by the council Sita became a council tenant and, when the council resold the block, no longer able to afford to maintain it, had been transferred to her current one-bedroom council flat in a pleasant area. Here another early interest had reasserted itself, and this was gardening. Her childhood experience of gardening had come about when war broke out and all the family's servants disappeared to join the army. Her stepmother was not prepared to curtail any part of her lifestyle so the children had to do the work the servants had done. Despite these circumstances, she had enjoyed the gardening because the hard physical labour had provided an outlet for some of her anger, and now she still derived considerable pleasure and satisfaction from tending a nearby patch, relishing the physical work involved. This, in turn, led to a sense of contributing to her neighbourhood. She proudly told me:

> "Because I'm fit and not ailing in any way, I took over a small triangle of ground that is a communal area outside my window and I have looked after it for the last ten years since I moved into this council flat. It gives me a place to work in, to plant things in and care for them. Before I came, I was told by a neighbour that it was waste ground; she said that people used to throw all their rubbish there, and after I came somebody dumped a mattress there, and broken furniture. But now they so appreciate what I'm doing, the local people, that not even a piece of paper is thrown in. So it does work."

This observation of the apparently beneficial social effect of cultivating a little public plot was the new aspect of her life that intrigued Sita and she was keen to develop it. She regarded this activity as an experiment in changing the attitudes of people around her, something which she was able to do, she felt, as a result of the greater maturity that comes with old age. She thought it possible that her little garden was the inspiration for others in the neighbourhood who had subsequently transformed a patch of common land which had been full of weeds and used by cats and dogs. Another intervention concerned a young neighbour whose behaviour, the result of serious mental health issues, brought her to the attention of the council which Sita successfully resolved. She was delighted with her new social experiences, and believed they were only possible because she had plenty of time to have contact with her neighbours, being retired.

The things that were important to Sita now, she said, were a willingness to help others; to shun excess in any form – "Because it's always a path of imbalance, ill-health, maladjustment and conflict"; to value social responsibility, always accord to everyone the human dignity which is their right, and treat everyone as an equal or superior; to develop and use the gifts with which you are endowed; to have a sense of humour; never to sit in judgement; to practise acceptance; and to seek to understand an opponent. These priorities were very much in keeping with the encouragement to examine moral values and ethical conduct which Sita felt had influenced the way she lived. It was on these questions that she now had the time to reflect and experiment. Contrary to many people's negative assumptions about old age, Sita saw this phase of her life in terms of fresh possibilities, possibilities that had little to do with material consumption: "I often joke about this and say to people that I have now entered a new incarnation; it's a whole new ball game when you are old, it's a whole set of new interests and new opportunities, and new enjoyments and new openings which come with old age".

§

Emerging questions

What generates satisfaction with life? What are our personal understandings and values, and where do they originate? Can we change them? How do we experience our relationship with the natural world? What is security? Where does the spiritual fit in to everyday life? These are just some of the questions that have began to emerge as themes in the ten accounts we have just heard. We have encountered some recurrent threads running through the experience and thinking of a diversity of individuals, whose only wholly shared characteristic is their own perception that they live a relatively modest material lifestyle, one which they find satisfying. We can learn more about these and other salient questions from these women and men and from the rest of the participants in the Modest Consumers study. Informed by their words, I will explore and illustrate these and other issues in the following chapters which consider many aspects of personal existence that are core to both human wellbeing and to environmental sustainability.

Caveat – the meanings of words

Before going on, however, it is necessary to acknowledge the ambiguities and limitations of the English language when it comes to discussions of material consumption. This expression will crop up unavoidably often, given the focus of the book and the dearth of alternative terms. Due to the multiple meanings and senses of the word *material* it is important to be clear about what I am and am not intending to convey. I do not use the term material in this context to denote the concrete, the antithesis of the abstract or ethereal. The material world of objects and substances, of tables and chairs, plates and forks, guitars and pianos, books and buildings, plants and animals, and of soil, rock, metal, water, fabric, paint and so on *per se* is not problematic. The world is, after all, made up of naturally occurring matter. Some of this is transformed by human creativity into objects which may be useful or beautiful or neither. Material consumption is problematic when the form and extent of acquisition of the manufactured product and the processed substance involves damage to the ecosphere.

Consumption is also a somewhat tricky word in this context. Car engines consume petrol simply to make them work, as animals consume food and plants consume oxygen. But human consumption is not limited to material products. Ugly though the image is, it is also sometimes said that music, literature, theatrical performances and so on are consumed, as increasingly are education and health services. These kinds of consumption are conceptual and relatively non-material. Whatever the case, consumption involves the internalising of something taken in from the external environment by the individual. In the chapters that follow, the expression material consumption is used to signal a sense of unsustainable excess, hard though it may sometimes be for us to distinguish excess from sufficiency, living as we do in a society steeped in the habits and expectations that characterise consumer culture.

4

No Wonder They Were Living Happily!

What is Wellbeing?

Material poverty of a degree which deprives people of the basic requirements and dignities of a decent roof and sanitation, and adequate food, water, warmth, clothing and transport, is a wretched state of affairs which makes life miserable. So is the financial inability to take part, like others, in the life of one's society. But this does not mean, conversely, that wealth is any guarantee of happiness. We see so in the self-destructive behaviour of certain multi-millionaire celebrities and recognise it in the phrase 'poor little rich girl'. It is perfectly possible to be conventionally rich but emotionally and spiritually impoverished, and, conversely, economically wanting but psychologically well-off. So what is wellbeing actually made of? And what is its relationship with consumption? This chapter will explore these questions.

Happiness and wellbeing are words that are bandied about a lot these days and refer to a condition that everyone knows intuitively to be desirable. Wellbeing has been defined in various ways; one particularly succinct definition is, 'a positive and sustainable condition which allows individuals to thrive'.[180] This on-going state is different from the often fleeting emotion of happiness, but the distinction between wellbeing and happiness is frequently overlooked in everyday parlance. Such fudging may have something to do with the lack of an adjective to go with the noun wellbeing, which means that there is no way to describe the state of wellbeing in the way that happy denotes the state of happiness. It does not usually much matter, however, if wellbeing and happiness are used interchangeably, as everyone has a working understanding of what these expressions mean, in context.

Another way in which both individual and social wellbeing have been conceptualised is in terms of prosperity,[181] as we saw in Chapter 1; flourishing is one more. Flourishing has been defined as, 'a combination of feeling good and functioning effectively.'[182] It is seen as one end of the mental health spectrum, where the other is actual mental disorder.[183] Flourishing is a more attractive term than the rather worthy, humdrum word wellbeing. As the present participle of a verb, 'flourishing' has a more dynamic sense. In addition, it contrives to be both a noun and an adjective, and is thus more versatile and elegant. Finally, flourishing means flowering – blooming, indeed – and thus embodies the notion of a lively process of growth which is both healthy and delightful.

Recent developments in considering wellbeing

Whatever name we choose to give the condition, it has attracted a great deal of academic, popular and political interest in recent years. The burgeoning market for books and articles on wellbeing, and tips for enhancing happiness, is complemented by a growing trend among certain economists[184] and politicians to take wellbeing more seriously as an aim of society. In September 2009, French president Nicolas Sarkozy published the report of his Commission on the Measurement of Economic Performance and Social Progress[185] headed by Nobel prize-winning economists Joseph Stiglitz, and Amartya Sen. A key message of the report was that the time was, 'ripe for our measurement system to shift emphasis from measuring economic production to measuring people's wellbeing'. Interestingly, in terms of the double concern of this book, the report recognised further that, 'measures of wellbeing should be put in a context of sustainability'. A year later British Prime Minister David Cameron announced that he was asking the Office of National Statistics to develop happiness measures.[186] The first UK happiness index was published in 2012. It showed that 16-19 year-olds and over 65s rated their overall satisfaction with life at 7.75 out of 10, while those aged 40-59 were less satisfied, with an average rating of 7.15.[187] Also in the UK, Action for Happiness,[188] an independent movement for positive social change, was launched in London in April 2011, bringing together people with a desire to play a part in creating a happier society for everyone. There is increasing recognition, then, that wellbeing is important and that its development and maintenance need active support both on the part of the individual themselves and from society.

Foundations of Wellbeing

While we might have a general sense of what wellbeing feels and looks like, a number of schools of thought have formulated their own frameworks to explain what generates this state which we all, consciously or unconsciously strive to attain. Let's look at what they propose.

Positive Psychology, an approach pioneered by American psychologist Martin Seligman, has been gaining considerable currency in recent years. In concentrating on factors which actively nurture wellbeing it diverges from the original approach of psychology which focused entirely on mental illness.[189] Positive Psychology is based on the notion that there are particular *character strengths* which will favour wellbeing in the individuals who have them. These are:

- Wisdom and knowledge: creativity, curiosity, critical thinking, perspective, etc
- Courage: speaking up for what is right, taking responsibility for your actions, zest, etc
- Love, eg, sharing and caring relationships, kindness
- Justice, eg, citizenship, fairness, leadership
- Temperance, eg, modesty, prudence, self-control
- Transcendence, eg, appreciation, gratitude, playfulness, spirituality[190]

A second way of understanding the underpinnings of wellbeing has been to see them in terms of the *satisfaction of certain psychological needs* (in addition to basic physical survival needs). *Self-determination Theory*,[191] which has been developed principally by Edward Deci and Richard Ryan at Rochester University, New York, proposes a set of three human needs:

- Competence – feeling confident and effective in one's interactions with the social environment
- Relatedness – a feeling of connectedness to others, belonging, and of caring for and being cared for by others
- Autonomy – being the source of one's own behaviour, that is, acting in a particular way out of one's own volition, rather than being driven by the expectation of any form of external 'reward' (eg monetary gain, admiration) or 'punishment' (eg, social disapproval)

A more expansive structure of needs-to-be-met for optimal emotional health has been termed the *Human Givens*.[192]

This understanding has been developed in the UK by Joe Griffin and Ivan Tyrrell as the basis of a distinctive approach to psychotherapy. It also encompasses the supposed innate human potential to be able to meet these needs. The Human Givens are:

- Security – of close relationships, a physically safe environment, and security in the knowledge of one's competence to deal with situations that may arise;
- Attention, both giving and receiving
- Sense of autonomy and control
- Emotional connection to others
- Being part of a wider community
- Friendship and intimacy
- Sense of status within social groupings
- Sense of competence and achievement
- Meaning and purpose

A somewhat different approach is the idea that *deliberate activity* is key to wellbeing. In order to help individuals to be proactive in nurturing their own wellbeing the new economics foundation published advice in their *Five Ways to Mental Wellbeing*,[193] encouraging people to partake daily of the following five types of activity. It is based on the much publicised message that eating five-a-day helpings of fruit and vegetables is beneficial to physical health.

- Connecting with other people
- Being physically active
- Taking notice of small things
- Developing skills and interests
- Doing something for others

All these perceptions and exhortations, which share a certain individualistic stance, are firmly rooted in western culture. Rather different perspectives have arrived from the east. Akin to the notion of self-determination but with a very different slant, arising not out of psychology but out of the economics of development, is the idea promulgated by Amartya Sen, in writings such as his book, *Development as Freedom*, that wellbeing resides in what he calls *capabilities*, that is, "capabilities of persons to lead the kind of lives they value – and have reason to value".[194] By this token, a family or individual whose income is not sufficient to provide the kinds of possessions and possibilities which are the norm in their society are prevented from taking part fully in the life of their society. In our society, such norms might include, say, internet access; and the ability to travel to civil society meetings or job interviews, to pay a club subscription, or buy tickets for the odd cultural event. But while financial poverty clearly has a bearing on capability deprivation, income is not the whole story of capabilities because, as Sen points out, "It is possible for a person to have genuine advantages *and* still to 'muff' them. *Or* to sacrifice one's own wellbeing for other goals, and not to make full use of one's freedom to achieve a high level of wellbeing."[195] Sen sees such freedom as enhancing the ability of people to help themselves and also to influence the world.[196]

While Sen conceptualises the wellbeing of an individual in terms of his or her own freedom of action relative to that of other members of the same society, the Buddhist view is very different. Matthieu Ricard, a French scientist who, over forty years ago, gave up his European life for that of a Buddhist monk in the Himalayas, has written a book called *Happiness: a guide to developing life's most important skill*,[197] in which he states that, "Happiness is a state of inner fulfilment, not the gratification of inexhaustible desires for outward things".[198] According to this view, outward things are not only money, reputation and so on, but any aspect of the external world, including health, family, friends, peace, and justice. These may be perfectly legitimate expectations but, as Ricard points out, we can have everything we need and still be unhappy and, in any case, such assets may disappear at any time. Thus life satisfaction which depends on favourable conditions is fragile and vulnerable, so durable happiness is independent of external circumstances. Cultivating happiness is a skill, he says, which requires honest analysis of our thoughts; only with this skill will we be able to see the true nature of things and develop a way of being that brings a state of lasting wellbeing. Achieving a stable sense of wellbeing, according to the Buddhist perspective, depends on the development of the potential, present in every individual, for loving-kindness, compassion and inner peace. We may not be able to change things but we can change the way we see them, and, "as we free ourselves of all insecurities and inner fears (which are often connected to excessive self-centredness), we have less to dread and are naturally more open to others and better armed to face the vagaries of life".[199]

All the elements captured by these different understandings of the foundations of wellbeing did indeed surface in various guises amongst the personal accounts of the modest consumers, as we have begun to see, and will continue to see in further contributions from them in the course of the book.

How Happy were the Modest Consumers?

Research into happiness has been conducted since the 1950s and a standard question of researchers has been *On a scale of 1 (low) and 10 (high) how would you rate your overall satisfaction with your life?*[200] Among the ninety-four people who participated in the first stage of the (fairly small-scale) Modest Consumers study the overall average life satisfaction rating was 8.3 out of 10. This appears to compare well with the British national average life satisfaction rating at the same time of 7.38,[201] although it is not possible to conduct the statistical analysis that would definitively confirm this impression. What can be said is that their relative material modesty did not detract from the level of life satisfaction they experienced. Most of the men and women who gave themselves lower ratings did so not because they were dissatisfied with their material situation, but due to personal circumstances beyond their control, such as terminal illness, a chronic and disabling physical condition or bereavement, situations which would naturally compromise anyone's enjoyment of life. One or two frankly admitted that they currently lacked purpose in life or fulfilling work, and it is no surprise that these individuals were dissatisfied, as work that has meaning for the individual is a crucial ingredient of wellbeing for most people.[202] Indeed, unemployment is the condition (apart from chronic pain) that is most likely to detract seriously from wellbeing,[203] for worklessness erodes those vital assets of identity, role and everyday social connectedness, in addition to the difficulty of loss of income. But even in a situation of unemployment, there can be hope: one respondent remarked that her high score of 9 had taken her three years to achieve since being made redundant. What is more telling, perhaps, is that a third of the participants gave themselves a score of 8, a quarter 9, and five rated their satisfaction with life at 10 out of 10.

Greater financial security was desired by a few; otherwise what the modest consumers felt would increase their sense of wellbeing was some change of attitude in themselves, eg, *to be able to deal with things more cheerfully* or *cutting myself more slack*, or a change of attitude in others: *peace on earth and goodwill to all people*. Other thoughts on what would enhance personal wellbeing were: greater equality, having children or a partner, pleasanter neighbours, nicer surroundings, better health, less stress at work, or more time. No-one attributed their satisfaction deficit, as one might describe it, to any perceived gap in their material lives. Indeed, a number declared that they revelled in their modest lifestyle for its simplicity, absence of the stresses created by more conventional levels of acquisition, and lack of clutter or waste. Seventeen cited active enjoyment of or greater happiness with a modest lifestyle as their reason for pursuing one. In short, if one has enough for a basically decent existence, wellbeing is not dependent on material consumption.

What Gave the Modest Consumers Satisfaction?

People

Significant relationships counted for a lot; family and friends were mentioned more often than anything else among the things they regarded as most important in life. But here the modest consumers were not at all unusual, for most people consider family and friends to be central to their lives.[204] People who have a number of friends with whom they can discuss things that are important to them are much more likely than those who don't to feel 'very happy', and those whose families and friends support and encourage them and show interest in their goals rate their wellbeing higher.[205] Indeed, there is solid evidence of the crucial importance of close relationships for wellbeing throughout life, and that the foundation for these is built early in life. Powerful witness to this is found in the American Grant Study which followed nearly three hundred men from the age of 19 for seventy-five years or until they died, from when they were first year college students in the years 1938 to 1941, collecting a huge amount of qualitative and quantitative data about them. One use to which correlations amongst the data were put was to enquire into the antecedents of flourishing. The study's most important finding, in the view of George Vaillant, one of the chief researchers, was that the only thing that really matters in life is the quality of your relations with other people.[206]

What was more striking about the modest consumers than their valuing of family and friends was the level of their involvement with people beyond their own social circle. *Helping others/being useful/ contributing* was frequently specified as being an 'important thing in life' to them. Indeed, second in popularity among interests and spare-time activities, close behind physical activities,[207] was voluntary work. Many, too, belonged to campaigning organisations, to churches and to specifically local groups. Twenty-nine political or campaigning organisations were named (including fourteen references to membership of Amnesty International), as well as twenty-seven religious affiliations (all Christian). Specifically local organisations (including nine Transition Town groups) were popular, as were volunteering groups and charities, and overseas aid or development organisations. Here we begin to get a glimpse into one reason why people who choose material modesty might tend to be more fulfilled on average than others. For the wellbeing of other people and making a contribution to wider society were active concerns, and being orientated in these directions is known to enhance wellbeing: you get more out of life if you try to 'do good' than to 'do well'.[208] If, at the other end of the spectrum, a person's attention is mostly focused on themselves, devoted to earning a lot of money or enhancing their reputation, or if their spare time is swallowed up in shopping, in order to enhance themselves or their home, they will not have time, attention or energy to give away. Of course, these different concerns are not mutually exclusive and most of us direct some degree of effort to both. But while nearly half of the modest consumers did enough volunteering to regard it as one of their interests and activities, nearly a third of Britons, in contrast, do not apparently give anybody their time, formally, eg as a school governor, or informally, say helping a neighbour, even once; in 2009 the UK was apparently ranked only 29th internationally for 'giving time'.[209]

Meaning

To look at the question of volunteering another way, to spend one's precious time, thought and energy on the needs of others beyond one's own family or social circle or on a situation outside one's own immediate circumstances, implies the serving of something bigger than oneself. Acting for the good of others or a particular cause lends life meaning, and having meaning is another important aspect of attaining an optimum psychological state.[210] Religious or political affiliations or voluntary work of any kind will lend meaning and purpose to life. But, the rationale that many of the modest consumers gave for their whole way of living, meant that their lifestyles were fundamentally shaped by some framework of meaning which acknowledged their place in the global scheme of things, human or natural or both.

§

LYNN

Lynn exemplified someone whose life now revolved largely around her desire to help people in her community who needed serious support. A woman of 54, she lived on the south coast with the two youngest of her four daughters, aged 17 and 19, in a three-bedroom rented house. Her financial means were limited; the house was decorated and furnished with simple second-hand items. Given the finances, Lynn would have put in insulation and double glazing against the winter cold, and would have put up curtains, but did not yet have curtain poles. But, even if she'd had more money she would not have made major changes, for her modesty was a choice as well as the result of financial constraints:

I think it is responsible to the rest of mankind to limit my consumption of finite resources, she wrote. *Consumerism does not provide lasting satisfaction, I prefer to celebrate relationship. As a Christian I try to identify more with the poor. Reading the life and teachings of Jesus gave me a background to simplicity, then seeing some Christians seeking to live in community, sharing resources, challenged me. Taking an interest in other societies made me aware of the huge difference in lifestyles. Now the consumerism of our society and the emphasis on externals lead me to make a stand (no matter how small).*

Lynn did, however, probe in her own mind the extent to which she was choosing to live so modestly. She turned the question over when we met, saying:

"Sometimes I wonder if it's just through necessity that I live like I do and then I remember back to when we were choosing to have children and I remember wanting four and wondering if that was responsible and thinking I'm sure I could bring up four on less than some people bring up one, and even right at the beginning I had a commitment to not needing to consume resources, in fact I rarely buy things new. It is a challenge to me to find ways to do things, and I enjoy it. I mean I make cards, and on these freebie leaflets that are given out if there's a little picture I'll cut it out and make birthday and Christmas cards out of them."

Lynn had never experienced material plenty. The eldest of five daughters of a military father who moved around and earned a limited income, she remembered a simple early life, eating her main meal of the day at school, playing out all the time, with one bike shared between her and her sisters. But, as far as she and the other children on the army estate were concerned, this kind of life was normal.

Now, Lynn had been separated for four years. Her husband's values had begun to diverge from hers before they went their separate ways, so Lynn found that she was now freer to make her own choices, such as eating less meat and more pulses. How about her daughters?

> "They're aware that you can live on a low income and they will do when they have to but they would like more money, and at this stage, the two younger ones would like more money to get what they would like to get. But actually they are quite content really, they are aware there's more values than having lots of things. They will make comments sometimes, I'm not sure how much is just for me, but they'll say, 'Oh, our friends get what they want when they want and they won't know how to manage when they're older, but we'll know how to manage'; they appreciate those kind of experiences. They're not into the bigger global values though."

Herein lay the difficulty that Lynn experienced in living a materially modest lifestyle. She found it hard to live by her ideals, to explain them to her four girls, and also to respect their right to decide for themselves how they wished to live.

For herself, becoming a Christian as a student had, Lynn felt, given her direction and the resources to become who she was now, "free from guilt and open to people and experiences". In addition, mental illness and counselling had caused her to examine her expectations and to expose her defences. These experiences had enabled her to discover "the way I'm made" and that her gifts and faith found their expression "in getting alongside people who struggle". Hence Lynn worked as a community family worker with Children's Services, and derived particular satisfaction from witnessing another person's successful striving, such as a child struggling to do up their shoelaces, and seeing their joy in achievement. For this reason she had recently applied to be assessed for respite disability fostering. She also regularly cooked and served food for rough sleepers and people living in lodgings or bed and breakfast accommodation, having had what she found to be an amazing experience of a church camp for the homeless. Drawing in people who were struggling with life was absolutely in tune with her core values.

Lynn's satisfaction with her life of work, church, family, friends, volunteering and card-making was at a level of 9 out of 10; "Yes", she said, "Things are all coming together at the moment. Just the way life fits with my Christianity and my interests each day".

Meaningful work

Having work that makes some form of contribution is an important aspect of an individual's way of creating meaning in their life. We have already seen this exemplified by Naomi as well as Lynn. Someone else for whom it was central was Becky.

BECKY

Becky wrote on her questionnaire, *I'm poor as a mouse but happier than I've ever been because I'm doing what I want to do.* She was a young woman of 32, for whom the process of dealing with personal crisis had led to the remodelling of her life and the devoting of it to work which, like Lynn's, addressed human inequalities close to home. Her financial constraints were self-imposed, the result of quitting her well-paid full-time job to set up a workers' co-operative, and she rated her satisfaction with her life now at 10 out of 10.

Starting at the beginning of her story, Becky told me how she came from what she described as an aspiring middle class background in south Wales. Her parents were not hugely acquisitive, but saw money as security and, feeling that security was the most important thing, believed that it was necessary to have a good job. Becky, though, had come to question this value system early on. A history teacher at school had made a great impression on her when she was 15 or 16 with lessons about the Levellers, the Diggers and the English civil war: "There was this phrase, I'm not religious in any way, I'm an atheist, but there was a phrase that the Levellers used that Jesus was the great leveller, meaning, basically like communism, that we're all the same, and that really appealed to me. I believe that wholeheartedly, and have done for many years, that we're all equally deserving". But her detachment from money went further back than her teenage years. She explained:

> "Money's been a kind of weird thing in my family. One of the things that my parents rowed about before they got divorced was money, and I've got a very clear memory, it was back in the days of pound notes, maybe I was six, I knew there was a money problem in the family and I remember trying to give my dad two pound notes because I knew that he didn't have very much money at the time. It's a horrible memory, a really sad memory, but it's always been there for me that money's not the answer, and it's actually quite unpleasant at times."

Becky's different attitude to worldly things was not without problems when it came to family relationships and she, like others, was aware that talking about her values might be interpreted by others as a judgement on their own:

> "I'm struggling with how I articulate my passion and my absolute fear and horror at certain things, cheap chickens, cheap clothes, whatever, without sounding like I'm saying to somebody 'goodness me you're awful for buying whatever'. I've set up this workers' co-op making gorgeous ethical knickers and then my mother gives me clothes that she's bought in Tesco's, and while I do appreciate that she buys me warm things and thinks about what I need, I'm thinking, 'you really just don't get me, do you', but that's a different thing, she really doesn't, and that's what it is. Yeah it is awkward at times."

Becky's current stance towards money and possessions did not, however, fully come to the fore until quite late. At 15 she was raped, which "threw all my choices up in the air for a long time". She then worked in a series of jobs in sales, which appeared to be her forte, selling wine and insurance, then software to large companies, before working in a university in the department that turned academic knowledge into businesses. "I've had highly paid sales jobs where I took home over £5,000 a month, and you know I don't know what I did with that, it's just money". Her modesty in spending now, though, was marked. She was almost vegan, took holidays by visiting friends or staying at home doing her garden, sourced some of her furniture in skips, and was still wearing some clothes that she had had since she was 16. Her only more expensive habit was to shop at Waitrose for items she could not get elsewhere, choosing to do so because it was a partnership store. Though in some ways a recent change, Becky's modesty had roots going back a long way, invigorated now by environmental and ethical concerns, which had made her unable to countenance filling her house with stuff which had travelled thousands of miles round the world, perhaps made in sweatshops and from depleting materials; everything in her house was second-hand except a sofa, an armchair and her mattress.

When Becky was 29, she eventually went to Rape Crisis for counselling, and it was during this process that her own values emerged clearly, distinct from those of her parents.

"One of the things that really came through was that I had been given a lot of lessons in life about what it meant to be happy and they kind of involved earning. It was really, really low level stuff, and it really didn't work for me. That was their way of being in the world. I know my parents would probably be horrified to think that this was how I experienced them, as I'm sure they meant very well, but it's how I remember things. Through my counsellor I realised that this stuff had happened and that it wasn't my stuff it was someone else's, and I threw it all away and promptly left my job earning shedloads of money in the public sector!"

It was this experience that enabled Becky to start a co-op:

"What Rape Crisis did was give me the courage – it helped me find my own courage to say this is what I really want to do and this is what will really make me happy. I think I've always believed that buying stuff doesn't make you happy, I do get that in a huge way, but for me there was a big thing about saying, 'do you know what, I can probably manage without a guaranteed income, I can probably do it'."

She was helped with an award of £15,000 from UnLtd[211] an organisation that funds social entrepreneurs, to cover her living expenses for a year, and found this income 'hilarious' and 'exciting' in comparison with her previous salary of almost £40,000, despite wondering each month how she would meet her £700 mortgage repayment.

The critical moment for Becky had come in a counselling session when her counsellor said something to her that she later learned was something called a power statement:

"She said, 'don't you think that the most important thing a parent can do for their child is to give them the message that they're alright just as they are' and that hit me like a train cos I thought 'my God, yes of course that's true'. I was told, like I suspect a lot of children are, 'be better, do better, look better, be neater', and I somehow got the message I wasn't up to much. It was implicit rather than explicit, it was never having time and always being cross and that sort of stuff and I do understand they had problems and that was what I got. So when she said that to me, I felt ten feet tall because I thought clearly if every child deserves that message every adult does too because children turn into adults. And I thought well I am just good enough, and it was this really enormous moment for me, and I've still got that sentence written on my fridge and my bedroom mirror."

The workers' co-op that Becky then set up was, in fact, the crystallisation of a combination of several experiences in her life:

"I'd been involved in work for Amnesty locally; I'd done work on business and human rights and for the Open University. I'd written a letter to the mother of a woman who was killed on her way home from working in a sweatshop in Central America and they filmed me writing the letter and they filmed the mother reading it and it was just this immensely powerful thing and this woman was reading my letter which said, 'Even though the police and the state aren't caring about what's happened to your daughter, there are people on the other side of the world who do care'. And I've always loved underwear; and the more I got involved in this human rights stuff the more I started thinking how can I wear this when it might have been made by a woman who was forced to take the contraceptive pill or a woman who was forced to have an internal examination, or by children or whatever? So that was kind of rocking around in the back of my mind but I also knew through Amnesty that there was a massive refugee population in Southampton, and all of these things kind of came together with that sentence from counselling where I just thought I want other women to have this feeling that I've got now. Cos I felt that I could do anything now, I felt I could take on the world. And I thought if I can feel like this, other women can feel like this, and the thing for me was that I never realised before how bad I'd felt until I felt better, and this is a sort of evangelical thing I suppose, I look at a lot of the women that I work with, some of them might be relatively liberated compared to some of their friends and colleagues. I want to make choices available to people if I can. So all of that came through in this idea that I want really nice underwear that I know has had a really happy start in life, and I know there are women who are having a really hard time in Southampton, and I put it all together."

There was an environmental strand to the initiative, too, for the knickers Becky's co-operative produced were made from materials rescued from the lingerie industry's waste stream. Becky did not use organic cotton because

111

she was adamant that the land and water required for growing cotton would be better used for growing food.

The effect on Becky of setting up the knicker-making co-op was that:

"I really am very, very happy; I mean my job is very hard, and very stressful and difficult and complicated and frustrating because I'm working with refugee women, some of them have got no work ethic, no understanding, but our job is instilling that. So we're working with people who haven't got a bloody clue about punctuality, but that's what my job is now, to teach them these things and I still wouldn't want to do anything else. And I know that this makes me happy, deeply and on a really proper and profound level I'm satisfied by this. I love what I do, it's making a difference to people's lives in a real way.

"There's an equation, a business idea," said Becky, "which is fast, cheap and good – in any situation you can have two of the three. My life currently is filled up with cheap and good, which means that it's slow. I think for a lot of people what money gives them is fast and cheap so they're missing out on the good. For me happiness is not a transient fleeting thing, it's really deep down solid, because on a daily basis I'm stressed out and in a panic and whatever, but I'm happy, really, really, fundamentally very happy."

§

LUCY

Lucy, who was 58, also put a great deal of emphasis on the fulfilment she derived from her work. She was the co-ordinator of a therapeutic horticultural project which she had devised and developed. The scheme was designed to support the personal development of individuals suffering social exclusion as a result of mental ill-health, for instance, or being an asylum-seeker or refugee, or assuming the role of a carer. Feeling connected to other people and to her work was what gave Lucy a real sense of satisfaction. Relationships and having meaning in life were the most important things for her, she said, and her therapeutic garden project, together with the therapy training she was doing, gave her both of these. Though crucial in her estimation, meaning in life was not something that had come easily to Lucy. She told me, "It's something I've struggled with, and I think since I've got into this therapeutic work, which I've discovered is what I like and what I'm good at, it's given me meaning and it's revitalised me. I think that often in my life I've been a bit depressed and I think it's because I've been struggling to find meaning. One of the things I've struggled with for a long time is what to do, how to be effective." She also found it immensely rewarding and gratifying that other people, and the environment, were benefitting from her work.

Lucy believed that it was important to have balance in life, nurturing every aspect of oneself, body, soul and mind, and compared this with her observation of her rich London former gardening clients, concluding:

> "One of the things I do think is that wealth is a drug and the acquisition of money is an addiction, and I think wealthy people can hide behind their wealth and can deceive themselves and it can make them unhappy because they can't face the void or their human condition. I really felt for some of those people in London, they were kidding themselves. They were probably wrecking their children's lives, racing around here, there and everywhere. I just sense that there are a lot of people who are not happy and they are deluded by material gain. I think there's something to be said for not having that option really."

Lucy did feel somewhat weighed down by having debts to repay, and she would have liked to be able to afford to have her little terraced house properly insulated and double glazed so as to reduce her energy use. If she had had more disposable income she would also have gone to the cinema, theatre and concerts more often, been more generous with hospitality, visited her brother abroad, and bought herself more clothes, books and pictures. But any purchase would have been made with a keen eye on its origins, mindful of how its production affected people and the environment. Consumption really did not attract Lucy, and she was very aware that it often came at a human and environmental cost: "I know in my heart that it really doesn't make any difference to how I feel, and so what's the point of it?"

§

Gratitude

Asked what gave them particular enjoyment and satisfaction, the modest consumers named sources from amongst the possibilities around them, or which were within their grasp if they extended themselves. These fell into several categories: conviviality, physical exercise, being out of doors, the natural world, intellectual challenge, and independence, for example:

Good conversations; A good pub or tearoom when out walking or cycling with friends; Dancing; Things that make me feel loved; Playing and singing in a band and choir in worship and practice; Being comfortably tired after a long walk on a beautiful day; Outdoor scents: blossom, new mown grass, heather in bloom; A sunny day; Fresh air; Gardening, seeing things grow: the tadpoles in our garden pond, the seven cobnut trees I grew from local nuts from the farmers market; Puzzles and mathematical challenges; Fixing something by myself, eg, nesting box on garden wall; Learning new skills; Being able to go out every day and do my own shopping; Having time to myself.

It is easy to see that these everyday occasions and opportunities, while identified as founts of enjoyment and satisfaction, were found to be so because they were received in the spirit of appreciation and gratitude. A sunny day, the smell of new mown grass, being able to go for a long walk, the ability to do one's own shopping. These and other simple experiences which money can't buy, are easily taken for granted and often pass unnoticed. Most of us have them but how often do we perceive them as gifts? Most of us are more inclined to complain about being stuck in traffic, than to welcome the experience which Becky described with characteristic zest:

> "I love cycling to work, even though it is hard. There's a level crossing and the longest I've ever sat there is eighteen minutes. I can go over the pedestrian bridge but I kind of like waiting because what I'm doing then is waiting, and even if it's raining I'm waiting in the rain, that's what I'm doing, it's a real experience. It's visceral rather than cerebral. Those sorts of things are the things I like having in my day."

Real riches lie in the capacity to notice and to appreciate small things and to perceive situations as opportunities. An approach to life which finds pleasure and satisfaction in the ordinary will fashion delight and fulfilment out of everyday details. This capacity is closely related to the exercise of mindfulness meditation, the giving of attention to the thoughts, feelings and physical sensations of the present, which, if practised regularly, has been found to be notably effective in reducing stress and depression, as well as pain and other physical symptoms.[212] Indeed, it is not surprising that an attitude to life which is inclined to perceive experience in a positive light and as worthy of conscious appreciation, will result in a greater sense of wellbeing than one that fails to notice details, takes things for granted, or is disposed to moan. And, while gratitude does not come readily to everyone, it can be learnt. Experiments have shown that writing down five things for which one is grateful or appreciates, whether major or trivial, every week for ten weeks, generates a lasting increase in levels of personal wellbeing,[213] because actively looking for positives beneficially alters perceptions.

Engagement

The modest consumers spent little time on non-essential shopping – other than having fun hunting for treasures in charity shops. They did not, apparently, spend much time on the passive pastime of watching television either, and there was no mention of playing computer games. Again, there is a contrast here with typical British behaviour, the average time spent watching television being four hours a day.[214] The men and women who took part in the study preferred to be active, physically, culturally and socially, indoors or out, frequently enjoying walking, cycling, gardening, yoga, reading, going to the cinema, eating out with friends, following intellectual pursuits such as learning a language, and creative activities such as music, writing, photography and knitting. Their most frequent non-essential purchases were books, CDs and DVDs (some of them second-hand), tickets for theatre and live music events, good food, and beer and wine.

The impression the modest consumers gave was of a proactive, motivated collection of people, and this profile throws light on one more reason why they were happier with their lives than others, on average. It is that deliberate engagement of some kind, in whatever form, as captured in nef's *Five Ways* above, is an important factor in determining an individual's characteristic level of happiness.[215] In fact, 40% of our level of wellbeing is reckoned to be generated by intentional activity,[216] that is activity which is freely chosen and requires effort, be it behavioural (such as regular physical exercise), cognitive (such as reframing a situation in a more positive light), or volitional (such as initiating and pursuing a personal project).[217]

The experience of putting in time and energy was certainly one with which many of the modest consumers were familiar, and they were keenly aware of the feeling of achievement which this generated: *Successfully completing a complicated task; Singing (both for social/relaxation reasons and also for a sense of achievement); I feel happy when I have mastered a challenge, and when I have mastered a crisis; When I know that I have done something to the best of my ability; Becoming competent at something (e.g. playing an instrument, learning a new martial arts move); A good result (relative to my fairly low expectations!) in a fell race or orienteering event.*

A proactive, enthusiastic attitude, a willingness to try new things and to persevere with them so as to get better at them, is not something that can be bought; neither does it, in itself, exact any environmental toll.

Emotions

So much for cognitive self-assessment of satisfaction with life. There is, of course, an important affective aspect to wellbeing too. In order to have a sense of wellbeing we need to experience more positive than negative emotion.[218] This is not at all to say that difficult or uncomfortable emotions are to be avoided; feelings of sadness, regret, and righteous anger, for example, have a very real and important place in human affairs. There would be no brake on armed conflict, and social injustice would have free rein, without the stab of grief and the drive of outrage. A life of only upbeat, fluffy feelings would be two-dimensional and anodyne. So enjoying a high level of wellbeing does not mean that one constantly experiences the positive emotion we call happiness. The point is that it's better to experience patience than agitation, enthusiasm than indifference, admiration than disdain, and forgiveness than bitterness.

Good relationships certainly ensure plenty of positive feelings, as does an attitude of ready appreciation. Another means of generating positive affect is to engage in self-chosen activities of a kind that make demands on us. While we do gain benefit from enjoying pleasurable moments which need no effort (and which may be the result of someone else's deliberate act), we also need the more lasting fulfilment generated by activities which require the investment of attention and energy. Being immersed in any pursuit, be it badminton, cooking, hill walking, poetry-writing, carpentry, music-making, calligraphy, bird-watching or any number of other activities which require concentration and which utilise and stretch personal skills, induces a gratifying sense that has been termed 'flow',[219] the state in which time passes unnoticed and one loses oneself. At these times we feel a tangible connection with the others with whom we are engaged in the activity, or a loosening of ego if the occupation is solitary.[220] This release from the self is the antithesis of the focus on self that is involved in the buying of clothes, video games, handbags, gadgets, cosmetics, and all the other merchandise that draws crowds into stores week after week, seeking to better their image or their repertoire of possessions. For all that shopping is usually about 'me', the acquisition of 'stuff' generally recognises only the surface of life; it is by involvement in solo or collaborative pursuits that we find self-knowledge and develop inner resources.

Much of what the modest consumers conveyed about their satisfying lives was very much in keeping with what is known about the generators of wellbeing. But two themes which recurred amongst some of their accounts were more unusual. These were the feeling of being a small part of something big, and the enjoyment of solitude and silence.

Being a small part of something big

A perception expressed by several of the modest consumers was of a sense of being a tiny part of something much larger. They did not experience this as a diminishment but as a source of comfort and of awe. Becky, for instance, unable for many years to come to terms with the trauma of having been raped, had found that feeling small and insignificant on a wide expanse of beach, looking out to sea, had put her problems into perspective, so that they were no longer so overwhelming. She recalled, "I remember sitting on this enormous rock one day and thinking, 'this rock's been here for thousands of years and it'll be here after me, and it doesn't care whether I'm sad or happy, and it doesn't care what's going on in my world, it's just going to sit here and do its thing, and then it will be sand.'" For Susan, her new perception of scale was a welcome revelation when she came to see in a wider context the working self she had formerly been, once she had developed a new, lower-key but satisfying existence after rheumatoid arthritis struck. Chris, as we have seen, saw his smallness in temporal terms when roaming amongst ancient trees. Here, then, is a paradox: that individuals who consider that their little everyday actions can make a difference to the collective human impact on the Earth or on humanity, are also glad to perceive themselves as almost insignificant in terms of the scale of the entirety of the natural and human worlds. This humility, seeing themselves as a fragment of something much greater, is a source of comfort that is unavailable to anyone who is exclusively preoccupied with themselves, their gaze trained myopically on their own money, possessions, appearance, power, pleasure, social status or reputation. It is modesty of a non-material, yet clearly related, sense.

Solitude and silence

Moments of stillness and sometimes solitude also surfaced amongst the modest consumers' narratives. These allowed them time for reflection and appreciation. Such moments were a special benefit that Lucy felt from being able to live in one place. Earlier, she had worked half the week a hundred miles away in London, as a garden designer and gardener. Since she had stopped commuting she'd loved being able to stay put. Why? "It's being quiet, and, maybe, at the risk of sounding corny, to some extent it's a spiritual thing I think, it's enjoying the stillness. Since I've been able to just be here I've had a lot of time just being quiet; I've felt very good, very connected with myself." After years of commuting, this enabled Lucy to "feel satisfied with where I am rather than constantly dreaming of where I might be."

Active appreciation of the benefits of solitude and silence was expressed by others too, including Clive and Gillian whom you'll meet later. But solitude and stillness are not to be regarded as the exclusive preserve of adults. Caroline, another woman you will meet in due course, recounted a seminal experience she had had when she was about nine years old and very unhappy at boarding school:

> "I sat on a lawn and looked at a daisy. Somehow this brought strength
> and comfort to me, thinking how pretty it was but also something
> about its capacity to survive, I think, and just taking comfort from
> it. And although I was very unhappy at that prep school it was in the
> most beautiful grounds, there were wonderful trees and woods, and of
> course in those days you were just allowed to amble off; we could go
> anywhere we liked, and that was just fantastic, hugely comforting."

This story speaks powerfully of the potential for personal development and nurture in moments of being alone with oneself. Had Caroline been in the company of another child or children, it seems unlikely that she would have been able to reflect in the same way on the little flower or drawn metaphorical lessons from it.

Times of solitude and its twin, silence, were highly valued by several of the cohort members, particularly members who lived alone. Ellen, a piano teacher, found that, "I need solitude to recoup my stability when people have gone. I don't feel lonely, I've got too much going on in my head to get lonely, but I need time for the sediment to settle and I'm very, very happy with solitude, so if I don't get a clear period of time I do feel I'm suffering from that." Susan had at last learnt positively to enjoy her own company, she said, some years after having to give up an active working life due to her serious health condition. Clive, whose life revolved largely around meditation, would from time to time spend two months at a time alone in a cave in India, with only his violin to distract him from his solitude. Being quietly and contentedly alone with oneself, though probably hard if it is unfamiliar, can be a nourishing experience. And it requires no consumption whatsoever.

Materialism and Wellbeing

Was there any relationship between the modest consumers' material modesty and their wellbeing? The extent of a person's leaning towards materialistic values, that is to say their prioritising of material success and public admiration over other possible life goals, such as social relationships, community and self-acceptance,[221] has been measured in a number of studies by a scale[222] which asks people to say how much they agree with statements like:

> I admire people who own expensive homes, cars, and clothes
> The things I own say a lot about how well I'm doing in life
> I don't pay much attention to the material objects other people own
> I usually buy only the things I need
> Buying things gives me a lot of pleasure
> I have all the things I really need to enjoy life
> I'd be happier if I could afford to buy more things

Marsha Richins, who has carried out a lot of research into materialism, has identified three interrelated themes associated with the concept: putting possessions at the centre of one's life, viewing possessions as essential to life satisfaction and wellbeing, and judging one's own and others' success by the number and quality of possessions accumulated.[223] "Because consumption is so important to [materialists]", she reasons, "they may have higher expectations for what a new possession will accomplish in their lives. With higher expectations, the chances for disappointment increase and, indeed, disappointment was greatest amongst those high in materialism".[224] Other studies have repeatedly shown an inverse relationship between materialism and wellbeing.[225] Materialistic people tend to be less satisfied with the quality of their relationships than are others; to believe their marriages are more prone to suffer from financial problems; to believe that they will need more income to satisfy their daily needs; and to experience more negative emotions. They experience less meaning in life, less relatedness to others, fewer feelings of competence, autonomy, and gratitude, and greater personal insecurity.[226]

Personal security

Intriguingly, some of the modest consumers independently introduced the very subject of personal security. The ways in which they perceived this issue were striking and probably rather different from the way it was conceptualised in the studies of materialistic people above. Chris, for instance, felt that his sense of inner security, which he'd developed through self-exploration over a long period of time, was one of the most important things in life to him. "Having a sense of security in myself doesn't mean I'm sorted", he said, "it just means I have a sense of who I am and what I want to do, what makes me thrive". For Becky, security developed more rapidly, the product of her Rape Crisis counselling, "And it's real, proper, deep down safe, it feels solid, it's the foundation to build other stuff on. And because I've got this it's much more exiting to poke the world and say, 'oh that's funny, what happens if I do this?'" Ruth, who lived with Robert in a simple hut they had built in a field, with no running water or electricity, had come to realise, she said, having suffered divorce and life-threatening illness, that nothing is secure in life other than the way you feel inside. For Clive, the only difficulty with the nomadic, meditative lifestyle he loved was the lack of financial security it gave him. He often ran out of money, not knowing where the next pounds would come from, and he sometimes worried about the future and his lack of security should he become ill. But he derived a great deal of personal security from his strong relationships, and realised in any case that there is no such thing as complete security:

> "The thing I think about security is it's a kind of construct. You know we live in a society that really tries to frighten us to buy goods and services that alleviate this fear of insecurity, you know buying a house and all that sort of thing. But I begin to realise that it's not that secure really, we might wake up with a tumour on the brain and that's it, it's all over."

Grapplers

While it was the modest consumers themselves who identified themselves as happy with their materially modest lifestyles, it would be wrong to give the impression that they all found their kinds of living plain sailing. Over half of them admitted to some difficulty. They weren't necessarily immune to the pressures of the consumer culture, for instance, and had to work hard to resist these at times:

- *Sometimes I see things which I find aesthetically pleasing or technologically interesting, but mostly I cannot justify their purchase for financial reasons or simply because I don't actually need them, and I know they won't make me any happier.*
- *You can't be perfect, and have to make compromises which you feel guilty about.*
- *You have to learn to measure your status and achievements in a different way to the standards of mainstream culture.*
- *There is huge pressure to buy stuff, and some of it is pretty attractive! eg, I would like to have many more music CDs for example, but try to balance my love of music and desire to have more of what I want on tap, with being able to access a lot of interesting music on the radio.*

Then there was sometimes an effect on personal relationships, as we have already heard. An 18-year-old student had found that:

It has excluded me from 'belonging' to my university. Everyone I met there seemed to have the same concept of social interaction and going out (everyone seemed to be pretty rich too), and that was a different one from mine, which made me be always far away from all my colleagues, which eventually led me to dislike it strongly enough to withdraw from the course and uni.

And a young man wrote:

The consumer world is hard to resist sometimes, you feel like you're not part of a community and that community is most of the people in this country and includes your friends.

Energetically committed to reducing her consumption, 31 year-old Lauren whom you'll meet in the next chapter, admitted that, despite her experience and strong convictions, refusal to conform to the consumerism all around her did require discipline. In fact she confessed that it was a constant battle. She had actively to check herself, and to help her overcome her urge to buy things, she had invented rules for herself to stop her hand reaching out towards, say, chocolates or a new T-shirt. For instance, if she was tempted to acquire something she had not thought about until the moment she saw it in the shop she would not buy it. "There's some instinct in our human brains that makes us reach out for this 'stuff' all the time. Then I have to say, 'Did you want it before you saw it? No. Don't have it then!'" I put it to her, wasn't her claim that she struggled with consumption a paradox in light of her stated claim on the questionnaire that not being materialistic was easy and made her happy? Her response: "Well, when I've made the small effort to say no to something I feel free!"

Another difficulty was the need for time to make things rather than buy them, or to ferret out technical information about products before deciding which to buy; and for the financial resources to acquire the expensive means to reduce energy consumption, such as double glazing, water butts and solar panels. A few expressed sadness at the curtailment of their possibilities for travel to new and interesting places or to visit old friends, having taken the decision to stop flying in order to reduce their carbon footprint. But the modest consumers were made of stern stuff, generally strong-minded and principled enough to stick with what they felt to be right.

Self-knowledge

The modest consumers were, indeed, a bunch with strength of conviction, world view and self-knowledge. One wrote, for example:

> *The realisation and the acceptance that I wasn't ambitious in the slightest enabled me to pursue work which wasn't about getting somewhere and more about enabling me to live a more authentic lifestyle.*

However gently many of them may have spoken, the message that came across loud and clear was that each was his or her own person, reflective, able to form critical views and to act on them, undeterred by the incomprehension or derision which their somewhat unconventional values and behaviour could arouse. For several, personal crisis had been a catalyst in revealing what was truly valuable to them, as we have already heard in some of the personal accounts. Other critical situations cited included near-drownings, marriage break-ups, estrangement from an adopted daughter, redundancy, business failure, life-threatening illnesses, and a serious dispute at work. One woman wrote:

My first sexual partner died of an accidental heroin overdose when I was 17 and he was 21, and I have also had family bereavements, mostly of a sudden nature. I have been involved in two traffic accidents which could have been fatal for me, and I luckily emerged uninjured. I have a chronic illness. Prior to separating with my husband I was severely depressed and felt suicidal. Each of these things made me look at my own life and consider what was really important. I realised that my happy memories had more to do with people and experiences and feeling I was doing the right thing than with material possessions. I am now more conscious of when I am happy, and value my time.

She added:

I spent my married life thinking that having a dream home with lovely things would make me happy but it didn't. I have adjusted my priorities.

Another woman, aged 70, wrote:

A close friend's death at an early age taught me to value life and use it. Being forced by parental pressure to waste too much of my best years on pointless study led me to put other things first, likewise working my butt off at an increasingly frustrating job led me to rethink my priorities and rate leisure (albeit filled with hard work at times) and freedom above financial gain.

This woman's satisfaction with her current life spent gardening, watching cricket, walking, reading, seeing friends, following current affairs, and doing voluntary work for Book Aid International and the local allotments association, and knitting for Oxfam was now 9.5 out 10.

Whether or not they had experienced some kind of trauma, a considerable number of the modest consumers had found that counselling, or another means of gaining self-knowledge, had been important to them. For Lynn, the therapy she had received for bouts of mental ill-health as a young adult had ultimately had a positive effect: "It's like breaking the pot and rebuilding it into a different shape," she said. Becky found, "When

I came out of counselling, I felt as though I had been reborn into this amazing world and it's not through religious fervour or anything transient or ephemeral, it's reality, I live in this world and it's really cool".

Having time and the opportunity to get to understand herself better was clearly an important aspect of Sita's enjoyment of later life. She had gained valuable insights from ten years of therapy and various forms of self-help, and was candid in explaining how it had helped her. She had come to realise, she explained, that her manner with people, which could apparently rub them up the wrong way, had been determined by her early experience, and that she could change it in ways that would bring her more rewarding social interactions. She recounted her therapist's theory and how it made sense to her:

> "She said, 'Because of the way your mother treated you as a little child you are somehow special'. And everywhere I go I have always had the experience of antagonising people, who see me as very middle class. They don't even notice that my face is brown. What they notice is that I'm ultra middle class, and there is so much prejudice among working people against the middle class after so many centuries of bad treatment."

This was compounded by Sita's habitual response to her stepmother which she had unwittingly transferred to others, as she discovered from the theory of role-modelling as propounded by the Neuro-linguistic Programming school of therapy:

> "As a result of all the beatings and canings, my whole attitude was coloured by it and what people see as my being very hoity-toity and arrogant. I relate to them in the way I related to my stepmother. I couldn't say a word to her so I held her in contempt. It was the only way I could hit back. So for a long time, I realised, when I spoke to people I spoke to them in a contemptuous way. In therapy many people say that you are responsible for the way that people treat you. I have taken that on board. So I have this rule for myself that I take it as read that people are reacting to something in my behaviour that I'm unconscious of, so I never retaliate, and as a result of that their behaviour changes. And as a result of that, my environment becomes much more friendly and so on. So these are all the things I said I could do in this period which is called old age!"

Bringing up children in a consumer culture

If the modest consumers were inclined to have considerable insight into themselves and to be disciplined in their own consumption, how did this affect their parenting? Bringing up children to be materially modest in a consumer society which exerts all sorts of pressures to conform to different values might be expected to be fraught at times. Few of the study participants had school-age children, but here is what two mothers of 5 – 12 year-olds wrote about their experience. I quote them at length as the issue is so important for the next generation, and of particular interest to readers who are themselves parents of growing children. Rosemary's household details tell their own story of real efforts and struggles to accommodate the needs of her family within principled consumption:

Travel and transport: we do have one car, which is second-hand and we try to structure our lives so that we cut down on its use (although this is not always possible as there are five of us and our eldest son plays cricket at county level which requires a lot of equipment and sends us round the country quite a bit). We try not to use the car for the school run – my son (12) goes by public transport four days a week (he has to take his cricket kit the other day, so we give him – and the boy over the road – a lift). One of us cycles our daughter (5) to and from school, but we usually take our youngest (3) to preschool by car – due to the length of the journey and time constraints. We recycle everything we can, not just what the council will collect, and have reduced our weekly rubbish for a family of five to ¼ of a small wheelie bin most weeks. We try to buy locally/British by preference for fruit and veg/meat/honey etc, but exceptions made for bananas and tomatoes, and occasional treats (eg. clementines at Xmas). Xmas, birthdays etc, always tell relatives what to buy for kids or to give them money, which we save. Often give our children presents from charity shops or (for younger two) things their elder brother had and we have kept in loft. We don't tend to do celebrations like Valentine's and father's day, but I did once get three bags of manure for mother's day. We subscribe to the basic cable TV package, plus Sky sports (sports is a big thing in our family, esp cricket) and

Sky movies. (We encourage the children to watch only public service channels and they know that advertisers are only trying to get them to want things they don't need and can't have). Holidays are usually camping in the UK; we do fly every 2 or 3 years to the South of France where my Mum has a house, and stay with her. The price of driving and/or going by train is prohibitive for a family of five, although we would much rather go by train. I don't think we do enough – I feel that time constraints, short cuts and children mean that we compromise.

Beyond the difficulties of transporting her family, Rosemary found it hard trying to compromise between the desire to live a sustainable lower impact life, and the children having a life which she and her husband were not always saying no, and in which they didn't feel so completely different from their peers. So how did her children feel? She and her husband talked to them about issues such as waste, deforestation and climate change, and explained that many people in the world had much less than they did. The eldest boy was well aware of his parents' feelings and largely supported them; he saved up birthday and Christmas money for things he wanted such as an ipod. The younger two did not yet have a sense of whether something was new or second-hand.

Kerry's experience was similar to Rosemary's in some ways. Her family's holidays were mostly in the UK too, with lots of walking, beaches, orienteering, camping and youth hostelling. As far as buying things was concerned, Kerry tried to stick to 'moderation in all things'. Her son of 8 and daughter of 10 differed from each other noticeably in their attitudes however. The boy was not concerned to have more clothes or toys but, left to his own devices would turn to the television or computer, and was very keen to be given a games console for Christmas, despite not knowing exactly what they were, because his friends talked about them.

As for how we deal with this, we try to use logic! We have held out a long time and we have explained that we do not want him to waste too much of his time playing computer games, or give up other activities as a result as some of his friends have. We have pointed out the cost and the fact that you have to spend a lot on games as well, once you have bought the equipment. However,

I think we are weakening simply because that is the only thing he wants for Xmas, so we may eventually get just one item - probably a Wii, with limits on playing time!

Kerry's daughter, on the other hand:

seems to be really adopting my non-consumerist views, much to my surprise and delight. She rarely asks for anything at all, and is not impressed by visits to friends' houses with TVs in every room and all the latest gadgets, seeing that as being wasteful. She was quite critical (privately) of a girl who asked for and got a new mobile phone just because it was pink!

A small dilemma that Kerry voiced was how to handle the need to buy presents for her children to take to all the parties to which they were invited: *You can rapidly end up disappearing under a sea of seldom-used plastic toys, and I struggle to find acceptable presents to give to other children that fit my ethics but would be enjoyed by the child!* Other parents, she found, did not share her concern. As far as her own children were concerned, the key, Kerry concluded, *was not just to deny them material stuff, but to concentrate on filling their lives with more meaningful things, thus leaving no room for the consumer rubbish! So we do lots of activities and sport after school and at weekend, and spend time reading, playing and listening to music.*

The quandaries did not appear to detract from these mothers' satisfaction with their lives, both of whom gave their rating as 8 out of 10.

Was it a different matter with teenage children? During their teens youngsters are more likely to want to disentangle themselves from their families, to become critical of their parents and more receptive to external influences. Lynn, for one, was reluctant to press her own values on her daughters, on the one hand recognising their right to develop their own views and, on the other, finding it hard to deal with the 'sarky' comments typical of their age. She therefore settled for a degree of compromise, for instance in providing more meat to eat than she really would have liked. However, she did feel that her daughters did not diverge seriously from her own outlook and did not long to be able to live a consumption-oriented lifestyle. The question of meat was one that exercised Jackie, too, and she planned to go vegan when her son and daughter left home; otherwise, her two teenagers did not find her modest lifestyle difficult. She said, "I'm lucky that the children aren't conned by the brand thing – they don't let anyone steal their dreams and sell them back again for the price of a product." Anne, whose daughters were now in their early twenties, told me, "My children always said that their friends' parents were more generous with pocket money and presents than we were. I suspect that was true. We always felt it was not a good idea to give our children too much in the way of money or presents. As soon as they could get jobs they did and we stopped giving them an allowance at that point." Now, the young women felt that they had had a good childhood, in that they had had lots of enjoyable and interesting experiences.

Jenny and her husband had grown up in make-do-and-mend families, and chose to continue living modestly because they wanted their 14 year-old daughter to know that who you are is more important than what you have. Their daughter understood and accepted her parents' environmental viewpoint and often got involved in in-depth discussions with them at the dinner table. It wasn't altogether easy for her, though, as her school peer group were quite different and not aware of environmental concerns, so she felt it wasn't 'cool' to admit at school to being green. Only once the old family television was updated, had she felt able to invite school friends home to watch DVDs. She did, however, maintain some differences, avoiding eating at McDonald's, choosing fair-trade goods, and not buying 'trashy' magazines.

So determined were these parents to be relatively modest in their consumption and to bring their children up to understand and share their principles that they went to some lengths to explain their beliefs and practices. But they recognised the psychological needs of their children in relation to fitting in with their peer group and realised that they needed to make some compromises in order to give their children a comfortable experience of growing up. Open, reasoned communication, empathy for the child's position, and the provision of plenty of opportunities to pursue active interests go a long way, then, to maintaining harmony within families in which parents insist on bucking the trend.

Because children tend to emulate the values transmitted by their families,[227] it is not altogether surprising that those (albeit few) modest consumers' children who were represented, did not apparently have too much difficulty with their parents' material consumption principles. But perhaps there was also something more subtle going on here, in terms of parenting style. Tim Kasser, an American psychologist with a long-time interest in values and materialism, has conducted research into the aspirations of 18 year-olds and the relationship between these and their mothers' approach to parenting.[228] His research found that more nurturing mothers, that is to say, mothers who were emotionally warm, allowed their children to express their views and feelings and made them feel appreciated, had teenage offspring who placed greater value on self-acceptance, good relationships and contributing to society, while the adolescent children of mothers who took a harsh, punitive approach to discipline, did not help their children to feel they could take care of themselves, and who were inconsistent with behavioural rules, had more materialistic values.[229] Kasser has interpreted his results as an indication that children who come from unaffectionate, unsupportive homes are more likely than children from warmer, more accepting backgrounds to grow up materialistic. This does indeed seem very credible, for young people who lack affirmation from their own parents will look for it elsewhere; and material objects frequently confer status. They also offer consolation and don't chide.

The idea that the emotional tone of a family somehow relates to its attitudes to material things also emerges from research that has looked at the meanings attached by people from three or four generations to domestic objects they regard as special.[230] Analysis of interviews showed that adults in families who came over as warm spoke about their possessions in terms of the associations they had with family ties far more often than those whose tone was neutral or negative. But we must beware over-generalisation, for there were some contrary indications amongst the stories of the adult modest consumers. Among our non-materialists were intellectual Anthony who had been misunderstood by his father and Mark who had been hectored by a critical and undermining mother. On the other hand, there were several who explicitly attributed their current values to their upbringing by warm, supportive, open-minded parents. As far as the next generation goes, a particular gift the modest consumer parents in this study gave their children in raising them in the way they were doing was a sense of control over their lives. Overtly practised in day-to-day decision-making, they transmitted the idea of making choices for well-informed reasons, rather than behaving in particular ways simply because it is the conventional expectation. And a feeling of personal control or autonomy is one more important contributor to a subjective sense of wellbeing.[231]

Conclusion: The Imperative to Increase Happiness and Decrease Consumption

The level of material consumption which is typical of contemporary lifestyles in the UK (indeed of the rich or relatively affluent all over the world) – and to which it is socially acceptable to aspire for those who cannot yet afford it – is responsible for much of the rapid and daily evidenced decline in the conditions which the Earth provides. Yet we utterly depend on these conditions for a reasonable quality of life. The services rendered by the Earth cannot actually afford to support this level of personal consumption if they are to be spread equitably between all people and to endure long enough to sustain even today's children to the end of their natural lifespan. We are already collectively overdrawn at the bank of the biosphere. The change in our ways which this uncomfortable truth demands of us may sound impossibly daunting to those of us who are paid up members of the consumer society, yet it also presents a huge incentive to us to discover an existence of as yet unknown individual and social thriving. What the modest consumers, like other voluntary simplifiers,[232] amply demonstrate is that satisfaction and pleasure are to be found, often abundantly, in lives of relatively low material consumption. A lifestyle of basic material sufficiency, entered into adventurously, is the route we can and must travel towards the dual, prized, destinations of personal wellbeing and a sustainable natural world. The more people who reject over-consumption and prioritise the true generators of happiness, the easier it will be for others to follow suit; and when enough of us live according to this principle, our future prospects can be transformed.

5

Happiness, Status, Money and Time

Why Happy People are Better for the Planet

Illbeing, wellbeing and consumption

It goes without saying that humans (and other life-forms) flourish best in the biophysical world within the balanced and complex conditions of which they have evolved. What is not so obvious is that, conversely, happy people are likely both to be more benign to the planet, and to adapt better to a changing world. There are several routes to this conclusion which I shall consider.

How many people, implicitly or explicitly, measure the love they receive in terms of the pounds spent on them at Christmas, or attempt to convey or extract affection by the proffering of a lavish gift? When it is socially acceptable to represent the extent of a person's wealth as a question of how much they are 'worth', then the amount one person is willing to spend on another can perhaps be understood in a symbolic way as how much of *themselves* they are prepared to give. When it comes to presents, however, a simple handmade item, designed specifically for a particular friend or relative, whose value lies not in its financial cost but in the thought, effort and time put into it, can very often express real giving far more meaningfully than the handing over of a mass-produced, much advertised, impersonal item or a cheque.

One way of looking at the relationship between *dis*satisfaction with life and eco-*un*friendliness is that it is all too easy for us, if our lives lack the ingredients of genuine wellbeing, to seek solace in material possessions. When under pressure from unmet emotional needs, moreover, it can be more difficult to resist the call of the shop window or catalogue or to ignore advertising that stokes anxieties about supposed personal inadequacies. Eating and drinking excessive quantities of food and alcohol are not the only forms of comfort consumption; within the jokey phrase 'retail therapy' lies a serious insight. We use consumption to try to fill holes in the tissue of our emotions, when we lack or lose self-esteem, or experience difficulties in expressing love, or fail to feel needed or appreciated. Surrounded at every turn by goods which appeal to us to buy them, a common response is to 'treat ourselves' to food, drink, or some new consumer item whenever we feel dispirited or rejected. At these times, though, some other activity, like a stroll in the woods, dancing to a CD, writing a diary, or a run in the park, would, in all probability, be a more effective treatment for our sorry state. Such a remedy would also be likely to be less taxing on the environment. The existence of a certain relationship between how people feel and how much they consume embodies a direct connection between ill-being and environmental damage. Being impelled to indulge oneself by buying a glossy magazine, some highly packaged cosmetics, a novel gadget, a new pair of shoes or a continental weekend break, simply to distract or cheer oneself up, is a tiny example of how, in our consumption-oriented culture, uncomfortable emotions often beget yet more pollution and resource depletion.

On a larger scale, the profound and prolonged distress involved in divorce or separation means that a family or couple, who have been living together in one home, now suddenly need two, effectively doubling (or nearly so) their need for bricks and mortar and everything that goes with them – bathroom and kitchen fittings and appliances, furniture, curtains, flooring, and so on. A greater likelihood of materialistic values and compulsive buying has, in addition, been found amongst children of divorced or separated parents, whether still at school or grown into young adults.[233]

From a more general perspective, it is logical to suppose that those with non-materialistic values live in a more environmentally-friendly way than people who prioritise material goals. When we add to this the large body of research evidence that indicates that people who have materialistic values experience lower wellbeing and life satisfaction than those who do not,[234] it seems that non-materialistic values, higher well-being and lower impact on the environment fit together as loosely associated characteristics. Moreover, the majority of common activities which most effectively generate wellbeing, such as getting lost in a book, tending the garden or window-box, talking to a friend, painting, bird-watching, making or listening to music, or helping others, inflict negligible irreversible damage on the world or none at all. We can therefore see that while personal wellbeing as an end in itself is certainly important for individuals and for society as a whole, its significance goes much further: when multiplied it has major implications for the state of the Earth. There is another, more subtle reason, too, why happier people are better for the environment. It is to do with perception and focus as I shall now explain.

Wellbeing and realism

Feeling happy inclines people to think in terms of the big picture, it makes their thinking more expansive.[235] Twenty years of experiments have shown that individuals experiencing positive emotions show patterns of thought which are flexible, integrative and open to information, while negative emotions narrow the attention.[236] Clearly, a capacity to see one's choices and actions in a wider context than one's own little life and likes is a pre-requisite for taking into account all the possible impacts of personal consumption, such as the demands for raw materials, polluting manufacturing processes, sweatshop labour, and so on.

Another important effect of an ability to step back and put issues into a broader framework is an aspect of what has been described as our 'relationship with reality'. This is the expression used by Nick Baylis, a psychologist who, through studying highly accomplished university students, elite members of the armed forces and young prisoners, identified three cognitive-behavioural processes in which most people partake to some degree; he terms these 'quick fixes', 'reality evasion' and 'reality-investing'.[237] Quick fixes are strategies such as eating or drinking too much, gambling and retail therapy, while reality evasion involves denial of circumstances, escapism through excessive television watching or computer games playing, or hard drugs. Reality investment, by contrast, involves planning, practising of skills, pursuit of learning and the cultivation of good health. According to Baylis, reality investment is the defining characteristic of a positive relationship with reality; and reality investment is likely to enhance well-being. It is also, surely, the only form of relationship with reality that can further the cause of environmental sustainability. This is because studies have shown that happy people are not starry eyed; those who have a positive outlook on life actually have a better grip on reality than the unhappy. They are better at attending to relevant information, including the negative and threatening, and are more realistic about what they can and cannot achieve.[238] They have also been found to have greater self-control and self-regulatory abilities, and tend to be more co-operative, pro-social, charitable and 'other-centred'.[239] These are all qualities which are likely to incline individuals to consider the ethical dimensions of their consumption decisions.

One more way in which human happiness favours environmental sustainability is that, as we have seen, an individual's wellbeing has a lot to do with their capacity to function autonomously, out of internal motivation rather than as a result of the pull and push of externally imposed expectations or sanctions; so autonomous individuals are more likely to take responsibility for their behaviour. Taking all these considerations into account, there is strong reason to suppose that individuals who enjoy a high level of wellbeing may well live in more environmentally-friendly and socially aware ways than those who don't, being psychologically better placed to make choices which entail less or no damage to the environment and to their fellow humans.

Meanings and Uses of Consumption

Although actively materialistic individuals may sometimes be contrasted with the willingly modest, and although a distinction can be drawn between the person motivated by perceived external pressures and someone who ploughs their own furrow, these divisions are an oversimplification: few people inhabit an extreme position at all times. Most of us can probably be found somewhere along the spectrum, and the exact position of anyone along it is likely to vary from one occasion or phase of life to another. Helga Dittmar, one of several researchers into material culture, has suggested that personal possessions can be divided into two broad categories, the instrumental and the symbolic.[240] Objects with instrumental uses are those which are used to make things happen, which give us the possibility of doing certain things, while the symbolic use of objects resides largely in their power to create and communicate aspects of individual identity. Individual possession is a deeply rooted feature of Western culture,[241] and it applies to both categories.

But the relationship between people and things is not simply a matter of a human subject making or acquiring a material object, for material goods themselves shape human culture. That is, not only do people choose their possessions but possessions influence aspects of the way people live. For instance, fridges have revolutionised shopping and eating habits; cars have increased geographical mobility, with all sorts of knock-on effects; and television has changed the way that family members organise their time and interact with one another.[242] Research by Ofcom has suggested that new technology in the form of mobile phones has "fundamentally changed the way that we communicate", texting seemingly having overtaken talking on the phone or face to face as the main means of communication between friends and family.[243]

Material objects play many roles in human life. For example, toys and games help babies and children to learn about themselves and the world;[244] the type and arrangement of furniture shapes the mode and tenor of human interactions within a particular space;[245] and religions and political ideologies express the immaterial through material means,[246] whether via candles, statues, posters or buildings. In fact it has been claimed that things make people as much as people make things.[247] We use objects both to differentiate ourselves from others and to integrate ourselves into society.[248] Wherever we live, it is the possessions with which we surround ourselves that make where we live into our home.[249] When people are asked about the objects on display in their homes, their responses quickly reveal that these are often closely tied up with their life history and family relationships, convey special associations and keep significant memories alive; gifts, photographs and the creations of children and grandchildren have a particular place in people's hearts.[250] Thus the things that are to be seen in people's homes construct meaning and tell stories about them – both to themselves and to other people; and the distress experienced at the loss of personal possessions in domestic burglaries is often due to a sense of losing of a part of the self along with those belongings.[251]

Understanding consumption and recognising limits

It is important to our understanding of the 'material' to acknowledge the deep personal significance of much of our stuff. But we also need to recognise, in this era in which the resources for manufacturing more stuff are shrinking, that many material objects, both on the domestic front and in other kinds of space, can be classified as unnecessary, dispensable clutter to which we have no emotional attachment or of which we make little practical use. We buy so much because the growth economy has identified the sensitive psychological buttons in us to push in order to propagate itself. In whatever ways our capacity to consume may be curtailed by economic and environmental crisis, those sensitive psychological buttons will still be there. It is therefore important to understand the functions served by non-essential material consumption and to consider other means of satisfying these needs – or, indeed, of finding ways to do away with them. Only with such an understanding will we have a chance of finding effective means of *radically* and *willingly* reducing our individual and collective buying habits. This requires us to examine the symbolic functions of material things. Many of these can be broadly summarised as meeting our need to express our personal identity and our social status.

135

Personal identity and possessions

Individualism is a distinctive attribute of Western societies which emphasise individual achievement and expression. This contrasts with the priority given to group loyalty and harmony found in collectivist cultures such as those found in East Asia – at least hitherto; collectivist cultures are likely to become more individualistic as consumerism spreads. The emergence of individualism and mass consumption has led people in Western Europe and the United States to define themselves and others in terms of the things they possess.[252] Psychologists Mihalyi Csikszentmihalyi and Eugene Rochberg-Halton carried out an investigation of the meaning attached by people living in a middleclass suburb of Chicago in the late 1970's to domestic objects they regarded as special.[253] The importance of particularly valued possessions, it turned out, as I have already indicated, tended to reside in the associations they had with certain people. It was noticeable, moreover, that those people who did not attach meaning to their belongings in terms of human ties lacked a network of close relationships. From this the researchers concluded that great involvement with possessions for their own sake, for what they were deemed to say about the owner, rather than for their affectionate associations, might be a sign of alienation. Csikszentmihalyi and Rochberg-Halton proposed a different division from that of Dittmar's between instrumental and symbolic objects, and distinguished instead between 'instrumental materialism' and 'terminal materialism'. Instrumental materialism, in their terms, is possession of things which a serve a purpose for a person or for the common good of the culture, which can include symbolic purpose. Terminal materialism, in contrast, is consumption for its own sake, a dead end.

However one might choose to characterise material objects and their consumption, there is a close association between people's possessions and their sense of identity. Identity can be understood according to numerous characteristics, some of them social, such as class, occupation and age, and some of them personal, such as political outlook, tastes and interests. It is extremely important to people, it seems, to convey the *right* messages about their identity through their possessions.[254] A class of possessions which is of special concern to most people is their clothes, for through our appearance we feel we publically mark out our personal style and values. Indeed, so important are clothes to us, that it was estimated in 2007, just before the economic crisis broke, that we each bought every year an estimated average of 77lb of clothes.[255] That's an awful lot of clothes. Even if the weight were halved, it would suggest that many people feel no personal bond of affection for their clothes and thus don't wear them from year to year. Rather, many people apparently buy clothes on a whim, or are primarily concerned to wear whatever is the current fashion. Statistics of quantities of clothes sent to landfill each year[256]certainly indicate that we cast them out without much thought. The vast array of styles and accoutrements on offer, all so readily available in the high street, the catalogue, or online, allow us to tell ourselves and the world who we are – on any given occasion – whether we go for jeans, a suit, 'bling', twin-set-and-pearls, Doc Martens, jogging bottoms, body piercing, 'ethnic', 'vintage', designer labels or chain store items.

The way we equip and decorate our homes is open to similar treatment, and the many 'make-over' television programmes and magazine features of recent years have encouraged us to change our styles frequently. As a consequence of the rise of individualism and mass consumption many people have come to interpret their feelings of wellbeing in terms of their levels of material consumption.[257] The dual development of individualism and mass production has also resulted in an increase in the relative importance of the *expressive*, rather than the functional use of goods.[258] Take handbags; though of practical use too, these are often purchased for expressive rather than functional purposes, such as the £23,000 Louis Vuitton Tribute bag sported by the singer Beyoncé,[259] or the many less expensive alternatives retailing in the region of £1,000 which provide no more functionality or aesthetic value than bags a tenth the price. For some purchasers the latest fashion is all, including one young actress who reportedly told the Daily Mail in 2007, "I bought three Chloe Paddington bags, which of course no one carries any more. And I bought a Dior saddle bag in every colour available. Again, they aren't fashionable anymore, so I can't use them".[260] Yet the desire for expensive bags that are thought to communicate a message about the owner is not confined to a few odd cases, otherwise upmarket handbag shops would not have become a target of raids by thieves as they have.[261]

Leaving aside the serious environmental toll taken by the scale of our demand for consumer goods and the stress sometimes induced by too much choice, one might think that the acquisition of identity-creating items amounted to no more than harmless fun. But a more critical and penetrating view, expressed by the sociologist Anthony Giddens, is that, "the consumption of ever-novel goods becomes in some part a substitute for the genuine development of self; appearance replaces essence".[262] Giddens agrees with fellow sociologist Zygmunt Bauman that, "…Individual needs of personal autonomy, self-definition, authentic life or personal perfection are all translated into the need to possess, and consume, market-offered goods. This translation… is intrinsically inadequate and ultimately self-defeating, leading to momentary assuagement of desires and lasting frustration of needs."[263] Another downside of increasing personal consumption is raised by Fred Hirsch's important 1977 analysis in his book *Social Limits to Growth*.[264] Hirsch pointed out that growth in the acquisition of positional goods can bring its own limitations. One example he gave is of car ownership: when this passes beyond a certain point, congestion, degraded air quality, a reduction in public transport and other unfortunate, unanticipated consequences follow, and "[C]onsumers, taken together, get a product they did not order."[265]

Every human being needs to have a sense of who they are, and in our deeply rooted individualistic culture there is nothing wrong in making our individuality apparent; indeed, human variety can be a source of social strength and personal pleasure. But our 'stuff' is far from the only means we have for asserting our individuality and, while visual appearance seems an easy and inviting means of signalling identity, our acquiring of ever more or new things is jeopardising our very future. Thus we need to put far greater emphasis, both as individuals and as a society, on the development of real personal qualities and skills, enabling us to throw off our dependence for identity on the thin veneer of style which consumerism makes possible. As I observed earlier, many of the modest consumers were notable for the strong sense of self, views and values they projected; they presented very varied individual identities and personal styles (in the most general sense of the word), quite independent of consumer goods. Identity construction does not actually require the immense choice of merchandise which saturates our society.

Social status

Closely related to identity is a person's social status; indeed there are those for whom their status seems to be the aspect of their identity which they feel the most urgent need to display. This is revealed, for example, in a study of the identity and educational engagement of 14-16 year-old working class pupils in London.[266] These young people, all of whom had been identified by their schools as at risk of dropping out of education[iii], dressed in brands which they felt represented their social class: "[Y]ou wouldn't really expect [upper class] people to come out in Nike tracksuits and stuff, we expect them to have that Gucci designer stuff. But people like us… we're Nike". Those

---

iii This was before the mandatory age for leaving education was raised from 16 to 18.

who could not afford to buy appropriately branded goods were regarded as morally inferior and bullied, the study found. Most of these young people had histories of educational failure, regarded themselves as 'stupid', and lived and went to school in deprived areas they described in terms like 'shit' and 'crap'. Many described their main hobby as shopping, and the reason they were keen to leave education was that their chief aspiration was to earn enough money, legally or otherwise, to "buy all the designer stuff".

When social status is as closely tied to display of buying power as it is, spending priorities can become distorted, an effect which emerges in this telling passage from Richard Wilkinson and Kate Pickett's 2009 book *The Spirit Level*[267] about the wide range of social ills created across society by large inequalities of wealth:

> [S]urveys of the 12.6 per cent of Americans living below the federal poverty line (an absolute income level rather than a relative standard such as half the average income) show that... almost 75 per cent own at least one car or truck and around 33 per cent have a computer, a dishwasher or a second car. What this means is that when people lack money for essentials such as food, it is usually a reflection of the strength of their desire to live up to the prevailing standards. You may, for instance, feel it more important to maintain appearances by spending on clothes while stinting on food. We knew of a young man who was unemployed and had spent a month's income on a new mobile phone because he said girls ignored people who hadn't got the right stuff.[268]

Thus we see how conspicuous consumption can also serve to disguise the lack of a sense of self-worth. It may be indulged in in order to try and avoid the shame of not having the same financial options as one's peers, but this urge to display worth through ownership of consumer goods is not confined to the poor. Returning to handbags, we can see how the need to display social status affects those with plenty of money too; in the explanation of Stefan Lindemann, shopping editor of the fashion magazine *Grazia*, some women are prepared to go to great lengths to acquire a particular bag: "It's a show-off thing. It's even better if you can have a limited edition one that no-one else can have... Bags are a status symbol. They show you have class and that you clearly understand fashion. Plus getting your hands on one that is hard to get... shows you are well connected."[269]

The relationship between social status and wealth is circular. Social status is accorded largely on the basis of wealth, so the display of acquisitions, more than anything else, is the way social status tends to be communicated. This is far from new but now, mass production and increasing affluence have blurred the boundaries between the rich and the relatively poor to some degree. In his 1925 book *The Theory of the Leisure Class*, American economist and social philosopher Thorstein Veblen observed that, "conspicuous consumption of valuable goods" had long been the basis of the reputation of 'gentlemen of leisure'.[270] "[D]uring the earlier stages of economic development", he wrote, "consumption of goods without stint, especially consumption of the better grades of goods – ideally all consumption in excess of the subsistence minimum – pertains normally to the leisure class", but that, "This restriction tends to disappear... with private ownership of goods and an industrial system based on wage labour or on the petty household economy".[271]

Status and autonomy

Desirable as popular buying power may feel, wellbeing is not actually nourished by keeping up with or out-doing the Joneses. The difference between outward show and personal control over a satisfying existence is captured in these lines of Carol Ann Duffy's poem *Mrs Faust*.[272]

> We worked. We saved.
> We moved again.
> Fast cars. A boat with sails.
> A second home in Wales.
> The latest toys – computers,
> mobile phones. Prospered...
>
> I grew to love the lifestyle,
> Not the life.
> He grew to love the kudos
> not the wife.

Having control over one's life, rather than achieving success in the eyes of others, is what matters for genuine wellbeing. This distinction is not necessarily easy to detect but medical researcher Michael Marmot discerned it when considering the evidence of his Whitehall Studies, in which he investigated the consistent health gradient found within the ranks of civil servants. Health, in the form of longevity, is often used as a proxy measure for the more difficult-to-measure phenomenon of wellbeing,[273] and Marmot found that those on the lowest grade suffered from the highest rates of stress-related physical ill-health such as heart disease, while those at the top of the hierarchy, whose jobs might have been expected to be more stressful due to greater responsibility, experienced the least such illness. Marmot concluded that the higher a person's social status, the more freedom of action and scope they are likely to have for influencing their situation, and that this has crucial importance for a sense of wellbeing. It was not, then, the disparity in income *per se* between grades which accounted for the marked difference in health profiles but the disparity in personal autonomy.[274]

A new perspective on social status
Without in any way undermining Marmot's findings on the relationship between social status and autonomy, it is necessary to reiterate the very close association between social status and money, ie, buying power. Human beings are by nature status-seeking creatures, as indeed are many other species (just think 'pecking order'). Throughout history the possession of money has been the pre-eminent factor according to which social status has been bestowed and recognised. Indeed level of wealth and place on the social ladder are very nearly synonymous. This, it seems to me, is why: it is logical that human beings should early on develop an attraction to material things when survival and successful breeding was once crucially dependant on the possession of secure shelter and sources of food, water and warmth. The possession and outward display of material resources can therefore be seen to have originated as the marker of this survival characteristic; it would attract potential mates and therefore ensure the propagation of the species. And the meeting of this human need has long brought environmental damage in its wake: Roman mining and metal-smelting activities, copper in the Jordanian pre-desert and gold in Spain, limited in extent only by lack of technological capability, caused desertification and pollution centuries ago, the extensive damaging effects of which are still present today.[275]

In today's consumer culture, the urge to possess and display has become so grotesquely bloated that the situation has now, ironically, been reversed: the contemporary scale of manufacture and consumption threatens to damage beyond repair the very ecological conditions on which the human species and many others depend. It actually beckons our demise. This desperate state of affairs has arisen because human instincts, which evolved millennia ago, in the context of hunting and gathering, have not changed, even though human existence is now very different.[276]

Against this macro-scale evolutionary rationale for the common human weakness for material wealth, another biological insight, arising from the observation of a detail of bird behaviour, perhaps offers an unexpected second explanation for our attraction to 'stuff'. When biologist and Nobel laureate Niko Tinbergen was studying oystercatchers, birds which lay small blue eggs with grey speckles, he found that under experimental conditions they actually preferred to sit on the large fake bright blue eggs with black spots which he provided. This led him to suggest that problems can arise when animals are disconnected from their natural environment: in these circumstances the exaggerated imitation, which he termed 'supernormal stimulus', can exert a stronger pull than the real thing.[277] Could it be, then, that this perspective sheds a wholly new light on human beings' tendency to find the luxury model more appealing than the economy version, to desire more than basic necessities? Maybe the most supposedly sophisticated material inclinations are actually horribly crude. There is no doubt that goods have a powerful appeal for most human beings. Karl Marx regarded it as the 'fetishistic' character of commodities,[278] which he interpreted, perhaps rather romantically, as the attachment of value to the products of human labour. But the near-universal pull towards material possessions that human beings have felt throughout history surely demands to be explained in more fundamental and enduring terms than the flimsy, transient, human artefact of economic theory. The phenomenon seems, rather, to be explicable in terms of an evolutionary trait, one whose usefulness, now that the human species is firmly established, is long outlived. The thought that our increasingly unnatural lives may nudge us towards consumption behaviour which separates us ever further from the essential sources of life-support is one with which we must engage without delay. Tinbergen's oystercatchers may have thrown us a crucial life-line, if only we will grasp it. They could be telling us that, "we need not be slaves to instincts gone berserk".[279]

Certainly, nothing less than our future hinges on our getting our impulses under rational control and constructing an informed view of our material needs and wants in relation to what the Earth can afford. We may resist this emotionally unwelcome demand but we do so at our peril. We urgently need to use our peculiarly human abilities to reason, to be creative, and to exercise a moral sense, that we so proudly claim as elevating us above the rest of the animal kingdom, to redirect the trajectory of our own existence and that of all other species. We must move onto a different track from that on which our original instincts have set us, and beat a new path to a more promising future.

The recognition of the importance of social status to human beings actually offers us a powerful means of attempting to reduce material consumption – if only we can establish new and better markers than money to recognise (in both senses) social status. In any case, just being rich should not raise a person above their peers – many of whom may be their betters in many ways. After all, while money may be earned in return for hard work or skill, fortunes are often acquired by chance, via inheritance, lottery winnings or the vagaries of the market (such as a rise in property prices), or by downright dishonesty or criminality. Much of the most worthwhile or demanding work, which makes a tangible contribution to society, such as fostering severely disturbed children, caring round the clock for a completely dependent person, or campaigning to bring to light and end human rights abuses, is poorly paid or not recompensed at all, while the bankers whose recklessly risky practices which brought many countries' economies to the brink of disaster continue to earn millions. So money is in no way a reliable indicator of personal excellence, and should not constitute the primary basis for social esteem and an exalted position in society.

In order to reduce individuals' need to prove their worth by spending on outward-facing, supposed enhancement we need to create a culture that values and identifies individual worth in quite other ways. Some radically different rewards have been proposed to this end. They are: the temporary provision of shopping, cooking, cleaning, and house maintenance services; the loan for a period of a treasure such as a renowned painting; or the gift of a prestige seat at soccer stadium for a season.[280] We need to generate a culture which elevates to the highest level of social regard such humanity-supporting qualities as wisdom, kindness, integrity, courage, perseverance, compassion, imagination, and public-spiritedness.

This does not mean that money can ever be expected to lose its appeal – it does, after all, deliver a significant degree of that genuinely valuable asset, autonomy. Having spare money allows a person to go straight to a private osteopath or chiropractor to treat their back pain, rather than waiting for a clinic appointment, for example. Control over one's life is vitally important for wellbeing, as Marmot discerned in his findings on the correlation between physical health and social hierarchy. We need to find ways to increase the control which *everyone* has over their lives. Also, with proper understanding of its environmental repercussions, conspicuous expenditure and consumption should come to be seen as vulgar and anti-social. Anthropologist Daniel Miller has proposed that much consumption is driven by a desire to achieve normality, stability and continuity, by having what other people have.[281] Our challenge now is to normalise low consumption. Fortunately, while we may be largely pre-programmed to be attracted to material things, the lifelong modest consumers of the world, and the converts to voluntary simplicity, demonstrate that such a trait is neither universal nor immutable.

Bypassing process

'Time is money' is a well-known aphorism, and one which is often perfectly true in practical terms, as we rush through our days from one role or responsibility to another. By dint of the purchase of manufactured goods, many of which we could, in principle, make ourselves, as well as the acquisition of labour-saving devices and use of electrical energy, we use consumption to bypass the process of arriving at a product. We simply reheat a highly processed and packaged meal instead of preparing it from raw ingredients, or use food processors to spare us the trouble of having to chop, grate and beat; we dry washing in a tumble-drier rather than hanging it out in the sun and wind; and buy clothes, toys, soft furnishings, greetings cards and all manner of other things that could be made at home, if only we had the time, and the skills. In doing so, we often deprive ourselves of sensory pleasures – the delight to the nose and fingers of squeezing a lemon until the juice runs, the stress-release of mashing potatoes, the satisfaction of the even slicing of cucumber, the aesthetic satisfaction of generating silky peaks of beaten egg white, the sense of order or randomness emerging along the washing line, and the achievement of something made with our own hands and head. By focusing on the product and its consumption, and forgetting the process by which it is created, we short-circuit our relationship with it. In doing so we deprive ourselves of gifts to the senses and opportunities for the mind to disengage and wander. We do ourselves out of the therapeutic sense of efficacy, connectedness and meaning that involvement in physical processes bestows, as well as time to reflect. Many of the activities that are basic to life, such as cooking and washing, are usually associated with low status rather than high; but if we constantly distance ourselves from them we are the poorer for it.

Making usually costs less than buying; sometimes a choice can be made between earning money and having time. This choice was particularly reflected in the stories of two of the modest consumers, Toni and Mark, who, like several others, put a premium on having control over their own time.

§

144

TONI

Toni was a life coach and trainer in mindfulness-based strategies for pain and stress management. Her life was determined, she said, by a conscious choice to simplify her lifestyle in order to minimise the work involved in daily living. "Being healthy and having good friends is what matters. As I've got older I've needed to feel that the work I do is meaningful, not just something that happens to be interesting. I want a sense of using my abilities in ways that contribute to other people's wellbeing, a way of me 'giving something back'. If I earn enough for 'basics', and a bit extra for a few treats, then that's fine by me." Treats for Toni were a drink and a piece of cake in a café, plants, a flute, occasional concerts or films, a Friends' pass to the Royal Academy, train fares and painting materials.

Although she had lived modestly all her life, about fifteen years earlier, she told me, "I got to the point where I realised very strongly that to be content I needed to find a means of income that allowed me to work/live in ways that fitted comfortably with my values". In fact, Toni was well prepared for this approach to life by her 1950s and 60s childhood:

> "Money was quite limited. My parents did put a new carpet in the hall after I left home, but when we cleared the house after my dad died the rest of the carpets were still the same as we'd always had. Our holidays were always two weeks on the south coast in a B & B. We hired a beach hut and had soup and sandwiches for lunch. It was a huge treat to go to a local cafeteria restaurant to eat in the evening. My clothes were often hand-me-downs from my sister. Good shoes were thought to be important; I had one pair in the winter and a pair of sandals in the summer. It was very frugal. Dad was an insurance clerk and didn't earn much so there wasn't much spare money. Mum suffered a lot from severe depression."

In this household Toni experienced hours of lonely boredom which, she believed, was the impetus for the development of her creative ability. "I don't know at what age I first had paint and paper but it must have been very early because my mum painted and she valued that, she allowed me to be messy. There was very little in terms of toys but I did have paint and brushes and paper."

It was as a reaction to the atmosphere of relative fear and sadness at home and her mother's sometimes harsh words, the result of her mental condition, that Toni later became drawn to the Buddhist precepts of non-harming and loving-kindness. Now she was a great believer in kindness to self and others. Simplicity, she felt, can be seen as kindness to oneself because a complicated life is stressful. Buddhist precepts resonated with her, and their discovery was 'like coming home to a sort of truth'. As a result, Toni often helped out on Buddhist retreats. Wwoofing (World Wide Opportunities on Organic Farms) was another voluntary activity of hers, undertaken in order to connect with the cycles of nature. She felt she had an inborn affinity with the outdoors, remembering how as a child she loved being outside and feeling the air, wanting to be out on summer evenings, or, when it was snowy, running around pretending to be a horse drawing a sleigh; she loved playing in the mud and making things with sticks. It was reading Frances Moore Lappé's *Diet for a Small Planet* in 1972 that first made her aware of environmental issues, in connection with food, and this also informed the way she now lived: "Knowing I can have an infinitesimal effect I feel I need to do my bit" she said.

§

MARK
This is how Mark lived...

> Don't have TV, fridge, freezer, microwave, toaster, washing machine, dishwasher, car, constant hot water. I travel by bicycle, on foot or public transport. Don't fly. Buy second-hand furniture mostly or make using reclaimed materials. Buy food mostly from markets (no packaging) or grow it. Don't do Christmas. Holidays usually cycling or staying with friends. Put an extra layer on rather than heating.

On paper Mark sounded somewhat ascetic, but this impression was short-lived: on meeting on the South Bank he suggested that we go to his favourite café for almond croissants. The reasons Mark gave for choosing to live the way he did were:

> Because 'more' isn't better. Because I hate waste and greed, and chattels are weighty and unsatisfying while nature is free, generous, delightful and uplifting. Because consuming only what I find I need reduces my carbon footprint and allows me to feel good about myself and my place in this environment.

Had he chosen to earn relatively little, or did he simply not spend much of what he did earn? He explained that he had worked for a local council which had been flexible about working patterns so had been able to have two separate jobs. This meant that whenever he ran out of savings and a situation came up where he could expand the number of hours he worked, he'd do that for a while and save as much as he could, because he couldn't see any point in earning more than he needed. Mark's working life had, in fact, come to an end eighteen months earlier when he had been made redundant from his job as a library manager. But he was an artist and craftsman too, and he enjoyed having variety in his life. "I earn money to live, I don't live to earn money... why would you want to do that? I really enjoyed my job at the library, but when they offered me voluntary severance I just thought that's it, I'm out." I quickly learnt that Mark had strong opinions which he expressed with vigour.

He was passionate on the subject of waste; for example, waste of time and personal ability as well as of physical resources:

> "It doesn't matter what aspect it is, to me it is utterly wasteful for me to spend valuable time doing a job to earn more money than I need to keep me ticking over, when someone else could have that job that actually needs it. I think it's appallingly narrow, deeply boring, just to be doing the same thing every day. But the key I think is the waste. I think the problem now is that people think you have to be doing. I remember as a kid I spent a lot of time sitting with a book on my lap, just sitting thinking, which was absolutely not allowed. If you had a book on your lap you were reading, if you were not doing anything you were wasting time. And this is wrong because some of the most valuable time is spent just standing looking, being, walking, whatever, doing apparently nothing. Stuff is always happening, not just outside you but inside your head, and if you don't stop it never gets to the front of your head, it just gets knotted up at the back. So I actually think that the most important time is what most people probably call wasted time, and I've always been, certainly in my adult life, very clear that I have to have time to waste."

A worthwhile use of time in Mark's experience was going out and about and taking in what was to be found outside in the surrounding world. Going out on a bike, he declared, "Is a glorious thing to be doing, out in the countryside or in the city or wherever, just being a witness actually, because most people are paying no attention to what is ordinary stuff going on, and I think it's important, we should be appreciating what's around us."

Mark was similarly independent in his thinking about most things, and I quote him at some length because his unconventional perceptions cast an interesting and unusual light in a number of corners. He cycled from south to north London every week to tend a friend's garden and bring a box of vegetables home. "In some ways it doesn't matter whether you like the food, if you grow it yourself there is something magical about it. I grow spinach because it's good for you, I can't stand it but I'll eat it if I've grown it." His home was a one-bedroom housing co-op basement flat, into which he had recently moved, and where he applied his characteristic and economical approach to setting up his new kitchen. The units came from Ikea but he had made his own adjustments to them such as installing a pull-out cooker. His Baby Belling had, in fact, apparently been one of the reasons why he was allocated a place in the co-op, on the basis that it indicated that he was deprived. This attitude outraged him; "I just bit my lip cos I was going to say 'How dare you!' Because nobody needs more than that – I've got two rings, I've got a grill and a little oven, what more do you need?" The cooker fitted in a drawer so that when it was not in use there was a smooth kitchen surface which could be used for art work or anything else. He put a lot of thought into what he bought: "If I buy things, I don't just buy something that will do the job, I buy something that pleases me and will do the job because I'm going to have to live with it. I bought an armchair which is an original Arts and Crafts armchair and it's absolutely beautiful. It's got a flap-up table on one side and shelves on the other." He had also bought an Arts and Crafts table for 50p in a jumble sale many years before, which he had used for "absolutely everything", even as a workshop table.

Mark was quite clear about the personal value of the table to him:

"People say, 'you can't use the table like that', but it's my table, I have it because I love it and I use it for everything I need, end of story. In fact the Arts and Crafts chair is probably going to have a cut made in it to take a tile, when I've designed the tile. Because, although I like good stuff, I'm not precious about it, it does its job and OK if it gets scarred or it gets scratched, or I decide to alter it to do something else, then that's what happens. If someone else thinks that's buggered the value of it, well no, it's doubled the value to me."

He was not afraid of putting his own view of possessions to other people, in fact he felt it was his responsibility to do so: "It might come out in conversation that I have no TV, for instance, and the person I am talking to will be appalled and want to know how I can survive without one. Once they understand, they are further appalled that I live so chattel-free and it is by choice." I suppose often it's that kind of thing where someone will ask your opinion when what they actually want is for you to agree with what they've said. People who don't know me that well will say, 'I've seen such and such and it's really brilliant and I'm going to get one', and I'll say, 'Why?', 'Well because it's...', and either they haven't got a reason, it's just because, it's all the adverts really, when asked they can't think of why because they don't need it, they'll just try and kind of bluff it."

Mark saw it as his responsibility to challenge people's values on such occasions because:

> "I'm responding to the fact that I don't live on an island, as nobody does, therefore what other people think affects me, and what other people do affects me, and I think one of the reasons we're in the mess we're in is because people don't question, they don't stand up and say, 'I don't think that's right'. And I think unless you are prepared to stand up and be counted nothing is going to change."

Born in 1954, Mark was accustomed to fairly basic provision from his childhood. No new furniture was ever bought in his family home, and sheets were patched, sides to middle, when they wore out. This made good sense to him. Moreover, he didn't like having stuff around him that wasn't really useful. He did not like having things that needed dusting, not even his own paintings on the wall. He disliked carpets because they required the use of a vacuum cleaner, and vacuum cleaners are inimical to spiders. Living in this way was extremely comfortable for Mark, and relieved him, he felt, of much decision-making that can cause people stress: "I've got what I need, I haven't got anything extra, I haven't got a huge amount of clutter. I have a pile of T shirts and I don't think about what to wear cos I just take one off the top."

A formative experience that had led to what Mark valued and enjoyed, he believed, was a very early memory, of being carried by his father along a lane dappled in early sunlight through spring green leaves of trees, with the sound of blackbirds singing. Despite this idyllic image, though, his childhood had been largely unhappy, his older sisters vindictive, vicious bullies, and his mother, he felt, always raising objections to what he did or creating contradictions. Partly as a result of this, trees were top of his list of the most important things in life:

> "Because I was brought up on the edge of Epping Forest and the forest was the only thing in my childhood that didn't fuck me up, and I spent a lot of time up trees and they were just there, solid, constant, and didn't do anything nasty. That's probably where it comes from, I was always more comfortable around trees than anything else in my childhood. They're just beautiful. And that's stayed with me."

Sea and sky were also important to Mark, because their huge size and constancy put human life into perspective. Indeed he found the environment as a whole endlessly magical, beautiful and fascinating, and being in it a privilege. He was intrigued by how, "Nature doesn't give a fuck, it just gets on with it, and if you elbow it in the ribs in one place it will hit you in the face somewhere else. But the somewhere in the face may be nothing to do with you".

Mark had now lost any desire to travel abroad, and had decided that air travel was no longer acceptable. In any case, he realised that it was the travelling he enjoyed, more than the destinations, so he was going to stay in the UK. He had cycled around most of southern England, but was keen to explore other parts, positively relishing the process of travelling from place to place, for instance noticing, the first time he cycled from London to Bath, which took a whole day, that daylight lasted thirty minutes longer in the west: "I find that so amazing and wonderful, a real sense of time moving, that you can't get if you're flying into the sunset all day".

Communication was also important to Mark, but in his experience, the sense of having been fully heard and understood by another person, though "absolutely glorious", was very rare. This he put down to most people lacking the time to talk things through properly. He mentioned several friends and intense conversations he had had with them. Friendships that were nurturing were of special importance to him as his relationships with his family were so difficult. Communication in his childhood home had been anything but constructive. His mother was given to taking exception to what Mark said, frequently telling him, "You can't do that", and his retorting, "Well I have!" From always having been constrained in this way, expected to care about the supposed disparaging opinions of others, Mark came to realise that the most important thing was to decide things for himself. Having been kicked out of more than one art class for his independent approach, he had come to realise that, "It isn't *what* you do, being an artist is *how* you do things."

Conclusion: Time for Radical Change

There is no getting away from the fact that social status is important to human beings. But outlooks such as those exemplified by the modest consumers show how concern for financial status need not drive our behaviour, albeit even unconsciously. Rather, they illustrate how, with our basic needs met, other facets of life, such as having time and control over how we spend it, are ultimately more valuable. It is high time that society learned to elevate more genuinely personally and socially enhancing achievements above the accumulation of wealth. For the sake of our wellbeing and that of the planet we need to move away from economic standing as the principal marker of an individual's social status and instead to give full recognition to other aspects of personal worth, to more genuine grounds for admiration and more enduring forms of excellence.

6

The Significance of Experience

A preference for material modesty

Many signals from the bio-physical environment are telling us that we urgently need to subdue our impulses to consume. Statistics and a few moments' honest reflection remind us that material things are really not the source of fundamental happiness. Yet most of us resist the idea of seriously changing our buying habits or lowering our material expectations. How much better it would be if we actually *preferred* to live in ways that involve less stuff and less energy. In fact, if we don't learn pretty quickly how to enjoy a different way of living, the requirement to shrink our appetites is likely to be forced on us by the depletion of natural resources. Indeed, at this time of economic uncertainty, the diminishing of personal finances in many western countries is already limiting the scope of many people to buy stuff. In the light of rapidly changing conditions it would help us enormously if we could develop some understanding of the psychological origins of the active preference that some individuals have for a life of material consumption that is more modest than the current norm. Such awareness, it might be hoped, would help us to find ways of cultivating both personal wellbeing and more sustainable life-styles.

The Way We're Born?

Some of the modest consumers sensed that their inclination towards material modesty was an aspect of their personality. One young woman wrote, for example, *I've always felt that way*, and another told me, "My younger sister wanted things around her all the time, but I was never interested in 'stuff'. It has to be partly because of my personality because my sister grew up in my house,

152

with the same parents and grandparents, so why else would we be different?"[iv]

When we talk about personality we mean a person's characteristic way of being; we describe people as laid back, bubbly, kind, dour, single-minded and so on, recognising in them lasting dispositions that shape the individuals they are and the way they respond to life. It is therefore a perfectly reasonable claim that a marked interest in possessions, or its lack, is a facet of personality. But this raises a question about how personality is constituted. Anthony was clear in his belief that his characteristic material modesty was somehow inborn, declaring, "I often feel it's almost in some genes within me, it kind of has that feel, because there are some people who in their youth are brought up in conditions of frugality and their great ambition is to get away from it, but I never wanted that, I'm just naturally frugal. I don't count it as a virtue." Far more of the modest consumers, however, attributed their modest lifestyles to the way they had been brought up. Either they felt that they had taken on their parents' values or that the thrifty practical ways of war-time or post-war living during their childhood had become ingrained habits. It is the old nature/nurture divide. The origins of personality, attitudes, values and behaviour are a huge field to penetrate but a brief foray into this highly complex subject can, nevertheless, be instructive, and in this chapter I will attempt to shed light on some of the factors which seem to motivate a positive preference for modest material consumption.

How powerful are genes?

We have just heard a reference to a sister with different likes, so what about the siblings of other modest consumers? Most of the thirty-seven who told me their stories, described a mixture of lifestyles and outlooks amongst their adult brothers and sisters. Only four out of thirty-six (one was an only child) felt that their siblings all shared their values, and five of those who had just one brother or sister said their sibling's values were very different from their own. The perception of the modest consumers of some of their siblings' divergence from themselves in orientation towards material things could be striking:

> "She's quite arty but wouldn't pursue something at length. I think she'd rather have more money. If I told you that she was made bankrupt a few years ago because she overspent on her credit card up to £40,000, 50,000, that's the difference.

---

iv I won't say which cohort member said what, so as to conceal the identity of siblings who were not asked for consent to inclusion in this research.

"She and her husband drive a large, brand new four-wheel drive Landrover, they've got a huge mortgage, spend a lot of money on clothes, spend a lot of money on stuff."

One study member said he had a good understanding with his brother who was an artist and whose life was financially insecure, but described his other two, well paid, brothers as, "almost polar opposites in some ways"; one of these, a legal consultant, felt he could not afford to retire. Another man said, "My sister and I have completely different lifestyles; what I see is quite a materialistic lifestyle compared with mine. The next brother down went to the States in the '80s to make a fortune. Then my younger brother, who's eight years younger than me, is closer to me in values. But I think they secretly all think I'm a bit odd, really. I've ceased trying to explain some of the things I do." A woman, whose siblings varied in their values, had a brother who was a "big saver" who didn't own a house or drive a car or have any aspirations to do so, and two sisters who were more materialistically-minded: one of them, with her husband, always had a new car, and the other who scraped by on benefits with her children and partner and who, on getting £1,000 in a back payment of benefits, had immediately bought a wide-screen television and a video games console.

One woman described a half-sister to whom she had been very close as a child, saying:

"She has many times our income and she regards us as the poor relations because we buy in charity shops and holiday in this country and that sort of thing. We regard her as the poor relation as we have enough and we can't imagine her ever having enough! My partner said, 'Come on, you're being a bit hard on her, check it out', so I asked her how much she would need to earn to feel that she had enough, and she thought about it for a few minutes and came back to me and said, 'I don't think I'd ever have enough cos however much you've got you could always do with a bit more!' I suppose she would say that she works extremely hard for every penny she gets and she's entitled to do what she wants with it – and she *is* quite generous."

Similarities and differences

Such differences within families are not at all uncommon and these huge discrepancies beg for an explanation. That siblings have approximately half their genes in common might suggest a degree of similarity between brothers and sisters greater than that between strangers. Indeed, psychological research on the origins of personality has repeatedly found significant *similarities* in personality traits between blood brothers and sisters – even if they are brought up in different families. From a large number of studies of many identical (monozygotic) twins, some reared together and some apart, fraternal (dizygotic) twins, and biological and adoptive siblings, psychologists have attempted to deduce the distinction between the influence of genetic inheritance and that of the environment. These studies are mostly based on questionnaires in which parents and adult twins and other subjects are asked to rate their child or themselves with regard to particular character traits.[282] Correlations between identical twins, who share all their genes, are always significantly higher than those between fraternal twins who, on average, share half their genes;[283] indeed, identical twins have on occasion been found to be staggeringly similar in their adult tastes and habits even if separated at birth and brought up in very different homes.[284] This points to a clear genetic influence on personality. The results of many such familial studies have suggested that personality traits – or at least the potential for particular traits to develop in certain environments – are inborn to a significant extent. To put a figure on it, it is believed that genes account for 40-50 per cent of personality[285] (though the degree of genetic input seems not to be the same for every trait;[286] genes apparently have a greater bearing, for example, on Extroversion than on Neuroticism.[287]

Although siblings share roughly half their genes, sexual reproduction does, in fact, produce diversity: when the father's and the mother's genes mix, the normal number of twenty-three pairs of chromosomes from each parent means that a total of over eight million different combinations of genes is possible. Not only that, but when pairs of chromosomes come together during the process of 'meiosis' or cell division, they exchange segments in a recombining of genes which generates an almost unlimited amount of variation in the sperm and the egg.[288] The complexity doesn't end there either, for genes are not always expressed; one gene can have different effects; a single trait can be influenced by many genes; and genes can mutate.[289] When the naked biological make-up of each individual is spelled out in this way it is easy to appreciate the immensity of the scope for differences to arise between siblings' personalities on the basis of genes alone. In the view of neuroscientist Susan Greenfield, genes are necessary but not sufficient for the development of personality traits.[290] However, some geneticists are cautious about attributing personality traits directly to genes at all. Eva Jablonka and Marion Lamb, for instance, whose particular interest is in evolutionary genetics, warn that, "Usually it is not at all clear that the DNA sequence is *causally* related to the character, and it is almost always very clear that 'the gene' is neither a sufficient nor a necessary condition for the character's development".[291] They declare that the popular belief, fuelled by the press, that there is a straightforward causal relationship between genes and traits is simplistic and very mistaken:

> Not long ago, an amazed public was informed by the media that the gene for 'adventurousness' or, as the scientists preferred to call it, 'novelty-seeking', had been isolated. A person's decision to do something exciting like becoming a fighter pilot or a revolutionary, or alternatively to be an orderly and conscientious librarian or accountant, is, the journalists told us, determined to a large extent by which alleles,[v] [292] one particular gene they have. However, if we turn to the original scientific papers... [W]e discover that some people who have the allele that is correlated with adventurousness are in fact very cautious and conventional, whereas some of those who lack it are nevertheless impulsive, thrill-seeking risk-takers... In fact, only four per cent of the difference among people with respect to their adventurous behaviour can be attributed to the particular gene that was investigated... Even the four per cent that got so much media attention is somewhat problematical, because it is not always easy to classify a person as adventurous or not adventurous. People can be adventurous in some aspects of life, but very conventional in others... Even when a study shows that there is a correlation between the presence of a particular allele and some aspect of human behaviour, we have to be very cautious about accepting that the relationship is causal.[293]

It is known that there are specific genes, such as those associated with Huntingdon's Disease, that definitely do determine particular characteristics. On the whole, however, the role of genes is to contribute to certain predispositions which interact with the environment, developing different effects. The Human Genome Project made this clearer than it had been before. By the time of its conclusion in 2003, the project, which had been set up to identify all the genes in human DNA and determine the sequences of the chemical base pairs that make up human DNA, had

---

v An allele is one member of a pair of genes that is located at a specific position on a specific chromosome.

discovered that the relationship between genes and experience is more dynamic than was previously realised: that not only can genes influence experience but that experience can alter the expression of genes. Science writer Matt Ridley concluded at the time that, though deeply entrenched, the apparent dichotomy between nature and nurture is a false one. He summed up the outcome of the Human Genome Project thus:

> The more we lift the lid on the genome, the more vulnerable to experience genes appear to be...In this new view, genes allow the human mind to learn, remember, imitate, imprint language, absorb culture and express instincts. Genes are not puppet masters or blueprints, nor are they just the carriers of heredity. They are active during life; they switch one another on and off; they respond to the environment... They are both cause and consequence of our actions."[294] The implication of this discovery, concluded Ridley, is that genes do not determine behaviour and that environmental influences are often less reversible than genetic ones. In the words of Susan Greenfield, "[G]enes themselves do *not* set an autocratic agenda but rather are key players in a complex interaction... [i]t's surprising how even traits that one might assume were impervious to interference from the environment are none the less influenced by it.[295]

One particular example to emerge from studies comparing identical and fraternal twins, raised together and apart, tellingly illustrates how genes normally need particular conditions in order to be activated. It is this: it has been found that abused boys who happen to have genes which code for low levels of the enzyme MAO-A have a higher tendency to become violent or criminal than abused boys who do not have these genes, but that when boys with the same genes are brought up in normal, non-abusing homes the gene does not appear to affect their behaviour.[296] Here we see how the genetic predisposition towards anti-social behaviour has to encounter a particular environmental influence in order to become expressed. For an effect to be felt, neither a gene alone nor experience on its own is usually enough. As a general point, then, in the course of development, "individuals with the same genotype may respond to their environments in innumerable and sometimes qualitatively distinct ways",[297] and the process of learning, by which an individual acquires their characteristics, and which is usually considered as belonging to early life, in fact continues in some way throughout life.[298]

What about Experience? The Many Facets of Environment

The conclusion of twin and familial studies that genes account for up to 50 per cent of personality implies, in turn, that experience – referred to as environment – accounts for half of the development of an individual's personality, or more. We cannot know, nor have a say in, the genetic inheritance of an individual which might be likely to favour an inclination towards material modesty; nor would it be desirable to embark on genetic interventions of such a nature. However, there *is* much scope for us to develop our understanding of the kinds of experience that could encourage its development, and to act accordingly. In order better to understand the role of environment in the development of material modesty and other associated characteristics, we need to explore the general area of the impact of experience. So let us now consider the main kinds of environment that a developing human being experiences, for any of them may contain clues as to potential influences on the development of leanings towards or away from material things, or indeed other aspects of happy, materially modest ways of living.

Childhood home

The first environment a child will experience is the physical and emotional environment of his or her family home (or that provided by another primary carer-giver). There is a substantial body of well-established knowledge about the major effects of secure or insecure attachment to the main care-giver in the early years of life,[299] a subject to which I shall return in greater depth in the last chapter. In addition, more narrowly focused studies have shown the effects of other specific aspects of carer-child interaction. One example is that children with over-controlling mothers who assert a high level of power over them are very likely to display chronically high levels of physical aggression from kindergarten onwards;[300] another is that emotionally supportive, warm, responsive parents tend to produce empathically responsive children.[301]

A different aspect is apparent in the life's work of American psychologist Jerome Kagan who has studied children at intervals from the age of four months to eleven years. He accumulated robust evidence which indicates that the tenor of parental handling is crucial in deciding how inborn biological temperaments (revealed in physiological measures such as heart rate, muscle tone and brain activity, as well as in emotional responses) play out in the development of a child's personality. To illustrate this, one of his findings was that very protective parenting of a child with a temperamental bias towards anxiety will result in the development of a different personality from parenting which actively helps a child with a similar inborn temperament to handle his or her natural fretfulness. While inborn temperament remained constant, as evidenced by physiological measures, the children whose parents had gradually and supportively exposed them to new situations found ways to overcome their fear, while those with over-solicitous parents continued to feel and express anxiety in the face of the unfamiliar.[302] While the main point of describing this research is to show some of the evidence that different experiences of parental handling produce significantly different effects on children's developing personalities, this illustration is also particularly relevant to our present context because materialistic values have been shown repeatedly to be positively associated with anxiety.[303] So this seems to be one direct, if hidden, way in which there can be an association between upbringing and personal consumption.

A somewhat different perspective on the relative importance of infancy for shaping later behaviour is offered by others studying child development, such as Ann Clarke and Alan Clarke who advance the view that early experience represents no more than a first (and important) step on a long and complex path through life. Such experience does not *by itself* set for the child a predetermined future, they say. Indeed, *by itself* its long-term influence may be negligible. When reinforced, however, its effects may be strengthened.[304] This view is based on findings of longitudinal studies dating as far back as the 1930s that children removed from homes where they suffered cruelty or neglect recovered from its effects when placed in homes with normal conditions. Clarke and Clarke point out that the effects of early experience, important as they are at the time, will be perpetuated only if they are reinforced by further similar experiences, and that this is what generally happens – children usually receive continuity of care, be it good, bad or indifferent. Their assertion has gained support from the findings of a large, more recent study of children in care[305] which has found that even late entry into care in adolescence after experience of abuse or neglect at home, can reduce the risk of offending if it provides support which capitalises on the protective potential of relationships and involvement in constructive activities.

Whatever the significance of the home environment for development at different stages of childhood, it is generally assumed that the home will exert a powerful influence over the way a child develops, as expressed in his or her behaviour. The way parents interact with their children and the example they set them is an issue for many parents, as it is for society as a whole: if we come across brattishness in a child or thoughtless or unruly behaviour in a teenager we are often quick to criticise the parents, perhaps even if the child in question is our own. If our child behaves in what appears to be an undesirable way we may blame ourselves, or at least question our approach to our parental role. Parents who do not respond in this way to their children's anti-social behaviour are usually viewed by society as neglectful or irresponsible. Such responses assume that parents influence their children's behaviour, as illustrated by the attempt by Wandsworth council in London to evict a tenant whose son appeared in court, charged in connection with rioting and looting at Clapham Junction during the disturbances in August 2011.[306]

On the other side of the coin, one often comes across instances of people attributing particular characteristics of their own to their early experience or the tenor of their upbringing. Take renowned clinical psychologist Oliver James, who has ascribed to his own infant circumstances an important aspect of the adult he became: in the context of the writing of his book on parenting, How Not to F*** Them Up,[307] he explained, "Basically I was fucked up by my mother. She had four children under the age of five and found it difficult to cope. Often I was left crying in my pram at the bottom of the garden… If I have achieved anything much in my professional life, at root it has been powered by a nuclear rage, that of the three-month-old screaming in his pram."[308] Another, different kind of example is that of award-winning actress Naomie Harris. She has said that her mother, who gave birth to her at the age of 18, worked in the Post Office, then went to university while bringing her up and became a successful writer, was her inspiration. Her mother's telling her that you can achieve absolutely anything, and that obstacles are to be seen as challenges which can be overcome with hard work, says Harris, "is an amazing, empowering belief to instil in your child."[309]

Whichever way one looks at it, there is plenty of evidence that parents influence their children's attitudes and behaviours. So what about those related to material consumption in particular? The previous chapter has already touched on the question of the influence of parents on the development of materialism in children, but what did the modest consumers feel about the influence, in the widest sense, of their own childhood homes with regard to the way they lived now? In fact they were inclined to believe that the environment provided by their parents, and sometimes other close relatives, as well as external circumstances, had had a bearing of some kind on their current lifestyle. It is, perhaps, a moot point whether or not these types of experience can be considered as having influenced their personalities per se. But if personality is to be defined as broadly as, "enduring dispositions that cause characteristic patterns of interaction with one's environment",[310] as it is in psychological literature, then the experiences regarded by some of them as influences on their current lifestyles did influence the development of their personalities in some sense. Those they specified fell into three broad categories. One was to do with the emotional climate of the family home, such as *A fairly rigid but stable family with undemonstrative love* and *Secure, contented, loving, interesting childhood*. A second revolved around material conditions, like *Wartime rationing and working class background; Seeing Grandmother and Grandfather growing fruit and veg and keeping livestock, also Aunt lived with us - talented dressmaker - once saw her making a wedding dress from a parachute (silk of course), everyone sewed and knitted - I was often called upon to darn socks, replace buttons from the age of 7 onwards; My family always lived frugally, so that's how I grew up, although their reasons for doing it were different from mine;* and *I grew up in a household of books*. The third was to do with social attitudes and values, such as, *Very liberal parents who encouraged debate and discussion of 'issues';* and *My growing up in WW2 in the port of Grimsby, ALL nationalities came here, and Mam and Dad helped, and we made them welcome*.

Nature or nurture?
While nobody can ever actually know if or how they or someone else would have developed differently in a different family or under other circumstances, a great deal of research bears out the significance of experience within the home for the way a child develops. It has, however, been suggested, not altogether unreasonably, by Judith Rich Harris in her iconoclastic book *The Nurture Assumption*,[311] that the distinction between nature and nurture is an illusion. As she sees it, any parent's style of parenting is shaped by their own genes. But her assertion that, "It's not that good parenting produces good children, it's that good children produce good parenting... It's not that good *parenting* produces good children, it's that good *parents* produce good children",[312] assumes an unwarranted degree of similarity between any parental couple. After all, in terms of personality, opposites often attract couples to each other, and in any case some mothers and fathers disagree about how their children

should be brought up. Her argument implies, too, the existence of an unrealistic degree of similarity between parents and their children down the generations, and of unalloyed 'goodness' or its lack in any individual. Rich Harris also neglects the possibility that people can and often do learn to do things differently and better. In fact, many people have made a conscious decision to raise their own children very differently from the way in which they were themselves brought up, and programmes of support and guidance for parents have been shown to improve the quality of parenting.[313] Both these factors indicate that style of parenting is not simply an outcome of parents' biological inheritance.

The 'non-shared environment'

Now for a conundrum. In the light of the popular belief and the wealth of evidence that the home environment plays a significant role in a child's development, the second apparent finding of the battery of sibling studies comes as a big surprise for, in addition to indicating that genes contribute roughly half the stuff of personality, these studies have repeatedly concluded that the family environment plays little or no part in the formation of personality or social attitudes.[314] Rather, it has been concluded, the experience which interacts with an individual's genetic make-up in the development of personality arises out of the 'non-shared environment' encountered beyond the home. This might be at school, say, or particular to one sibling within the family[315] (such as being treated as the favourite or as unwanted). Evidence that a non-familial environmental influence can overpower genetic predisposition comes from cases such as that of the well-known hair stylist Vidal Sassoon who told a newspaper, "My mother left me for seven years in an orphanage. I cowered at everything, then fortuitously my nature adapted. I fought through it. I became a fighter."[316]

However, while family study after family study has apparently revealed a lack of influence exerted by the parental home, it seems hard to believe that any child would grow up with exactly the same personality and response to life regardless of whether their parents constantly criticised and ridiculed them or encouraged and affirmed them. It seems to stand to reason that different styles of interaction draw out and strengthen different inborn potentials – or indeed leave them undeveloped. The conflicting conclusions regarding the impact of upbringing, based on very different research methodologies, are hard to reconcile. Perhaps the contradictory evidence base, which makes it extremely difficult to identify causality, just goes to show how very complex and subtle is the development of each human being, how difficult to pin down influences on that process, and how tricky to come up with a wholly satisfactory definition of personality.

The world beyond the home

Whatever the nature of the influence of the home, the wider environment does also play a role, and the testimony of the modest consumers included many references to influences they perceived from the 'non-shared environment'. Again, to what extent these can be considered to have had an impact on their actual personality is open to question, but they certainly coloured the way these individuals now responded to life. Here are some experiences they cited in answer to the questions about what experiences had led to what they enjoyed and valued and what influences had helped to shape the way they now lived. These reflected experiences at school, as well as substitutes for the family home.

Firstly, there was the learning of creative subjects: *Teachers at school instilling a love of language, literature and music; Shown by nuns at convent school to do embroidery and fine sewing; Music at (convent) school probably gave me a love of it;* and *The school I attended focused on arts and creativity*. Then there was learning about the environment: *A brilliant primary school teacher at the age of about 10 or 11 who got her classes doing recycling projects and 'save the world' campaigns;* and *Getting interested in environmental issues in Geography at school*. And thirdly, being valued oneself and taught to value others: *Going to a comprehensive school where I felt that I was valued as an individual; My high school education was big on being kind to other people, social responsibility and living ethically; Kindness shown to me when young and evacuated from London during WW2;* and *Spent some time in a children's home and was taught with care the right way to live*.

The role of the peer group

While promulgating the view that parents' 'nurture' is no more than an expression of their own 'nature', and that environmental influences therefore all emanate from outside the home, Judith Rich Harris has advanced a particular case for the power of a child or young person's peer group to influence the development of his or her personality.[317] But friends, classmates and other young associates from childhood and youth were notably absent from the modest consumers' accounts of what had influenced them; indeed, several gave glimpses of how they had swum against the tide when young. Rachel, for instance, said she had had a reputation at school and university, "of being somebody who did have quite strong views about political things" such as ethical trade and human rights, and Chris described how, "When I went to university I was quite rebellious in a way, in that I wasn't interested in what, apparently, a lot of my peers were interested in, which was a lot of material stuff, a career and all the rest, I didn't really feel sort of drawn to that."

§

LAUREN

Lauren's expulsion from school for refusing to accept rules that her contemporaries went along with suggested an early character trait that had come to express itself in her chosen way of living. Now 31, she explained why she had decided to live modestly, writing:

> As I have grown older I have become steadily more aware of the fact that most of the energy and resources that our society is built on are finite (coal, oil, gas) - and they are being wasted and used for unfair short-term selfish monetary gain for a select few. I have also witnessed first-hand the destruction and pollution caused by industry such as intensive farming (in India and Costa Rica) and believe strongly that humans must learn to demonstrate better respect for what nature offers us and operate more sustainable practices before we drain our precious resources dry.
>
> I have always been prepared to stand up for the values I believe in and in this issue I am unquestionably correct so I am prepared to make sacrifices and fight for what I know to be true. I find it hard to fathom why others don't care enough to act when faced with these facts. I also care a lot about the lives of people, animals and plants in natural habitats in this world, all of whom are indirectly adversely affected by my western consumption and waste, (and that of the businesses providing my lifestyle), and I care about those coming after me on this planet, whoever they are.

Lauren's lively and thoughtful approach to living was evident throughout our long conversation in a room over a busy pub in central London. Her spare time was filled with activity in keeping with her priorities. She belonged to her local Transition Town group, went to environmental workshops and seminars, to London 'green drinks' to network with likeminded people, and was planning to start a green street group to share her newfound knowledge and experience. She rated her satisfaction with her life at 9 out of 10, and felt that she couldn't have a better life. Never a great consumer, she told me, her lifestyle had become more modest in recent years, as a result of a combination of factors:

I happened to volunteer to work with young people for a charity 'Raleigh International' a few years ago, and spent 3 months living a very basic life and working with the locals in Costa Rica. Since then I have also travelled to India, Nepal and Peru where I witnessed first-hand lots of poverty and economic and environmental corruption. This clearly showed me a) the adverse effects of large-scale industrialisation - especially in parts of the world less regulated than the West, and b) that I am personally (and it is generally possible to be) very happy with very little possessions and simple food. Since then I have made a conscious effort to cut out 'stuff' from my life and live in an environmentally and socially aware way, while also setting an example and influencing others to make similar changes as much as I can.

During our conversation Lauren talked about family influences:

"My grandparents were a part of the Second World War and everything associated with living at that time, like rationing, and they know the value of things around them from that experience so they just quite simply don't waste things. They use up every last scrap of everything around them: food, plastic bags; whatever comes through the door gets used properly; they just don't throw it away before it's finished its useful life. So my parents did the same because they're the children of that generation (and because until the late 70's there wasn't much 'stuff' available anyway), and it must have passed on to me this way. Not being wasteful and respecting things around us was just a natural part of what my family did while I was growing up, but I heard about and began to understand environmentalism in the context of sustainability of resources, and the concepts interested me. So I started to be more aware of the choices I was making. I was being drawn into consumerism as I was living and working in a city environment full of shops and people who appeared to have lots of money – and I decided to make a conscious effort to stop myself from being drawn into that just because it was there."

Lauren went on, however, "I've made my own decisions to really try and be green. That has to be a personal thing, because nobody's influenced me to do that. I don't have any friends that are doing it, it's just me, I'm totally out on a limb." Her boyfriend, with whom she lived, sympathised with her views but did not share her passion for living in an environmentally-friendly way. Wasn't it difficult to be out of step with those around her? "Yes, it is, but it's the same with lots of things. I've always been a bit of a crusader, I tend to find an issue and fight for it, whatever it is, and so I think this is just my crusading issue. I'm often very surprised that I am in the minority on things that appear to be such common sense to me, but that's even more reason for me to explain to everyone why it's so important."

§

JAN

One more modest consumer who indicated an earlier, youthful resistance to the norm of his peer group was Jan. He was a scientist in his early 40's from Germany. The emphasis in his thinking was firmly on peace: "I try to choose my values and to shape the way I live based on my understanding of the world I'm part of, and not to be influenced by anything else. The principle of potential sustainable equality is an important basis for my choices and decisions. I derive this from pacifist principles, which I consider fundamental." Understanding and promoting peace was one of the most important things in life for him. Jan clearly took an intellectual approach to the question of how he lived, and an ethical stance that originated in his teenage years. He had joined a youth group which happened to be Christian, so had this informed his view? His emphasis on peace, it turned out, was actually very much tied up with the time and place of his growing up:

"My awareness of the natural environment is probably based on my interest in the biosciences more than on a religious basis. The conversations and thoughts shared in the youth group certainly have contributed to the development of my pacifist position. Parts of the group frequently engaged in long discussions of theological or spiritual topics, including implications of these for choices that one had to make. The issue of being conscripted into the German (at that time West German) army, or conscientiously objecting to that, regularly featured in such discussions. Pacifism and conscientious objection were not a majority position in the group, and I would say that I have developed my position relatively autonomously."

§

In contrast to these accounts of independence of one's peer group, one particular anecdote, however, supports the notion that the peer group might play an important role in the development of the individual. Caroline now had a large number of friends and, because, as we have seen, friends are important for wellbeing, it felt important to me to ask her why she thought she had come to have friend-making skills. Her explanation:

"I can put my finger on that. When I first went to boarding school when I was 9, I was profoundly unhappy, and didn't have friends for a long time, really struggled to make friends and to keep friends, and got bullied and was bottom of the pecking order. It absolutely shook me. When I was about 13½ I realised that if I was going to make anything of all of this I had to slightly change my tune and it was no good being limp and pathetic; I realised that I could be quite comic, people could find me quite engaging if I was a bit more kind of oomphy. And I remember where it happened, it was one of these weird moments, I was in a classroom called Willow and I got called Village Idiot, and I realised instead of kind of wincing, if I laughed and kind of played up to it in some way it shifted the dynamic. And from then on I felt more confident and that I could actually make people like me somehow. I did learn something, it was a real revelation."

The modest consumers' accounts show clearly how all forms of experience, whether inside or outside the family environment, and not only in the early years, can have an impact on an individual's developing responses to life. Incidental learning, conveyed by several of them in such comments as, *just looking around me and seeing that people with more stuff are not necessarily happier; being a teenage mum, single parent, living on benefits;* and *in my 20s walking taught me to observe nature, to take time to get to places and to enjoy the journey*, and the reading of certain books and writers,[318] seemed to be more important than formal education in contributing to the current lifestyles of most of them. Ed's pivotal experience of a chance undergraduate module on energy supply, which we learnt about in Chapter 3, was a striking example of how academic learning can have a real impact in changing an individual's perspective, but it was exceptional amongst the experiences related in the study.

Later experience

The transformative experience described by Ed belonged to adulthood rather than childhood, and he was not the only modest consumer to have adopted his low-consumption lifestyle as a result of adult experience. What seemed to set him apart, however, was the apparent lack of earlier experience which might have predisposed him to respond to his later academic learning in this way. Three people who had had some formative experience which might have primed them to respond to later occurrences by taking steps to reduce their environmental impact were Michael, Martin and Gillian.

MICHAEL

Michael's awareness of the coming environmental crisis was initially ignited by a seminal film, *The End of Suburbia*; and his first glimpse of a solution came from a talk by an author, Helena Norberg-Hodge. As a result he made deliberate efforts to simplify his life. His experience of this change was so positive that it provided him with a further incentive to pursue sustainable living. Now in his late thirties, Michael dated the beginning of his lifestyle back four years. Before this, when he was working in central London, he would go out most nights and spend a lot of money in bars and restaurants, would often go to football matches, and would travel quite a bit. It was towards the end of a four-year period of travelling the world that his gradually developing recognition of the environmental emergency began to have an impact on his behaviour. He explained, amongst the roar of double-decker buses as we sat at a pavement café in central London:

> "I kind of always knew about climate change and knew that I should be
> doing something about it but never really thought about it too much, and
> then I saw the film *The End of Suburbia*; Peak Oil was different altogether,
> I went into what somebody describes as 'Peak Oil Shock'. You look
> around yourself at everything and think well that's not going to be here,
> and we're not going to be able to do that, that kind of thing, and it was

168

so different to climate change, and I think it brought home to me more starkly the challenges that lay ahead, and from that I've obviously learnt a lot more about climate change as well. I've always recycled, but before that I was kind of talking the talk and not walking the walk".

So, towards the end of his travels, Michael began to add up his airmiles and see how he could get around without flying; he therefore hitch-hiked half-way up Argentina in order to avoid a flight. When he got back to England he looked for a job involved with the environment, and was now running a reminiscence project for an environmental charity. At home he started cutting back and had continued to "chip away at my lifestyle, doing less and less." This involved reducing his expenditure which he now felt had been somewhat uncontrolled, perhaps as a reaction against his parents' watching of the pennies when he was young.

The moment of realisation of the environmental damage being done and how to prevent it came when Michael happened to be in Ladakh in India at the same time as Helena Norberg-Hodge, the author of *Ancient Futures: Learning from Ladakh*,[319] and heard her speak.

"The fascinating thing about Ladakh was the Indians really only took an interest in it in the '70s because of the Kashmiri problem. So all of a sudden these Indians moved in, and the sustainable lifestyle that the people of Ladakh had been living started to be eroded, and so you can see within living memory the changes that happened in our culture over hundreds of years. I saw her lecture, and that was the first time I saw somebody say there's all these problems and the answer to it is this, it's localisation. So that was a big catalyst, I think, to be able to think OK, well now I can go back home and apply those kind of theories to the way I live."

So how could localisation be applied to a person's life in England? This is how Michael explained the changes he had made in his own:

"Well I don't think it happened straight away but now I live a lot more locally because I only work four miles from home and can cycle there; I grow food locally, I get most of my own food from a box scheme which is relatively local. And really with things like Making Colliers Wood Happy [a community initiative inspired by the 2005 BBC Two television series *Making Slough Happy*] it's possible to get all your entertainment locally. I mean before, I used to work in town, I used to entertain myself in town, I only went back home to sleep, I wasn't involved in the community at all. Now it's different, I sing in the local choir, I get involved in local events and things like that, I think my life is more centred around where I live. This Making Colliers Wood Happy thing, the sense of belonging that people involved in it now have, mainly because of the formation of the choir, I walk to the Tube and I walk past people that I can say hello to that I could never do before, and so it has an immeasurable effect; just having the choir creates an amazing sense of community. When I moved into the flat I loved it because it was just next to this massive Sainsbury's but now I loath to go into Sainsbury's, it's a kind of almost 180 degree reversal."

The other change that happened in Michael's life on his return from his travels was that he met and married his wife. Now they had an eighteen-month old daughter. However, his family were also a cause of tension for him, for his wife, like her family and friends, did not share his environmental perspective; she took a rather longer-term view, saying that species come and go, but for Michael sustainability was:

"almost like a kind of a religion, a religious code to live by. I'm not religious, if anything I'm probably humanist. A friend once quoted Gandhi to me, he said this phrase to me: 'to know and not to do is not to know', and I really feel that once you're really aware of the real effects of things like climate change, to know that and not do anything about it, you have obviously misunderstood it. Anyone who isn't doing whatever they can about climate change hasn't really grasped the seriousness of the problem."

For the moment, Michael's life revolved largely around his small daughter, in whose company he delighted. He wanted to strive for a situation in which his life was much simpler, much slower, one in which he was satisfied with what he had. "I think that if you're satisfied with your lot then you're content, you're happy, but if you're always striving for things, that you never actually attain happiness because there's always a bigger car or a bigger TV or the latest this or that."

The stories of the older people he heard during his reminiscence work, as well as the particular modesty of the lives of some of his colleagues at the environmental charity, worked on Michael; his own childhood had left its mark too. His parents had been neither poor nor rich; the family had always had enough, but he remembered that he and his sister were given less expensive toys than other children. For holidays they camped in the UK, and when they did once go to France they could not afford to eat in restaurants. But this did not feel like serious deprivation and his memories were warm: he remembered playing in car-free streets, and "I kind of equate my school days more with the kind of traditional school days you see in the media; we used to play with conkers; my mum grew all her veg in the back garden and my aunts and uncles grew quite a lot of food and stuff like that, the neighbours had chickens. We grew up in a kind of make do and mend environment." The influence of this was still so ingrained in Michael that he felt he would compost food even if there wasn't an environmental need to do so.

Something hugely positive for Michael had been his discovery of his connection with nature. Previously, his appreciation of it was little more than an intellectual understanding that we must not destroy nature, "that thing over there". But now he had an immediate and personal sense of the interconnectedness of everything. What made the difference was his starting actively to interact with nature, having taken a bee-keeping course, and begun to make his own wine:

"I suddenly realised how many elder trees there are. I never noticed them before. I can see now that the elderberries are already ripening, the blackberries are already there, I recognise the hawthorn berries are out, the berries on the rowan trees and things like that. Before I might have said, 'look at the red berries on that tree' but I never knew what they were or why they were there, or certainly I wouldn't have known they were early this year or anything like that, and I think that just being able to look at things around me and know what they are and what they're doing is very satisfying. Certainly the idea of keeping bees, just making that connection with the natural world is more satisfying than I imagined it would be."

It also palpably enhanced Michael's sense of wellbeing, "simply because the bits of nature that surrounded me, I seemed to be in their club, do you know what I mean, they were now part of my life rather than just being scenery. It just occurred to me when I was cycling back from the apiary after one of the sessions, just feeling really, really good about it, almost taking me by surprise". His feeling for his relationship with the natural world and its sustainability was shifting from the intellectual to the emotional.

Another revelatory moment had arrived while reading Joanna Macy's *Coming Back to Life*.[320] As well as talking about the interconnectedness of things, and that, "You don't have to go out and convert everybody, and I think that just knowing that just living a sustainable life is almost as good as going out and trying to convince other people." He drew as well on the words of Bill Mollison, the inventor of the term Permaculture,[321] who, he thought, had suggested that the world would be changed by "what they call revolution over the garden fence", that the individual can influence others just by living a contented life and causing them to reflect on what creates this contentment. As a parent, Michael had an immediate task, he said, to bring up his daughter with material modesty yet a sense of abundance, of belonging to her local community, of having everything she needed.

§

GILLIAN

Gillian definitely saw it as her role to set an example. Aged 56, she ran a natural health and wellbeing centre, and lived over her business in a, light, airy modern two bedroom attic flat. Although she had lived here for several years, she still did not feel that she had put her stamp on her home. Why not? Waving across the open plan floor space, Gillian explained, "Well, making it my own feels like a total extravagance because when I moved in, this carpet was here and it's a really good carpet, but it's not my sort of colour and for me it's one of the first things that I would change, but at the moment I can't because I can't bear to get rid of something that is absolutely serviceable." This was typical of her attitude to living. She had given up her car and had decided four years earlier not to fly anymore; she didn't use household cleaning products if she could help it, preferring the use of such materials as microfibre cloths, vinegar, lemon juice, bicarbonate of soda, ecoballs and soap nuts; she collected the cold water run-off preceding the hot water and used it to flush the toilet and water the plants, and had replaced most daily showers with a stand up wash at the basin; she did most of her food shopping in the market, at small independent stores, and the Co-op; and such clothes as she bought were second-hand or good quality new garments made from natural fibres rather than oil-based synthetics. She agreed that she had a keen sense of personal responsibility and that she felt she could have an individual impact: "I feel that even though it's only me doing it I then talk to other people about it and it spreads. Someone's got to start somewhere". But she was human; as far as buying 'stuff' went, Gillian did have weak moments too: "I do try not to buy things, but occasionally I have a blip and then I think, 'why did I buy that?'"

Life had not always been like this. Twelve years earlier Gillian was living in a three-bedroom house and owned a yacht, ate out a lot, and had expensive clothes and generally expensive tastes. It was a fantastic time in her life, she said, that had given her a lot of fun. What changed it all was a breakdown, brought on by a combination of very stressful work as an educational psychologist, the increasing pressure of yacht racing, and the suicide of a close friend. Gillian gave up her job and realised that she was going to have to cut down expenditure. At first she was worried at the prospect of having to live on a quarter of her previous income, "But in fact it didn't have that much effect in terms of how I felt, I just found other things to do. I didn't sell the yacht because I didn't have enough money, I sold it because I'd moved out of that sphere. I didn't want to drink heavily any more, I didn't want to go out to balls and restaurants, I didn't feel I needed that anymore." Gillian felt that her changed lifestyle, which arose out her doing lots of personal development activities and, finding that she got pleasure out of simple things had contributed to her recovery. Had she known earlier about climate change, peak oil and other threats to the environment, she would have changed her lifestyle more quickly, she thought.

But in fact, looking back, Gillian felt that, although the self-development work she did was important in redirecting her attention and interests, "I think I sort of had it in me from the start, and although the extravagant period of my lifestyle was twenty years of my life it was a sort of blip really. I mean even when I took up sailing it was very much this is nature, it's wind, it's natural". But then the social side of belonging to the sailing fraternity and all the wining, dining and balls it entailed, meant her sailing activities reshaped her life to some extent. When crisis brought this period to an end, Gillian realised that most of her sailing friends, who were mainly men, were little more than acquaintances. Now she had closer friendships, and more female than male friends. These days she found that dancing, singing in a community choir, reading, swimming, environmental campaigning, camping and running her business created a satisfying life.

So what had preceded the sailing phase? Gillian came from a working class family. Her father had grown up in a one-room flat and his parents didn't have a bathroom until they retired to a caravan in the 1960s. Gillian remembered how her childhood home had lino and hardboard floors, and that the first carpet was bought with a prize of £20 won on the football pools one week when she had filled in the numbers. Both her parents worked, and her father came home in the evening and worked in his workshop making and mending things in metal. In fact he turned his hand to all sorts of things: "Our only heating was a two bar electric fire in the living room which we all huddled around and a paraffin heater in the hall. My dad later made an electric convector heater which my parents had in their bedroom or occasionally in ours if we were ill. Eventually he made electric blankets for us! They were made out of wires and canvas, which my grandfather probably stitched."

Gillian's current modest material lifestyle was not, then, such a far cry from her early life which also saw the beginnings of some of her interests. Her love of dancing had begun with lessons at the age of three, and she often danced with her parents at family parties, holiday camps and Freemasons' Ladies' nights. She said, "I've noticed over the years that in the periods when I'm not dancing I'm quite low, physically and emotionally, maybe a bit depressed. I've had moments of ecstasy in dancing, it's like meditation. My head can clear." When she had been in the sailing fleet she had made her own ball dresses. She had learnt to sew from her father and grandmother who used to make all her dance costumes and clothing; "It was very much what we did at home."

Her grandfather worked in a canvas factory; indeed, Gillian still used a tent he'd made, and camping was another early activity that was still of great importance to her. Having time to relax and enjoy nature was one of the things that was most important in life to her, and walking and sleeping on the ground gave her a very tangible, spiritual sense of connection with the Earth: "When I did a walk last year from Cornwall to Glastonbury, just being out, it was like a meditation. It didn't matter if it was raining or what was going on, I just felt so much part of nature. It really hit me the following day when I came home and was sitting here [looking up at the large skylights] and it was really windy and wet outside and I realised I was in a sort of bubble, and the previous two weeks I'd been part of it".

"It's interesting", she said, "I have a friend who's very rich and a few weeks ago he said to me something like, 'you're poor' and I said, 'but I have a very rich life, and I'm happy'. For me a rich life is something that's internal, it's very much the way I feel about life, and appreciating what I have and what there is around me."

§

MARTIN

Martin, who was 38 and from Germany, had lived modestly for three years. It dated from the time he had come to live in England to join his partner. Before this, as a single man, responsible only for himself, he described his lifestyle as 'ambiguous'. He had not put any savings away and spent what he earned, but at the same time did not feel comfortable spending money extravagantly, on expensive holidays and the like. He had worked as a social worker which he felt was a reasonably well paid job, though less well paid than in England. He had owned a car, but his most prized possession had been his motorbike. He also spent money on gym membership, going out with friends, and on DVDs, CDs and books that took his fancy.

> "My colleagues used to make jokes about me because I would spend all my money and nobody, including myself, knew what I was spending it on. I wouldn't plan my shopping for instance, I would go shopping after work in a gas station and would buy very expensive products rather than going to a supermarket and buying the same product for half the price, so I wasn't really bothered about money at that time."

Everything changed when Martin moved to England, quitting his job, giving away his personal possessions and paying off his debts, in order to be able to set up home with the woman who later became his wife. They now lived with their 8 month-old baby in a former council house in an area of north-east England with a rough reputation, unable to afford a house in a more salubrious area. Martin's wife had given up work to look after their son and Martin had got a job as a Structured Day Care Worker. They lived without a car, organised their shopping to avoid unnecessary expenditure, for example by using discount stores such as ALDI and Netto, used community facilities and resources such as the library and church groups, and often visited or invited friends round rather than going out. Martin rated his satisfaction with his current life at 8 or 9 out of 10, writing,

I feel that I am very happy with my life, I appreciate what I have got and I do not wish for anything different. My decision to leave my home country behind, as well as all my material belongings, in order to commit to my partner, made me realise that I do not need such things to lead a fulfilling life. Riding my motorbike was a very pleasurable experience and it was hard to imagine living without it, but

leaving it and everything else behind, made me realise that
true happiness comes from leading a spiritually rich life,
with healthy and meaningful relationships.

Although Martin's previous lifestyle had been financially unconstrained and happy-go-lucky, he found the change in his life created a sense of freedom:

> "It was a really liberating experience to give everything away and I literally started a new chapter in my life, only having two bags of clothes and really very personal belongings with me, and some other stuff I stored at my father's place. We had a very small apartment at that time, we only had basic furniture, most of which belonged to the apartment, but I felt really free, and experienced that I wasn't missing my car or my motorbike or the gym and I was actually enjoying this simple life... For instance one of the first things that I bought over here was a book at a car boot sale, and it was only 50p. I really enjoyed that book and that I didn't need much to have a good experience, small things like if it's a good meal or time that I spend with my family or friends."

The 'ambiguity' of which Martin was aware, was the mismatch between his carefree attitude to money and certain other values he held. These other values seemed to arise from two sources. One was his upbringing. His family was upper middle class but, while his father, a consultant surgeon, was quite affluent, their lifestyle was relatively modest as a result of the earlier influence of wartime poverty and his parents' consequent emotional need for financial security. The other aspect was his religious background. He had spent much of his childhood with his Roman Catholic grandparents and every Sunday his parents would take the children to church. This, Martin felt, had formed his moral values, highlighting the conditions in which other people live and the need to care for one's neighbours. He had lost his faith during his teens, but had still felt the need for an explanation of how the world functions, the meaning, sense and purpose behind it all, so looked at other religions, including Buddhism. This added a further dimension to his perspective on life:

> "What I have realised for myself through getting acquainted with Buddhism is that happiness lies within; what Buddhism teaches is that as soon as somebody gets attached to something, material or a person

or whatever, it's always related to suffering because there is this form of dependence, attachment or whatever, and what I have learnt is that I can be happy even if sometimes circumstances are not as easy or ideal as I would like them to be but if I see things more or less from an optimistic way, so not putting how I would like them to be but adapting and realising how my perception, my interpretation of the situation, affects whether I am happy or not.

I think that I've always appreciated what I had got, it's just part of my personality and childhood or teenager years that I really was aware that I actually had very fortunate life conditions and that I've always felt gratitude for that. From my personality and being the oldest and always having to be the most responsible one I think it has always been more important for me to be more modest; things like going on holidays and stuff, or cars, have never been as important for me as I think for my younger brother, for instance, the second oldest."

It was Martin's wife who brought about the reassertion of Martin's core values. She was Portuguese and also came from a Roman Catholic background but had, in contrast, grown up with significant financial limitations: "She actually taught me to save money, even before our son was born and we both had an income so we had lots of money to spend. And at that time I realised that I actually felt much happier and content with that lifestyle, appreciating the smaller things, such as my morning coffee or reading a good book. From my perspective now, I can understand that for instance a monk can be very happy and content living in very simple conditions if this is the life that makes him/her complete. But for myself it is definitely my relationship to my wife and my son that makes me complete."

§

And the Soul?

All the discussion of the relative roles of biology and environment in determining personality and behaviour can leave one feeling that each of us is no more than an effect of chance forces, rather than an active being. James Hillman, a psychologist and scholar who has continued to develop the theory of archetypal psychology originated by Carl Jung, rejects the notion that each human being can simply be reduced to the result of a "subtle buffeting between heredity and social forces".[322] He challenges the Western mode of thought that is characterised by an oppositional, either/or stance, and bases his 'acorn theory' on the idea that stretches back centuries and across cultures of the existence of an individualised 'soul image'. While he accepts that genes, parenting, social class, economics and so on, have an influence on the child, he points out that reading a life backwards enables one to see "how early obsessions are the sketchy preformation of behaviour now",[323] suggesting that it is mistaken to put too much emphasis on development.

Hillman believes that there is also something else at work, that each of us is born with what has been referred to as a calling, destiny or soul. This is guided by a constant companion, an entity the ancient Greeks called a 'daimon', which remembers what is in one's image and is therefore the carrier of one's destiny. The Greeks, he points out, believed that happiness, 'eudaimonia', resides in a well-pleased daimon. Hillman calls the image 'which asks to be lived' the 'acorn' as an acorn contains within it a potential oak tree. The acorn is often most evident in people of outstanding talent who are impelled to follow their talent regardless. An exemplar of this is Donovan, the 1960s folk icon, who has written:

> "My father wanted me to be a tradesman, but I knew I couldn't do anything but make music. I felt the call to adventure. When you hear the call, you can either heed it or not. I chose to heed it and that meant leaving society and all forms of conditioning behind me. It broke the family a little, but I had no choice. I had a spiritual calling for my tribe."[324]

While it is most obvious in individuals with exceptional talent, Hillman believes that the acorn does not tell us *what* to be but *how* to be. A calling, he suggests, "may be postponed, avoided, intermittently missed. It may also possess you completely."[325] It may guide you into dramatic, visible, even eccentric identity, or it may guide you into subtle, unobtrusive ways of being. While Hillman's concept sits outside the mainstream and may be difficult for many Westerners to accept, the single-mindedness of certain individuals amongst the study cohort in the way they chose to live can perhaps be understood in terms of 'calling'. But experience of some kind must have played a part, too, in giving form to their calling; and some of them identified in their conversation with me a moment that had led to their current way of living.

In short then, it is ultimately impossible to trace precisely all the factors and influences that interact dynamically in the creation of any individual personality. The effects of a particular set of genes depend critically on the environment in which they are expressed.[326] Ethologists Patrick Bateson and Paul Martin use the metaphor of cooking in a vivid image of the impossibility of untangling these constituents; "a baked cake," they point out, "cannot be disaggregated into its original raw ingredients and the various cooking processes, any more than a behaviour pattern or psychological characteristic can be disaggregated into its genetic and environmental influences and the developmental processes that gave rise to it".[327]

Personality Traits

Personality has been defined very generally by psychologists as the typical way in which an individual interacts with their environment. This, as we have seen, raises questions about the boundaries of what can be termed personality. A more specific framework for conceptualising personality emerged during the 1990's, however, when psychologists arrived at a consensus around a model which posits five overarching personality domains.[328] These have been dubbed Extroversion, Neuroticism, Agreeableness, Conscientiousness and Openness to Experience. Each of these umbrella terms describes a spectrum of *kinds* of trait (hence Extroversion also encompasses introversion, and so on). From all the different sources of influence the modest consumers enumerated, and the effects these had in moulding their lives, it is apparent that this collection of people were 'open to experience'. What might be regarded as the high end of this domain encompasses such traits as intellectual curiosity, aesthetic sensitivity, imaginativeness, a philosophical capacity, flexibility and unconventionality.[329] The traits of the other four domains can be found in the Endnotes and References.[330]

Personality traits clearly play important roles in the way people live and experience their lives, and it is pertinent for our present interests of personal wellbeing and environmental sustainability that people high in Agreeableness have been found to be less consumerist, and those high in both Agreeableness and Openness to Experience to exhibit pro-environmental motivation and concern at environmental degradation.[331] There are, though, conflicting findings: while there is consistent evidence that Extroversion predisposes people towards happiness,[332] and introverts have been found to be relatively immune to the lures of wealth and fame,[333] non-materialistic people clearly seem to experience higher levels of subjective wellbeing than their materialistic fellows.[334] Whatever the case may be, we may not be stuck forever in a groove of traits.

Changing traits

Personality traits have generally been considered by psychologists to remain remarkably stable throughout adulthood,[335] but there are indications that this may not necessarily be the case. A rare longitudinal study which has considered the question is the seventy-five year Grant Study,[336] which I have mentioned before, which revealed unequivocally "that adult development continues long after adolescence, that character is not set in plaster, and that people do change".[337] Its findings suggest that personal development is a life-long process. Increasing maturity over time was found to bring growth in the development of coping styles, a sense of responsibility for others, and wisdom, for example. Its reading of lives backwards from old age produced the opposite emphasis from Hillman's.

While the maturing process often just happens, change can also sometimes come about as a result of conscious effort. A figure for whom this was the case was Mahatma Gandhi, one of the world's greatest proponents and exemplars of non-violence, who deliberately had to transform what was for him a particularly salient trait, working hard to overcome his towering temper.[338] The actor, director and screenwriter Julian Fellowes is another who by strength of will changed an aspect of his personality: he has described how, having just left school and boarded a ship bound for Colombia, "I had climbed the gangplank as a shy and insecure bore, an awkward, spotty teenager, only to be danced with as the partner of last resort. But I resolved to walk down it an outgoing, gregarious, confident young man, up for anything, eager for adventure. And that is what I did."[339] Here, then, is evidence that it is possible to change one's characteristic responses if one has the desire and determination to do so. There is real reason to suppose that it is possible to reduce our susceptibility to consumption, to nurture a rejection of material things, and cultivate different responses at moments of potential acquisition, as did Lauren who had taught herself to say to herself, "Did you want it before you saw it? No. Don't have it then!" and embrace the non-material possibilities of life instead.

It is absolutely reasonable to believe that, as with other aspects of personality, there is an innate element to a personal inclination towards or away from material possessions. However, experience is required to activate genetic potential; and, by the same token, absence of particular experiences is likely to leave that potential undeveloped. There is a great deal of scope, therefore, through the types of experience we make possible for our children and ourselves, to encourage the development of a leaning towards the non-material and away from material consumption as the focus of living and the route to enjoyment of a rich and satisfying life. Very little research has been carried out to investigate whether the origins of a materialistic attitude are chiefly genetic or environmental,[340] but one study has set out to do this. It concluded that the valuing of acquisition as a sign of success and of possessions as bestowing a sense of self was entirely down to experience, and that genes played no part.[341]

But even if, as seems likely, genes are responsible for some degree of susceptibility to a fondness for unnecessary consumption, we cannot allow the future viability of the Earth as a habitat for humans and all other species, to be destroyed by that susceptibility. Genes, after all, provide only a *potential* motivator of a desire for stuff. It is now well understood that genes do not bring about effects in a vacuum but are activated by environmental factors. In order to protect the Earth's carrying capacity on which we and all species depend, we must make every effort to avoid triggering or succouring the common human weakness for things and dependence on large quantities of energy. Conversely, innate predispositions towards the non-material aspects of life deserve every encouragement. We therefore need to devise means, as individuals and as a society, of strengthening our desires for and our capacities to enjoy the multitude of life-enhancing experiences that human existence has to offer, and to help children to develop personalities and values accordingly. This may sound sinister, but the social engineering involved, if indeed it can be regarded as such, would be very much more benevolent than that of an education system designed primarily to turn out young people to fit and serve a profit-driven world.

Conclusion: The Power of Experience to Carry us Towards a Better Future

In the light of the current prospects for the future quality of human life we cannot justify *not* taking steps to facilitate the kind of character building which would benefit both the individual and the world as a whole. The route surely lies in paying close, deliberate, sensitive attention to the types of experience that people, particularly children, have available to them. Perhaps the importance of experience for personal development is a truism but this understanding needs to be fully acknowledged and acted upon in order to help us create a happier, more sustainable future. It is certainly true that much of our experience lies beyond our control, and that in any case the same experience will be perceived differently by each individual and by the same individual at different times, for anyone's response to any given situation is unpredictable. Nevertheless, the considerable proportion of *type* of experience which it is within our means to determine or shape for ourselves and others, individually and collectively, formally and informally, is the key to the realm we now need to enter. Only by having plenty of truly nourishing experiences can anyone become aware that such possibilities exist, and then be able to choose these in preference to superficial material enhancement.

7

The Vital Role of Values

What are Values?

Lauren taught herself to respond differently in shops. She was not the only modest consumer to have done so. Katarina recognised that, "it's part of human nature to want to buy things and I have that too, you know just in a supermarket you're trying to find something to buy". Her way of dealing with this was to think, 'will that be useful?' Or 'will it fill a niche?'... Often, if we're on holiday and we're popping into nice little shops because that's part of what you do on holiday, I can feel myself looking at everything and wanting to buy something, but I'm aware that that's not actually useful, we don't actually need that! And I have learnt from previous purchases that you just forget about them when you get home."

Do Lauren's and Katarina's responses in those shops actually demonstrate a change in personality? Neither woman had ever been actively interested in possessions. Like Lauren, Katarina felt that she was someone with a personality that 'doesn't really care about stuff'. Maybe their new efforts at self-restraint, in the face of the common human impulse to buy, were more a question of shifting values. Like personality traits, values have been classified, their domains identified as Achievement, Benevolence, Conformity, Hedonism, Power, Self-direction, Stimulation, Tradition and Universalism; and again, each domain encompasses an illuminating collection of associated values.[342] It is easy to see how particular personality traits are likely to be drawn to certain values. For instance, the considerate, nurturing, altruistic aspects of the personality domain of Agreeableness seem thoroughly in tune with value of Benevolence which has the wellbeing of others at its heart, while the narrow-minded, shallow end of Openness to Experience is likely to be drawn to the value of Conformity. Hedonism might be found as either type of value, depending on the type of sources in which pleasure and sensuous gratification are found: luxury hotels, catwalk clothes and extravagant meals in sophisticated restaurants, or nights under the stars, favourite old garments, and feasts of home-made food with friends round the kitchen table. Values are formed in response to social interaction, new information and introspection, and are more likely than personality to change during the course of adult life.[343]

Preferences as principles

In the most general terms, values refer to what is deemed to be valuable, or desirable. They can be divided into distinct types. One distinction is between values as preferences and values as principles.[344] Values as preferences are essentially positive likes, specific situations that an individual holds dear, such as being one's own boss, easy access to cultural activities, or living in the country. Values as principles, on the other hand, often termed personal values, transcend particular circumstances and guide the individual's ideas as to the right way to behave, such as commitment to honesty and integrity. Both types of value were to be found amongst the reasons given by the modest consumers for their lifestyles. Indeed the kind and strength of these people's convictions, combined with the sorts of activities and interests they enjoyed, was what they loosely had in common. But while both forms of value applied to some extent to most of them, some individuals gave more emphasis to their personal liking of a simple life and others were more overt in pursuing their chosen ways of living primarily because they felt it was the right thing to do.

So let's look at how some of the variations on the theme of values appeared in individual stories. Often, more than one value or type of value would be in play simultaneously.

Environmental Concern and Social Justice as Drivers

KATARINA

Katarina was one person who clearly fell equally into both value camps. She was a medical student aged 26 who lived in a rented house with her husband, Ed, whom we met in Chapter 3, and two others. She had chosen to live modestly to conserve resources for other people now, for other people in the future and for the rest of the ecosystem, to combat climate change and running out of resources like water, "Because it's just a waste!" Waste was a particular bugbear of many of the modest consumers.

Katarina's environmental concern was expressed in her daily life by, for instance, having taken up quilting to make use of damaged clothes that could not be given to charity shops, and finding gadgets that relied on renewable energy, such as a wind-up radio, water battery clock and solar phone-charger. For her wedding Katarina had asked for charity presents, had a caterer who sourced food locally, decorated the hall with her own scarves and the like, used a cycle rickshaw for transport, had a dress made from things she already owned, had no bridesmaids or groomsmen to get clothes for, used potted plants which she gave away afterwards instead of cut flowers, and carried an artificial bouquet which she later passed on to another bride.

Katarina could not pin-point exactly when environmentalism had become an important motivation for her; it had developed gradually, influenced from a number of quarters. She remembered beginning to live independently as an undergraduate, having "a gradual realisation that when you're buying everything and doing everything for yourself, that you're responsible for those decisions, and then slowly kind of investigating and reading books and things." It was at this time that she made the decision not to take any short-haul flights. Before that, during her last three years at school, Katarina had been a member of a Jewish youth group where she took part in a lot of very explicit discussions about values. She thought that these may have been part of the route to her starting to think actively about values, which later made it more logical to make certain lifestyle changes, due to the realisation that climate change would particularly affect poor people. But the process of working out the implications of it all happened later, at university.

After her first degree, Katarina had volunteered in Uganda, and this is where she met Ed. The experience of living in Uganda for six months, without running water or electricity, also left its mark, partly from the point of view of witnessing extreme poverty, but more because it showed that it was possible to live even without these basics: "So when I came back I would really feel horrible about having the tap running to wash my toothbrush because in Uganda you just had a little cupful. And then just to be able to leave the tap on seemed so wasteful; so in a way it was wasteful on its own but also in comparison to what other people have."

During her childhood Katarina had experienced a mixture of values. Her parents were divorced when she was six, after which she lived with her mother who did not have a lot of money. She did, though, go to a private school which was paid for by her father who was well-to-do, and she benefited from what he could provide materially when she visited him. Now, she felt, she had quite a different value set from her father. Her mother was not particularly anti-materialistic but did not have great financial means; she "believed in being nice to people" and Katarina felt she had adopted this aspect of her mother's values. This expressed itself in her opting for medicine and her involvement in a number of voluntary organisations and charities, including Amnesty, Actionaid, Practical Action and a local befriending network. Being compassionate, responsible and helping people was important to her and contributed to her happiness, she believed.

Other influences on her were encouragement of reading by her family. Reading had led her to the book *A Life Stripped Bare* by Leo Hickman, based on his columns for *The Guardian* newspaper, in which he set himself the challenge of reducing carbon in his lifestyle as much as possible, with lots of practical hints and discussion. Reading this book had proved quite a turning point for Katarina in realising the extent of how her lifestyle would be affected by attempts to reduce her carbon emissions. Most of Katarina's friends were "more normal, more average" consumers than she was, buying more clothes than she did and never thinking of giving up flying. But actively trying to persuade people to change their ways was not something that Katarina felt comfortable doing. When opportunities arose, though, she did slip things into the conversation, such as when discussing holiday plans: "I say, 'Of course we don't fly, we're going by train', so that people are exposed to the idea that other people have taken those decisions, because I think that that can be a little bit effective, just to know that other people can live life differently and it's not so hard or so crazy".

§

ANNE

Another woman who was driven by her need to live according to her environmental principles but who also found that this way of living suited her was Anne. Anne had originally led a fairly modest adult life because she believed it was wrong for people to have a big disparity of incomes. In recent years, however, she had reduced her consumption due to her growing awareness of the level of individual carbon emissions that is sustainable. She had been a member of Friends of the Earth since her twenties in the 1970s, but had more recently come to see how urgent the situation was and how serious the consequences would be if we don't get global warming under control. Her biggest decision was not to fly, and she also started to use the car less and tried to make the house more energy efficient. Her domestic arrangements were complemented by active involvement in the Campaign against Climate Change, Norwich Peace Council, Quakers, Transition Norwich and the Green Party.

Anne did not find her relatively low consumption lifestyle a hardship because she could still do all the things she had loved doing since childhood: tennis, swimming, walking, cycling and reading. She had grown up in a comfortable home, her father a GP. They lived in a village near the sea so the children had to make their own entertainment (for Anne this was mostly reading) and the family swam in the sea and went for walks. At school Anne developed a love of history, and remembered a formative sixth form history trip to York where her eyes were opened to the beauty of the medieval city which made her want to go and visit other places. She thought her history teacher had had much more influence on her in this respect than her parents. In London as a young adult, she had come to enjoy the art available in the many galleries, and since moving to Norfolk, had developed her historical interest on discovering its wealth of medieval churches.

Acknowledging that her life was not yet modest enough to reach her ideal of a one-tonne limit on carbon emissions and that to do so would involve hardship, Anne felt that her relatively modest life was rich and that she was not missing out, other than flying to see places she would love to visit or enjoying some sun in the winter. She said, "I've had to accept that there are some places I cannot travel to even though I would like to visit them. I have had to turn down invitations I would have liked to accept. It has caused some friction with some family and friends who feel that my lifestyle is a criticism of their less modest lifestyles."

Did she ever feel that she had to resist the temptation to buy things? "Occasionally with food, especially in winter, the thought of buying something which is more associated with summer, seems rather appealing, and occasionally I do give in. Interestingly my daughter bought some tomatoes yesterday [it was January when we spoke] and I was really excited about these tomatoes! But I do try and be very firm with myself about not giving in, it's a very minor hardship, and especially when I'm aware how very difficult life is for many people it's absolutely not an issue."

Anne felt "happiest and most sane when I'm surrounded by the beauty of nature; it gives me a sense of peace. The same thing can be achieved at a concert, a piece of music; it's this thing of being transcended, being taken out of yourself and your existing at a slightly different level of being". But her top priority for well-being was having good relationships, first of all with family, then with friends, and, "You don't need money to have good times with friends and family".

§

CLARISSA

Clarissa was another for whom the imperatives of environmental sustainability and social justice coincided with her own preferred way of living. A single woman of 69, Clarissa had lived in the same small Victorian terraced house since the early 1970's. Gesturing towards the curtains, carpet and wallpaper in the living room, she told me she had never changed them; they still looked quite unblemished. As a chartered physiotherapist in the NHS she had not earned a generous salary, but it had met all her needs: "because of my early training in thrift it's always been enough". Although she still owned a car for going on occasional sailing trips or into the country for walks, she preferred to bike short distances or use public transport for longer journeys. Her last holiday abroad had been four years before, travelling around north Germany on a month's railway ticket; now she and a friend were considering taking their bikes to Holland. Clarissa had no desire for luxury and wouldn't choose to go away with somebody who wanted to stay in a grand hotel; she had once gone on holiday with a friend in Sri Lanka but, "The hotel was on the beach and we'd obviously pushed the local fishermen aside and I didn't feel comfortable in that situation". Now, moreover, that she was aware of the contribution of flying to climate change, Clarissa would, on principle, no longer fly unless there was no other way.

Her knowledge of environmental issues came largely from the daily reports issued by Christian Ecology Link to which she belonged; she felt that these reinforced her life-long love of nature, and her awareness of the threats posed to it which began with hearing about Rachel Carson's book *Silent Spring*. Similarly, her experience in Uganda of working with VSO amongst the very poorest people who had absolutely nothing had powerfully reinforced her pre-existing values regarding money. But what had led to what she enjoyed and valued, she believed, predated this experience; it was a secure, contented, loving childhood:

"A series of different places that you can look back on and share memories of, that my brothers would remember. As for being secure, my parents were always very interested in what I was doing or achieving or being,

188

and appreciative of letters written, and that's part of it. I always feel extremely sad to know of children who've had a dreary upbringing or are unloved. There's no base, no mattress you can bounce on."

Clarissa came from a military background. Her parents were prudent with money, and pocket money was always carefully considered. The family lived partly on the Continent and partly in rural areas of England where, "there were nothing like the same temptations there are now. I remember buying one gramophone record when I was 12 or 13, it was a treat. Our amusements were bicycling and picnics and messing about in the garden, no temptations of shopping. We used to spend our pocket money on presents or saving up for something."

Later, the student life did not provide any spending money. "We didn't have money to go to the pub, let alone to buy meat to eat; we used to live on things like baked beans and sardines", she said, and felt this had set her up for life. She still regarded going out to a restaurant occasionally as a treat, but a different lifestyle had never held any attraction for her and amongst the things which gave her particular enjoyment and satisfaction in life was hospitality given or received by friends or family. Clarissa's appreciation of her house and garden in its peaceful environment, being able to go to films, concerts and the library, country walks and dinghy sailing, and the feeling of belonging to a community, be that her church, her friends from Health Service days or the organisation with which she volunteered, generated a satisfaction with her life of 9 out of 10.

But despite earlier pleasures, there had been a time when she had not found life so satisfying: "I remember when I was in Hong Kong and went through a period of a lot of amusements and parties and I got a sense that life ought to offer more than that, even though I had an interesting job. It was superficial. Seasons, one could say, of feeling that life ought to be more interesting than this."

The Religious Imperative

While environmental concern was by far the most common reason given by the modest consumers for their choice to live as they did, this often shaded both into religious tenets and the desire for social justice. Three people who were primarily driven by their religious beliefs were Andrew, Molly and Luzie.

ANDREW

Andrew was a man of pretty comfortable means, a lawyer in the civil service, his wife a GP. They lived in a four-bedroom, two hundred year-old cottage on the green in an East Midlands village with their 7½ year-old daughter. They spent about half of what they earned and saved the rest. Andrew had come into close contact with poverty, having been born in the West Indies and spent much of his childhood in the Caribbean and the South Atlantic where his father was a colonial civil servant, and where the local people were very poor. Andrew himself had more recently had very little money during a period of unemployment. Religion was an important factor in the shaping his lifestyle now, but so were *green considerations and hatred of waste and ostentatious spending on fripperies.*

Andrew's parents had been thrifty so he felt he had had a modest lifestyle for most of his life, but particularly so in the last few years. He and his wife had not had the desire to go abroad since their daughter was born, and had decided they would probably not fly again anyway. The birth of their baby also reduced their consumption, he told me, in that they had stopped going out in the evening and lost their former habit of meeting friends for a meal at the pub on Friday nights and of often eating lunch out at the weekend. Their eating habits changed further when Andrew's wife became interested in growing vegetables and got an allotment in addition to the vegetable patch in the garden.

It was in 2004 that Andrew moved from the Church of England, in which he had been brought up, to the Greek Orthodox church, and it was to this that he attributed his increased modesty in consumption, for he saw a clear parallel between Orthodox Christianity and environmentalism:

> "We were put on the earth as its guardians or stewards. The earth is not ours, it is God's. Everything that we have comes from God. Although God gave us dominion over all the earth he did not mean that we should exploit it. Since it is not ours, we must treat it with respect. We are to tread gently. Therefore we are required to live in harmony with creation. We do that by being responsible, by not unnecessarily consuming, by ensuring that we protect the environment so that, as good stewards, we can pass it on to the next generation more or less intact. It seems to me that this is little different from what the green movement thinks."

It was for a mixture of reasons, then, that Andrew consciously consumed considerably less than he could afford. His wife shared his environmental point of view, though not his religious one. He said, "We do have concern as to the planet and all that sort of thing, but from my point of view it's a religious thing really. We're stewards of the world, we're not there to exploit or rape it or whatever, you've just got to tread gently."

I wondered if Andrew found that the way he lived was very different from his civil service colleagues, or from the barristers with whom he used to work:

A Oh yeah, I think they think we're nuts! I'm sure they do.
T So do you ever discuss lifestyle and values?
A No, because my office is in London but I go there five days a fortnight so the rest of the time I'm here at home, so when I go to London it's go there do my work and come home. No, you might have a deal of banter but you don't talk that much.
T But if you say they think you're nuts they must be aware of it.
A Oh yes. Maybe 'they think I'm nuts' is a bit strong but I think they think we're unusual.
T And how would you characterise the way they live?
A They're normal I suppose… I suppose they're more materialistic really, and have aspirations towards more materialism.

Our telephone conversation was interrupted by a neighbour coming round to make arrangements for going together to a beer festival the following night. Andrew valued the fact that, as well as having close friends, he felt embedded in the local community and that, "we know our neighbours and help each other out without necessarily being in each other's pockets". Alcohol, better quality food and eating out were things which Andrew, like many others in the study, enjoyed spending spare cash on. But one aspect of his attitude to spending money was more unusual: "Having a child is one of the most selfless things a person can do," he said. "Choosing not to have one (when you are married and physically capable) can be considered selfish. For a start, it gives you a lot more disposable income. People in that position tend to dispose of it on themselves." He and his wife paid for private education for their daughter. They had both been privately educated themselves. Andrew's daughter also went with him to church, where they were both taught to be 'in the world but not of the world', that is, "We are 'in the world' in that we live in the world amongst others of all different faiths and value systems. We are not 'of the world' in that we do not share the desire for what the 'world' wants – worldly goods, possessions and values."

§

MOLLY

For Molly, who had lived all her 75 years, apart from war-time evacuation, in a deprived east coast town, her Christian faith was absolutely fundamental to how she saw the world and lived her life. It was first in her list of the things that were most important to her, although it was not at the forefront of her stated reason for living modestly, which was, *To help the planet because we are all too greedy. I could be short of money if I lived a 'spending' lifestyle, but I feel I have plenty! I have an A-rated washing machine and dish washer etc. Things to use and enjoy. A long time ago I read in a church 'Live simply that others may simply live' – it seemed to be the right thing to do, BUT I don't always get it right!* Her stance meant that Molly refused to fly, got around locally on an "aid assisted electric bike", bought fair trade and organic goods whenever possible, found furniture in charity shops, and did not give her family expensive presents.

Molly's deep faith had been integral to her life since childhood. She described her early life:

> "My grandfather and my father and my uncle were fishermen. My grandfather had a small boat, he was a longshore fisherman. I can remember we lived on fish. I suppose they sold the rest and got a little bit of money to run the boat and shared it like that. But it was a good home. I had a really good mum, who had a Christian faith right from the beginning. She took us to church, she cared about us. I can remember some of the hymns she'd sing round the house. And when my father was in from sea, they would go to a little mission that used to be by the railway on a Wednesday evening and sing… I think I decided to follow Christ when I was about eleven, and this goes back to my mother and my father, they took us to church and we went as a family, and I can remember her saying that we're going to the church up at the top of the town because that's the one that's got a good Sunday school. And that had quite a strong influence on me."

Times had changed and Molly was keen to be consciously aware of the needs of the contemporary world and to try to live accordingly. Looking around her living room, at the second-hand furniture, the new television she had bought because she couldn't read the text on the old one any more, the chairs that she and her husband had re-covered two or three times, and the shelves her husband had put up years ago, she said, "We have to care about our environment, and part of our Christian care is thinking about other people in the world who, let's face it, haven't got any of this."

Molly's husband, a former maths teacher, who had died five years before, had shared her faith and her eagerness to bring their three daughters up to live in a similarly thoughtful way; all now married, they did indeed share their parents' values. Apart from her Christianity, the most important things in life for Molly, she said, were her daughters and grandchildren; also, to be able to go into the natural world and share in its great beauty and do her bit to preserve and care for it. It was an urge that had grown partly out of seeing the beauty of natural places while on camping holidays with her children in Scotland. When her family were young and they were strapped for cash, they went to Scotland for a month for eight successive years: "We walked and swam. We watched birds, dug cockles (which we cooked and ate), picked wild raspberries and blackberries. We made our own fun. It was wonderful! We got a second-hand trailer and we used to pile all the stuff in it, and that month's camping cost us less than our next door neighbours who were fairly well off who had five days in Butlin's." Later, Molly and her husband camped and caravanned in France, not for lack of money now, but for the pure enjoyment of it.

Molly's love of nature had actually begun long before, during her own childhood; her parents had taken the children for local walks and they had picked wild flowers, as you could then. She also remembered as a little girl, getting a lot of ear infections and her auntie suggesting she pass the time while home from school by threading nuts and watching the birds eat them. As she got older, her love of God's creation took on a clear association with Christian teaching: "I think I owe that to a wonderful man who lived in this town. At the time when we were growing up some of the church leaders arranged holidays for young people. When I was around 21, we went to Derbyshire and climbed the hills there; he talked about God's love and Christian living". He read from an inspirational book, *The Great Outlaw*, by Geoffrey Hoyland which tried to describe what the love of Christ was like, using the idea of being in the countryside, with Jesus in the hills. Now she sometimes caught a train and just sat in the countryside, away from everything, "in God's world". She also derived much pleasure from her garden and new-found vegetable-growing activities.

Although Molly still missed her husband very much, she rated her satisfaction with her life as 9 out of 10. She said, "I think I'm very happy with life generally... I just feel I'd like to get more involved in doing something for other people. There's a new thing in the town that's opened up to help other races and I went down last week to see them, and I thought this is something that I could do, I could be a befriender".

§

LUZIE

For Luzie, a 43 year-old scientist who had settled in England from Germany, the overriding concern was with poverty and exploitation; for her, environmental damage was to be addressed primarily for the effect it would have on human beings, and Christianity was clearly a continuing influence on her view.

Luzie had always lived fairly modestly. Her parents were neither well-off nor poor; the family owned a car, but she was made fun of by her richer classmates at secondary school because she bought her clothes in high street shops, rather than the boutiques where they bought theirs. This did not worry her, however, as she was generally not a great spender, and she had other friends outside school whom she met at her scout group who dressed more like she did. When she first started work, Luzie did splash out on clothes a bit more but found she did not wear everything she bought and that the extra clothes annoyingly cluttered up her wardrobe. She then made the decision to spend her money on ethical goods. Where did she think that decision to spend ethically came from? "That's all within the context of religion. I was brought up as a Roman Catholic, in fact the Scouts were Catholic, and when I was about seventeen, that time in your life when your emotions are high and you discover new things, we looked into the life of Jesus and how he preached that everyone is equal. So it stems from then that I thought we should treat people equally."

Luzie did not deny herself every pleasure, but took account of their implications: "I do have pleasures, but I can't enjoy them if I know that there is nothing left for the future but also for the people currently living. I was thinking one day of buying a carpet and investigated how they are produced and found they are produced very much with child labour, these large oriental rugs. So I decided that I couldn't actually buy one, knowing how much the kids had suffered". A luxury she allowed, however, was a very expensive laptop computer, to higher specifications than she needed.

What was really important to Luzie was that her work should be of value: "I started my Biology study naively in the hope that it would help to tackle the hunger problem in the world; I think that's what work should be about, this world is about people. We should try to improve, help others to live a happy life and I would love my job to be helpful in that greater sense." Ultimately for Luzie the environmental question was about people:

> "Well of course environmental costs are in the end human costs as well. If we don't sort out our ecological problems people will drown in Bangladesh and so on. For me most problems about ecology mean we spoil our world and we can't live very well on it any more. Nature itself will find a way, there will always be something living. If humans die out mice or rats will take over, something will happen, so I'm not really worried about that. I'm worried about human suffering."

§

Global Inequality

ELLEN

Human suffering in terms of gross inequality certainly drove Ellen's way of living. The plight of other human beings and her sense of privilege at having access to resources was much the more powerful in determining her priorities than her concern for the health of the planet. No stranger to living with limited means herself, she explained:

> "I'm used to it. When it's so much part of your life you don't take it for granted, for example, that you can throw water away; everything becomes a resource, and you are aware that people in Africa have it a load harder than you. Turning on a light switch or a tap is something magical, you're aware that the machine can stop. You don't do it out of sanctimony or anything like that, you just wouldn't dream of squandering things."

Money had not been absent during her childhood, but her father had restricted its flow, she thought, as a means of maintaining power in the family. But her mother had enjoyed jumble sales and making meals out of leftovers, not wasting anything, as was the norm in the post-war era. When Ellen was a student her father chose not to support her financially, so after a very lean period her university gave her a grant for refugees and aliens. "In retrospect", she said, "It seems like a good thing because I never expected that money would be forthcoming." While married, she and her husband were both self-employed and low earners. At the outset they had no running hot water, central heating, car or washing machine but it did not seem to matter. They did not at all feel hard up: they earned a tiny amount but simply lived within their means and even paid off their mortgage.

Later, family difficulties did result in several worrying years of severe financial hardship when coping on very little was absolutely essential. Now, separated and financially more comfortable, Ellen still had no desire to change her way of living. Luxury for her meant leaving a light on unnecessarily and, "being able to get water out of the tap for a cup of tea, being able to put a fire on. I don't know how many years it is since I heated water by the boiler: that strikes me as profligate, having the boiler on every day, I can't conceive how I would do that." She heated water in a kettle on the gas hob, and if she heated more water than was actually needed she poured it into a thermos flask to use later for the washing up.

Counterbalancing Ellen's meagre use of resources was a lively enjoyment of many other, largely non-material things that life offers: art, "natural beauty", "simple fresh food such as apples and porridge", solitude, being out on a bike, running in the early morning, making music with friends and playing the piano to elderly people. As an enthusiastic piano teacher and music lecturer, music was 54 year-old Ellen's passion; yet she was content to play CD's on a couple of ghetto blasters rather than expensive sound equipment. She did, though, spend a lot on musical texts and books. Her spending could be inconsistent and unpredictable:

> "In the summer I blew money on a sculpture which I loved. I com-
> missioned it. Unexpected things like that. It doesn't happen a lot. Oh
> pictures, I like having pictures by people I know. I can't predict, and
> when I spend money on non-essentials it may be a huge amount; it can
> be, 'Right, I'll have a conservatory now!' I rarely regret impulse buys!"

The possession of books was of constant and major importance for Ellen, in an interesting contrast to the preference of book-worm Anthony who would have liked books to be communal possessions held in libraries. "Books I've always been obsessed with," Ellen told me. "When I was a child I was banned when I was about eight from changing my library books more than once a day. Now she felt that books were friends, "sources of information and contact with worlds other than my own". One of her early memories was that she longed to have books; "obsession with books was a big thing".

Ellen was certainly a person who went whole-heartedly into all her endeavours. She believed that deriving deep pleasure and joy from any activity required real effort. "I teach music and there are people who'll say, 'I want my child to learn the piano because I want her to have fun', not realising that to have fun there has to be some commitment, some application and that that way you can get a huge amount out of it". Another 'obsession' was for pelargoniums, the beauty of one particular species. In fact, she said:

"Without an obsession I'm miserable, and if I have an obsession I'm as happy as Larry. I went through an obsession with embroidery, never having been able to sew as a child, and getting very keen on Jacobean embroidery, and calligraphy, and Bartok. If you have an obsession and go into something deeply the pleasure becomes a real joy. But I don't think that simple exposure to various different arts will get you very far. It may be great at the time but you have to go deeper, and there has to be some application on your part, not just exposure and opportunities. I worry for children because we all want to give them so many different opportunities, but they don't know how to choose and end up bedazzled, with a sense of disappointment. If they had had fewer opportunities, if they'd been allowed to go deeper it might have been better. I know that when I really apply myself I get a million times more out of anything I do."

Concern for others, including people she didn't know, far away across the world, was as thorough and profound for Ellen as the characteristic way she went deeply into every one of her interests. It coloured her whole stance: while at first she rated her satisfaction with her life to be 9 out of 10, she later reconsidered the question and it incensed her:

E I found I hated the question, I loathed the question, the word satisfaction is awful, awful, awful, awful. In fact I disown the answer. I have no satisfaction with my life. I think there are lots of ways of doing it better, what does the question mean? Is it my experience of how life is impacting on me? Or is it my response to life? I think it's a completely spurious question and I hate it and I'd like to say either 9 or nil.
T It's trying to get at how happy you are with the way that you live your life
E I'll never be happy with it, I'll never be happy. I was talking to someone yesterday and I was saying it's dreadful because at the moment life is dealing

me really good cards, it's really fine, but I'm absolutely on the rack because various friends of mine are ill, there are awful wars, there's everything else, and I can't make any difference about it. I'm completely dissatisfied with it. But the impact of what life is doing for me is perfectly fine. How I'm living my life and failing to do anything about these other things is absolutely loathsome. So I think you could say my satisfaction is nought.

Ellen's friendships were important to her, though not necessarily based on regular contact. Her take on social relationships was unusual:

> "What I like doing is having lots of low key connections with other people and building family elsewhere and feeling that I am part of a goodwill community. When I was younger I had a real revelation that it didn't matter whether people liked me or not. For me to like them, and perhaps if they liked me later that was a real bonus, but I really didn't care. That's been fantastic. And I do like most people. Wondering how people are and hoping they're OK, worrying about them if they're not, and wanting them to feel good is very, very important... I just like to be friends and for them to know if there's anything they need then I'll do it, just community. I've so often been on the receiving end of friendship from people and sheer human kindness, and that really matters desperately."

For Ellen, that sense of community extended to the impoverished of the world: "I feel very edgy at having more than people have in Saharan Africa sometimes, and at having an easy time. I can't feel happy when people don't have sanitation and clean water, I can't feel happy rolling round in luxury, I just want to walk more and more lightly on the world."

Personal Responsibility

A sense of ethics or personal responsibility was high on the list of many of the modest consumers when explaining their lifestyles. Indeed, it was the second most frequently cited reason, given by nineteen people.

§

RUTH
Ruth was one of those who took her personal responsibility deeply to heart. 63, and the partner of Robert whom we met earlier, she also took what she believed was her moral obligation to its logical conclusion by living

an existence which had minimal impact on the environment. She had always lived modestly but more so in the last twenty-five years. She wrote, *I believe in personal responsibility, so I must live according to my moral code. Also it's fun, life is good when I remember I am part of a wonderful whole, I don't fill the universe.* Moreover, she had grandchildren and wanted a future for them.

Ruth told me how her current life had come about:

"We did live in a house, but I've never really had a lot of money so I wasn't taking a great big backward step in that sense. I have a couple of boys. I was married and then I was divorced, and Robert and I have been together for thirty-two years, and we fished for our living and all sorts of things, so it's always been a bit hand to mouth anyway. When we were children, and when my children were little, there wasn't much money, and again I was sometimes hungry and I would never want to go back to those levels. But no, we're comfortable.

When my children were old enough to stand on their own feet we decided to do something different. We started off with a horse and cart, just travelling round the country, but we had beliefs in creating something as well. We discovered every single inch of land is owned by somebody, I borrowed enough from my mum and dad to buy a field, and we set up so that we could put our own beliefs into practice. At that time the sewage went into the North Sea here and I'd been arguing with the council for years about it, and I said we'll make ourselves *responsible* for our own actions; that was what we were trying to do. We bought some more land when Robert's father died and he inherited a little bit of money so we bought the next land on to us, and ended up with 17 acres. In those days nobody wanted it, it was pasture and woods in very bad condition; it isn't now, it's in really good heart, we've done it all by hand because we don't use electricity, and we don't use poison or anything like that."

It was not straightforward or even possible, however, to become entirely independent of society, and Ruth found that life was constantly a compromise, but ultimately rewarding: "You have to fit in with so many other people for a start, you can't cut yourself off and that, and you have to work out what does the most harm and what does the most good; you can stick to principles and damage your family, you've got to do the best you can. But I must admit it's a *pleasure* living like this you know, there's no hardship in it whatsoever, really."

I wanted to know more about the practical details of life in the field. Did they have running water, for instance? The answer was that they lived on a spring line but resisted suggestions to pipe the water to the hut: "I mean what housewife sees a tree creeper or something like that, like I sometimes do, when I go to the spring for water!" Instead, Robert had carved out a log by one of their woods where the spring bubbled up and attached a pipe, raising it off the ground, so that they could fill their water containers. And did they keep animals? They had had two horses when they started, but these had both died and been replaced with a shire horse for the sheer enjoyment of his company and ornamental value. Friends' horses were also sometimes accommodated on their land; and they had sheep to help keep the grass down, though they didn't eat meat themselves. Ruth and Robert grew their own vegetables and firewood. Indeed, they had grown about 2,500 trees. Everything was composted, including the contents of the eco-lavatory, using a very thorough, careful, five-year cycle of turning between bays. Cooking had been done on a primus stove for seventeen years, but Ruth now used a little gas cooker taken from a friend's caravan. She admitted that living like this was hard work, but she found it to be rewarding because it was so *real*:

> "It takes quite a lot of discipline, you've got to tackle all the jobs that need doing, and work out the order of them, because there are so many and not enough time. It is quite hard work. But it's not the bad sort of tension. Whatever problem arises it's the sort of thing you deal with because the problems are usually physical. If something happens to the hut you set to and mend it, you're not faced with enormous bills that you don't know how you're going to pay, and they're always immediate problems and I think there's a lot less tension because they're much nearer reality."

Ruth and Robert were a mile and half from the bus stop, and their nearest neighbours were a field away. Ruth felt slightly ambivalent about being so cut off from other people: "Sometimes there's a sort of frustration because other people don't live like us, the frustration of not being able to just do things as easily and join and socialise; and also living on very little money you just can't participate in the same way, it does have its frustrations, and there's a slight isolation feeling sometimes, you know. To be perfectly honest, most of the time I'm extremely happy living here. I don't miss having other people around me and then I have Robert and the animals to share with". When people found out how they lived, their response tended to be one of admiration, but Ruth felt that this was misplaced – there was nothing to admire because they found their life good.

Had living so long so close to the natural world given Ruth a sort of rootedness? "Well yes it does. It's nice to be not too separated; we actually have a wooden house so you can really hear the rain hitting it. It does bring a feeling of belonging." Indeed, what was most important in life for Ruth was, "to know that I belong to the wonderful magical world. I don't belong to any religion, but I have a feeling that there is a completeness and we should be, we are, part of that completeness, and it's absolutely wonderful, magical, it's just unbelievably wonderful".

Ruth had written, *I was lucky in having a mum and dad who taught me to think, to care about fairness*, by which she meant:

> "Mum and Dad grew up in an era when there wasn't a lot of chance to move on education-wise if you didn't have money. I mean they both won scholarships to grammar schools but it really wasn't possible to go much beyond that. And then of course the war came and one thing and another, but it left them both with a desire that the children should have a chance to go on, in a way that wasn't particularly material, it was that one should follow, to some extent, your dreams. My dad used to have a saying that if you dream about climbing Mount Everest it's better that you die half way up than never set off. So yes, apart from the fact that they took us to the library, they did teach us to think and make decisions about things."

So Ruth had enjoyed reading since she was a small child, and now reading and music gave her increasing pleasure. Beethoven above all showed her joy and beauty and restored her courage. Although she felt she had grown away from her parents to an extent and developed her own ideas, she readily acknowledged that she owed them a lot in that initial way of thinking. "I didn't pass my 11-plus but they didn't want that to be a limitation. One of my sisters went off to university and one went to college. When we went fishing mum and dad were thrilled to bits you know, because they weren't ambitious for us to have conventionally good jobs so much as a fulfilled life. I do think I was lucky like that." While formal education is constantly held up as the means to building an informed and worthwhile life, Ruth's parents' attitude encouraged the building of a rewarding life through other channels, and her limited schooling was no barrier to her love of reading or her ecological understanding.

Tough as their way of living was, Ruth found it extremely satisfying and had no regrets:

> "No, on the contrary. Everything you do has got a purpose in doing it. You know if you don't go out and get your own firewood, basically at the bottom of the line you could die of the cold. It's a very satisfying way of living, real things to do. I go out and do a bit of gardening and a bit of cleaning work, just enough for the things we can't produce for ourselves really. But again they are jobs that are very satisfying because they are things that are needed. I work for people who need me basically. So there's always a satisfaction in what you're doing, which I really think, well it's important, much more important than anything you can own actually, because what you can really own is yourself and your time."

In fact, Ruth's efforts stretched in a very tangible way beyond the meeting of human needs: "we ought to be adding to things, it's important to give as we go along rather than just take. Life is only worth having if we're contributing towards the end of it". So she and Robert had bought their land in a very run down state, putting in more hedges and ponds, adding compost and manure, and watched it come back to life again, providing a big habitat for all sorts of other living creatures, "so that you have put yourself into just a small bit of the Earth".

§

Intrinsic and extrinsic values

Another way in which values have been differentiated is between the intrinsic and the extrinsic. Intrinsic values determine goals which are worthwhile in themselves.[345] These are oriented towards personal growth, knowledge or experience for its inherent worth, cordial relationships, or the common good. Extrinsic values, in contrast, focus on the outward-facing attributes of financial success, image and popularity which are prized largely as means to the worldly end of social status. Straight away, it is clear that the values of the modest consumers were pretty well exclusively intrinsic; as a group, these people simply weren't motivated by money, acquisition, appearance or public acclaim; they constructed their lives instead around friendship, usefulness, contact with nature, creativity, moral frameworks, and physical activity, all pursuits which have value in their own right.

Parental transmission of values?

The learning of values begins early in life, and it is common for adults to identify themselves by the extent to which they have adopted or rejected their parents' values. For example, in a newspaper interview the actor Natascha McElhone explained that it was due to having been brought up by a "Marxist, rationalist" stepfather that she did not believe in the supernatural, religion or horoscopes,[346] and another actor, Jeremy Northam, has recalled with warmth, "My dad was an academic and the things that were valued in our household were conversation, sharing, books, music. We didn't have money and my folks had to be cautious people, so there was a sense of sharing and fairness among the family."[347] Journalist Zoe Lewis has written, "My family have always defied convention, and I do the same with the way I dress... I enjoy designer labels. One reason for my occasional over-indulgence in luxurious clothes is that my father was a fervent anti-materialist which made me go the other way, to rebel".[348] The singer Seal has recounted a different form of influence, in that, "I always say my father is my most important role model, because he showed me everything I shouldn't be".[349]

As far as parental influence on the values of the modest consumers went, the testimony of many of them supported the belief that values are learnt from parents, and suggested that their mother and/or father were often positive role models. They cited, among others, these influences on their current lifestyles: parents who *CARED and took us to interesting places and helped us discern what was valuable and set us an example*; parents who *shaped my whole view of life and showed me the value of non-material things - they taught me that love was more important than money, that waste is criminal and that there is so much enjoyment to be found in the natural world*, and *parents who did not try to limit my life or my thinking, which has helped me to gain a sense of independence and personal responsibility*. One woman wondered, *How much was I influenced by knowing my mother had built the kitchen cupboards - or by seeing my mum's oil paintings?* and another cited, *My mum and her campaigning/concern on local and environmental issues, my grandfather who was a shop steward at his work and actively political, my other grandparents who were keen gardeners*. Growing up in an uncongenial atmosphere could also have an effect in this respect, as illustrated by these remarks: *Having a workaholic mother and father*, and *Being brought up in church-going suburbia where 'being seen to be' seemed to matter more than really being, influenced my politics away from the right wing.*

Values are based on past experience and in turn influence the way we assess subsequent experience. They are the drivers of thought and feeling,[350] and feelings are often more important influences than facts when it comes to making judgements. Many studies have established substantial correlations between people's values and their corresponding behaviours.[351] So, though very personal, the significance and implications of individual values are vital because their effects on behaviour are felt far beyond the individual. Our values determine, at least as much as our personality, how each one of us interacts with and therefore impacts on the wider world. Crucially, values, even more than personality, grow out of experience.

Crossing Thresholds

The 'threshold concept'

For people who are basically content with their lives, material consumption often adds a thick varnish of additional pleasure. So how does it happen that a person's spontaneous initial response to a situation, such as to the possible purchase of an attractive article in a shop which cries out, "Make me mine and I will give you aesthetic pleasure (or convenience, or the admiration of others)", can be trumped by what they consider to be of greater importance in the larger scheme of things? This, after all, is what happened for Katarina when she asked herself if an appealing little item sighted while on holiday really would find a use at home, and for Lauren when she consciously stopped her hand from reaching out to take something that caught her fancy in a high street store. Answering this question could clearly support a widespread shift towards willing reduction in consumption. Here our exploration changes direction.

Nearly half the modest consumers dated their modest lifestyle not from birth or from the point of becoming an independent adult, but from a more recent time. This was the result of their broadening perception of consumption. On the one hand, it concerned sustainability and justice, and on the other, it expressed the realisation that consumption is not actually satisfying. People with perceptions changed in such a way as to compel them to significantly restrict their buying, home energy use or travel have crossed some kind of threshold in their understanding. The notion of a 'threshold concept' is one that has been developed to support teachers in helping students in higher education to overcome intellectual barriers to formal learning in any subject area,[352] but it is equally useful in understanding informal, incidental learning that happens in the course of everyday life. An example of a threshold concept from the study of History would be when a student comes to realise that a particular historical event or situation cannot be properly understood by viewing it through the lens of today's perspective but must be considered from the point of view of the world at the time it took place; this requires intellectual engagement.[353] An example from Cultural Studies is the grasping of 'otherness' in learning about different social identities; this requires affective as well as intellectual engagement and may result in personal discomfort, particularly if a student themselves belongs to a minority group.[354] Such thresholds have been explained like this:

> A threshold concept can be considered as akin to a portal, opening up a new and previously inaccessible way of thinking about something. It represents a transformed way of understanding, or interpreting, or viewing something… As a consequence of comprehending a threshold concept there may be a transformed internal view of subject matter, subject landscape, or even world view. This transformation may be sudden or it may be protracted over a considerable period, with the transition to understanding proving troublesome.[355]

The power of crossing thresholds

A threshold concept is both transformative and irreversible; once learned it is unlikely to be forgotten or unlearned. It can also, as we have just seen, be troublesome. Problems can ensue if a particular threshold is intellectually difficult for us or if it comes from a perspective that conflicts with our own.[356] Thus, people who have difficulty in making abstract connections will find it hard to translate their travel or eating habits into greenhouse gases and the damaging climatic effects these inflict. Similarly, those who believe that status is conferred by shows of wealth and that happiness resides in acquisition are likely to find it hard to appreciate the idea that mastering the art of story-telling, jazz improvisation or conflict mediation could enhance their social status, or that helping a neighbour with a leaking pipe will increase their own wellbeing. Those who assume that it is their inalienable right to fly around the world as they please are likely, when confronted by the data on planes' CO_2 emissions and climate change, to find this threshold of learning uncomfortable, and so ignore it. Likewise, figures that demonstrate the mushrooming of the world population and its implications for future availability of resources are unlikely make the slightest difference to individuals who believe it is their right to produce any number of children without consideration for the wider ramifications. So, crossing any conceptual threshold is not simply a matter of intellectual activity, it will also involve the 'learner's' emotional position in relation to the information in question.[357]

The testimony of the modest consumers regarding what had influenced their lifestyles presents plentiful glimpses of thresholds having been crossed, as the following reflections illustrate. It is interesting to note how each instance pivots on a particular person or people. One woman wrote how, *My husband introduced me to my love of the natural world and initiated my political awareness.* Another wrote, *Through a former landlady I got curious about living a greener lifestyle. Friends happy with their life and generous with their happiness showed me ways of life that I liked. Work colleagues in the NGO world also helped me to find alternative views to the consumer lifestyle. Finally, my sister made this journey with me and many of her discoveries became mine. She taught me to love truth and beauty. For one, living among people who cared deeply about under-privileged people opened my eyes about different political stances and to ethical thinking;* and someone remembered *Meeting a local green activist who taught me a lot about alternative ways of living in a conventional system – you don't have to live in a tipi on a hillside – that working within the system is just as valuable a way to achieve change in your own life and to help others change theirs; that small steps have big consequences.* The learning could be slow to take effect: *Mostly it is encounters with people that have helped me to make my lifestyle what it is today. It sometimes took me years to learn from them, and they were long gone from my life then, but they did influence me deeply.*

Emotional capital

Teachers have found that learners vary in their capacity and willingness to engage with threshold concepts and that a new one is not always fully integrated into a student's thinking. Some students will show a readiness to internalise learning and be transformed by it while others will be hostile and resistant.[358] So what determines an individual's readiness to cross certain conceptual thresholds? One possibility is that the deciding factor is 'emotional capital'. This is a term coined to denote a set of emotional resources which arise out of life experiences,[359] that have the effect of priming the individual to respond to later experience in a particular way. Emotional capital is different from emotional intelligence which is the facility to process emotional issues, and is analogous to the concept of 'cultural capital' posited by the French sociologist and philosopher Pierre Bourdieu.[360] Bourdieu pointed out that the outcome of a person's education is not only the result of their natural intelligence and the quality of their education but is also a question of how much cultural capital they have imbibed from their family that predisposes them towards learning. This might consist in such experiences as living in a home where books and reading are valued, receiving a positive response to childhood curiosity, and being provided with a quiet place to do homework. It might also come from outside the home, from the local provision of a good library, perhaps, or cultural activities for children and young people.

The notion of analogous emotional capital is compelling, but what might generate such a resource is rather more difficult to say. One type of experience which had had a big and relevant impact on a number of the modest consumers was travel in materially impoverished places. Several of them had had experiences of living in less developed parts of the world which were, as we have seen, clearly important in the evolution of their views on material consumption and lastingly altered their assumptions about how much it is really necessary to consume in order to live happily if basic needs are met. Encountering the huge discrepancy between contented, or at least viable, ways of living in poverty-stricken parts of the world and the material superabundance which is taken for granted in the rich world, yet is somehow never enough, engendered a shift in perception. This experience changed understanding and values at a gut level. Some people gave quite specific reasons why travelling had had this impact on them. One, for instance, specified, *seeing the destruction man has caused to the environment, especially in Africa*, and another wrote:

> *I lived in Africa for six months with a poor local family, where I was running a business. This, perhaps more than anything else, has taught me the value of relationship with other people, and with this, how humans can survive well with little (or perish, where there is a lack of knowledge). It has made me value enormously just how lucky people are in the West to enjoy a deal of personal freedom, and safety and access to knowledge and entertainment, not to mention access to healthcare, food, etc.*

Impressionable adolescence

While parents' values may clearly be an important factor in shaping any individual's own values, either in their adoption or rejection, a change in values can arise at any point in life; indeed we see in the accounts of several of those who participated in the study how such a change is sometimes precipitated by major crisis. The most turbulent time for values, however, is likely to be during adolescence and young adulthood, when children are turning away from the family towards the wider world. Young adulthood is especially salient for value formation for someone who goes to university;[361] we have only to think here of Ed and his module on environmental issues and geosciences, and of Sarah who identified intellectual and political discussions at university and encounters as a student with people committed to political action, as having been crucial to the way they had decided to live. But new values are not learnt only at university. One young man noted that something that had influenced him had been *learning about climate change at the impressionable age of* 14. Becky, in her early 30s now, dated her political awareness to history lessons, declaring, "There was a history teacher when I was at school who taught me about the Levellers and the Diggers and the English civil war and basically socialism and I got very excited about it and thought this stuff is really good. I was 15, 16. It just really lit my fire."

Indeed the teenage years turned out to be a time that had been of particular importance for a number of other modest consumers, and not only specifically in terms of their education. Luzie referred to the age of about 17 as, "that time in your life when your emotions are high and you discover new things". In fact, both she and Jan, both now in their early 40's, made a point of the stimulus to their thinking about moral questions imbibed from Christian youth groups. Katarina, still in her mid-20s, believed, too, that her understanding of human inequalities and personal responsibility originated in discussions of moral issues in her Jewish youth group. For another woman, the teens had not been easy but had offered a valuable opportunity: *as a teenager who had difficulty finding her place in society, I went through a few years of when I had a lot of time to think, to formulate questions and look for answers for myself,* while a 72 year-old respondent felt that experience of living in digs with wonderful landladies when young was one that still influenced the way she lived now. For some of the older study participants it was the social and cultural climate of their youth that had had a lasting impact: three people cited being a teenager in the 1960s as significant, one because it encouraged independent thought, one because being a hippy was *the profoundest influence – LOVE!* and the third was influenced by *the sense of optimism and wholeness of that time and the great music that was so available.*

These days, children are sucked early into consumerism, the attention and desires of many drawn towards mobile phones, fashion, and so on long before they reach their teens. With the successive cuts in local authority funding, youth services have been decimated. The provision of regular meeting places and activities for adolescents is largely left to the commercial world. Loud music, that drowns out the possibility of searching exchanges of views, is a frequent feature, and activities on offer are likely to favour financially profitable entertainment rather than to set out to develop practical skills or stretch social and moral thinking. The testimony above suggests, however, that people going through the transition from childhood to adulthood, in whatever generation, are at a particularly receptive stage of development, possibly more open to new ideas about ethics, politics and ways of living than at other times of life. While it is not, of course, possible to legislate for personal moments of meaning, it seems that many young people, as well as society as a whole, would benefit from having more opportunities and encouragement to critically explore ideas appertaining to how best to live and to organise society. At this point in our history, crucial in terms of the human relationship to the Earth, creating possibilities and encouragement for such discussions is more important than it has ever been.

Vital thresholds of understanding and building emotional capital
Placing familiar experiences, perceptions and expectations into a wider context somehow sharpens our focus and alters our perspective on reality. Although it is certainly not impossible to empathise strongly with the plight of the disadvantaged from a great distance, as was amply demonstrated by Ellen, such fierce solidarity with strangers is rare. Lauren enthusiastically suggested that all teenagers be sent away for a spell in a developing country, and this would no doubt have a salutary effect on the ideas of many young people in Britain, for as she found, "I went away and worked with people who had nothing and I saw how they lived, and they were quite alright. So ever since then I've really appreciated what we have. I appreciated it before but you don't really truly know until you see it and live through it, do you?" But the practical and ethical issues involved in temporarily transplanting large numbers of young people from rich to poor countries unfortunately renders this idea impossible.

There is, though, another form of emotional capital, and in some ways it is more constructive and certainly more achievable. It is familiarity with the exhilaration, fascination, contentment, curiosity, sense of achievement, transcendence and other such valuable emotions offered by all the non-material possibilities of human life. Among these, respectful, trustworthy human relationships; personal creativity and ingenuity; encounters with nature; a sense of being useful; and of working with others to make a better world, are important ones. The widespread development of personal priorities such as these would be likely to see envy, greed, competitiveness, a sense of social inferiority and a considerable degree of stress decline dramatically. Familiarity with non-material rewards creates its own demand for more; a life which seeks such returns brings the individual the greatest satisfaction. When we come to realise that putting time, thought and energy into the kinds of experiences that produce these sorts of effects is far more rewarding, and its effects more sustained, than the constant pursuit of possessions, convenience, comfort and admiration, we have crossed a vital threshold towards the cultivation of our own well-being. This, together with the crossing of a second threshold, the realisation that every single purchase we make contributes in some measure to the erosion and contamination of the Earth's precious resources (unless that purchase is second-hand or locally hand-made out of renewable, biodegradable materials), will also reduce our personal toll on the planet. It is no longer tenable to declare, as a philosopher did as recently as the end of 2010, that, "Given a choice between being quite happy at a modest standard of living and being equally happy at a significantly higher standard of living, it is not irrational to prefer the second option".[362] Knowledge of the largely irreversible destruction being wrought to our life support system by that higher standard of living renders such a preference utterly *ir*rational.

Being able to burst through the emotional and intellectual barrier which makes it possible, against the powerful undertow of consumer culture, fully to take to heart the destructive impacts of our personal consumption, requires certain forms of emotional capital. One is empathy for the other, unknown, probably far distant person who is exploited in producing goods for our market or whose home will be washed away by rising seas. Another is a deep love of the Earth together with some understanding of the interconnectedness of human activities with its systems. A third is the sense of personal agency which enables an individual to feel that their own decisions and actions can and do make a difference. To change our consumer behaviour radically enough to minimise the damage it inflicts requires not only intellectual knowledge of its destructive impact, but also a visceral sense of revulsion at our profligacy, on the one hand, and a familiarity, on the other, with the deep personal fulfilment and delight that can be reached only by a non-material path.

It can take time for any threshold of learning to be fully crossed, and this is surely particularly true when that learning dictates the overhaul of an entire, deeply engrained way of living. After all, we have until relatively recently partaken in all innocence, at least as far as carbon dioxide and the global climate is concerned, in travel and acquisition of personal possessions; and fed, clothed, decorated, entertained and heated or cooled ourselves as freely as our financial resources allowed, taking such practices to be normal, 'natural', and without serious consequences beyond our own purse. Now that it is plain that these activities are anything but cost-free, we cannot allow the common human fondness for material consumption far beyond what is required to live perfectly well, to undermine life on Earth as we know it. We must alter our perception of material consumption and learn to see it not in terms of what it gives us but in terms of what it takes from the Earth's atmosphere, soils and waters, and exudes into them. Material profligacy does not, after all, even deliver happiness. With certain modest material provision in place, the sources of true wellbeing lie in the non-material realm. These are the critical twin thresholds of understanding to be crossed by affluent and materially aspirant individuals and societies.

Conclusion: The Cultivation of Intrinsic Values – A New Priority

Nothing short of a cultural transformation is needed in order to secure personal and environmental wellbeing. The means to achieving both is the cultivation of intrinsic values, values which prioritise personal growth and common purpose. This runs completely counter to the imperative of 'wealth creation' and the dogma of perpetual economic growth which demands and fuels constant consumption. Our society's priorities must change and change fast. Talk of the 'end of nature'[363] and the 'end of history'[364] confronts us with the possibility of the demise of life on the Earth as it has existed for many millennia. If the macro-scale of this scenario is too vast to get to grips with, the micro-level can help: Bronnie Ware, a palliative care nurse who spent many years caring for terminally ill patients who had gone home to die, found that amongst her patients' regrets when faced with imminent death, the most common included regret that they had not been true to themselves; these patients wished that they had not led the life that others

211

expected of them, that they had spent so much time working to attain a certain income that they had missed their children's youth and partner's companionship, and that they had limited their own happiness by fearing change and denying their discontent, and so had stuck with the familiar rather than choosing to do things differently.[365]

The much larger lesson is there for us to learn. Our values need to change.

8

The Place of Spirituality

Some Contemporart Perspectives on Spirituality

A growing interest

At various points in this book I use the phrase 'non-material world' or 'non-material consumption' to indicate aspects of life or sources of personal enrichment that have nothing at all to do with money or possessions. Another way of expressing this notion is in terms of the *spiritual*. I have used this word hesitantly until now as I believe it can be off-putting, suggesting some idea of religiousness or an elevated state far removed from the everyday. However, there has recently been an enormous upsurge of interest in spirituality and a growing recognition of its importance in daily life. In the field of health, the World Health Organisation acknowledged in 1984 the need to attend to the spiritual aspects of health,[366] and twenty years later the Department of Health established for the first time in the UK the requirement that patients' spiritual needs be taken into account.[367] The Royal College of Psychiatrists had already set up a Spirituality and Psychiatry special interest group in 1999, which by 2011 had attracted over 2,500 members.[368] However, in practice there are many barriers which may prevent health professionals from engaging with spirituality in their dealings with patients,[369] shortage of time being one major factor.

In the realm of education the question of children's and young people's spiritual development is a concern among educationalists in many countries around the world.[370] In Britain, reference was made to it as long ago as the Education Act of 1944. At that time spiritual development was considered to be more or less synonymous with the daily act of Christian worship,[371] an expression of spirituality which is no longer appropriate in contemporary society. Now, Ofsted guidelines require schools to take account of the spiritual, moral, social and cultural development of pupils,[372] and spirituality is understood as something much broader, as "encapsulating those very qualities that make us human".[373] As in the realm of health, however, implementation is not straightforward. It is not clear to every teacher how best to nurture or develop children's spirituality in school or in wider educational settings,[374] and Ofsted reports have noted how provision for social, moral and cultural development can be more successful than for the spiritual.[375] This is not to say, though, that there are not teachers who give considerable thought and energy to including spiritual dimensions of their subjects across the curriculum.[376]

What is spirituality?

What, then, is this somewhat elusive phenomenon we call spirituality? At the most fundamental level the concept has been said to express a sense that human life involves more than biology.[377] Somewhat conversely, it has also been described as a way of living that balances the ego and the eco, that harmonises the individual with the planet.[378] In the view of theologian Ursula King, spirituality is "fundamentally about becoming a person in the fullest sense... developing one's capacity for going out and beyond oneself." This ability, she says, "makes possible all our understanding, pursuit of knowledge, experience of beauty, quest of the good, and outreach of love toward the other, leading to responsibility and the creation of community".[379] From a more individual perspective it has been described as, "the search for that which gives zest, energy, meaning and identity to a person's life, in relation to other people, and to the wider world... [t]hose moments of life which take you beyond the mundane into a sacred place".[380] Another theologian, Philip Sheldrake, proposes that, whether religious or secular in inspiration, all forms of spirituality aim to promote the development of such humane qualities as compassion, patience, contentment, responsibility, harmony and concern for our fellow human beings. Further, that the pursuit of spirituality as a way of life promotes a certain self-discipline and detachment from material possessions.[381] In fact, one could view the pursuit of a distinctively spiritual life as the polar opposite of out-and-out materialism. For most of us life is lived somewhere along this continuum, at some distance from either extreme, incorporating aspects of both interests.

The stories of the modest consumers offer numerous glimpses of many aspects of spirituality, even though not often spoken of explicitly in these terms.

§

PAUL

One study participant who had shaped his life around a conscious exploration of the spiritual was Paul who had been on a deliberate spiritual journey for five years. He had chosen to live modestly in order to create more time and space *for the non-material things which I consider truly important* and *to do the work I love.*

He later explained: "I'm constantly growing and gaining new insights, so this answer is only a snapshot of where I am now. At the moment I'm reading books by Eckhart Tolle. His key idea is that living in the now, in consciousness, is our primary purpose, that our 'inner' purpose is to bring presence into the world." Paul's journey had begun when he started reading personal development books such as Wayne Dyer's, which introduced him to the idea that we are spiritual beings having a human experience, not merely bodies, and that at some level we are all one. Then he discovered Quakerism, about which he had read on the BBC Religion and Ethics website, and had since joined the Religious Society of Friends. Spirituality and personal development were now central to Paul's life. He had reduced his working week to four days so that he could spend more time concentrating on the writing that was emerging from it, and had been able to transfer his civil service job to a local office rather than having to commute five hours a day into and out of London. He tried as consciously as possible to live in the present: "In the past I've had goals, and I still have goals, but now the journey is at least as important as the destination, and I like to have a lot of space in my life, to take my time over things, to have a depth and a being, a presence, rather than being in a rush because I've got other things to do." Spirituality and personal development were so important to him because, "It goes back to the reason why I'm here, why any of us are here. If you go on holiday, after a couple of weeks it's over; if you buy a new car, you may have a bit of fun for a couple of weeks, but then you get bored with it. Spirituality is perhaps the only thing that you can take away with you when you go. It's the Quaker phrase, 'the things that are eternal', it's not transient, it has more depth of meaning maybe."

Paul addressed the spiritual by working on himself:

"It's a gradual thing. Little by little I'm making small changes to my life. At the end of each month I do an exercise called the examen and consider what changes I want to make in my life in the light of those observations. I reflect on the month and ask myself, when did I feel most in-spirit? What made my heart sing? I also ask myself what

I would have preferred to do differently. Is there anything I regret having done or failed to do? So I identify things about myself to work on and to change."

Despite his current focus, Paul did not think that he was living much more simply now than he had previously because he had never been particularly drawn to material things. Moreover, he believed that it wasn't right that "some people are drowning in luxuries while others haven't the essentials, like enough to eat or clean running water." Allied to his spiritual consciousness, and to his recently increased awareness of environmental issues, Paul was keen to reduce his environmental impact. He had not flown since 2000 when he attended his grandmother's funeral in Hungary; kept his old 1991 car; rarely took overseas holidays; had a budget of £1,000 a year to spend on meeting friends and going on courses, and if it wasn't all spent gave what was left over to charity; and aimed to own not more than fifty CDs.

Paul's childhood had not been lavishly provided for. His parents divorced when he was three, after which his mother worked as a live-in nurse until Paul was seven. Then they moved into their own maisonette, but there wasn't much money left after the mortgage and bills were paid. He and his mother felt quite differently about this:

> "We're actually quite different in that I value a simple lifestyle and she has a need to surround herself with nice material possessions, and she says that comes from her own childhood when she was poverty-stricken. She was brought up in Hungary just after the war; there was a two-room flat in which six people lived, they really were very poor. Her dad died when she was eleven of TB, so that carries through for her now, she perhaps compensates for her poverty in childhood by wanting nice things now, whereas my childhood wasn't so deprived: we weren't rich, but we had enough."

Paul's mother's love of beautiful things was a matter of aesthetics rather than materialism, however. She would now regularly buy flowers, regarded by Paul as a luxury, and liked to have pictures on the walls. Paul did not want to remain single for the rest of his life, and the one difficulty of his modest lifestyle that he saw was a potential one, should he live with someone who did not share it and who might, for instance, have a need to beautify the home like his mum.

Having withdrawn somewhat from the world, Paul was now keen to give something back. He had discovered, he felt, a reasonable talent for writing, and was hoping to be able to help other people by writing books through which he would be able to share some of his own experience and understandings. What did he mean by giving back? "I have been given life for a start, and within life I've been given opportunities, like a nice home; I'm in a position at the moment where I only have to work four days a week; I have my needs met, life has been generous with me, I should not kind of hoard all that to myself, but rather give something back to the Universe, whether it's materially, financially, or whether it's in time or in whatever way I see fit."

The Universe? He described what he meant by referring to an image that he had shared during a Quaker Meeting for Worship:

"I think of all life as One. So when I say give something back to the universe I mean give something back to the whole of which I am a part, and obviously all people are part of that Whole. Humans have a lot more consciousness than any other form, but all the forms that we see are an illusion on some level. Ultimately, it's all One."

§

SANDRA

To Sandra, a mature student midwife of 39, spirituality had a somewhat different hue. She had always wanted to travel and had been to more than thirty-five countries, mostly in Africa and the Middle East, usually going alone. She belonged to Women Welcome Women Worldwide whose members offer each other hospitality. She had grown up in Switzerland where, as a teenager, she had earned money with babysitting and Saturday jobs in order to be able to save to travel. Despite her parents' lack of funds, Sandra had never felt she was missing out; in her home, family and friends were more valued than success and money. Her work was more important to her than money too. Her Masters degree had been in Anthropology, and with it she could have earned £5,000 a month: her friends who did the same degree were all now working for development agencies, government organisations or NGOs, some in exotic locations. But she soon realised that this work is done in offices and that it was not for her. While studying, she had found a part-time job as an outreach social worker, trying to contact young people on the streets who were at risk of becoming criminal or caught up in prostitution. She was pleased to be able to support herself on these earnings and not rely on her parents' contribution to her studies. Later on, while unemployed because of ill health and living on benefits amounting to 80% of her previous rather meagre salary, she lived so frugally that she was still able to save money for travelling. What gave her enjoyment was being with or talking on the telephone to friends and being outside.

Now, however, Sandra was embarking on a new career, recently having begun a degree in midwifery, a skill which she planned to take overseas, despite the fact that while travelling in West Africa in 2004 she had been involved in a head-on bus crash in which all the passengers on the other bus were killed. Sandra's hip was dislocated in the accident. It was agonising at the time and she had suffered debilitating, chronic pain ever since. Sitting for any length of time was difficult for her, so she decided to go back to one of her early ideas, to train as a midwife, as this work would not involve too much sitting.

Spirituality, she said, had always been part of her life. She grew up in a Catholic family; "There was no doubt for me that there was God. But for me it's not a man with a white beard, it's more like a positive energy that we can access. I don't know whether my experience comes from how I was brought up, going to church. Later on I keep meeting people from the Baha'i faith, and I just like going to their prayer meetings but I have never signed or anything." Sandra's faith was a constant source of comfort to her. "When I was in a lot of pain I think it helped me, I wasn't alone, or when my pain was really, really bad I did say, 'Why did I survive the accident if the rest of my life is just pain? Why didn't I get killed?' And I think the will to continue to live comes from my family and friends but definitely from my faith as well."

Sandra was resolutely unimpressed by money and possessions. She remembered a time when she was a teenager when some boys were trying to show off with their motorbikes, which did not have the desired effect on her. She also remembered other people having been impressed with her at the age of eighteen because she was fluent in three languages, and realised that you can be valued for things other than possessions. For her now, luxury would be being able to pay to go to an osteopath to have her pain sorted out. She did not even know if she would be able to find the money to continue her course, but did not consider herself to be poor. "Come with me to Africa", she said, "and see what poverty's really about. Actually, it doesn't need to be Africa, some parts of England would do."

§

CLIVE

Clive's version of spirituality was different again, yet encompassed both his own inner exploration and wholehearted outward action intended to address suffering in the world. Clive had never established himself in the world of work. Although he loved working hard, he found the idea of working forty-eight weeks of the year and becoming dependent on the organisation for which he worked a terrifying idea. When he left school he had tried to start a career, having felt the pressure to do so. He quite enjoyed working in a bio-medical lab but felt uncomfortable with the constraints of the working life and started travelling, hitchhiking round Europe; he also went to Israel and worked on kibbutzim and became very interested in their way of life. Later, after doing a degree in photography, he worked for a while as a teacher at an art college, but then the old discontent returned and he gave up his job. Now Clive worked as a decorator and floor-sander, as and when he needed to, but his life revolved around meditation and voluntary work in a leprosy community in India and with olive growers in Palestine, living in essence as a nomad with no home base, staying from time to time with his brother on the south coast.

Clive was accustomed to living on little. His mother divorced his father, whom he had never seen again, when Clive was three. The maintenance allowance his mother received from his father was twenty-one shillings a week. But, like Gloria and Mary and others in similar financial circumstances, Clive did not feel that he had missed out:

"We lived on a council estate, and I think in those days this sort of post-war welfare state was a very different beast to what it is now. There wasn't the stigma, Britain was a more socialist kind of country so this council estate was kind of teachers and, it was middle class and a mixture. And the house was nice. It was cold, there was ice on the windows inside in the winter, but it seemed OK to me, I never felt that I had a deprived childhood. And I think Britain in the early 60s was a poorer place, it didn't have this kind of consumerism that we have now. I can honestly say that I had a very good childhood, I mean there was a lot of freedom. By today's terms it may have seemed there was an element of neglect because my mother was out doing what she could to provide for us, but within that I think I had a lot of freedom. I just remember having a lot of freedom to go fishing, getting up to mischief you know, bird nesting, collecting insects, a lot of time with nature; I think that's how I developed the love of nature that I've sort of carried with me really."

Travelling had had a huge influence on Clive. In 1988 he went on his first visit to India. On a later trip there he took up meditation, and had now been practising regularly for ten years. It had had an immense impact on his life. He explained: "If we drop thought, sense, ideas, identification, position, if all those things are suddenly not there, what remains? And for me what remains is a wonderful sense of peace, spaciousness, an incredible sense of wellbeing which we can then carry into our daily lives. And for me, that sense of wellbeing has infused itself into every area of my life, I'd say it's extraordinary, and it's mysterious, not just for me but for my whole community of people who do this strange thing, for quite long hours sometimes; it has an incredible impact on their lives, always positive."

Meditation had led Clive to find great contentment in simply being.

> "I just love having unplanned time, I just sit around not doing very much, reading, or not even doing that. I think there's a lot of value in it, personally. My belief is that we are obsessed with doing and completely ignore the sense of being, so completely miss out on this sense of experience. There's a stigma to it, you're not supposed to sit around doing nothing. We're expected to define ourselves by what we do. It's always in the realm of doing, 'what do *you* do?' And for me it's very hard to answer that question because a lot of the time I don't do very much, but it's difficult for me to articulate that because people don't understand, there's not any understanding, no faculty to understand this idea that it's possible to live a very wonderful life without doing very much."

Because Clive emphasised the sense of wellbeing he gained from meditation, I pressed him to say more about his experience. His explanation was intricate, and elements of what he said were reminiscent of things that others told me too, for instance the discussion of what is *real*:

> "I've recently become interested in solitude so there's a place I go in India where I spend quite long periods in a cave and spend up to two months without seeing anyone. The process of meditation is about letting go of our need to control what's going on around us, so a sense of allowing things to be as they are, rather than constantly trying to manipulate it. And what it also does is create a huge amount of space in our lives; a lot of what seems to appear is this sense of peace and contentment. It's not easy. At first it's frustrating because we've become accepting

of the fact that our thinking process never stops. It is about being able to experience spaces within thoughts, and to go into those spaces and make the spaces longer, and then to be able to drop thought completely, and with the dropping of thought, the dropping of identification, then ultimately the dropping of self really. This idea of self as a separate entity no longer exists so where the self and other conflicts, this conflict begins to break down and there is a much greater intimacy with reality, rather than our reality being constructed round what the Buddha would have called dukkha, unsatisfactoriness, that we try and fulfil; you know, I want an apple, I want a cup of tea, I need to go and buy a new car, I want promotion in my job, I want more sex or more drink. It's always something reaching out for, ways of wanting, that I think takes us away from this wonderful sense of being which I think is our essence."

Clive had written that he had had a modest lifestyle consciously for about 25 years, but the timing was actually more to do with the realisation that it was something he had always had, that, "I just wasn't interested in this hamster wheel mentality, this running after happiness and buying things and trying to maintain some sort of satisfaction through exterior things. I think perhaps I always realised it and perhaps going to India was a big trigger for me because just seeing the way of life there, the way people live, was just incredible." He found the people he met in India to be open and inquisitive, because they had the time to sit around and not do very much. He had now spent a total of about five years in the country, bringing back to Britain the lessons that less is more, simplicity is life-affirming and satisfying, and that comfort encourages laziness. But he readily acknowledged that the way he had chosen to live was possible only for a single person without family to consider.

India was not the only influence on Clive's modesty, nor non-doing his only mode of living. He also attributed his modest lifestyle to an instinctive mistrust of capitalism and his interest in politics and counter culture. Describing himself as a socialist who had come to distrust ideologies as a means of liberation, he had been politically active through most of his life, with groups like CND, the Anti-Nazi League, anti-apartheid, the Socialist Workers Party, the anti-road movement and the anti-war movement which opposed the invasion of Iraq. But he had got fed up with being anti: "I'd rather be for peace than anti-war really, and I realised I was surrounded by a lot of angry people, and I think this triggered my own anger that was perhaps something left from my childhood, whatever, injustice. I always felt this very strong sense of injustice."

T How has your meditation experience interacted with your anger at injustice?

C Yeah, good question. It's an ongoing process I think. I've begun doing more service-orientated, not exactly political, more humanitarian work. I go to Palestine every year with a group and work with the Palestinian olive farmers where they get a lot of harassment from the illegal Israeli settlers... So to answer your question... It's good for me to be in that sort of situation to see all my potential anger but not to explode with it, not to seal it in but to see it for what it is and just to say my anger's not going to change anything, in fact it's going to make things worse. I don't think anger can ever have a positive effect on the world. The opposite is usually true. Look out there [pointing out of the window], look at how we live, look at the anger out there, there's a lot of it about.

So Clive's quiet contentment was counter-balanced by his active engagement in the world. His loss of self in meditation was complemented by connecting with global events, and he was an avid follower of current affairs on the internet. He saw the very inner and the very outer as two halves of a whole, "This balance between nourishing myself and trying to be engaged with the world. It's really important for me that that balance is somehow maintained".

One of his favourite activities was cooking for friends: "Give me a kitchen and some food and I'm really happy, a nice bottle of wine and some music and it's great, a really nice thing to do." Generosity was important to Clive. Because he did not have the financial resources to be materially generous he tried to be bountiful with his time, "especially as it is so rare that people give each other their full attention." Indeed, the things that were most important in life to Clive were friendship, generosity, kindness, silence, health, good food and playing the fiddle. He also enjoyed long hikes, a good train journey and a pint in the pub. The way he lived meant that he was "surrounded by interesting people and things that give life meaning." What was this meaning? "For me the meaning of life is happiness, it's as simple as that. I think if we're happy we can have a huge impact on the world. Just being happy and joyful I think rebounds; just like the anger rebounds in a negative way. If we feel happy we can cultivate lots of other positive attributes. From happiness comes compassion, from happiness comes love. I think that's all we can do really."

* * *

Enquiries into how people define their own spirituality reveal myriad interpretations of the word.[382] But there is amongst them an overarching sense that spirituality is closely bound to questions of meaning and purpose, wholeness and belonging, values and principles. It inhabits or engenders a sense of connection between the deeply personal and the universal. In my own view, an experience or perception felt by an individual to be *uplifting* can also be characterised as spiritual. Feeling uplifted could be described as having a sense of being picked up and held aloft for a while, above the routine, the mediocrity and the distress that can form a significant part of daily life, in a realm which offers succour, inspiration, or delight. Moments of enlightenment can also be seen to have a spiritual aspect, for they involve new insights, and depth of understanding of the meaning or the connectedness of things. While descriptions of the spiritual can have a decidedly ethereal quality, my own understanding is that spiritual experience is firmly rooted in actual bodily, social or emotional experience. It originates with the senses, with the sight of the vast and distant night sky maybe, or a tender photograph; with the sound of children playing happily, the wind in the trees, or a sublime or cheerful piece of music; with the movement of dancing or digging; the touch of a stranger's helping hand, or the smell of growing woods in the rain. While spirituality may be an abstract concept it is not theoretical. Its wellspring is essentially experiential.

Effects of a sense of the spiritual

Although it is necessary to define the general territory of the spiritual, it is perhaps more helpful to ask what spirituality *does* than to try and pin down more closely what it *is*.[383] I would say that conscious awareness of a spiritual dimension may inspire a sense of transcendence, a glimpse of a mysterious greater reality beyond the familiar. At least as much, however, it can deepen and enrich concrete experience of the here and now. In either case, for a spiritual dimension to become discernible to the individual requires that they reflect on their experience with an open, receptive heart and mind. For Ursula King, spirituality can be linked to all human experiences but has a particularly close connection with relationships – whether with ourselves, with others, or with a transcendent entity, often called the Divine, God or Spirit.[384] Thus, while religion is a particular form or expression of spirituality, spirituality need have nothing to do with religion. Whether found in religious or in secular discourse, spirituality is generally understood to refer to many different experiences and practices, and to be life-enhancing.[385] Indeed, people who are in touch with their spirituality appear to be in a better state of mental health than those who are not.[386] This surely has much to do with the greater subjective wellbeing experienced by people who feel some sense of meaning and purpose in their lives.

Our power to create meaning depends partly on the kinds of experience and experiences we have,[vi] but also on our capacity for perceptiveness, reflection and making connections. Although nobody is entirely immune from moments of uplift or enlightenment or feelings of relatedness, there is clearly a huge range in the individual susceptibility to such moments, and it seems likely, as with other human attributes, that there are innate differences in inclination towards spiritual sensitivity. Also, one person may come to understand and label some life-enhancing experience as spiritual while another may not. Major life events may awaken an inkling of a dimension beyond the everyday; so too may small incidents or interactions. But it might take deliberate consciousness-raising efforts regarding spirituality to stimulate the necessary reflection. An example of how a specifically designed intervention can awaken a sense of the spiritual is expressed in the declaration of an Occupational Therapy student who, after taking a module on spirituality for her professional group, declared, "The word spirituality opens up a whole new world – I'm starting to explore and find myself. I am making changes in my life that I never thought I would, and it has made me understand myself a lot better."[387] At its most powerful then, spirituality is an *active* inclination, involving conscious awareness of and engagement with those facets of life which speak to the spirit rather than to worldly needs and desires.

The group and the individual

While spirituality is generally beneficial for wellbeing, one must beware naiveté in assuming that the spiritual is exclusively benevolent. There is such a thing as a negative spiritual belief.[388] For example, Hitler claimed a spiritual basis for his political philosophy,[389] and it is easy to see how his speeches whipped up a sense of belonging, meaning and greater purpose amongst attendees at Nazi rallies. The massed singing of hymns or anthems (national or otherwise) may also have these effects, with benign or malign significance, according to the context.

However, the growing weight now given to that which we call spiritual is generally a positive development. This is not only from a personal point of view but also from the point of view of the wellbeing of society as

---

vi Experience is a word that can be used in a general, overall sense, as in a particular individual's experience of life, or can to refer to a specific occasion, feeling or perception.

a whole, for there seems to be a connection between spiritual awareness and ethical behaviour. For example, a thirty-year study of spiritual experience in Britain[390] found that almost without exception, people link their spiritual or religious experience with a moral imperative. Typically the initial effect of their experience is to make them look beyond themselves; they have an increased desire to care for those closest to them, to take issues of social justice more seriously and to be concerned about the total environment. One person told David Hay, the author of this research, "I now have far more respect for my physical surroundings as well as my fellow humans… I don't think they were important to me before".[391] Others, Hay found, associated their moment of spiritual insight with a radical shift in their life's purpose. An illustration of this was the account of a woman who told him that she gave up a job that was meaningless to her in order to look after troubled children, dating her decision from half an hour of sitting in the park on a sunny evening."[392] But spirituality is not an exclusively adult domain; children as young as six can communicate a sense of it. In a study with primary school children, Ruth Nye, a collaborator of Hay's, found children's spirituality to be rich and individual. She described it as 'relational consciousness'.[393] This was based on how the children's 'spiritual' conversation was unusually perceptive, and expressed thoughts about how the child related to things, to other people, to him/herself, and to God. Out of this 'relational consciousness' arose meaningful aesthetic experiences, personal and traditional responses to mystery and being, and moral insights.

Conclusion: The Importance of Spiritual Values

The role and clear benefits of conscious spirituality contain a vital message for the contemporary world: that is, that we need to give prominence to the spiritual dimensions of life, our own and others', if individual and societal wellbeing is really to be addressed. While well-intentioned policy rhetoric is in place in the areas of health and education in Britain, as well as in some business contexts, everyday experience and observation leads me to believe that the realisation of policy in day-to-day practice is patchy, to say the least. The spiritual side of a person is still usually the poor relation of those aspects which fit our current social and economic model. Spiritual values such as trust, kindness, generosity, humility, honesty, wisdom, discernment, patience, beauty and compassion, values which link us with each other and with the natural world,[394] are in striking contrast to the worldly, exclusive, often profit-driven, values of self-interest, competitiveness, expediency, secrecy, self-protection and short-sightedness which are usually more evident in public and business life, and are also to be found in institutional settings.

While it is certainly true that there is a growing interest among certain individuals in activities and alternative approaches that promote community and interdependence, such as using farmers markets and food co-ops, sharing little-used equipment, and co-housing, as well as support for voluntary work, ethical investment, fair trade, and other altruistic and co-operative endeavours, individualism and materialism still dominate our culture. These values are sadly at odds with the universal, boundless, interconnected quality of the spiritual. On the larger scale, commercial interests as well as some institutional organisations tend to treat people as pawns in a life-sized chess match and behave as though the human race (and other species) were not intrinsically of value in themselves, nor part of one and the same interconnected biosphere. If we are serious about human wellbeing and environmental sustainability we need to build a society in which the many sources of uplift and enlightenment, and the numerous forms of connectedness are the direct and indirect priorities for investment – together, of course, with the provision of a reasonable basic standard of living for *all*.

This may sound madly impractical and hopelessly utopian – even perhaps to those to whom such a change of values appeals. It is certainly not altogether clear what such a society would look like. One thing that is certain about such a society, though, is that the generation of private wealth would no longer be the primary objective of political economy as it is now. Rather, it is the many facets of the spiritual which could actually best guide the construction of a personal and collective value system which would most effectively support human and ecological flourishing. If such a value system were to be adopted across society, a set of practical priorities would emerge. These would accord with the belief that the human spirit thrives best in a social and political environment in which the individual and all their community are safe, housed, fed, respected, cared for, nurtured and interdependent; where responsible freedom of action, expression and association are the norm. This society would operate in a natural environment of biodiversity, clean air and water, and fine landscapes. It would be very different from our current society of desperately unjust inequalities, a society which pushes luxury bathrooms and kitchens, costly cars, watches and jewellery, gimmicky devices, designer clothes and exotic holidays, and thinks of investment as stocks and shares and gold bars. The only form of monetary wealth which truly sustains us and which can itself be sustained is that which is distributed evenly enough to enable everyone to have a decent existence, and to support the common good from which all benefit. It is the common good made palpable, rather than individual, competitive, worldly 'success', which offers enduring connectedness, belonging and meaning.

9

Creativity – A Human Need

A Means of Communication and the Essence of Generation

Creativity and spirituality, creativity and innovation

Spirituality is intertwined in complex ways with creativity. While the individual's experience of spirituality involves the taking in of inspiration from the external world, in the form of some kind of discernment, creativity entails the outward communication of new ideas from the mind of the individual. But although the relative emphasis on inward and outward processes is rather different, spirituality and creativity share important features. Both tend to involve periods of communing with the self; both require an active, open, reflective, questing stance; both also require the capacity to entertain memories from the past, perceptions in the present, and notions of things impalpable or not yet in existence; and both involve the making of connections and/or meaning.

While studies of creativity have tended to focus on exceptionally creative individuals, whether scientists or artists, all human beings have some capacity to plan, to design, to imagine, to perform and to make. Archaeologists well know this from their investigations of past cultures and artefacts.[395] We are all born with certain types and strengths of innate creative potential. In fact, researchers into creativity draw a distinction between what they call 'Big-C', the kind of creativity which makes a major contribution to a particular field, and 'Little-c', that which produces something new but which does not have a wider impact.[396] In other words, creativity is involved in producing new ideas of any scale, from paradigm shifts in scientific or artistic thought to simply rearranging your kitchen.[397] There is also the important distinction to be made between the creativity whose motivation is expressive or aesthetic and that which aims to advance knowledge or improve practice. While there is always destructive potential in creativity if skills are applied to such ends as the development of new weapons or insidious methods of persuasion, creativity in general has an inestimable role to play in making a better world.

The importance of creativity in human life, like that of spirituality, has also, at least in theory, become more widely recognised in recent years. Around the turn of the twenty-first century it became common in a number of western countries for governments to enshrine the intention to foster creativity in educational policy documents.[398] One of these was the UK Department of Education and Employment's 1999 publication, *All our Futures: creativity, culture and education*,[399] which advocated the development of skills and approaches which would foster people who could adapt, see connections, innovate, communicate and work collaboratively – for employers.[400] In 2004 the Scottish Executive's[401] website contended that it was the Executive's duty to create the conditions that allow creativity to flourish, adding that "Creativity is as valuable in retail, education, health, government and business as culture".[402] Some commentators have argued that although such policy appears to be value-neutral it actually arises out of a cultural context which is over-marketised at global, local and personal levels, and is thus motivated primarily by the desire to enhance productivity and competitiveness[403] – and profit.

The commercial impetus for the nurturing of creativity may, however, be misplaced as the capacity to produce marketable innovation may not be as rosy a proposition as is commonly assumed. For one thing, the production of new consumer goods is highly likely to carry an environmental cost.[404] For another, according to the recent analysis of one economist, Robert Gordon,[405] the scope left for large scale fundamental innovation is now limited, and the potential for novelty largely resides simply in the further development of existing products. Gordon identifies three industrial revolutions: the period 1750 – 1830 which saw the invention of steam engines, cotton gins, early railways and steamships; 1870 -1900 which witnessed the introduction of electric light, workable internal combustion engines, fresh running water to urban homes, and the telephone; and 1960 – 1995 which was when computers were adopted and the worldwide web invented. Many of the inventions and innovations that have led to better living conditions and contributed to economic growth, Gordon points out, have been one-offs or capable of little further development. Furthermore, he suggests, just one of the many late nineteenth century inventions has done incomparably more to improve the quality of life than any of the portable electronic devices developed recently.

While this is unarguable, however, we cannot know what beneficial technological paradigm shifts may yet be possible; nanotechnology and gene therapy, for instance, are still in their infancy. But we certainly do not need novelty for its own sake. Wisdom is required to distinguish between ideas whose effects will be positive from those whose impacts will not.[406]

Leaving novel consumer goods and commercially-driven calls for the support of creativity behind, there is no doubt that we do urgently need imaginatively gifted individuals who have the skills and vision to come up with the agricultural, economic, political, technological, and social innovations that will carry us into a more sustainable future. This, and the major role that personal creativity plays in supporting wellbeing, are the real reasons why creativity requires every encouragement. We do not all to need to be an Einstein, Picasso or Beethoven, a Dyson, Spielberg or Lennon, but there are low-key, everyday kinds of creative and imaginative capacity that everyone can exercise, both for sheer enjoyment and for the role I will propose they have in contributing to environmental sustainability.

Creativity for Health and Wellbeing

Taking part in creative activity of any kind can bring immense pleasure and personal fulfilment. Some people find in addition that creative recreation enhances their occupational performance. One such is a physician-scientist who believes that investing serious time and energy in sculpting have made him a better scientist and teacher. He speculates that, "being creative with the hands or the heart in satisfying ways might open up more circuits in the brain and allow more alternative neuronal pathways to fire."[407] Creativity is thus of great significance for its power to enhance our enjoyment of and effectiveness in life, as well as our sense of purpose, efficacy and identity. Anybody who has made or devised anything, even everyday, be it a recipe, a book case, a story, a Christmas card, a clay pot, a flower arrangement, a plumbing system, a bird table or a costume for a school play, will have experienced this to some degree. There is something mysterious and marvellous about producing a new entity from raw materials or simply out of one's head. The activities of the fulfilled modest consumers encompassed many and various examples as we have heard and are still to hear, including the creation of a fold-away kitchen space, the setting up of a workers' co-operative, sewing banners, planning a smallholding, making wine, and the cultivation of productive land out of undernourished acres. If objective evidence were needed in addition to the positive subjective feeling that accompanies creativity, it has been observed that levels of the neurotransmitter serotonin, which influences wellbeing and happiness, rise during involvement in satisfying creative activity.[408]

The arts

There are many types of creativity. The arts are a vital manifestation, but many art forms are less integral to everyday life today than they were in past millennia.[409] Now, 'the arts' have become largely separated from daily life, tucked away in concert halls and art galleries, and tend in Britain, to be associated particularly with the middle class. Indeed, in recent decades the arts have become increasingly colonised by the market economy.[410] Some less culturally inclined people might regard music, dance, visual, dramatic and literary arts as optional extras to what they see as more essential aspects of life, but human existence would be poor indeed without the flesh that arts activities and products add to its bare bones. Artistic expression, moreover, is in principle available to everyone, either as creator or audience. While the talent necessary to direct a film or design a workable building is thinly spread, many forms of artistic activity are wide open to everyone to try. And a beginner's attempts might one day, in return for much practice and dedication, turn into a virtuoso performance. But even if the gain in skill is limited, creative or performance activity can be a source of untold enjoyment and fulfilment, solitary or collective. Indeed, it has been suggested that the experience of getting involved in creative activities can reduce the pull of extrinsic values.[411] Given the importance I have suggested is to be attached to intrinsic values both for personal wellbeing and for sustainable living, and the need to resist extrinsic motivation, this effect of creative involvement is one to be taken very seriously.

Whether for practitioner or recipient, artistic creations and enterprises offer aesthetic pleasure and intellectual fascination. They open up new dimensions and perspectives that broaden and deepen our understanding of ourselves, other people and our surroundings. They stimulate new ways of seeing the world and thinking about it. The arts constitute a site of connection-making, where meaning is contested, empathy evoked, sensibility honed, values challenged or reinforced, longing quenched, new possibilities illuminated, questioning instigated, and a sense of belonging to a wide world and a greater reality perceived. Artistic creativity is a uniquely human capacity, and visual arts, drama, literature, music, poetry, sculpture, and every other form together play a crucial part in turning mere existence into worthwhile living. In whatever era human beings have lived or will

231

live, we have personal needs which can partly and powerfully be met by art. Josephine Hart, a novelist who had a 'love affair' with poetry and set up regular public readings of works of the great poets, found that poetry, "this trinity of sound, sense and sensibility... expressed the inexpressible". "For a girl with no sense of direction", she wrote, "poetry was a route map through life" – and a lifeline during her terminal illness.[412]

Music

Or take music. Music has been a significant part of human culture since prehistoric times.[413] Indeed, eminent neurologist Oliver Sacks believes that we are an innately musical species no less than a linguistic one.[414] Now as ever, whether making music, or as an audience, music plays a special role for most people. Music has undoubted psychological and physiological benefits and research is attempting to understand them.[415] For instance, one study found that music by Mozart reduced the stress levels of critically ill patients;[416] another that introducing live music and visual arts into antenatal and postnatal wards, a day surgery unit, a trauma and orthopaedic ward and a HIV/AIDS unit was beneficial for a wide variety of patients. It brought about a reduction in anxiety and depression and resulted in measurable psychological and physiological benefits such as lowered blood pressure, shorter duration of labour, less need for analgesia and shorter hospital stays.[417] Music can help fluid movement in Parkinson's patients who are generally unable to move, and enhance some kinds of functioning in people with advanced Alzheimer's.[418]

It is good for the healthy as well as the sick. This is important to realise as health and wellbeing need active maintenance. Making music is probably the richest human emotional, sensorimotor, and cognitive experience. It involves listening, watching, feeling, moving and coordinating, remembering and expecting, as well as frequently giving rise to profound emotional states.[419] Music brings people together, to play, to dance or to listen, and thus generates common purpose and shared experience. Singing with others has a particular ability (with absolutely no environmental cost) to boost a sense of emotional wellbeing, in addition to its benefits to physical health.[420] Many people find themselves uplifted on particular occasions when it is customary to burst into communal song, such as at a football match or singing carols at Christmas, while regular singers with choirs have been found to sense an enhancement to their wellbeing from their singing activity, through improved mood, focused concentration, deep controlled breathing, social support, cognitive stimulation and regular commitment.[421]

This effect has been made visible to millions in the several television series chronicling the development of choirs by musician Gareth Malone with different groups of people in Britain, including inhabitants of Slough, military wives and teenage schoolboys. Another model of musical activity is El Sistema, the approach pioneered in Venezuela from 1975 and now acknowledged worldwide as the most significant example of collective musical education, and the inspiration for a profusion of similar initiatives on all continents.[422] The founder, José Abreu, adopted a particular, large-scale approach to instrumental instruction and the practice of music, through the performance of symphony orchestras, as an exercise in social integration, an antidote to economic deprivation and an alternative for children to joining gangs, drug-dealing and violence. A musician involved with Sistema Scotland, which was set up in 2008 in one of the most disadvantaged areas of the country, remarked, "Four years ago you'd be lucky if you got five minutes work out of the class in 40 minutes. Now, the children will rehearse for up to three hours a night... That's a huge change – motivation, concentration and being aware of themselves, that they are achieving something. Their families tell us they do more things now as a family because of their involvement in music."[423]

Creative engagement

The impact of music-making on wellbeing in clear. But the new field of neuro-aesthetics has claimed that the arts in all their forms have a unique value, in that perception of the out-of-the-ordinary in the creative stimulates all areas of the brain and their multiple connectors like nothing else: the mapping of the brains of people watching dance, looking at visual art or listening to music has shown that these activities increase synaptic activity and result in greater interaction between the left and right hemispheres.[424] In respect of active creative engagement, beneficial effects were observed when children in England were given the opportunity to take part in a variety of creative activities via the Creative Partnerships scheme.[425] This initiative, which ran from 2002 to 2011, brought creative workers such as artists, architects and scientists into certain schools to work with teachers in the most challenged communities in the country; they worked with over one million children and 90,000 teachers. The great majority of head teachers whose schools participated reported an improvement in pupils' confidence, motivation, enjoyment of school, ability to learn independently, and communication skills. A study of 13,000 of the young people who had taken part in Creative Partnership activities found that these students outperformed the national average at Key Stage 3.[426] In one of the primary schools involved it was noted that, regardless of type of creativity involved, the more that young children developed their attention and their ability to focus on details, the greater their ability to link features of one situation to another, and then to see the bigger picture. They thus began to practise 'vital habits of mind', which could be applied to science and everyday problem-solving as well as the arts.[427] In today's complex and globalised world, the ability to see the bigger picture is more crucial than ever.

Arts, economics, politics

Engagement in artistic endeavour clearly has a beneficial impact, both immediate and long-term. But, while it is true that artists from a variety of disciplines have been increasingly engaged in a wide range of healthcare and community settings, supporting clinical care, enhancing healthcare environments, and promoting community wellbeing,[428] the British Coalition government demonstrated its lack of understanding of the vital role of the arts for individual health and wellbeing and social cohesion, not only in its cuts to public expenditure on arts and culture, which were predictable at a time of recession, but by withdrawing funding from Creative Partnerships and planning to remove all creative subjects from the curriculum of the proposed English Baccalaureate 'performance measure' for all 16 year-old students.[429] This decision was, in fact, overturned in response to public criticism, but it reveals, nevertheless, a barren, narrowly mechanistic understanding of education.

The thought of giving such exclusive weight to academic subjects certainly seems at odds with the requirement that schools actively promote the spiritual, moral, social and cultural development of all pupils. Official pressure to emphasise a narrow, easily assessed group of core subjects to the detriment of physical, moral, civic and artistic education has also been felt from beyond British shores, in the OECD's escalation of three-yearly standardised testing of 15-year-olds in maths, science and reading in order to construct international rankings. Many educators have expressed concern at this development, believing that education is not only preparation for working life, but also for participation in democracy and a life of personal growth and wellbeing.[430] Artistic creativity and communication are not for the good times only. They are a constant human need. In the view of American clinical psychologist, Seymour Saracen, there is a universal human capacity for artistic expression and development which is not generally understood or valued in young children and is therefore usually allowed to whither. "The need, indeed yearning, for artistic expression is never truly extinguished", he says, and claims that, "It goes underground, a festering source of dissatisfaction in quotidian living".[431]

So far I have concentrated on the benefits to be gained from the arts, culture and creativity for the nurture and maintenance of individual and social health and wellbeing, but there is also an important dimension to their potential role in social transformation. There is in fact a smudged distinction between the personal and the collective here, to be found in the observation that discontent at the conditions of everyday life, either for the artist him- or herself or on behalf of his or her fellow human beings, often stimulates or finds expression in artistic creativity. There are many examples of art born of social injustice and political frustration.[432] It is also notable that in the areas of Europe hardest hit by the economic crisis, artistic activity is thriving. Spaniards have flocked to theatres in record numbers, despite huge funding cuts, and in Italy the foundation that organises Romaeuropa festival has found it difficult to meet audience demand.[433] The art scene in Greece has also flourished, adapting to the new economic conditions with touring exhibitions, one-off performances, and other events, not driven by motivation to cater to rich buyers. Athens has been able to boast more than fifty non-profit, non-hierarchical and self-organised art collectives, many occupying temporary spaces and collaborating with other institutions and groups.[434] This frenzy of artistic activity in the context of huge economic hardship, social upheaval and political uncertainty bears out the judgement of the influential behavioural psychologist and social philosopher B.F. Skinner, that, "Although sometimes questioned, the survival value of art, music, literature, games and other activities not tied to the serious business of life is clear enough... A world which has been made beautiful and exciting by artists, composers, writers, and performers, is as important for survival as one which satisfies biological needs."[435] Art, moreover, is vital to stimulating our way of thinking about solutions to the problems we find ourselves grappling with, to finding radically new ways of living. It can contribute much to "the gigantic influx of hope, resourcefulness and social innovation" that we so urgently need;[436] that is, the practice of art has a 'path-finding role'.[437]

At a time when the biological survival of much of humanity is threatened by the very way that the human style of living has developed in the age of mass production and consumption, the arts embody a particular potential to influence the direction of our future trajectory. As Robyn Archer, an Australian advocate of the arts, herself a singer, writer, and director, has declared, art is not just entertainment, art is not just creative industry; it is "the imaginative and often sublimely pleasurable safe place where you can have a dangerous conversation. It is primarily a philosophical and ethical platform sorely needed in today's world... Because the arts employ metaphor and abstraction, allegory and illusion, analogy and experimentation, they help us to think through our human situation... We need to nurture revolutionary thinking to create evolutionary futures."[438]

Creativity and sustainability

There are reasons of a different kind, too, why creativity is of particular significance if we are to embrace the future in a constructive, hopeful spirit. One is that whole-hearted involvement in creative activity is rather inimical to an enthusiasm for material consumption. Time, thought and energy devoted to amateur dramatics, mapping special features of your locality or working on a novel is time and – more importantly – attention not spent on shopping. Another is that many forms of creative activity, such as poetry-writing, collage, drawing, papier mâché, mime, patchwork, organic gardening, and musical composition to name some obvious examples, do not demand much, if anything at all, in the way of virgin materials or non-human energy. They thus incur a vanishingly small environmental cost. In a world of shrinking material resources, which is likely one day to make easy dependence on physical materials and equipment less possible, the cultivation of imagination, resourcefulness and creative skills will become all the more relevant. We need to learn how to accept the unavailability of materials and energy in a creative way by developing our ingenuity and ability to improvise.

Words, especially if spoken or sung rather than written down, make no physical (or financial) demands, while their human impact can be profound. The oral traditions of story-telling, song, and wandering players have been rich sources of imaginative production, shared spiritual nourishment and moral lore down the centuries and across cultures, yet have left no physical scar or scarcity behind. Amongst the 10-12 year-old children whose story-making I investigated in a study of the influence of television on children's story-making,[439] the most prolific and imaginative writer, Mike, took enormous joy in story and words. He came from a family, he told me, in which his parents, cousins, aunt and grandmother all took special pleasure in word games, and making up stories and poems. These activities not only provided much entertainment for them but bound them together in shared experience, both in terms of playing together and in communicating their memories, exploits and perceptions to one another.

§

GLORIA

Gloria, 39, was a study participant for whom words were of particular importance. She lived with her husband, 18 year-old daughter and 13 year-old son, and worked part-time as a learning mentor and drama tutor. She had deliberately chosen to work only three days a week so as to be able to exercise her creativity. Raising children, she'd never really wanted to work full-time, "But a lot of it's just been the way I live my life. I don't like working that much, I'd much rather be doing other things, so I try and do work I mainly enjoy and do enough so we can manage." She preferred to devote her time to writing and had got a place to do an MA in creative writing the following autumn. Being creative was very important to Gloria, who had been involved in drama since she was a child. Her father had got her into a Saturday morning drama group when she was 9 to help her overcome her shyness, and at 15 she had successfully auditioned for the Birmingham Youth Theatre. When she was 18 she became pregnant, and then had another baby at 21. She realised that in order to support herself she would need to gain a qualification so, while her children were very young, she did a degree in Drama.

Living on benefits as a single parent had been tough. But Gloria wasn't used to prosperity:

> "The material lifestyle of my childhood was very modest. I come from a working class background, white mother, father from the Caribbean, and my dad wasn't around very much. My mum and dad were together but they weren't married and he didn't live with us full-time but they had a relationship so he came and went as he pleased. And he didn't really give any financial help apart from if we desperately needed school shoes he might; he could disappear for weeks and months on end so we grew up on benefits on a council estate in the Midlands. It sounds really clichéd but we didn't seem to go without. Lots of people say that don't they. I grew up in the 70s and the 80s and I think it was very different to how it is now. There were less things to spend money on. I think we had two holidays in my childhood, so we didn't do things like that. But what was nice was there was a real sense of community on the estates that we lived in. They were built for people in what they called overspill, people in high rise or in housing that wasn't in very good condition; if you wanted to move out of where

you were there were these houses twenty miles away. A community centre was built and Mum was part of that, and a playgroup and a summer play scheme and an old age pensioners' group, and you'd pay a bit of money and every summer they took us to the seaside for the day, and at Christmas they took us to Coventry, Belgrave Theatre, to see a pantomime. Like I say, looking back we didn't have much but it didn't feel like it."

Now Gloria lived with her family in a four bedroom Victorian terraced house in a quiet London street. Her husband shared her approach to life, indeed he also enjoyed writing, and they had at one time run drama workshops together. However, he had recently exchanged his part-time work for a full-time job as an advocate for young people with learning difficulties, because he got fed up with getting overdrawn and not having enough money to carry out essential maintenance to the house or even to go into central London to an art gallery or occasionally buy sandwiches for lunch. Now he was earning £25,000 a year, which was a lot for them, and this had enabled them to camp in France for the first time, and made Gloria's MA possible.

If she had more money, she wouldn't live very differently though, Gloria thought. Comparing herself to her younger sister who was struggling on benefits she said, "I think I have choices. I'm lucky to say that I have a modest lifestyle because I'm choosing. I'm lucky really". Limited finances meant that her family often bought clothes and books in charity shops, cooked fresh food and did not own a dish washer or tumble dryer, or subscribe to extra-terrestrial television.

I wondered why she was not more part of the consumer culture in which everyone is saturated:

"I'm suspicious of capitalism, I suppose. I kind of think that having 'things' doesn't necessarily make us happy, it's not good for us, and it's not good for the environment, the throwaway culture, and I think it can enslave you, the more you want the more you have to work to get it and I think there has to be another way of living your life and I suppose that's what I'm more interested in. I'm not that attracted to things. I find shopping boring, shopping for clothes. There's almost too much choice these days and I can get really anxious and unhappy in a shopping environment. I think it's really the link between work and not being able to do what you want to do. I know people who work very hard, have very good jobs, and buy a lot of things, but they're not happy people and I don't like this idea that we work and work and work and then we retire. I'd rather work a little bit until I drop dead!"

Gloria was an avid reader, a habit she had picked up at home as a child. Keeping up with current affairs was important to her too. Her reading had been a strong influence, she felt, and had given her a sense of the injustices that exist and the inequality of wealth in the world. But this sense started with her parents because, "My dad wasn't around much but when he was at home, my dad doesn't do small talk it's all politics, and even now when he comes to visit we have massive debates, the whole family, about the state of the world. And my dad was a member of the communist party for a while, and my mum was always heavily involved in community things. So that was my background so I think everything else stemmed from that."

§

Enjoying arts and good health

Simply entering into the imagination of another, in whatever form they express themselves, and enjoying the fruits of their talent, clearly adds much to the quality of anyone's life. In fact, the enjoyment of vicarious creativity through actively appreciating the work of creative people appears to have a measurable benefit on health and wellbeing: the results of a major study of 12,000 adults in Sweden suggested that those who attended cinemas, concerts, museums and art galleries lived longer than those who were less culturally active.[440] Personal creativity can also serve a therapeutic function at times of difficulty. Deep-seated issues that are suppressed, avoided or denied can generate serious health risks, but there is a growing body of evidence that indicates that facing and working through grief, shock, fear, conflict and so on in some art form can have invaluable healing effects.[441] One study found, for example, that writing about troubles such as loneliness, death, divorce and trauma improved psychological wellbeing and resilience so much that immune status was still enhanced six weeks later. It is thought that the positive impact of putting experience into words in such a situation is brought about because conscious, controlled, and deliberate processing, as happens in narrative construction, leads to deeper understanding and lower reactivity.[442]

Creativity is, then, clearly significant for our wellbeing in a whole range of proactive and responsive ways. Yet it is not apparently particularly appreciated as a personal attribute.[443] Indeed, there is often little tolerance in society of unconventional, nonconformist thinking, and difference can be pathologised as 'abnormal'.[444] We need to understand that independent thinking, imagination, inventiveness and ingenuity are precious potentials, peculiar to the human species, and to make sure that we derive maximum benefit from them.

Imagination

To create anything new, even if it is only an idea which is new to the thinker but not new in the absolute sense, requires imagination. Unlike creativity, imagination does not necessarily materialise into a tangible product but may remain in thoughts and mental images. It has to do with our capacity to think of the possible rather than the actual.[445] For poet Ted Hughes, imagination was "the faculty without which humanity cannot really exist": it is imagination, he thought, "which embraces both outer and inner worlds in a creative spirit".[446] Alan Moore, highly successful creator of graphic novels *V for Vendetta* and *Watchmen*, likens imagination to a muscle which gets stronger with use. He is of the arresting view, of particular relevance to our present concerns, that if you've got lots of imagination you don't need money, and has declined large payments from Hollywood as a consequence.[447] Spurning of money is also characteristic of another immensely imaginative and successful children's author and illustrator, Raymond Briggs, who told a journalist, "Huge amounts of money have been generated by *The Snowman*. I'm not interested... I don't spend anything... I buy clothes from charity shops".[448] In contrast to these inwardly focused views, radical possibilities for the social world can also been seen to be contained in individual and collective imagination. Imagination is therefore a potentially political characteristic which enables us to challenge an unsatisfactory status quo and try new social arrangements.

This is all rather abstract. Taking a different approach, J.P. Guilford brought an analytical approach to the study of the skills or processes involved in imagination, based on many years spent investigating creative thinking. Guilford distinguished between 'convergent' thinkers whose style of thinking gives them a narrow focus, and 'divergent' thinkers who think in broader terms.[449] By asking people to suggest uses for certain everyday objects, such as a brick, he found that those with a convergent thinking style produced a few rather literal and predictable uses, while a divergent thinking style produced a larger number of less obvious yet still plausible uses. The three abilities which he regarded as crucial for creativity were fluency (number of ideas a person generates); originality (unusualness of ideas); and flexibility (the ability to switch easily from one category to another). But Guilford did not think that creativity was exclusive to certain people. He wrote, "Whatever the nature of creative talent may be, those persons who are recognised as creative merely have more of what all of us have."[450]

E. Paul Torrance, an American psychologist who made a particular study of creativity, built on this framework, developing The Torrance Tests of Creative Thinking, and put much thought into how creative thinking might best be nurtured. "To learn creatively", he asserted, "we question, inquire, experiment, manipulate, or play with ideas and materials... Certainly we cannot say that a child is fully functioning mentally, if the abilities involved in learning and thinking creatively remain undeveloped". He contrasted creative thinking with learning by authority, which is what happens when we accept the word of a teacher, parent, text book, or newspaper. The influence of majority or peer group opinion also often acts as such an authority.[451] Torrance went on to warn that, "Children who are systematically conditioned for brainwashing can hardly be expected to work out solutions to society's problems".[452] Belief in the significance of creative thinking for a positive future was even more forcefully put by the eminent Russian psychologist Lev Vygotsky who wrote in 1967, "We should emphasise the particular importance of cultivating creativity in school-age children. The entire future of humanity will be attained through the creative imagination; orientation to the future... is the most important function of the imagination."[453] Yet the many social pressures which Torrance saw fifty years ago as interfering with creative processes, such as success orientation, fear of making mistakes, pressure to conform, the desire for perfection and the valuing by society of knowledge over attitudes, are no less active today.

Encouraging imagination and creativity

Given that imagination and creativity are both so beneficial to our wellbeing, so necessary for constructing a better future, and are traits apparently latent in every human being, how can they be fostered? Torrance believed that children must be given the chance to think by being allowed to question, doubt, test and prove; this would encourage divergent thinking rather than the convergent kind of thinking which moves towards the 'right' answer, the one accepted or approved solution to a problem.[454] Parents and teachers, he felt, tend to place too many restrictions on children's desire to manipulate the world around them and exercise their curiosity, and that supervising children too closely hinders their development.

Others have continued to pursue this thinking, and more recently it has been pointed out that, "Creativity is wasted if it simply translates into occasional outbursts of 'light relief'... Enjoyable though such activities may be, there is little evidence that, without any stronger rationale, they make a lasting impact on children's development".[455] Rather, creativity needs to be promoted in an integrated fashion. Teachers can help children to develop a creative disposition by stretching them in a such a way that their habitual ways of making sense will no longer suffice, and by encouraging reflection on perspectives other than their own, so that they make their own connections, and their meaning-making capacity expands.[456] But in practice, as we have seen above, nurturing creative potential is still often viewed as separate from the mainstream academic curriculum, and teaching methods are still dominated by the convergent thinking style and a drive for the acquisition of facts.[457]

Living Creatively

One of the two particular sources of inspiration of my own which crystallised in the writing of this book has been the Quaker camp I have attended almost every summer for over twenty years, a week during which families, couples and single people, old hands and newcomers, Quaker or not, from babies to septuagenarians, live together in a field as an eighty-strong community. With only the communal basics of tents, food, wood, water, eco-toilets, tables and chairs and some form of transport in place, I never fail to be impressed at what a good time we generate between us, out of *ourselves* and what is around us. Campers contribute their skills and share their interests in such a way that there is plenty to occupy everyone when they are not just hanging out and enjoying *being*, whatever their taste or age.

There might be story-telling, star-gazing, charcoal-burning, poetry-writing, weaving, pokerwork, foot massage, music-making, pond-dipping, making or flying of kites, and so on. The simplicity of the situation stimulates much experimentation and improvisation: the making of a turf oven for the baking of Chelsea buns; knitting with tent pegs; a solar-heated shower; rigging up a rain shelter over the large fire pit from odd pieces of tent and tent pole; a rapidly put together shadow play on the long marquee wall when the sun was shining brightly on it; a banner sewn by many hands at once, started during the day and so enjoyed that sewing continued in the evening by lamplight; a throwing challenge using the many teabags to emerge out of the several great pots of tea drunk in a single day by such a large gathering. Many campers discover imagination and ingenuity they never knew they had when they come to devise sketches and songs based on the week's happenings for the last evening's Entertainment. Notwithstanding the brief, communal and holiday nature of this burst of basic communal existence, the experience has given me an invigorating glimpse of the possibility of gaining profound satisfaction and pleasure from a simple life, relatively unreliant on material goods and electricity, that draws on and draws out individual and pooled resourcefulness, and the human potential for inventiveness and co-operation. It is a satisfaction and pleasure of lasting value that becomes built into those who experience it, and many campers return for more of these spiritual riches, year after year.

Discussions of creativity usually focus on artistic activity and scientific discovery, yet the concept also has much wider and more immediate, everyday application, as it does at the camp. Indeed, for Donald Winnicott, the renowned English psychotherapist and paediatrician, creativity signified not a work of art but a colouring of the whole attitude to external reality:[458] "It is creative apperception more than anything else", he said, "That makes the individual feel that life is worth living. Contrasted with this is a relationship to external reality which is one of compliance".[459] Thus Winnicott believed that creativity enriches the whole experience of life. Torrance saw creative living in a comparable light, but his understanding conveys a greater energy and an urge to live to some constructive effect. For him, one mark of a person who lives creatively is that "he always has some thorn in his flesh. Always bothered by some problem, always aware of some defect, some need, some deficiency, he is concerned about finding remedies and solutions."[460] One of the characteristics of a creative person is considered to be the ability to see problems where others do not.[461] This is surely complemented by an ability also to spot hidden opportunities. Indeed, the individual with a disposition towards 'wise creativity' looks below the surface and detects a wider range of possibilities and constraints within a situation than others might see.[462]

§

JACKIE

A modest consumer who embodied a creative approach to the whole of her life was Jackie from Reading. Born in 1959, she was very much a doer. Along with family and friends, Jackie's personal list of the things that were important in life included: *working with others for global/*

local sustainability and for global/local justice; having my own role in these activities; keeping up to date, i.e. time to read the paper, check emails, etc; doing the right thing and meaningful work: (love made visible). Her spare time activities and interests included peace and environmental campaigning, volunteering at a refugee women's group and collating a local community e-newsletter, as well as reading, singing, t'ai chi, dancing, playing the flute, cycling and camping.

Jackie found she derived a number of personal benefits from her campaigning activities. One was the frequent company of friends. Now, an important part of her enjoyment of campaigning was the knowledge that she would see friends at meetings, and that they would share the tasks and concerns and nurture each other. To her, working on campaigning with others was a way of creating a sense of belonging, much as going to a football match might be for others. Another, rather unlooked for benefit of Jackie's campaigning involvement had been the development of her creativity: "I regard banner-making as my creative activity. I didn't at first, it was just a job that needed doing but I've got more and more into it. I don't do very much that's just for fun and nothing else, but neither do I do much that is purely hard slog, so I see the campaigning and the banner-making and all that as quite creative."

Jackie took energy and inspiration from the words of others. She related, for instance, how:

> "I was quite moved by a talk that Bruce Kent gave years and years ago about people going to Faslane [the nuclear submarine base on the River Clyde] and they said it's a submarine, we can't get to it, so they learnt how to canoe and got to it that way! It can be like that when I'm learning a new skill and I think what do I need to do, and actually canoeing is great fun, and so is sewing. And I've learnt to how to speak publically in the last couple of years. It's not a job I would have chosen but it was one that needed doing."

Jackie's lifestyle had always been fairly modest. She remembered a childhood lived in the least posh house in a posh, snobby area, where her family had everything they needed but not a lot more.

> "I didn't know at the time but there were times when Dad was unemployed and Mum didn't know where the next meal was coming from, but it was kept quite well hidden from us as kids. We were surrounded by people

who were very wealthy, but as a child I wasn't aware of inequality as an issue, just that we couldn't do lots of things some people could – like horse riding, holidays abroad, fashionable clothes."

But in the last couple of years Jackie's life had become more modest, and more consciously so, "The kind of realisation that reducing our consumption is not an optional extra any more, it's a must-do because the climate threats are just so dire. I think the mainstream view is to bury your head in the sand, whereas if you look out for the tide coming in you can adapt and get out the way". In a sense Jackie saw it as her responsibility to live modestly: "Because I've seen the tide coming in before the majority of other people have, I can kind of set an example. That sounds horribly holier than thou-ish, but I like my life and the example I would like to set is that this is actually quite a fun thing to do; doing the right thing and enjoying your life go together, they're not mutually exclusive." She remained in the same 'crowded' little nineteenth century worker's cottage with her partner and two teenage children to avoid the trap of having to earn ever more money to pay for a bigger house, and had paid off the mortgage so as to reduce her working hours as a nurse, in order to spend more time with her family and on campaigning. But her low consumption lifestyle was not entirely a matter of principle; although it was important to her that the way she lived in practice should be consistent with her beliefs, she also regarded her approach to life in terms of 'enlightened self-interest'. Sitting in her friendly, unkempt little kitchen, which nobody had had time to clear up, I asked what she meant by this. "In terms of my family I want to hand on something to my kids that's worth hanging on to, a liveable planet. I don't want to be part of the generation that saved the banks and lost the biosphere. But it seems that that's quite likely to happen."

Jackie was philosophical about the one aspect of life that she felt she was losing out on, putting her forfeit into a wider context, "The only thing that I'd like to do that I don't do is travel – but in the scheme of things that's not such a big loss, is it?" In fact, Jackie had a philosophical approach to many things, and this seemed to help her to accept the sacrifices she saw as essential: "I think there's an issue about recognising that you're not going to get everything you want but you are going to get some of it, maybe quite a lot of it, and the stuff you're not going to get you have to learn to let go of. In my situation I can do that and it's no big deal, I think if you're used to having more of what you want it's a harder struggle to let go of it".

So much of Jackie's time now was occupied with campaigning that once she had done all the have-to-do stuff, all the want-to-do stuff was just another chore. Her idea of taking time out to relax, however, would be to walk in a wood, by a river. She could not remember a time when she did not enjoy being out in natural surroundings, and had warm memories of her childhood interaction with small, local nature. This, it turned out, prefigured her current campaigning concerns and spirit, and her capacity to derive inspiration for her practical grappling with difficult issues:

> "Down the road there was a wood and a stream and we used to play, and we used to have this kind of fantasy life based on the den, and I just loved this little stream and making bridges and dams and that sort of thing. And I remember one time when it was full of detergent and going to see someone who lived in the street who was a local councillor to moan about it, when I was maybe 10… And I fell in once and had to hold on to nettles to get out and they didn't sting me, and from that I learnt that physically grasping the nettles is sometimes easier than not grasping them."

Conclusion: Cultivating Creativity is Crucial

In a world that is changing so rapidly we need to nurture and encourage creative living on a grand scale. The less we reorder our lives now so as to shrink our dependence on energy and goods, the more the overhauling of our way of life will be forced upon us in the not-so-distant future. In any case, a creative, exploratory approach to the ordinary opens up all sorts of possibilities for enriched everyday experience and sheer enjoyment. It offers dimensions to living that are closed off to those who simply follow a well-trodden path through day-to-day choices and actions.

10

Nurturing Playfulness

Play and creativity

While creativity can certainly be encouraged and cultivated, it is an attribute that cannot be carved into a blank slate. It develops organically out of the experience of playing. Play is known to have a special role in animal development, and Patrick Bateson and Paul Martin are two scholars of the biology of behaviour who have set out examples of play as a driver of problem-solving and creativity in a large number of animal and bird species. They argue that in humans, as in animals, new modes of thought and new forms of behaviour frequently derive from play, especially from 'playful play' (i.e, play without formal rules).[463] Play in a general sense can be defined as any activity which is engaged in for its own sake, for the immediate, pleasurable rewards it brings, rather than for any instrumental purpose. It may be, however, that the experiences acquired during play do result in certain advantages that are felt months or years later.[464] The findings of studies of brown bears in Alaska, for example, even go as far as to suggest that play might enhance these animals' survival chances, through producing behaviourally and immunologically resilient individuals.[465] In view of the weight of evidence to be found in animal studies, Bateson and Martin argue that new forms of human behaviour and new modes of thought frequently derive from 'playful play', play that happens in situations in which the activities have no real world consequences.[466] Such play is an interesting parallel to the arts which, as we have heard, have been said to offer a "sublimely pleasurable safe place where you can have a dangerous conversation".

As far as human beings are concerned there is certainly a strong belief amongst a number of theorists, supported by a considerable body of empirical evidence, that the roots of imagination and problem-solving abilities are to be found in the pretend play of the very young.[467] The Russian psychologist Vygotsky, whose work on cognitive development has proved seminal, was one of these. For him, play is "a novel form of behaviour in which the child is liberated from situational restraints through his activity in an imaginary situation."[468] Vygotsky considered it to be immensely significant that in play a piece of wood could become a doll and a stick could become a horse, because this meant that the thought and activity of play arise out of ideas rather than objects, allowing the child to enact a very changed relationship with his or her immediate, concrete situation.[469]

Remembering transformational play

Memories of just such transformational play were shared by adults at a day of workshops held in1994 by Play for Life, an organisation I shall explain below. Reminiscences included turning the living branch of a willow tree with rope reins into a horse and carriage; setting up an outdoor shop with objects found around the garden such as seeds, apples and cucumbers; making indoor tents out of feather bedding and hoops; games of doctors and nurses using potions made from plants; putting on circus shows using the garden swing as a trapeze; and making an ocean-going liner out of the garden seat, with the clothes prop for a mast, the whole thing festooned with parents' holiday-souvenir pennants. These adults believed they were still reaping the benefits of such childhood episodes, in terms of resourcefulness, creativity and self-confidence.[470]

Play for Life

Play for Life was a small voluntary organisation of the 1980s and1990s which arose out of the anti-war-toy movement of the time. My involvement in its work was the second source of inspiration that resulted in my embarking on this book, the nub of both being attention to the foundations of life-affirming, future-enhancing attitudes, values and behaviours. The group's thinking was that to give a child an imitation weapon as a toy (and later, violent video games) implies endorsement of real-world adult hostility, violence and preparedness to kill and maim, and is thus potentially harmful to the child's developing perceptions, attitudes and values. This is not the same as saying that children should be denied the scope to discharge aggressive feelings in play. A stick or a Lego construction could serve perfectly well as a symbolic weapon, or something to be hurled or broken at moments of emotional need. Later, however, rather than lying around, encouraging aggressive stances, a stick could become a magic wand, a fishing rod, a javelin for testing strength, a spear for hunting mammoths, or a conductor's baton; it could be thrown for the dog to catch, used to draw a picture in the mud or to light a fire, or simply abandoned harmlessly in the garden; Lego bricks would become part of some other construction.

Rather than joining the 'anti' campaign against war toys, Play for Life was set up to stimulate fresh 'pro' thinking about the kinds of play which we believed give positive support to children's social, emotional, cultural and spiritual development, particularly in the context of home life. At this time the Pre-school Playgroups Association was hugely influential in providing varied, sociable and regular play opportunities for the under-5s. From the age of 5 upwards, however, children's play was largely determined by the 'educational', ie, chiefly cognitive concerns of school, by what the market offered, and by what local authorities provided in the way of playgrounds. Out of school, while the commercial world was exerting ever more influence on children at an ever younger age, the freedom to roam and to meet other children and create occupations unsupervised, which previous generations had enjoyed, had shrunk drastically in the face of the real and perceived dangers of traffic and strangers, and the limitations on open space imposed by building development.

Research evidence

While personal memories of transformative play and beliefs about its benefits, such as those of the workshop participants we have just heard, may perhaps be interpreted as rose-tinted nostalgia, objective insights into the effects of such play have come from empirical research. Much has been carried out by Jerome Singer and Dorothy Singer, psychologists at Yale University, who devoted considerable attention to investigating young children's imaginative processes. Together they designed numerous experiments and instruments which allowed them to carry out systematic studies of make-believe play. They found that children played more imaginatively in free play with unstructured toys such as blocks and puppets than in controlled play settings with structured toys, such as those that are battery operated to perform in particular ways.[471]

But the benefits were not confined to play itself, for the Singers found, too, that children who played at make-believe smiled more, were happier, showed empathy, appeared more interested in their surroundings and in activities, and were less likely to engage in aggressive behaviour, than those who did not. In addition, imaginatively playing children also tended to be more civil and better behaved, more co-operative and patient, and better able to take turns and share.[472] Those children who played at make-believe early on, taking on many roles and using materials symbolically, employed advanced language and elaborate scripts. They were also likely to be more amiable, persevering, conscientious, co-operative with teachers, and to show more initiative. These are traits which have been found to persist into adulthood, and which predict greater positive emotionality, less aggression, and more self-control.[473] It is not hard to see that these characteristics promote the personal wellbeing of both the individuals themselves and of those around them. It is not hard to see either why play has these beneficial effects, when one understands that free play actively nurtures communication, social skills, flexibility and problem-solving skills, and relieves stress.[474]

The benefits of playing in natural surroundings

Another relief from stress is time spent in natural surroundings; there are over a hundred studies that testify to this effect.[475] Studies further suggest that being in natural settings may be useful for the treatment of Attention Deficit Hyperactivity Disorder in children, even perhaps able to be used in place of medication or behavioural therapies in some cases.[476] All children, though, can find freedom, fantasy and privacy in nature, it has been suggested by Richard Louv, author of the acclaimed book, *Last Child in the Woods: Saving our Children from Nature Deficit Disorder.*[477] "Time in nature", he believes, "is not leisure time; it's an essential investment in our children's health (and also, by the way, in our own)".[478] Studies in Sweden, Australia, Canada and the US have found that the quality of play varies significantly between school playgrounds with manufactured play areas and those with natural spaces: the more natural environment stimulates more make-believe play. In these surroundings, the basis of leadership is language skills and inventiveness rather than physical competence, which is the case in environments dominated by specially designed play structures.[479]

This finding surely relates, as Richard Louv suggests, to the 'loose parts theory' of play arrived at by architect Simon Nicholson, the son of Ben Nicholson and Barbara Hepworth, two of Britain's foremost 20th century artists. Nicholson's theory is that, "In any environment, both the degree of inventiveness and creativity, and the possibility of discovery, are directly proportional to the number of kinds of variable" and a 'loose parts' toy or environment offers scope to the imagination and creativity by allowing elements to be combined in many ways.[480] Nature is full of 'loose parts', the less tamed it is the more there will be.

Playful play

Make-believe or pretend play is a peculiarly human form of 'playful play', depending as it does on the use of symbolism – as, for instance, when sitting on the stairs is transformed into going for a ride on a bus. The capacity for imaginative thought begins to appear by the third year of life, but some toddlers already show signs as early as eighteen months, in such ways as feeding their inanimate teddy with a spoon.[481] By the age of 3 or 4, children can sustain co-operative play for long periods, taking on different roles and following a simple storyline and appropriate self-imposed rules.[482] This kind of imaginative, child-directed, unstructured play, has also been termed 'free-flow play', described as the kind of play in which children "wallow in ideas, experiences, feelings and relationships", integrating through original thinking what they know, understand, feel and are competent to do.[483] It can be a solitary activity but is more likely to be sociable, co-operative and negotiated, the children involved being sensitively attuned to each other. While such play may appear to be inconsequential to adults – and is deceptively difficult for parents, teachers and researchers to interpret[484] – such play is important for fostering imagination. This has particular relevance in our present context of preparing for a fast changing future world, for such play, which is stimulated by the possibilities provided by the surroundings in which it takes place, represents an experimental dialogue with the environment, and thus develops the child's adaptability to altering circumstances.[485] But for play of this kind to be an option for a child, the child must have gained a well-stocked pool of first-hand experiences on which to draw. This is another facet of the importance of experience, which has emerged as a recurring theme of this book.

Encouraging playfulness

If playfulness is the root of creativity then it is useful to consider how playfulness itself may be encouraged. We commonly assume that children are naturally playful, but this isn't necessarily the case. Certainly, every child is born with the innate potential for playfulness, but this potential needs to encounter a nurturing human relationship in order to be activated. The listlessness of the children in Romanian orphanages, isolated in cots from babyhood onwards, demonstrated the terrible effect of a coldly impersonal and uncommunicative human environment on infants and young children. The vacant apathy of these children that so shocked those who saw film of the orphanages is all the more understandable if, as has been claimed, humans are unique in being the only species in which play is first initiated by a parent.[486] This would constitute a big contrast with other species, in which it is the young animals themselves who instigate play. One of the most universal forms of play between adult and infant humans is the game of peekaboo, in which the adult approaches the infant from a distance, coming close with a "Boo!"[487] Peepo may follow, with the parent or another playmate pretending to disappear, hiding their face behind a hand, chair back, cloth, or such like, then quickly reappearing. This game almost always generates mutual fun and laughter for the players.

In Winnicott's view, "... *for the baby* [original italics] (if the mother can supply the right conditions) every detail of the baby's life is an example of creative living. Every object is a 'found' object. Given the chance the baby begins to live creatively, and to use actual objects to be creative into and with. If the baby is not given this chance then there is no area in which the baby may have play..."[488] Those mothers who cannot supply the right conditions are the severely depressed or distressed who are too distracted by their own circumstances to be able to interact joyfully and proactively with their babies. But, even for the great majority who can, playful communication between parent and baby is only the start. Having ignited the spark of playfulness that's waiting, dormant, in their offspring, the parent's role in assisting the development of this trait continues. Observations have made clear, for instance, that telling and reading stories to pre-school children stimulates make-believe play.[489] Yet the reading of bedtime stories is no longer the common practice it once was in many families.[490]

More generally, the most important support that can be given to the encouraging of pretend or symbolic play, according to the Singers, is for a child's parents and teachers to understand the importance of imaginative play and to provide time, space and simple toys or props accordingly. The space need not be large, but does need to be recognised as sacred and protected. This requirement is not, in fact, limited to pre-school children, as one mother illustrated beautifully in an article written in 1994.[491] She wrote:

> The lack of opportunity to roam wild and free and have some sense of
> adventure is one of my main concerns, living as we do in the centre
> of town on a very busy main road. But youthful imagination and
> enterprise will out! My children have created their own out-of-the
> way, slightly dangerous, adult-free zone by playing on top of the garden
> shed. How the garden shed roof was ever considered a suitable place
> for play is now forgotten, but for the past five years it has been a firm
> favourite with my children and their friends... With fencing on one

side and a brick wall to the rear... with a few bricks removed to create foot holds... the shed is screened to the front by a lilac bush... Access to the roof is via a ladder for the younger children, by the wall for the older children... From the ground it all looks very interesting: various bits of wood, plastic-coated wire fencing, plastic guttering and bicycle baskets are piled around making, I am told, a 'base'. They type of game often played is some sort of combat, castles-under-siege type game, and elaborate building, shifting and constructing goes on. We never seem to have an 'us and them' situation develop, everyone is united on the shed roof against some common invisible enemy below... In five years no-one has ever fallen off.

The sacredness of this space for the children who played in it was revealed when the question of a possible house move arose and a visiting friend aged 10 ½ plaintively asked, "But what about the shed roof?"

Many adults do not realise that children prosper in the absence of sophisticated and expensive toys and equipment if given space, time and simple, versatile materials. Many manufactured toys incorporate a great deal of specific detail, which directs and restricts the play to which they give rise – including merchandise based on television and film characters. The spurious belief that imagination is stimulated by such playthings is compounded by the greater value which the Singers found parents tend to attach to activities regarded as directly educational than to a child's own invented activities and self-directed exploration.

The Importance for Imagination of Real Experience

The kind of supposedly educational activities which have come massively to the fore in recent years are specially designed television programmes, DVD's, computer games and online material. In the view of Aric Sigman who has made a particular study of the neurological and educational effects of screen technology on children, the marketing of these has "perpetrated the view that learning and experiencing via a screen rivals, and often exceeds, the process of learning via real-life interactions".[492] Yet practical knowledge cannot be downloaded, it must be lived. "Getting an adequate *grasp* on the world, intellectually, depends on getting a handle on it in the same literal and active sense". This is the well-informed view of Matthew Crawford who swapped the work of the executive director of a Washington think-tank for that of a motorcycle repair expert.[493]

And as we have seen, real-life, hands-on experience is emotionally very powerful. First-hand, direct, organically and unpredictably unfolding, three-dimensional experience, the development of which one can influence, is very different from the mediated, edited, pre-programmed, vicarious 'experience' available within the boundary of the television or computer screen. This was forcefully borne in on me when reading (and in some cases listening to) approximately four hundred stories in the course of a study I carried out into the influence of television and videos on 10-12 year-old children's story-making. My overall conclusion was that the effect of television on the imagination was to stifle rather than stimulate it.

For the most part, the scenarios of courtrooms, operating theatres, jungles and numerous other unfamiliar and exciting environments into which television and film must have transported the children, apparently instigated little, if any, new thinking. But screen material certainly did capture the imagination of some children and, as I have said, entering into the imaginative world of other, particularly gifted individuals is often life-enhancing. Such processes did offer children material to include or vary in their own narratives, thus inspiring an *imitative* form of imagination in some stories. But rare were the instances when stories that borrowed from the screen showed any evidence of *transformative* imagination, that is, the development of quite new ideas by the recasting of borrowed material and combining it with other elements.

The principal ingredient of the children's writing was in fact their own, direct experience, be it social, emotional, cultural or physical, unusual or routine. Let me illustrate the transformation of first-hand experience with descriptions of a few stories titled *The Face at the Window* (that all the study participants wrote). In one, a boy's reflection in the window smiled at him and turned into a faint figure sitting on the bed which could tell him anything he wanted or needed to know; a moral dilemma was introduced when the boy asked the figure for the correct answers to questions in a school test. Another began with the narrator moving to a new house and seeing the smiling face of an old man in the supposedly abandoned house opposite. Asked why he had written this story, the author explained, "I couldn't think of anything and then I thought of when I was little and looked out of my window and I thought I saw a green old man sitting in the window in a rocking chair, rocking about, smoking a pipe and I got really scared." His story, however, exhibited empathy for the old man, not fear. All the stories of one girl vividly described different tragic circumstances of homelessness, abandonment and death. These were also closely related to personal experience it became clear when she told me that she had been adopted and that her adoptive parents had later divorced, following which her mother now had a new boyfriend. Her description of her history, given in the course of attempting a response to an imaginative exercise about changes she would like to make to her home, showed that the circumstances of her life were woven into her stories, and that she currently felt unsure as to where her home was.

The Screen and Play

Television's stifling effect on creative imagination

In general, real experiences were more likely than screen content to be treated creatively. But, even if derived from first-hand experience, many of the stories were downright dull, often accounts of the walk to school, an ordinary school day, how hum-drum weekends were spent. They lacked the 'effective surprise' that has been described by educationalist Jerome Bruner as the distinguishing feature of the creative act. In reading through the sheaf of children's stories, I agreed with Bruner that, "It is the unexpected that strikes one with wonder or astonishment. What is curious about effective surprise is that it need not be rare or infrequent or bizarre and is often none of these things... [It is the] connecting of diverse experiences by the mediation of symbol, metaphor and image".[494]

So can the screen be held at least partly responsible for the lack of imagination to be found in so many of the stories? I believe it can. It is of course true that some children are naturally more imaginative than others, but the type of stimulus is a factor to be considered too, and a number of studies that have compared children's imaginative responses to audio-visual and purely audio stimuli, indicate that exposure to material on the screen inhibits the development of imaginative thinking, whereas that presented on the radio or an audio-recording encourages it.[495] Such an effect is likely to occur, it seems to me, because images that are developed in the mind's eye of a listener need to be actively constructed, and depend entirely on their imagination, unlike those presented as finished products on the screen. Images on the screen are complete, detailed, technically perfect and carefully edited. Mental visualisations are usually quite different: impressionistic, incomplete, indeterminate, fluid and dream-like.

From television to internet

Since the time when my study was carried out in the 1990's computers in general and the internet in particular have come to play a much bigger role in children's lives. Now, social networking is cultivating the habit of quick thinking about the outward projection of largely superficial messages for the approval of others. This is inimical to the slow, inner, mulling over of ideas, the trying out, and the staying-with-the-problem, that is a vital part of the creative process. It is certainly true that interactive digital technology presents us with many new, exciting and powerful creative opportunities to which to put our minds. But if it is unthinkingly used as the default means of killing time or filling inactive moments it is also a potential block to experiences on which the imagination can draw; for time spent in front of a screen is time that is not spent interacting with the immediate, unpredictable, physical and social world, experiencing subjective reality which is the chief grist of imagination. When attention is focused on a screen, moreover, it is unable to wander along its own path and is thus closed to the kinds of creative thinking and ideas that have a way of arriving unbidden.

By 2005 eighty per-cent of 5–16 year-olds in the UK had a television set in their bedrooms,[496] and the almost universal ability to turn on a television, DVD player, computer or mobile phone more or less whenever there appears to be 'nothing to do' means that children are being robbed of the need and time to learn how to initiate their own occupations and pursue their own thought processes, or just to be. They have no incentive to watch the world go by and no space to assimilate and reflect on their experience. Farmers learnt long ago that land is more fertile if allowed to lie fallow from time to time; it is possible that the human mind also needs periods of inactivity in order to bring forth new ideas. Constant bombardment by fast-paced distraction and noisy external stimuli crowds out the possibility of cultivating an inner life.

Given the extent of television-watching, it is a matter of concern for imaginative development that the medium is unlikely to fire the *creative* imagination in new directions except in the case of exceptionally imaginative individuals. Unhelpful as this is, the more alarming is the idea that too much exposure to television viewing and computer use during early childhood and beyond can seriously affect neurological development. There is much evidence pointing to damaging effects. During childhood, explains Susan Greenfield, "there is huge potential for anything and everything to leave its mark, almost literally, on the brain".[497] Until early adolescence the human brain makes an enormous number of connections and is exquisitely sensitive to the environment. Thus if screen technology constitutes a significant part of that environment it will inevitably have an impact on the brain, she says. In Britain four out of ten children aged 0 to 4 now use games consoles, one in ten own their own, and one-quarter of the same age group access the internet at least weekly.[498]

Research carried out by two academics at the London School of Economics[499] has found that children in the UK are among the youngest in Europe when they begin to use the internet, at the average age of 8. Of those who used the internet in 2010, 95% did so at home (over half of them in their bedrooms). The average length of time that children aged 9-16 spent online was relatively long, at 102 minutes a day compared with the EU average of 88 minutes. (In the US the figures are higher.)[500] 71% of this age group in the UK who used the internet went online to use social networking sites, and social networking is now the main reason that children in Britain go online.[501] We cannot know yet how the human brain adapts to screen technology but Greenfield's familiarity with the malleability of the human brain has led her to predict that spending so much time in cyberspace will inevitably lead to minds very different from any others in human history, as she argues in detail in her book *The Quest for Identity in the 21st Century*.[502] For some youngsters the pull of the internet becomes addictive, and Internet Addiction Disorder is increasing in prevalence.[503] IAD results in multiple structural changes in the grey matter and white matter of the brain, and in impaired psychological wellbeing, impulsivity and academic failure.[504] Effects short of addiction that have also been noted include reduced playfulness, reduced attention span, slowed language development, and a marked decline in reading and mathematical skills.

Attitudes to play and consumption

It's hard even for pre-school children and their parents to escape the internet. In 2008 the UK government introduced the Early Years Foundation Stage (EYFS)[505] curriculum which is legally binding on all organisations with the care of pre-school children, including child minders. So important for educational advancement is information and communication technology (ICT) held to be by the government, that the EYFS document directs that from the age of 30 months children's attention should be drawn to ICT apparatus, from 40 months children should be able to "use a mouse and keyboard to interact with age-appropriate computer software" and that teachers should "teach and encourage children to click on different icons to cause things to happen in a computer program. Provide a range of programmable toys, as well as equipment involving ICT, such as computers".[506]

One London-based EYFS team have made the following suggestions to help others to embed ICTS across the curriculum, indoors and out: "Use the computer in role play… MP3 recorders can be used to record environmental sounds, then downloaded and played back at later times or inserted into digital books… Data loggers can be used to explore and measure environmental changes and differences… Import photos into SMART notebook to use as additional resources (eg storytelling)."[507] Following their advice would rob the youngest children of the opportunity to learn about weather and seasons by feeling the sun on their faces, hearing the wind in the trees, the crunch of dry leaves, and the splash of rain in puddles, and seeing the filigree patterns of frost, and so much more, by substituting lively, memorable personal experience with impersonal, quantitative 'data'. Abstract numbers, technologically gathered and stored, would take the place of opening all the senses to patient and perceptive observation and sensuous delight. Learning which neglects emotion has shallow roots. Imposing on young children computer simulation and photography as advised by the team means depriving them of vital opportunities to evoke their own memories, reinforce their own experience of the natural world and exercise their imaginations.

This kind of educational development is a woeful misuse of technology, combined with exaggerated risk aversion and litigiousness. It compounds the effective withdrawal over the last twenty years of many opportunities for outdoor play in the name of health and safety.[508] A survey carried out in 2002 found that children were being prohibited from all kinds of previously enjoyed activities ranging from climbing trees, to playing football, snowballs, and even making daisy chains.[509] These bans amount to no less than the proscription of opportunities for building important foundations for wellbeing, creativity and spirituality that should be every child's birthright. The technological slant applied to play in the early years is perverse. Not only does it incur an unnecessary financial cost to the over-stretched early education budget at school and in many homes, but also encourages dependency on a particularly sophisticated form of material consumption. It violates the rightful development of the child and interferes with the growth of affective and affectionate relationships with the natural environment. What could be more wrong-headed for the foundations of human wellbeing and environmental sustainability?

When it comes to attitudes to children and material consumption, plenty of parents, it seems, consider shopping in stores to be play. According to a cross-cultural comparison of parental attitudes toward play, learning and time by the LEGO Learning Institute, 38% of parents in the UK, US, Japan, France and Germany are of this view.[510] And there is the virtual consumption in return for real money that has passed for play on sites such as *BarbieGirls* which we heard about in Chapter 1. These snapshots return us to another facet of the connections between playfulness, wellbeing, material consumption and sustainability, flagging up one more aspect of how the general values and particular parenting style a child encounters in the home have an impact on whether and how his or her creative capacity will develop.

Parenting Style and Creativity

While twin studies have concluded that genes account for twenty-two per cent of variance in a person's creativity, other studies have found that certain child-rearing styles are either positively or negatively associated with creative development. These have suggested that parents who encourage curiosity and exploration and the expression of feelings, allow their children time to daydream and to 'loaf', and give them permission to question and discuss and to make their own decisions, produce creative children.[511] Also that homes in which parents consult each other about decisions, explain the reasons for their rules to their children, and try to avoid being arbitrary while providing adequate control, produce children who are inquisitive, original and constructive in their play and general behaviour. Autocratic homes, it seems on the other hand, which emphasise restrictions without much consultation and expect relatively unquestioning obedience from children, tend to have offspring who are quiet, conforming, and limited in curiosity, originality and fancifulness.[512] While modest consumer and independent thinker Mark, whose mother had expected his behaviour to comply with certain social expectations, is a useful reminder that general patterns may not apply in every case, these observations can help us to understand that parenting style is likely impact on the development of creativity in one way or another.

The Whole of Life

The hand-brain connection

A quite different reason why children need plentiful hands-on play is that cognitive and motor development are intimately tied up with the use of the hands. So close is the interaction of hand and brain that the neurologist Frank Wilson concluded from extensive study of the human hand in evolution and in contemporary use[513] that, "The curious, exploratory, improvisational interaction of the hand with objects in the real world gives rise to what we call 'ideas'".[514] Anyone who has whittled a piece of wood, moulded a lump of clay, tinkered under a car bonnet, or designed textile items will recognise how the thoughts about the unfolding handiwork they are engaged in arise in a wordless conversation between their head and the touch and feel of the materials they are bringing into a new form of existence, or with which they are solving a mechanical problem. Such hand–head interaction begins early in life, from the time a child first handles the toys and games and learns from the behaviour of innumerable other objects grasped and manipulated by the hands. However, hands clutching games consoles or curled round a mouse, fingers clicking on icons or tapping a touch screen are not feeling for conkers among the leaves and threading them on string, building with Lego, cutting with scissors, grasping branches while climbing trees, balancing and arranging furniture, planks and blankets to construct dens, placing pieces precisely on a chess board, skimming stones across water, sorting and arranging collections of found objects, pressing flowers, holding a pencil or paint brush, dressing and undressing dolls, or any of the other myriad activities that a growing child might enjoy and from which they would benefit in numerous ways.

More than a limited entry into the virtual world will deprive a child of any age of irreplaceable tactile experience, manipulating and controlling elements of the environment around them. Yet the changing world will require us to alter the things we make and how we use them, to become "good craftsmen of the environment", in the view of sociologist Richard Sennett in his acclaimed book *The Craftsman*.[515] Sennett points out that, while play can appear to be an escape from reality, it can also instil obedience to rules and allow experimentation with them. Play engages the child, too, in dialogue with physical materials which behave according to their own very real rules, a process essential to the development of new forms.

Attachment, play and creativity

In the last chapter I will advocate the active offer of support to parents to facilitate the development of secure attachment in their children for the sake of their general emotional wellbeing. Secure attachment is also an advantage in the context of creativity, for a securely attached child is one who feels safe to explore his or her physical and social environment, taking little 'risks' and gaining in a sense of personal competence.[516] These are qualities which are necessary for a later personal sense of creative self-efficacy. Parallel with support for security of attachment there is also much work to be done in helping parents, teachers and educational policy-makers to appreciate the importance of imaginative play in the real world for the cultivation of happy, adaptable, creative, pro-social people, and how to help it happen. Between the constant call of a screen, the demands of homework and perhaps sporting or other organised activities, today's children, whatever their age, have few opportunities to come face to face with the unprocessed world. They are largely denied the possibilities contained in a quiet, empty hour, or the beckoning of the great outdoors. How are they to cut themselves loose from of the multiple pressures of the social world to find and develop their inner selves, to begin to gather their own collection of the kinds of experiences which we can, given the discussion of spirituality in the previous chapter, call spiritual? They need adults to clear the way.

Play is for life
How will today's children look back on their childhood play? It is hard to believe that those who spend a large part of their non-school time interacting online, or with slick games whose graphic style is highly sophisticated and rules of engagement pre-ordained, will reminisce with the same warmth, and recall the same variety or originality of ideas that we have heard from the parents taking part in the workshop or the mother of the children playing on the roof of the garden shed. There is no doubt real enjoyment and benefit are to be had from using digital technology. But there is a stark disparity between children who have a rich experience of encounters with real world objects and phenomena and with actual people face-to-face, and those who spend hours sitting alone or side by side in virtual space, in bogus interaction with virtual reality. The online children miss out on a great deal of vital opportunity to learn to interpret the subtleties of body language, facial expression and tone of voice that are thought to make up 90% of verbal communication, or to respond to other people's pheromones or manage physical contact.[517] Their understanding of immediate encounter and their skills in negotiating social situations will surely remain underdeveloped. They also risk a future of manual incompetence. The implications of this lack, both for the wellbeing of the individuals themselves and for the coherence and resilience of society as a whole should be a serious and urgent concern.

§

ADAM
Modest consumer Adam, aged 33, largely put his current lifestyle down to his play-filled childhood. What had influenced him, he thought, was being involved in lots of activities with other children when he was young, as well as a supportive family, travel and education. He had spent the first six years of his life in the Middle East and had:

"Loads of memories of deserts, mountains, Arab souks, and playing outside, but hardly any recollection of television programmes other than Sesame Street. Lego is the only indoor toy I remember having for a long time. And abundance of sand meant Tonka toys were great for the outdoors! Since living in the UK from the age of 6, I seem to have been out the house every night of the week, doing things like singing in church choirs, cubs, scouts, swimming, water polo. I was definitely jealous of friends who had televisions in their rooms, but we spent most time playing in rivers and on bikes."

The effect of this experience, he said, was that he learnt a lot about the intrinsic rewards that hobbies and interests can bring. His current activities of capoeira and drumming were in fact becoming more than hobbies as he was beginning to instruct in them, and they had grown to be "a real part of my identity". He wrote, *I love being able to spend an afternoon hitting the congas or thinking up drumming and capoeira classes. I also walk friends' dogs at lunchtime or pootle round the boat fixing things.* Adam had lived on a narrowboat for three years, having chosen to live modestly to keep a healthier work/lifestyle balance and because the very small outgoings of such a way of living meant there was no need to work full-time. Living on a small boat dictated minimal use of possessions and energy, and production of minimal waste for him and his girlfriend. Part-time employment as a lecturer and government-level IT contractor also enabled him, he felt, to be in better control of his personal impact on the environment, something of which he had been aware since he began university. His view now was that, "The environment is a big loser in the capitalist free market economy, of which I am not a great fan. The further I can remove myself from the economic food chain the better. A natural side effect of me not being part of that economy is that the environment is slightly better off." Overall Adam rated his satisfaction with his life as 10 on a good day, 8 on a bad day.

Education had been an influence that had shaped the way he lived, but not in the conventional sense; it was not the content of what he had learnt which had had the effect, but the circumstances under which he completed his doctorate, testing times during which he learnt a great deal about himself: tenacity, flexibility, an appreciation of the freedom to do things in his own way, and skill as a teacher. Here Adam brought an unusual view to bear on the relationship between modest consumption and belonging to the working world:

"None of these [characteristics] are directly linked to me leading a modest lifestyle (though living on a £7K PhD bursary for four years sure makes you think about where your money goes!). Maybe it's all part of a small rebellion against a system designed to extract as much labour from people in exchange for as little pay as possible. My programming work is a key example. People email me the work, I do the work, I email the work back. I do it pretty much in my own time, I'm paid for results. I don't have to look busy, or seek out extra work when it's quiet, or engage in pointless meetings etc., and I don't have to spend my money on pre-packed manufactured food because I haven't got time to cook from scratch, or spend hours in traffic burning fuel on a daily commute. I don't need a big car to express my rank or how successful I am, or a big house to store all the accumulated signs of wealth."

§

The importance of memories

The value and significance of experience at any age is not limited to the time that it happens – as we have seen in previous chapters. In the form of memories, be they positive or negative, particular experiences continue to play an important role in our lives. Neither is reminiscence the exclusive preserve of the old. Adults of all ages reminisce in order to understand, explore, and reinforce a sense of who they are now and who they were earlier in life, and shared memories – like Mike's tale of family word play – bind friends and families together.[518] Being able to look back on a happy or fulfilling time past, a mattress on which to bounce, as Clarissa described it, can clearly contribute to a person's sense of their satisfaction with life in the present. My neighbour Doreen, whom I interviewed about her childhood memories of play from just before and during World War II,[519] showed how true this is when she told me:

"I used to help in the garden. I think I must have been 4 or 5 when my father put some little round balls in my hand and said if you plant these (and I'll show you how) they'll be pretty flowers – they were sweet pea seeds. I think that started my interest in gardening. When I wasn't very old I had my own piece of garden, just a little sunny spot. There was lots of moss in the garden and we found some flat, oyster-type shells, and I thought I can make a lovely path. I worked out how many shells there were and I could put them in rows of three and put the moss between them. I just finished this and it looked beautiful and the next day the

263

men came to do the fence and my path went for a burton. I think about that sometimes when I'm getting moss out of the grass! It was a nice little path – one of my earlier achievements – landscape gardening!"

Another recollection, originally printed in *Reader's Digest* in 1949,[520] relates how the children of two families fly kites on bright, fresh blustery March day, and how the mothers prise themselves away from their spring cleaning and the fathers from their farming duties, unable to resist the urge to join in. The [American] author wrote:

> We played all our fresh line in to the boys' kites and still they soared. We could hardly distinguish the tiny, orange-coloured specks. Now and then we slowly reeled one in, finally bringing it dipping and tugging to earth, for the sheer joy of sending it up again. What a thrill to run with them, to the right, to the left, and see our poor, earth-bound movements reflected minutes later in the majestic sky-dance of the kites! We wrote wishes on slips of paper and slipped them over the string. Slowly, irresistibly, they climbed up until they reached the kites…

This is real interactivity. It is also a moment spent united and ego-free, alive to the present moment:

> We never knew where the hours went on that hill-top day. There were no hours, just a golden, breezy Now… parents forgot their duty and their dignity; children forgot their combativeness and petty spites…
> 'Perhaps it's like this in the *Kingdom of Heaven*', I thought confusedly.

But more telling still is the profound significance this experience had much later, as the author describes:

> I locked the memory up in that deepest part of me where we keep 'the things that cannot be and yet are'… [Twenty years later] we were in the aftermath of a great war. All evening we had been asking our returned soldier, the youngest Patrick boy, about his experiences as a prisoner of war. He had told freely, but now for a long time he had been silent. What was he thinking of – what dark and dreadful things?
> 'Say!' a smile twitched on his lips. 'Do you remember… I used to think of that day a lot in PW camp, when things weren't too good. Do you remember the day we flew the kites?'

> Winter came, and the sad duty of a call of condolence on Mrs
> Patrick, recently widowed… We talked a little… Then she was silent,
> looking down at her lap… Now I must say something about her loss,
> and she would begin to cry. When she looked up, Mrs Patrick was
> smiling. 'I was just sitting here thinking,' she said. 'Henry had such fun
> that day. Frances, do you remember the day we flew the kites?'

Not only was this playful occasion a joyful and nourishing one at the
time, combining contact with the elements, experimentation and human
bonding (as well, no doubt, as being a learning experience about the nature
and behaviour of wind and kites), but it later provided solace at times of
difficulty and grief.

Brenda Crowe, the first national advisor to the Pre-school Playgroups
Association, collected adults' memories of play in her book *Play is a Feeling*[521]
in order to try and find a deeper understanding of how "[I]t isn't just what
we do or what happens to us that we remember but how we felt about it,
which is what really matters – for that is the truth to which we react".[522]
She describes in it how she and her younger sister emulated in their own
play the features and routines of the farm on which they lived, drying grass-
cuttings in the airing cupboard with which to make hay fields, and raking
them with a broken comb to make haystacks and animal bedding; using
peas as potatoes to be planted, harvested and stored in earth clamps with
straw to keep them from frost; and sultanas as animal droppings cleared out
of the stable and cowsheds, carted to the dung heap, then later spread over
the fields before being ploughed in, and so on. For Brenda Crowe and her
sister, shared memories of childhood play resurfaced poignantly a life-time
later, as they had for the kite-fliers. In a letter she sent me during her sister's
short terminal illness, during which they spent much time together and
"felt the ties of a lifetime being deepened", Brenda wrote, "Much of our
time recalls our play – and almost none of it relates to toys or games that
adults would recognise as such."[523]

Conclusion: Playfulness Prepares us for the Future

Play is not the exclusive province of children; "Play," says Brenda Crowe,
"is for all of us, helping us to go on making good the past and preparing
for the future, helping to restore the balance between inner and outer
tensions and pressures".[524] In her understanding that "play isn't something
apart, but a positive and creative way of living, an impulse that springs

from within to meet each moment of opportunity and respond to it in such a way that we feel vitalised or calmed and enriched"[525] the close affinity between playfulness and creativity is clear. Examining the tangible features of playfulness and creativity, one can perhaps discern in one's peripheral vision, so to speak, something of the nature of the spiritual that so eludes precise definition. In order to make happy lives possible in a world in which old certainties will change with increasing speed, developing our capacity for playfulness, creativity and spirituality deserves a prominent role.

11

Bonding with Nature

Nature – The Missing Element in the Matrix of Wellbeing

Biophilia

The calming effect of pet birds was the reason that Geoff Capes, twice winner of the World's Strongest Man title, took to keeping and breeding budgerigars, on finding himself becoming very aggressive while competing in the Olympics. This large and powerful man has explained, "To see a chick struggling to get out of an egg as tiny as my thumbnail – and I am there with tweezers carefully prising off the cap of the egg to help it – then in a matter of weeks the ugly little chick develops into one of the most beautiful creatures alive…it's phenomenal".[526] And modest consumer Anne, as we have heard, felt "happiest and most sane when I'm surrounded by the beauty of nature". In fact it has been proposed by renowned biologist E.O. Wilson that human beings have an innate tendency, which he termed 'biophilia', to "affiliate with life",[527] that "our existence depends on this propensity, our spirit is woven from it."[528]

"There's a little bit of golden sandy cove but then there are big huge rocks to climb over and further round the beach there are cliffs and it engages all your senses", said Becky. For her, being out of doors signified "luxury" and "playing" because it meant not working. But the weather did not have to be conventionally "good": "Much as I love sunshine I love the wind and I love the rain. I grew up in Wales so I don't really get the idea of beaches being for sun, I like beaches in the drizzle," said Becky. She went on:

> "You can just walk along the path at the top or you can go and climb
> over all the rocks and you have to think about it and be careful because

you could fall off and hurt yourself. There are sea anemones and mussels and things to look at and smells to smell, and from south Wales you can see to north Devon, or if you look in a different direction you can just see the horizon... My ideal is a day like it is today, it's grey, it's cold, there's a bit of drizzle in the air, but it's not hammering rain. Wrap up in something with a waterproof on, sit on a big rock and look at the sea, then I am happy as Larry! I think it's about making myself have to think about stuff that's not in my head. If you're thinking about being cold and being in the rain then you're outside yourself immediately. The real stuff is for me getting out there."

The stories of the modest consumers included many images of and references to time spent out of doors, in natural surroundings, both from childhood and more recently, many of them with a definitely playful feel to them like this one. In these autobiographical snippets one senses immediately what an important role contact with the natural world plays for wellbeing. It is remarkable, then, that this recognition is completely absent from all the theoretical frameworks for the underpinnings of human wellbeing which I outlined at the beginning of Chapter 4. This lack is despite a great deal of evidence that shows that being in natural surroundings restores us and enables us to feel and function better.

The benefits of interacting with the natural world are now well established. They are recognised in certain areas of academic literature,[529] and in the practical work of a number of organisations. One of these, the British Trust for Conservation Volunteers, provides 'green gym' opportunities, combining physical conservation activities with time in green spaces; as a result of these, 99% of participants in one particular survey reported enhanced health and confidence.[530]

As we have seen, however, the prescriptions of psychologists and others who have codified the foundations of wellbeing have completely neglected to consider the inbuilt need of human beings to have contact with the natural world, which is, after all, the environment in which our species has evolved and in which we are therefore *at home*. This missing element is crucial because it unites the two issues of human wellbeing and environmental sustainability. Many of us know from our own experience that the mind is cleared and calmed by a walk in the country (albeit probably tamed by agriculture and habitation), amongst trees and hedges, across fields, along lanes and over hills, immanent with spring buds; in verdant summer plenty; glowing or drab in colour when transformed by autumnal processes; or winter-bare and biding. Or perhaps in the great expanse of world by the sea, with the constant crashing or creeping of waves and the gliding or bobbing of sea-birds. Gazing at natural landscapes and visiting parks have both, indeed, been found to have measurable physiological and stress-reducing effects.[531]

Nature overlooked

Yet this understanding is all too easily taken for granted. While twenty-three of the questionnaire respondents in the Modest Consumers study named nature as one of the most important things in life for them (compared with fifty-four mentions of family, twenty of work and thirteen of relationships, for example), some did not appear to have a particular affection for the natural world. And some of those who did were as likely as anyone to pass over the benefits they derived from contact with it. Several whose conversation clearly showed how much the natural world meant to them, had failed to include it when answering the question on the questionnaire about what was important to them in life. When challenged, Andrew explained the gap as an "oversight", Paul as an "omission", and Chris as, "it's probably just implicit to me". Clive was surprised by my query:

T Is nature important to you?
C It's hugely important. Have I not written it on my list?
T No
C Definitely. I'm glad you've mentioned that, it's hugely important
T In what way?
C I've always felt a connection with nature and it's been a fairly constant feature throughout my life. But more recently there's the kind of how much it complements a quiet and contemplative life, being out in a natural environment, actually interacting with it. I've just come back from France and I've been living in my tent for six weeks, camping by a stream. There's a source there so you can get fresh water, just living and cooking outside. I love it just lying in a meadow, sleeping under the stars, climbing the mountain, sitting under a tree.

Evidence of the benefits of time spent in natural surroundings

Despite our frequent failure explicitly to recognise the importance to us of experiencing nature, there is plenty of evidence which confirms that being in natural settings very definitely enhances human wellbeing, both mental and physical. The Outdoor Challenge Programme,[532] an initiative which was carried out over ten years in the 1970s and '80s in a seventeen-thousand acre area of Michigan wilderness, revealed just how much being fully in natural surroundings seems to call forth our optimal mental state. And its striking outcomes are particularly relevant to our present concerns. Adults and adolescents were recruited to participate in a two-week hike and in an investigation into the effects of the experience. It involved camping, map-reading, finding food, cooking, rock climbing and using a compass in groups, and spending forty-eight hours alone, out of sight and hearing of anyone.

At the beginning, participants were apprehensive and admitted to ignorance about the ways of the forest, yet after only two weeks, they felt happy and confident in this wild place. The experience resulted in their gaining in self-esteem, becoming more aware of their real personal strengths and weaknesses, feeling more self-sufficient in the use of their time and talents, showing a greater concern for others and developing a more positive view of themselves. What is more, these changes were still maintained six months later, when they continued to be more content with themselves than a control group. Their journal entries said things like, "I don't understand it I just feel so much alive I want to yell and scream and tell everybody" and, "The thing I think about most about the program is that I can see so much more beauty in the earth in its nature state than I ever could before". Living an existence reduced to the simple essentials gave participants the unhurried opportunity and encouragement to reflect, and many of them felt a sense of wholeness which they found exhilarating. Being absorbed into the natural world meant that they came to notice aspects of it that they had not been aware of before, and they found the realisation that they coexisted with other creatures and plant life uplifting. The very existence of wilderness became a comfort, and for some of the adults came the realisation that their normal everyday lives lacked satisfying depth.

It is, of course, unrealistic to suggest that wilderness immersion of this kind could be organised for everyone, so it is reassuring to learn that even little doses of nature and enjoyment of green spaces near to home can be beneficial. Gardening, even on a small plot, seems to be a particularly effective way of interacting with the natural environment.[533] It was certainly a frequent pastime among the modest consumers, to the extent that they put gardening or growing things on a par with being with family and friends. In fact, the pleasure to be found in the garden or on the allotment is not trivial, for the evidence is that green space not only helps short-term recovery from stress or mental fatigue but also aids faster physical recovery from illness, and long-term overall improvement in health and wellbeing.[534] So much so that people who have access to nearby natural settings have been found to be healthier than those who don't, and in the longer term to have higher levels of satisfaction with their home, job and life in general.[535]

It isn't even necessary to be out in the natural environment to feel its effect, a green view from a window has benefits too: people experience their jobs as less stressful if they can see trees, flowers, or other greenery from their desks,[536] and a study of prisoners found that those whose cells looked out over farmland or woods needed less frequent health care services than those whose cells overlooked the prison yard.[537] Another study found that recovering breast cancer patients who participated in at least twenty minutes of nature-based activity three times a week for three months were better able to concentrate, more likely to return to work full time, strikingly more inclined to start new projects such as volunteering and music lessons than a control group, and they also rated their quality of life as significantly higher.[538] These findings provide what one might call an epidemiological perspective on the effects of green surroundings; further insights into the balm that nature bestows come from personal experience in particular situations. Someone who has testified to this is Rufus May who, at the age of 18 was diagnosed as an incurable schizophrenic and locked away in a psychiatric hospital but who later undertook his own healing and emerged as a respected psychologist. He has described walking in close proximity to nature, while working as a night security guard in Highgate cemetery in north London straight after leaving psychiatric hospital, as "a very healing process".[539] This mentally and spiritually healing quality of nature is a matter which Oliver Sacks, the renowned neuroscientist, has described too from his own experience. It was a particular moment, four long and difficult weeks after having undergone surgery for a climbing injury, when he was taken out into the hospital garden:

> I was taken down to the little garden I had so yearningly gazed at... This was a great joy – to be out in the air... A pure and intense joy, a blessing, to feel the sun on my face and the wind in my hair, to hear birds, to see, touch and fondle the living plants. Some essential connection and communion with nature was re-established after the horrible isolation and alienation I had known. Some part of me came alive, when I was taken to the garden, which had been starved, and died, perhaps without my knowing it.[540]

So tangible is the therapeutic effect of natural surroundings on sufferers of depression and reduced mental wellbeing that MIND, the National Association for Mental Health, has recommended that green means be used to prevent and to treat mental ill-health via GP referrals for green exercise or conservation projects. MIND has even gone as far as to propose that inequality of access to green space be addressed as a human rights issue.[541] Not only plants, but also animals, enhance mental wellbeing. Contact with animals helps dementia suffers to smile and communicate more and to become less hostile to their carers, and interactions with an animal or bird can enable autistic children to produce more focused attention, speech, social interaction and positive emotion.[542] In fact, the significance of human affiliation with animal life goes far further, it seems, than simply support for individual mental wellbeing. Pat Shipman, a professor of anthropology at Pennsylvania State University, points out that our capacity and need for one-to-one association with other species is a uniquely human attribute. Referring to the 20,000 – 30,000 year-old cave paintings such as those in Lascaux and Chauvet in France, Shipman commented in a newspaper interview which marked the publication of her book *The Animal Connection* [543] in 2011:

> These paintings are stunningly beautiful and superbly crafted. Sometimes scaffolding was erected in the caves...artists went to enormous lengths to get their pigments mixed with the right binding agents and placed in exactly the right spot. And what did they depict when they got things just right? Animals, animals, and more animals. There are no landscapes and only a handful of poorly executed depictions of humans. By contrast, the paintings of lings, stags, horses, bulls and the rest are magnificent. We were besotted with animals because our lives depended on our relationships with them.[544]

Observing and interacting with animals on an intimate basis as they later domesticated them, led humans, Shipman suggests, to develop empathy and communication skills, and the special relationship which humans have with animals is now revealed in our desire to have pets. Shipman believes, moreover, that the consequences of our world becoming increasingly urbanised and our contact with animals therefore diminishing, are potentially catastrophic.[545]

§

CAROLINE

Caroline, a part-time psychotherapist, was one of the research participants who did express a strong connection with the natural world. And this, she believed, actually stemmed from early contact with animals. "Both the houses I was brought up in had quite a lot of land around them, and the second house had a paddock and a field attached to it. I think that has profoundly affected me and I feel very connected to and protective of nature. I actually think that having quite a close connection to animals all my life, particularly big animals – I've ridden all my life – has been very influential." It was the natural world that came first in Caroline's list of what was most important to her in life, but she found it difficult to explain why: "I don't know what to say about that really; it seems to me it's what we belong to, or should belong to anyway. I feel it's what contains me, it's from whence I came and where I will go, somehow. It feels like my alpha and omega, I can't put it in any other way." We have already heard, in the context of solitude, about Caroline's seminal experience with a daisy in the school lawn when she was 9 years old. She explained, "Although I was very unhappy at that prep school it was in the most beautiful grounds, there were wonderful trees and woods, and of course in those days you were just allowed to amble off; we could go anywhere we liked, and that was just fantastic, hugely comforting. Which may be partly why my kind of sense of nature is *so* strong, it is my creed in some way." Was her love of nature something Caroline had picked up from her parents? Not really: "My mother wasn't unsympathetic to nature, but she was more interested in sitting and smoking with her gin and tonic in all honesty. She wasn't a walker. But she always took me to the theatre, she thought it was part of my education. I do remember going blackberrying with my dad, and I remember my dad hand-rearing a baby owl, I think he was more actively interested. But for me, it was simply a matter of being in nature; I don't think anybody 'taught' me." Very early in her adult life Caroline joined the Conservation Society and Friends of the Earth.

So how did her crucial valuing of nature influence the way she lived now? Her early life had always been one of material comfort, having a father who was a doctor and a mother who thought of herself as quite upper class. Later, although Caroline and her husband had continued to be comfortably off, the couple had never lived lavishly, she told me; for instance, they had always owned only one house and one car, although other couples they knew with similar financial means had two. In the past eight to ten years they had become more proactive and conscious in their choices, with increasing awareness of global warming and that, "there's no such thing as a free lunch, everything you have will have an impact on somebody or something else," in Caroline's words. Their current car was a Blue Motion Polo, bought specifically because of its particularly low diesel consumption, and when her husband had left his job and was asked what he would like as a gift, they together chose a folding bike in order to enable them to use public transport more easily. Caroline had seen to it that when they moved to their current house they installed solar panels for water heating and a wood-burning stove. She kept chickens and bees and the couple grew a good deal of fruit and vegetables. Other food came mostly from local markets and shops. Caroline bought few new clothes; those that did not come from charity shops she sourced from fair trade businesses or local producers. She was, however, happy to spend money on experiences, such as going to concerts.

The one area of major tension that she experienced regarding consumption was over travel. "I like going places and want to go places and know that travel, particularly flying, can't possibly be described as environmentally OK. So it is the most difficult area and I haven't reached the point of saying never again, I just try and think about it and do it carefully when I go, but I'm still flying places." What was most important, Caroline believed, however, was the ability to find pleasure in small things. "I mean we don't know what's going to happen, we could all lose our pensions, all sorts of alarums and excursions could go on in the next twenty years. I do think about these things and think would I be alright if I had practically no money? I think I would. I think I would go on having neighbours and friends, looking out of the window, the pleasures of the natural world, the beauty of what is around us. I do think, though, that to be able to appreciate what we have, we have to eat. We do need basic food, but not a huge amount else in all honesty."

Ultimately, it was the natural world that was most important to Caroline, and the thing that would make her most unhappy would be the inability to get outside. "I would like to die outside," she told me, "I'll ask to be carried out. And when I die my spirit will re-merge with the energy of the world. Wonderful, thank you very much! That'll be fantastic."

§

ROBERT
Intense feelings towards the natural world had informed the absolute frugality of Robert, 63. The son of a Latin master, Robert had always lived modestly, and his life had just gone on getting steadily more modest as time went on. What mattered to him were, "those things that are free: kindness,

honesty, generosity, beauty, health, openness, freedom of thought, and curiosity". He gained particular enjoyment and satisfaction from, "the right sort of weather, a well ordered garden, a fine landscape or cloudscape, and excellence in any form". Over his lifetime, Robert had turned his hand to many kinds of work: "Hundreds of seasonal jobs and spells as a vagrant between leaving a surveying course in 1963 and doing a government training scheme in joinery in 1969. Since then fisherman, forestry and quasi farming." His choice to live modestly was a matter of "moral logic". He explained: "If you accept, as I do, that morality consists of an objective set of values which serve the collective needs of the commonwealth of Mankind, and then logic suggests to me that no one should try to grab more than a modest slice of the cake". For several years now he had lived with his partner Ruth in the midst of fields in an octagonal hut they had built themselves, a single space, diameter sixteen feet, with a wood burning stove in the middle. The hut was comfortable but functional, and brightly painted inside. The futon on which they slept doubled as seating during the day. *Living on less than fifty quid a week one is a relatively low consumer of virtually everything except fresh air*, Robert wrote. *Lighting is by paraffin lamp; cooking, a couple of cylinders of gas per annum; heating, firewood from our own land; most veg own grown; travel by bus pass; clothing recycled; music by portable CD.* Robert later explained that his work as a manual worker and joiner had barely earned him £1,000 in the first nine months of the year. He found it hard to pinpoint any particular influences on the way that he lived. There was, he said:

"Nothing seminal. It has been a lifelong, sedimental process. No Damascene revelations, apart, perhaps, from looking over a field gate across a Sussex valley with my father on an idyllic summer evening when I was sixteen. No words. Let's just say the spirit entered me. A physical love of my country. I think I was just overwhelmed by the beauty of it. It seemed to make sense of everything, of our presence on earth. It was a sort of harmony of man and nature really; it was a manmade landscape, well nature and man, which was a sort of ideal to me, which I have been trying to attain ever since. Things have been going in the opposite direction, with more and more mechanisation; the beauty of it doesn't matter, whereas I think it's the essence."

§

RACHEL

Rachel was a third person whose love of the countryside, developed in her early years, as well as awareness of issues of social justice, was palpable in the way she chose to live. Both she and her partner worked for the Countryside Service, managing nature reserves, country parks and green spaces and encouraging local community groups and landowners to improve their environment. They lived in a village in Shropshire with their 17-month old daughter, using permaculture techniques in their house and garden. They grew fruit and vegetables organically, were very involved in the local community, and tried to make ethical purchases. Rachel said that she had purchased quite ethically since her teenage years but now bought fewer clothes and shoes. She had decided to live more modestly because she had become increasingly aware of "the impact of being consumptive on the environment and human rights". Two years earlier her views had been reinforced by a visit to India to meet her sister who was travelling off the beaten track. Their upbringing had introduced them to these issues, as, "Mum and Dad always used to watch the news when we were children, were always interested in current affairs. If you're exposed to that kind of stuff it does sink in and make you think." She had developed "a healthy cynicism of corporations and materialism" in her teenage years, and still attempted to influence the people with whom she came into contact, but tried not to sound too pious.

It was Rachel's passion for caring for the environment, however, that was her principal motivation. This, she believed had originated from her father's love of the countryside and wildlife. He had been a farm labourer when she was young, later becoming director of an agricultural company, and she had grown up on a small-holding. "It was in Hampshire, it had a bit of woodland and it had an orchard and a wildlife pond. It had animals and it was just nice and idyllic really. We had a lot of time outdoors as children, we didn't have a lot of toys. My sister and I are really close and I think it's partly because we lived in such a nice position, and didn't really have other children round the corner to play with and we just had that sort of resource right there to be enjoyed."

Rachel's partner had had a similar childhood and absolutely shared her values. They lived in a semi-detached ex-council house in "a gorgeous location with a beautiful view of the Shropshire hills". It was all they wanted. The house was largely furnished with hand-made pieces made by Rachel's partner, who had trained as a cabinet-maker, from trees he had felled himself. They had, however, added some modern, good quality kitchen appliances –

a fridge, dishwasher and microwave. Rachel was entirely content with her life of working four days a week on a job she felt worthwhile, being with her "happy little girl", being involved in community activities and going to an eclectic variety of live music events, rating her satisfaction with her life as 9 out of 10.

It had not always been like this, however, for Rachel had suffered two bouts of depression as a result of the state of the world.

"It did start the first time, in 1998 or '99, with finding it difficult to cope with trying to have a positive outlook about the future of the planet. If you involve yourself in those things it is difficult to think positively." But she had been fine for the last few years, and was convinced that it was the way that she and her partner lived that had helped to combat the stress:

> "You know you hear this thing about how people are more consumptive than they've ever been and yet are less happy than they've ever been, and I think that's definitely true. I mean I remember having been on shopping trips in the high street buying clothes in my early twenties, and spending not a huge amount of money, maybe £70 or £80, and getting home and expecting to feel really happy about it, but actually you get home and it doesn't really make you feel happy. And I think that's true of a lot of people, that spending a lot of money on things can give you a quick hit but then it's not lasting happiness, and you can gain far more happiness through doing simple things, whether it's through gardening or going for a walk or helping others or whatever, and that's what I think provides you with sustainable happiness."

§

The Natural World and Proper Functioning in Children

When adults recall their childhood play, their minds generally turn to memories of the outdoors, as Rachel's did, to times when they enjoyed the freedom of fields, woods, gardens and parks, more often than not in the company of other children. Or there may have been solitary times, contented or curious, such as those evocatively and poignantly described by Elizabeth Stutz, the founder of Play for Life, as times of feeling at one with nature:

> Perhaps you were sitting in a meadow full of flowers, sucking honey from the tips of clover petals while watching swifts gliding across the horizon. The grass tickled your legs and the pollen your nose, the air

was filled with the sound of insects and the scent of plants. The sky, a canopy above you, carried mountainous clouds... Or you lay on your front by the side of a pond peering down into the darkness full of wonderful creatures, tall trees, towering above, touching the sky. Cool smells of moss and fungi, shafts of light falling in patches on the brambles, acorn cups and the jumble of crackling twigs surround you... For many of us it was one of the most important parts of our childhood. It never occurred to us that it could ever end.[546]

Interestingly, a 1950's study of three hundred volumes of autobiographical recollections by creative thinkers from many cultures and eras, revealed that middle childhood, the period between the ages of 5 or 6 and 11 or 12 had been a time of particularly intense experience of the natural world, an experience that stimulated creativity. It emerged, moreover, that is was common amongst the memoir writers to go back in their minds to this period in their childhood to "renew the power and impulse to create".[547] But conditions have changed. A report released by Natural England in 2009 revealed that less than 10% of children now play in woodlands, countryside and heaths.[548] Yet we have seen above how important contact with nature is to mental and physical wellbeing. Indeed, many schemes that have provided children with carefully designed activities out of doors bear out the power of natural settings to enhance children's emotional wellbeing and cognitive functioning. It is instructive to look at just how children respond to being in natural surroundings, and how rapidly the benefits are felt.

Forest School

The Forest School Programme is one such scheme. Begun in Scandinavia, it has been increasingly adopted in Britain.[549] It involves weekly sessions in woods or other green spaces, combining free play and carefully structured but essentially child-led activities, and is characterised by a number of features. It uses woodland or another wild setting within strict safety routines and established boundaries; a high ratio of adults to pupils, with highly trained leaders; the freedom to explore using all the senses; and regular contact for the children over a significant period of time, including all year round, and in all weathers.[550]

Here is a taste of what a Forest School is like:

Once children become familiar with the wood, they may run and lead the way to the site. So while they are learning to deal with the uneven terrain of the woodland floor, they are also developing a sense of independence and confidence in being outdoors. A later session…might include learning how to build a fire on which to toast marshmallows. If this is the case, the children… will be told that they need to gather firewood, and the practitioner will discuss which type of wood burns best by showing examples of green and dead wood. The children will be asked to find three or more different lengths and thicknesses of wood to start the fire, which leads them to practise their mathematical skills as they add and subtract different twigs and try to assess their thickness and dryness. These activities also allow the children to develop linguistically because they are describing spontaneously what they are doing as well as talking about the feel and appearance of the twigs they are collecting… The children may then be directed, with the help of an adult, to use a penknife to whittle long sticks into a point for holding their marshmallows over the fire… The children will learn about safe behaviour around the fire area, and the concept of melting points.[551]

A fourteen-week Forest School programme in Wales was found to have improved six areas of children's behaviour and skills,[28] namely, self-esteem and self-confidence, ability to focus and concentrate, social skills, language and communication skills, physical motor skills, motivation and concentration, and knowledge and understanding of the environment. The children were better able to tackle new tasks, participate in good teamwork without conflict, and show assertiveness and problem-solving skills. There was also an improvement in their physical confidence and stamina. Likewise, during a six-week pilot project in Norfolk, carried out with a rural primary school that had been classified as underachieving, the participating children's high motivation and levels of concentration on self-selected activities, "perseverance to achieve small goals such as tree climbing and threading elder pieces on string, consideration for others' feelings, compromising and problem-solving skills" was marked.[29] Observers also noticed that, "A sense of calm and peace prevailed in the group; this was so tangible it was noted by a number of visitors throughout the pilot…The elements of space and time seemed to eliminate most behavioural problems in the woodland". The Forest School approach has been adapted to meet the needs of certain groups of older pupils too. In Whitlingham Country Park in Norwich, youngsters aged between 14 and 19 were introduced to practical countryside and conservation skills, building fences, footpaths and steps, installing gates, coppicing, planting trees, cutting grass and interacting with wildlife. The park's manager was quoted in the local paper as saying, "The young people we have are not necessarily classroom shaped. They would struggle in the classroom environment but if you bring them into an outdoors environment they thrive. There are days when they do a fabulous job. We have a really good success rate in terms of attendance to the point where they want to come for another day out here as well."[552]

Wellie Wednesday

In East Anglia another scheme, small-scale and local, was Wellie Wednesday, an initiative designed to address the complex needs of children excluded from infant schools where they were unable to cope with learning in a mainstream setting and their behaviour could not be managed. It offered play-based nurturing, a developmental curriculum and a progressive outdoor learning experience for children excluded from Years 1–3 and their parent or carer.[vii] A six-week pilot project revealed how effective such an approach can be, even in a short space of time.[553] While the emphasis of the programme was not on the natural setting, the leaders deliberately chose an outdoor environment in order to nurture curiosity, exploration and a sense of wellbeing. Feedback from the children proved that this was an important part of their experience. Asked what he liked about the programme, one boy said, "It's loads and loads of fun. Going in the woods is really good for concentrating and looking." Another found that being in the group enabled him to come to terms with the death of his baby sister, and he used natural imagery to express his feelings:

> My brain can turn things round now. So I can have the sad thing at the back and happy thing at the front. When we did Beautiful Thoughts Time [guided imagery], at first sad things came into my mind. Once I was doing it, going to my special garden I found a tree house there to go to. I thought I could be there with Laura (she would be three now). Now I feel happy when I think about Laura. I like to think about her now, she was the most brilliant baby. I made a picture in my head of doing nice things like going in my tree house garden or being in my real garden. I feel the fresh air and I think the breeze is her love blowing kisses.

---

vii Wellie Wednesday continued in Norfolk until its original practitioners had to end the programme due to reorganisation of the pupil referral unit. Hopefully it will one day be picked up by others.

The parents were convinced that the natural setting was a crucial ingredient in the success of the scheme.[viii] One mother said of her son, whom she now regularly took to the beach, "He seems to absorb more when he's outdoors... There's a different side of him when he's in an open space, it's like a free spirit. When we go to Mousehold Heath or Thetford Forest Rick's climbing up the trees or going on his bike. But he likes to relax, as he says. When he's at the beach he's very calm and doesn't really say much, we just walk."

Tackle Learning

Then there was Tackle Learning. Launched in 2005, Tackle Learning was set up all over the country in partnerships between the (then) Department for Education and Skills, local authorities and sports clubs to raise achievement in numeracy, literacy and ICT, while improving confidence and self-esteem in children and young people using sport-themed learning. The Norfolk project was based in a learning centre at the rugby club in a small rural town. Most of what the children did there was directly related to rugby in some way; however, as the rugby pitch was bordered on two sides by woods, the co-ordinator decided to include some woodland sessions in the activities he provided. He was amazed at the difference their time in the woods made to the children.[554] Some time was spent in free play and the rest was used for fire-lighting and shelter building. These activities had stimulated two Year 5 boys (aged 10) spontaneously to write poetry. On stepping out of the back door of the mobile classroom into the woods one child who simply could not sit still indoors and constantly climbed on chairs and under tables, became immediately focused, seeking out sticks of equal length, attempting to bang them into the ground, and hiding them, like treasures, at the end of the session so that he could find them again next time. One girl wrote about her time in the woods as the best day she had ever had.

Earth Education

A third East Anglian project is run by Ringsfield Hall Trust in Suffolk.[555] Set in fourteen acres of parkland, meadow, woodland, pasture and garden, Ringsfield was established to enable children and young people to learn about the natural world and their relationship to it. It caters for residential and non-residential groups of children of pre-school to secondary age, providing programmes on energy, waste, shelter-building, team-building,

---

viii In interviews with me

art, drama and story-telling, and encourages free play. Its work uses the approach and programmes of the Institute of Earth Education in West Virginia, USA,[556] based on a concept of ecology which encompasses the individual's relationship to self, to others, to society and to the Earth, and the restoration of the connections between them.

The IEE's aim is to develop a sense in children and young people of being at home with the Earth, to engender in them a deep love of nature, because, "when you love something you will give things up for it, and that is what we must do for the Earth. We must sacrifice our appetites on behalf of the future... people fight for what they love much faster and much harder than for what they know".[557] This it does by providing "magical learning adventures", developing children's senses and awareness by such ingenious means as changing the vantage point to make the familiar unfamiliar, taking away the sense of sight or sound in order to heighten the other sense, role playing other creatures and objects, and spending all day out of doors from dawn until dusk. This appeal to the senses and emotions is complemented by the teaching of themes such as the flow of the sun's energy through plant life, the finite quantities of substances that make up life and how they are constantly recycled, and the specialised adaptations made by living things to their environments.

Solitude in nature, the IEE approach believes, heightens awareness of both the flow of life on the Earth and of one's innermost thoughts and feelings about it, so a few minutes of every day of a residential course at Ringsfield Hall is spent alone and in silence in a 'magic spot' where each child is out of sight of everyone else (though teachers can see them), beginning with five or six minutes, and getting longer. The effect can be extraordinary.[558] One little girl, who had never written at all before she came to Ringsfield, wrote two pages after her solitary experience, describing a beetle she had watched, and her description was so accurate that the beetle was identifiable to an entomologist, Chris Walton the director told me. A ten-year-old boy wrote of his experience of the magic spot:

> Leaning against the rough bark of a gnarled oak tree I could hear the birds go twit. At the opposite end of the field there was an enormous spiky bush. The smell of the flower is beautiful. The flowers were as bright red as a red ruby which is really bright. The thing I thought was that I never knew it could be like this, it is amazing;

and a London child wrote after her visit:

Before I went to Ringsfield when I was in Holloway all my thoughts and feelings were, like, in prison. But when I was in my magic spot thy all started to escape all over the place and I had to run around and catch them.

The impact on rural children is no less than on urban ones, and some children enjoy their moments of solitude so much that they are still seeking out opportunities for time alone three months later, in the garden, the park, their bedroom or somewhere else in the house. This is particularly pertinent in view of the value of solitude described by some of the modest consumers in the lives they found so satisfying.

One can only conclude from these many observations from differently constructed projects that even brief contact with nature contributes immediate and vital benefits to children's social, emotional, creative and academic thriving. Indeed, the evidence of these schemes suggests that being outdoors in relatively untamed, natural surroundings is a kind of default setting for children, a state in which their functioning is optimal. Finding themselves with earth, grass or leaves underfoot and branches or sky overhead, unrestricted by walls, surrounded by trees and fresh air, with freedom to move, explore and come into contact with other species, but firm boundaries keeping them safe, these children came into their own. They suddenly became more confident, independent, reflective, engaged and expressive and also more sensitive to others and willing to co-operate. In fact, the kinds of personal qualities and capacities so readily displayed by the children in natural surroundings resemble closely those which I propose will stand everyone in best stead to lead happy lives in the future.

Nature deprivation
If contact with the natural world is so vital for children's wellbeing, one may wonder about the effects of a lack of such contact. An American study[559] that examined the responses of urban children on school trips to wild locations found that the students felt disaffected and alienated from nature. They felt uncomfortable in the presence of thick undergrowth, obscured views, and unaccustomed smells, sights, sounds and other sensations. Some were afraid of stars and the vastness of the night sky, while one small inner-city child was frightened by tall trees. These children's entirely urban existence, cut off from the wider natural world to which they belonged and which belonged to them, had created a disconnect in their consciousness between their experience and their essence.

It is nothing short of tragic that children deprived of an early introduction to nature should feel fear at the sight of lofty trees and twinkling stars rather than the awe and wonder which would nourish their spirit. Sad, too, that there is little chance that such children will ever be able to derive inspiration or insight from the natural imagery and metaphor of poetry and prose, of proverbs and myths. In missing these, expressions of the place and experience of being human in relation to the life of the Earth and to the cosmos will also pass them by. Unacquainted with the cycle of growth, death, decay and rebirth of plant life through the seasons of the year, they will be deprived of the sights and symbols offered by the natural world which can bring comfort, understanding, acceptance and hope in the face of the human obstacles and losses with which they will inevitably be confronted.

Simple lack of acquaintance with nature is not the only reason that people may be afraid of nature or dismiss it, however. Such a reaction can arise by association, as an indirect result of severe social and financial deprivation, as the Houston Child Study showed.[560] Interviews with children aged 7, 9, and 11 revealed that many of them associated nature with drug-taking and human violence as these often occur out of doors in green spaces. One first grade child did not climb trees in case she fell as she might fall onto broken glass in the grass. In any case, she did not go to parks for fear of meeting someone with a gun who might shoot her, and she said that her cat was not important to her because, "I have other things that's important to me. If I eat or not. Or if anybody in my family is gonna die." Another insight into distorted perceptions of nature has been offered by a social worker who wrote about taking a teenage gang from Brooklyn to a park in New Jersey.[561] He discovered the importance in determining certain youngsters' responses to nature of the cultural conditioning of cartoons and action movies which represent even benign natural phenomena as threatening:

> They had asked endlessly about the presence of wild animals, and I had assured them that there was nothing wild within a thousand miles. Then the headlights picked up a strange beast on the road. They screamed in terror. "It's a lion! A goddam lion!" one shouted. It was a baby doe. It took a lot of talking to quiet them.
>
> The group also went fishing.
>
> I had to bait their hooks. They had seen worms, but they were afraid to put them on the hook. Baldie caught a sunfish smaller than his hand and screamed in terror as it flipped at his feet.

"Take him off the hook," I said, "He's good eating."

"I wouldn't touch that sonofabitch for nothin'," Baldie yelled. "Get him away from me."

So I unhooked a two-ounce sunfish for a seventeen-year-old boy who I knew had the courage to lead his friends into gang war where the kids fought with bats, knives and even guns.

The alienation these children and teenagers felt in reaction to non-threatening aspects of nature seems to be a perverse given the proposition that biophilia or an affinity with living things is an innate human characteristic.[562] It indicates the grave extent to which children can be impoverished, their human development distorted, by lack of simple experience of the natural world, restricted to representations conveyed by certain screen genres.

Ecological Literacy

The extinction of experience

As more and more land is 'developed' for housing, shops, retail parks, office space, roads and car parks, so the everyday opportunities for experiencing green places in and around towns and cities becomes reduced. The disappearance under asphalt and breeze blocks of local pockets of semi-wildness and the creatures whose habitats may be lost with them means the end for many of everyday glimpses of green spaces. A lack of contact with the natural, especially for children, can lead to an ignorance of nature that has been dubbed the 'extinction of experience'.[563] In turning our attention to the importance for individual mental wellbeing of time spent in natural places, we also find ourselves addressing the fundamental question of how to approach the huge challenge of environmental sustainability. For to be able to take effective steps to protect the natural environment, individuals need at least some degree of familiarity it. Without acquaintance with the natural world, we are at a loss to understand the ways in which human activity damages the environment and have no hope of halting ecological degradation. Ecological literacy is the understanding of how nature sustains life according to certain principles of organisation. Direct interaction with the natural world is not only necessary for our personal wellbeing but also constitutes crucial learning.

According to research, purely intellectual learning, in the absence of personal contact with and observation of the environment, simply doesn't have the power to develop a thorough understanding.[564] Yet the very survival of humanity will depend on our having this understanding.[565] In the view of Fritjof Capra, a leading thinker in the field, this means that eco-literacy is a critical skill and should be the most important element of education, from primary schools to universities. It is necessary, he believes, to teach our children, our students, and our corporate and political leaders, the fundamental facts of life – that one species' waste is another species' food; that matter cycles continually through the web of life; that the energy driving the ecological cycles flows from the sun; that diversity assures resilience; that life, from its beginning more than three billion years ago, did not take over the planet by combat but by networking...nature sustains life by creating and nurturing communities. No individual organism can exist in isolation. Animals depend on the photosynthesis of plants for their energy needs; plants depend on the carbon dioxide produced by animals, as well as on the nitrogen fixed by bacteria at their roots; and together plants, animals, and microorganisms regulate the entire biosphere and maintain the conditions conducive to life.[566] Yet, as writer Richard Louv has pointed out, the way that nature is understood has changed radically within a few decades: while today's children are taught about the global threats to the environment, their familiarity with the nature nearest to home is receding; nature is for them more of an abstraction than a reality.[567]

The need for love

Having made a case for the importance of familiarity with nature for its protection, it is also important to recognise that familiarity alone is not enough. We also need love. For one thing, what best galvanises action is threat of the loss of what we hold dear; and for the other, no matter how much information comes our way on the human damage being done to the natural world, this will only be taken to heart by individuals who are primed to do so. We select for attention and then retain only those media messages which chime with our own interests and sympathies.[568] If we *care* about football or fishing quotas we will take note of the news on those topics; if we don't we probably won't. In order that our emotional ties to nature are strong enough to make us change our behaviour in response to information, they have to grow profounder and more ardent than a superficial enjoyment of idyllic or dramatic landscapes or sentimental feelings for fluffy animals. Reports of the drying up of six chalk rivers in the west Thames area due to over-extraction by water companies in order to meet consumer demand, have no hope of persuading local residents to sacrifice the pleasure of their daily soak in the bath or to replace their power shower with less luxuriant plumbing if they have not experienced and revelled in the 'glory' of these natural sites once abundant with fish and other life, as John Betjeman described the River Kennet.[569] Only three-hundred-and sixty degree encounters with the natural world in the here and now are capable of inspiring the fierce affection and protectiveness that are called for. No television programme can cause one to search the sky for the source of the skylark's song or the woods for the smell of wild garlic. No book can provide the prickly sensation of walking bare-legged among thistles, the buffeting of the prevailing wind on the body, or the taste of a wild plum. Only feelings gained directly from the natural environment and a sense of our own small place in the greater order of things can sway us individually to change our habits so as to put the plight of over-stretched eco-systems before our own material desires.

Ecological literacy may sound abstract and academic, but purely cognitive learning is not enough for the development of an ecological sensibility. For ecological knowledge to become personally meaningful, for it to exert a profound influence on individual behaviour, emotional engagement is required too. A brief account by an Earth Education worker at Ringsfield Hall of one youngster's experience during the programme there is telling in this respect. It conveys the affective element which needs to complement cognitive learning if we are to take fully on board the interconnectedness of living things. The 13-year-old, wrote the worker, did not want to have anything to do with going in solitude to a magic spot, and spent the first occasion swatting flies. Then:

> On the second day, he went reluctantly to his appointed place, and then he saw a deer. He had never seen an animal so close before. He was thrilled and remained quiet and still. He felt the deer was so intently watching him that it walked into a tree! "The deer noticed me!" was his comment.
>
> On the third day, he willingly went to his magic spot. He commented afterwards that he was concerned about the flies: 'I felt I was invading their place, so I waited for them to go away.[570]

In order to live harmlessly within the natural world we need to be oriented towards it with this kind of perceptiveness, respect, affection and spirit of co-existence. Such emotions will also nourish our own sense of wellbeing.

The responsibility of education

David Orr, a prominent American environmentalist, lays the blame for our current environmental crisis on education. He believes that over-specialisation at all educational stages has brought about a general inability to think about ecological patterns, systems of cause and effect, and the long-term impacts of human actions.[571] The fault lies, in his view, with the failure to teach people to live as whole persons. Instead of teaching pigeon-holed, discrete subjects, and training for competition in the global economy, education should, he asserts, promote "the capacity to understand the ecological context in which humans live, to recognise limits, and to get the scale of things right...the ability to calibrate human purposes and natural constraints, and do so with grace and economy".[572] Orr's call for holistic education to replace the current fragmented approach is well made. Such education is urgently needed: we must not, as he points out, continue to produce economists who "add the price of the sale of a bushel of wheat to the gross national product while forgetting to subtract the three bushels of topsoil lost to grow it."[573]

An example of holistic education was begun at Charlton Manor Primary School in Greenwich, where beekeeping illustrates what can be done to approach a nature-based subject from several perspectives. Struck by how calm and how fascinated the children were when a swarm of bees descended on the school, the head teacher Tim Baker had the swarm caught, took some members of staff with him to bee-keeping classes, then integrated beekeeping into the school's curriculum. In PE the children study the waggle dance of scout bees which signals to the other bees where nectar is to be found. They use honey in cookery lessons, and in geography they learn how bees are used in different parts of the world. The children sell the honey they produce with the help of business advisors. An unexpected benefit has been the "massive effect" the bees have had on behaviour, especially that of some unruly pupils. For the first time, some of them began to think of other people and their responsibility to them. One pupil, who was given to violent outbursts of kicking, punching, and throwing furniture, and who struggled with academic work, discovered that he excelled at the practical side of beekeeping – the making of wooden frames and dismantling of the hive to get at the honey. Being with the bees made him feel peaceful, he said.[574]

We do indeed need to educate the whole person, heart and spirit as much as head, but we will always need specialists too. Those scientists who have been able to trace the history of global air temperatures by examining air bubbles in polar ice cores, and the historians whose skilled scrutiny of the details of past life can chart the effects of climatic changes, are essential to our understanding of long-term trends. Indeed, the narrow formal education which has been the norm around the world hitherto does not produce the same tunnel vision in every pupil and student. If it were purely the blinkered intellectual understanding fostered by an over-specialised education system that had led us into the environmental predicament in which we now find ourselves, how is it that the environmental movement has developed? Since the late 1960s tens of thousands of environmental campaigners in many countries, scientists and lay people alike, who have themselves been through that system, have had an intuitive appreciation of the natural world and the way we have been mistreating it. There must have been other factors at work in these individuals that enabled them to appreciate the wholeness and interconnectedness of life. It seems likely that they have had their own sensibility towards ecological connectedness, and personal priorities which led them to value the unspoilt natural world more highly than the considerations of personal consumption and corporate profitability which are largely responsible for environmental destruction.

The Origins of a Holistic Relationship with Nature

What is it, then, that determines an individual's appreciation of and attitude to the environment? An international research project[575] conducted in the 1990s in fourteen countries in six continents, which set out to investigate the origins of environmental awareness, knowledge and concern, sheds useful light on this question. Two thousand environmental educators were asked to write an autobiographical statement identifying those influences and experiences that led to their environmental interest, and to indicate any particularly memorable years of their lives in terms of the development of their environmental awareness. From the memories of these actively ecologically-minded people the study discovered that direct early experience of the natural world was the most influential factor in promoting their environmental appreciation. Personal outdoor experiences, often gained with a close family member or older friend, had been of far greater significance than any provided by formal education. The researchers concluded that, "early childhood is an absolutely critical time. During these formative years, impacts on thinking and feeling about the environment occur that will endure the passage of years".[576]

A similar verdict was reached by other researchers who investigated factors affecting individuals' levels of eco-literacy in several countries.[577] Ecological literacy demands specific knowledge as well as an understanding of principles, and these researchers assessed such knowledge by measuring how many local species of plants and animals, and physical components of ecosystems, such as soils and water, people could name. This study found, too, that people with the highest levels of eco-literacy, wherever they lived, acquired it from parents, relatives or friends, or from interacting with the natural environment in the course of work or hobbies. In the UK, the most important factor affecting ecological knowledge was found to be the frequency with which individuals visited the countryside. Those who were least competent in identifying local species had acquired their knowledge primarily from television and schooling. Yet more than eighty per cent of children in industrial regions receive their ecological information from school or television.[578]

For most adults with a delight in and reverence for the flora, fauna, geology, meteorology and so on that we refer to under the umbrella term 'nature', learning about its systems and its responsiveness to human activity has, in the first place, been the result of personal experiences of the natural world which have engaged the senses and emotions ahead of the intellect. Following such encounters, intellectual learning about the workings of natural phenomena can certainly enhance fascination and enjoyment, whether or not a person has a scientific bent. Discovering the moon's pull on the tide, for instance, or the metamorphosis of caterpillar to pupa to butterfly, can, like the figure of eight communication dance of honey bees, present knowledge which, for some, is mysterious and poetic rather than a mechanical matter of fact. It binds human sensibilities to the extra-human world.

There are many simple ways we can feel an emotional tie with the natural world through sheer sensory revelling, such as listening to a blackbird singing from a rooftop, spotting from a train window the purple spikes of buddleia waving improbably from the roof of a derelict factory, watching a spider spinning a web, noticing as the moon waxes or wanes from night to night, searching for shells on a beach, throwing sticks into a stream and watching their watery passage in a game of Pooh sticks, flying a kite, making a grass whistle, blackberry-picking, going out in a thunder storm or marvelling at a rainbow. Sufficient early moments of this sort can be enough to inculcate a lifelong love of nature and a desire to protect it from harm. This is not to say that it is not important to learn both about detail and about the bigger picture at every stage of education, but simply to emphasise that the deepest, most enduring learning depends in the first instance on direct, affective and sensory experience.

Autobiographical insights

Author after author, writing about what initiated a professional interest in some aspect of the natural environment, has recounted striking but ordinary, formative experiences. As David Orr has written, "Most of us do what we do as environmentalists and profess what we do as professors because of an early, deep, and vivid resonance between the natural world and ourselves."[579] Jules Pretty, Professor of Environment and Society at the University of Essex, who writes about the importance and relevance of nature, and was a co-author of the comparative eco-literacy research described above, is another. As a boy he lived mostly on the east coast of England where his bedroom overlooked the sea and the sunrise, and he has described how he and his brother, "would run across the promenade and down the cliff path, and swim and run and throw stones, and climb on the groynes and pier, and feel the dry salt crisp on our skins."[580] Memories from an urban childhood are still fully alive in the mind of sports and nature writer Simon Barnes, who has recounted:

> I remember my boyhood on Streatham Common... playing football and cricket, and better, climbing trees.
>
> We had a very close relationship with those trees. We knew them as individuals. Different trees presented different challenges. Some were pleasantly easy, and we climbed them for the playful rhythm of branches that grew like step ladders or spiral stairs. Some we cherished for the broadness of their branches, for the wobbling journey out towards their tips. Some we liked for the technical challenge: the big reach, the scrabbling of plimsoll against trunk, the hooking of the leading leg round the bough... There was one we called the Pigeon Tree, there was a pigeon nest when we first climbed it, just visible, a few feet above the highest climbable point... This tree-climbing youth was nothing less than a deep and intense relationship with non-human life.[581]

Early memories of nature were still alive for author Richard Adams, too, eighty years on. Well-known for his novel *Watership Down* about a warren of rabbits, and based on the known behaviour of the wild creatures, Adams reminisced in a newspaper interview how the first time he walked with his father to the River Kennett he saw trout rising, and his father pointed out herons and other wildlife, insisting that the little boy be able to name what he saw.[582]

Tony Juniper, the influential environmental campaigner, writer and sustainability advisor, perhaps best known as one-time Executive Director of Friends of the Earth, England, Wales and Northern Ireland and Vice Chair of Friends of the Earth International, who is author of an important book, *What has Nature Ever Done for Us?*[583] is another person whose career developed out of an early love of nature. He recalls different kinds of experience.[584] The first occurred when he was walking near his home with his grandfather at the age of about 4 and noticed some hairy caterpillars on a nettle patch; walking the same way again a few days later, he found the nettles and caterpillars withered and dead, having been sprayed with weed killer. "This incident," Juniper writes, "was just one in a long line of environmental experiences that shaped my views during childhood. As I got older I spent much of my time riding my bicycle in search of wildlife. I became obsessed first with birds, then reptiles, and then insects. I wanted to know more about plants and how they formed their communities...My passion for nature brought me into contact with filled-in ponds, drained marshes, polluted streams, new buildings covering little bits of wild green space, hedgerows and trees grubbed up to increase the size of fields."[585] Juniper was 13 when he took his first campaigning action, attempting (unsuccessfully) to prevent the bulldozing of a patch of swamp where reed warblers were nesting.

Nature and the non-specialist
While early close encounters with nature are usually of huge significance for individuals who choose, when they grow up, to pursue some aspect of the environment in their working lives, they can be very important, too, for the way others choose to live; indeed, several of the modest consumers, recounted unsolicited childhood memories of nature. Some of these were experienced alone and some with a parent or sibling, and they believed these had exerted a marked influence on their adult priorities. Only one, however, Rachel, subsequently took up related work. I, too, have always attributed my own long-standing and active concern for the environment to childhood experience. Growing up in upstairs flats in London, I treasure memories of frequent visits by pushchair, foot or bus, to beautiful parks where I fed the ducks and ran around enjoying the green surroundings, as well as trips to urban woods, and to the relative wildness of Hampstead

Heath. But I particularly think back to various quite undramatic moments during two holidays at the large home of family friends in the Lake District. In this beautiful part of the country I climbed fells amongst sheep, enjoying the limitless space, the height, the breeze and the sunshine, and the view across the valley. When at the bottom, I fished for tiddlers from the lush bank of the stately River Eden. Back at the house, I wondered at the lifeless moths on the doormat every morning, unaccountably having scorched themselves to death on the light outside the great front door, at the hedgehog which ventured onto the veranda and ate the food we put out for it, at the smell of the sweet peas I was invited to pick in the garden, at the rabbits which played on the lawn in the evening, and at the thinness of the stalks of the harebells in the grass – which I therefore assumed were hairbells.

Indeed, one of the great pleasures for me of those holidays was the variety of wild flowers we found, and their names. From my mother, who had attended Charlotte Mason teacher training college in Ambleside, where the observation, painting and naming of wild flowers was considered an important activity for teachers in training, I learnt the wonderfully quirky names of ivy leaved toadflax, shepherd's purse, ragged robin, ladies bedstraw and crow's foot trefoil. For me the delight and fascination of nature was, and still is, not the scientific whys and wherefores but the aesthetics of it, its striking sights, the elegance of its intertwined systems, and its language: hornbeam, galaxy, icicle, cirrus, mirage, marsupial, umbelliferae. Indeed, those childhood introductions to the Earth constitute a third major plank of the foundations of this book.

Late discovery of nature

An inference from all the evidence of the impact of contact with nature at a young age is that any child who is exposed to natural environments and encouraged to explore them freely will go on to develop a special relationship with nature, but this does not necessarily happen. Observations of siblings can illustrate how children within a family may respond very differently to essentially the same experience. Not every small child who noticed dried up caterpillars on withered nettles would be so distressed and anxious to know the reason as Tony Juniper was, after all! Some children simply seem to be born with a greater affinity for the natural world than others. This does not mean, though, that all should not have plentiful opportunities to experience it. Any child will benefit in the moment from such exposure, as demonstrated by the projects with school children described above, and it seems likely that some level of appreciation will follow, even if it is not overt. The scope for the employment of naturalists and associated experts is limited, but we all need to take account of our daily environmental impact, whatever our occupation.

Another possible inference is that it may seem that if a child is not fortunate enough to come to develop a personal relationship with nature while growing up then the opportunity is lost forever. This is not necessarily the case. Vince Cable, deputy leader of the Liberal Democrat Party, wrote in a newspaper piece when in his late 60s, "As an urban and suburban man, I have discovered late in life, the sounds of birdsong and wind in the trees and grass and the simple pleasures of walking in the fields and woods among deer, horses and cattle."[586] Even growing up in the midst of green, if cultivated, countryside is no guarantee of developing a love of nature. Having children was a factor which some of the environmental educators in the international study described above cited as having influenced their pro-environmental inclinations, and so it was for writer Geraldine Taylor. Life in the big city of Bristol had a frantic pace which she wanted to change, and her financial resources were stretched. So, as her 6-year-old son loved books about animals, Taylor, who had sad associations with the countryside from her own childhood, decided to see if her son's interest would transfer from the page to the outdoors. Because they lived in a flat without a garden, Taylor and her husband and son decided to 'adopt' a piece of ground, a small wooded clump of wild parkland. Mother and son visited the clump every day, at first joined on each occasion by a robin, and as the weeks and months passed, developed their skills of observation and noticed more and more species of bird and plant. How their enterprise unfolded and developed is engagingly described by Taylor in her book *Planting Acorns: an adventure story and guide book*,[587] and she has since become an established observer and writer on the wildlife of the Bristol Downs.

Another story of a 6-year-old son leading his mother to discover the depth of satisfaction to be found in natural surroundings was related to me by the mother of Rick, one of the children who went to Wellie Wednesday. Melissa herself, it seemed, was a changed person as a result of this project, for, having got into the habit of taking Rick to the beach every Sunday, realising how it benefitted him to be out of doors, this young mother started to go to the beach on her own, too, to run. She told me:

> "I escape, I don't have no phone, sometimes I'm the only person on the beach, it's lovely. That is where I feel really happy. A bit uncomfortable at first cos it's really strange being in your own company own without

distractions. It's took a long while, cos I was always on the go, but now it's really nice to take time and be comfortable. It's a big thing, it's a hard thing to do to be with your own company, to know what to do. You learn to like it, because if you just want to get away from everything, from people, cars, everyday things, the beach is the most beautiful place and most relaxing. Honey, before I discovered the beach I was a shopaholic and it's a real cliché cos the girls at work say, 'here comes the beach girl' cos I'm always at the beach, but now I get more enjoyment from the small things, and it's the small things in life that matter, just peace and quiet. Be thankful for what you've got really and enjoy what's around you but you never see it. There's nothing nicer than walking on the beach."

Before I discovered the beach I was a shopaholic. Not only did Melissa discover the restoring effect of physical exercise and solitude in a wild place, but this discovery resulted in her giving up her shopping habit. Once she had experienced the far more profound fulfilment of a sense of oneness with the wide open beach, she lost her desire to keep consuming things she didn't need. As the pull of the stores dropped away, she found enjoyment in the small things in life and realised that it was these that really mattered.

Time spent out of doors in natural environments is something that parents and children can enjoy together. Their shared experiences of different landscapes, terrains, weather conditions and seasons, of sightings of birds, insects, animals and plant life, will not only enhance their own experience of life and sense of relationship with nature, but it will also enrich family bonds. Anywhere, whether in the countryside, on the coast, in the park, or on the urban way to school, curiosity can be tickled and interest kindled by going on 'wondering walks',[588] thinking about the natural phenomena all around: I wonder how many rain drops made up that puddle? I wonder if there have ever been two clouds with exactly the same shape? I wonder how birds find their way back to the right tree in the forest to feed their babies? I wonder if waves ever come back to the same beach twice? There are many ways in which families can incorporate nature into their on-going lives. Building a garden weather station, collecting and polishing stones, making a nature table, adopting a tree, holidaying in a national park, taking part in a beach clean-up, and getting up to hear the dawn chorus are just a few of the suggestions that Richard Louv makes.[589]

Nature, the pivot of our wellbeing

The glimpses into a variety of experience I have shown in this chapter underline the major importance for children, and the adults they become, of immediate, personal encounters with nature. My reasons for these illustrations are of course twofold: the one is to find ways in which we can enhance personal wellbeing, the other to develop our collective capacity to love the natural world, and to understand ecological principles, so as to be best placed to protect it. A *sense* of nature is not something that can be taught mechanically like how to solve a quadrilateral equation or to write grammatically, or learnt by rote like the lines of a poem or the periodic table. A feeling for nature must come from watching it, listening to it, touching and smelling it, being immersed in it, discovering its possibilities and accepting its constraints. In an interesting twist on the emphasis I have put on modesty of a material kind, Richard Louv suggests that "[I]nexplicable nature provokes humility".[590] Rachel Carson, author of *Silent Spring*,[591] the book that has been seen as the original stimulus for the environmental movement, wrote in another book:

> I sincerely believe that for the child… it is not half so important to know as to feel. If facts are the seeds that later produce knowledge and wisdom, then the emotions and the impressions of the senses are the fertile soil in which the seeds must grow. The years of early childhood are the time to prepare the soil. Once the emotions have been aroused – a sense of the beautiful, the excitement of the new and the unknown, a feeling of sympathy, pity, admiration or love – then we wish for knowledge about the object of our emotional response. Once found, it has lasting meaning.[592]

Humanity is a not separate entity with a prerogative to 'conquer' nature, to be 'masters of the universe' as the old children's television cartoon would have it. Rachel Carson believed that it is important for parents who want to teach their children but who feel unfamiliar with nature, as well as for children themselves, to feel nature rather than to know it. She encouraged parents thus:

> Wherever you are and whatever your resources, you can still look up at the sky – its dawn and twilight beauties, its moving clouds, its stars by night. You can listen to the wind, whether it blows with majestic voice through a forest or sings a many-voiced chorus around the eves of your

house or the corners of your apartment building, and in the listening, you can gain magical release from your thoughts. You can feel the rain on your face and think of its long journey, its many transmutations, from sea to air to earth.[593]

Our culture accentuates individual independence, mastery and competition. Psychological theory has therefore come to emphasise the development of the child as a process of separation and individuation, and lacks understanding of the need to develop a complementary sense of integration with the wider physical world.[594] We need to rediscover that we are, individually and collectively, a small part of something very big. Eco-psychologist Anita Barrows believes that a sense of oneness with rather than separateness from the natural world is as critical to our development as human attachment, and has called for a new theory of child development which would acknowledge that the infant is born into an ecological context as well as a social world. Proper recognition of the personal and societal importance of developing a bond with nature in the early years of life would have huge significance for an array of policy areas, including child-rearing, land-use and the design of built environments,[595] as well as for education. Natural England recommends that for the sake of their health and wellbeing everyone, regardless of age, should have access to at least two hectares of natural green space no more than five minutes' walk from home, and a site of at least twenty hectares within two kilometres.[596] Were this right to be enshrined in law, attention and resources would need to be devoted to ensuring the protection of suitable pieces of undeveloped land within reasonable reach of every residential area, nursery and school. These more or less wild plots would benefit all town- and city-dwellers.

Conclusion: We Need to Regain a Sense of our Place in Nature

Contact with the natural environment should become an integral part of education at all ages – and, indeed, of life before school. All children need to experience the reality that they are part of nature, not apart from it, to have the opportunity to feel its great scale, its repeated rhythms, its intricacy and wholeness, the rawness of the elements. It is each child's birthright to discover his or her place in the natural order of things, and something of the workings of the non-human world with which humans are interconnected. This right should be regarded as inalienable. It also requires proactive support. We urgently need to find our way back into the fabric of the natural world, and rediscover the delight, calm and inspiration it can bestow on the human mind, its complexity, limits and awful power. Only then will we really be able to protect its vital systems and fully experience its beneficence.

12

Personal Qualities and Capacities for Building a Better Future

Optimising the Capability to Experience Wellbeing

Wellbeing can be thought about, in very simple terms, as enjoying life; both what we get out of life and what we put in. It's to do with optimal human functioning. In Chapter 4 we saw how Amartya Sen, an economist, focusing on individual functioning rather than material status, has proposed that the way to assess the level of a country's development is in terms of its people's freedoms to take part in the life of their society: he calls these their 'capabilities'. He warns that we should not concentrate exclusively on income when considering what determines wellbeing, for "income is not the only instrument in generating capabilities".[597] In this final chapter I consider a different way of looking at capabilities and the wellbeing they enable people to experience.

It is undoubtedly true that money is often needed to acquire contributors to wellbeing, such as access to the countryside from the city, say, or a musical instrument. But it is not, conversely, the case, however, that those assets that cannot be bought are necessarily readily available to everyone. It is all very well, for instance, to be encouraged to 'connect', but if we don't have good social skills, this is easier said than done. We need certain personal qualities and capacities in order to be able to optimise our wellbeing.[ix] We can regard them as personal capital.

---

ix   Capacities is a somewhat ambiguous word which can have both an actual and a potential sense. In using it I mean capacities that are realised, rather than simply potential. Clearly every human being has the potential capacity to experience essentially human abilities, but my point is that for such capacities to be able to contribute to a person's wellbeing they have to be realised. Such capacities and qualities constitute the capability of individuals to enter into and benefit from those aspects of and possibilities in life which nourish wellbeing.

Personal Capital

There are many desirable personal qualities and capacities which enhance our ability to extract the maximum benefit from our experience, and to make a worthwhile contribution to the world around us. They include such attributes as interest, enthusiasm, an inclination to be proactive, perseverance, empathy, perceptiveness, and appreciativeness.

The most important determinant of wellbeing is the quality of our relationships. These, particularly relationships with the people we have most to do with, are more likely to enhance wellbeing if both sides exhibit qualities like responsiveness, trustworthiness, dependability and kindness. Self-awareness and self-esteem are helpful too, in ensuring that the motives that prompt our behaviour are healthy, that is, that we treat other people for themselves and not in order to boost our own sense of relative worth. An ability to listen attentively to others helps build strong relationships, too, as does forbearance, and a sense of humour.

As I have said before, an inclination to experience appreciation is known to nourish wellbeing; but, in order to be able to do so, to notice small details and to gain pleasure or insight from them, we must have the capacities for stillness, observation, concentration, reflection and interest. In order to be able to draw out all the potential for interest, joy, comfort, humour or gratitude from the dew drop on the spider's web, the chance encounter, the bus driver's waiting for us as we run for the bus, the unusual architectural detail, or the sun shining on an event that is important to us, we also need to have the ability to put aside other concerns that may preoccupy us, and be wholly present in the moment.

Attention

The capacities I have highlighted may seem simple but not everyone actually has the ability to notice, to sit still, to feel interest, to pay attention or to experience simple enjoyment. Some people lack perceptiveness, or do not engage much with the possibilities of life and are easily bored. Some wellbeing-supportive attributes come naturally to some people; others need opportunity, encouragement and practice to develop. Any kind of activity that can bring fulfilment requires the ability to pay sustained attention, as well as the staying power to master skills and the confidence not to be deterred by obstacles, mistakes and failures. Attention is a system which is a three-step process of awareness (taking in information from the senses), orientation (sorting and shaping it) and focus (planning and decision-making).[598] In the view of Maggie Jackson, who has made a thorough investigation of attention, it forms the very basis of a wide range of activities and conditions, including learning, contentment, caring, morality, reflection and spirit.[599] It is Jackson's fear, however, that the nature of contemporary life is eroding our capacity to pay attention. For example, very young children have been found to play with toys for shorter periods and with less focus if a television showing even an adult programme is playing in the room, as they look up for a few seconds every minute or two and their concentration is interrupted. This finding has serious implications for later cognitive development.[600] So, too, does the observation of teachers of a reduction in the ability of little children starting school to listen.[601] For adults, Jackson points out, life now is characterised by restless multi-tasking, mobility and the constant call of emails, texts, tweets, phone calls and the like, which are wearing down our basic capacity and willingness to give undivided attention to anything. If we are serious as a society about enhancing wellbeing we must consider how to develop (as well as how not to lose) attentiveness and all those other personal qualities which will underpin each individual's capability to access the kinds of experience which nourish wellbeing.

Wellbeing and the Climate

Mitigation and adaptation

Prioritising the sources of true wellbeing and re-ordering society so as to facilitate the development of relevant skills would not only nurture happier individuals, it would tend to direct thought away from material acquisition. Increasing the capacity to gain enjoyment in life from non-material sources would also reduce the pain which is otherwise likely to be experienced in the future when resource scarcity constrains consumption. Enhancing this capacity can be seen as mitigating some of the emotional effects of the ecological changes in store. It is the psychological equivalent of mitigating the physical effects of climate change by measures such as the replacing of fossil fuels with renewable sources of energy and developing flood- and drought-resistant crops. Similarly, we need to build human qualities and capacities to help us to adapt emotionally and socially, as successfully as we can, to rapidly developing new situations. We should be looking into the future now and recognising the need to be well prepared psychologically for the unpredictable circumstances that lie ahead. The upheavals of the future will demand even more of our inner resources and personal attributes. If we are going to be able to enjoy life in a much tougher and less certain world we will all need a capacity for constructive responses to new scenarios. Of greater value than ever will be:

- warm, supportive relationships
- an appreciative perceptiveness and an ability to feel uplifted
- the capacity to live in the moment combined with a future-orientation
- a co-operative, collaborative spirit for the development of socially cohesive, socially just solutions to problems
- a sense of personal agency and competence, to know that one can have positive impacts on one's own life and our collective existence
- flexibility for responding to new situations
- imagination and resourcefulness for devising new, better ways of doing things
- a sense of personal responsibility towards the physical environment and social world, and a willingness to shape one's behaviour accordingly
- empathy for those particularly affected; for example, migrants displaced by flooding or drought
- grit for putting up with inevitable changes, many of them unwelcome

It is growth in positive human qualities and capacities that we now need, not growth in economic output for those who already have enough or more.

However much we are able to quell our appetites for consumption in future, the accumulating effects of greenhouse gases already released into the atmosphere will be keenly felt in years to come, in rising sea levels, hotter temperatures and more frequent, fiercer, extreme weather events. We will feel the effects of these climatic changes, directly or indirectly, in terms, among others, of food insecurity and the flight of people from one part of the country to another, or from another part of the world to ours. We will certainly need enhanced human strengths if we are going to be able to deal with changed circumstances in ways that avoid social conflict and eat away as little as possible at our personal sense of wellbeing. Learning to refocus now on *being* and *doing* rather than *having* would also mitigate the erosion of wellbeing which could well be incurred by a forced reduction in consumption brought about by the dwindling of resources, rising prices and the increase in demand from a growing population.

It is perhaps helpful to consider that the many personal qualities and capacities which are advantageous in the promotion of wellbeing in the present and preparedness for future life can be grouped under four general headings:

- those which facilitate good relationships, e.g. empathy, co-operation, humour, forbearance
- those which support personal nourishment, e.g. attention, stillness, practical skills, gratitude
- those which help engagement of various kinds, e.g. confidence, perseverance, enthusiasm, questioning
- those which will help bring about successful future adaptation, e.g. flexibility, a sense of fairness and justice, imagination, and communication

These are just some of the salient attributes, and many of them sit just as comfortably in more than one category.

Resilience

All the attributes I have named add up to enhanced resilience, the ability to withstand or even respond positively to stressors, crises or difficulties.[602] The underpinning importance of mental health generally, and of resilience in particular, is becoming increasingly recognised in the broad field of health, quite independently of any consideration of a changing world. In 2009 the Mental Health Foundation reported to the World Health Organisation:

> If we do not create and implement policies that promote mental health and build resilience in individuals and communities, then we will never achieve the flourishing society that we should be aiming for in the twenty-first century…The time has come for a radical change in our thinking about our mental health, and to develop a deeper understanding of why we need to put mental health at the very core of political thinking and policy-making…All policy-makers, from those in government to those in local communities, need to consider and take into account the mental health implications of all policies. There is an urgent need to create policies that underline precisely those characteristics that individuals and communities need to survive adversity: respect, dignity, self-esteem, positive identity and social connectedness.[603]

While resilience is discussed here in terms of dealing positively with the ups and downs of normal everyday life as we have known it hitherto, this passage also has a lot to tell us about its importance for our adaptation when some of the parameters of life we have always taken as given begin to shift. It hints, too, at the crucial roles in this respect of both public policies and individual attributes. We can make some informed guesses at how the world may look in time to come, and I outlined in the first chapter how it has been estimated that climate change is likely to affect the British Isles.[604] We will need to adapt not only to the changing physical character of the country but also to a new demographic profile as climate migrants head for our relatively less affected island. This will call for more than mere adjustment.

Another definition of resilience is the "psychological ability to let go of old internal structures of thinking and behaving that over the years have given us a sense of stability and coherence and…[an] ability to create and reintegrate new structures of thinking and behaving that provide us with a more mature sense of coherence".[605] That is, in order to respond constructively to the new conditions we will somehow need to change the way we think. For this we will all need an open mind-set. So, as long-established patterns and expectations are disrupted by climate change, dwindling oil, increasing global population, and all the associated effects, pre-existing wellbeing will be particularly important, for happy people tend to cope better with change than unhappy people.[606]

In addition, positive emotions facilitate creative problem-solving,[607] a skill which will certainly be called upon for devising means of adapting successfully to change. While little study has been made of the psychological dimensions of adaptation,[608] it is known that successful recovery after survival from natural disasters is more likely to occur where there is a high level of social capital, that is to say, close relationships between individuals, and networks of connections between different groups. Thus we see that individual wellbeing both benefits from and contributes to the resilience of the wider social group.

The Transition Town model

The concept of social resilience lies at the heart of the Transition Town movement, a movement of people coming together in their local communities, be they villages, market towns or neighbourhoods in cities, to develop ways of living which optimise the potential of the local, in producing or providing food and other essential needs, skills and interpersonal support.[609] This is an approach which was first articulated and implemented by Rob Hopkins in Kinsale, Ireland, in 2005 as a constructive response to the twin challenges of climate change and peak oil; more recently it has also incorporated the economic recession. The model is designed to address mitigation and adaptation simultaneously, socially as well as physically, on a community scale. At once pragmatic and philosophical, and based on empirical historical example, the Transition model set out by Hopkins in *The Transition Handbook*[610] is a vision of how individuals can come together and make changes on the personal and community level. The aim is to re-imagine and reconstruct the fabric of everyday living in such a way that it avoids dependence on oil and the generation of carbon emissions, and enriches the experience of life as it does so.

The Transition concept is based on the three assumptions. Firstly that a future of dramatically lower energy consumption is inevitable; secondly that it is better to plan for this than be taken by surprise; and thirdly that "by unleashing the collective genius of those around us to creatively and proactively design our energy descent, we can build ways of living that are more connected, more enriching and that recognise the biological limits of our planet".[611] Taking the position that the looming compound crises of climate change, peak oil and economic instability place us on "the cusp of... an unprecedented economic, cultural and social renaissance", it envisages, and has rapidly begun to inspire in hundreds of communities in Britain and across the world, a wealth of community-based initiatives. *The Transition Companion,*[612] the sequel to *The Transition Handbook,* outlines a wide range of them.

Many Transition initiatives revolve around social enterprises for growing vegetables, and baking bread and brewing beer with locally sourced ingredients. There are tool-making-for-sustainability initiatives such as oral history collecting, resilience-mapping, story-telling and public speaking, and some Transition groups have prepared energy descent action plans, set up community renewable energy companies, and established local currencies for trading locally produced goods to boost the local economy. There are re-skilling events and groups to help people learn how to knit, weave, sew, darn, maintain their bikes, preserve produce, build with straw bales, make herbal tinctures, practise permaculture, and so on. Other activities might include planting nut trees on common land, seed exchanges, setting up communal urban vegetable gardens, arts events and walks. Such skills and activities are the necessary foundations on which to build a radically different way of living, one that is resilient through being both materially modest and psychologically fulfilling. All are characterised by the common ethos of taking control of the essentials of life, creative communal problem-solving, and enjoyment in the basic processes of living.

Human wellbeing and resilience as a process

The understanding of practical resilience adopted in the Transition approach is based on what is known about the features which enable ecosystems to reorganise themselves following shocks,[613] namely, modularity (i.e. elements of the system are not too closely tied to each other), tightness of feedbacks (i.e. effects are directly observable) and diversity (i.e. variety of features). Human wellbeing and resilience can be said to have parallels with all of these, particularly diversity and feedback loops. For the individual, diversity in this context would mean that their life was characterised by variety – by social connectedness, engagement in learning, being creative, contributing to the community and so on. A person's investment in life would thus be spread, so that if one facet proved less satisfactory at a particular time there would still be others to provide fulfilment. This is the antithesis of the approach of the 'workaholic' who focuses on work to the exclusion of outside interests, a social network, community involvement and even, perhaps proper attention to family.

Feedback loops are about the ability to intervene and adjust processes in response to the development of undesired effects. Thus the individual who finds that the book they start to read proves uninspiring can leave it and try another; a disappointing attempt to paint a picture, design a garden or construct a built-in wardrobe can lead to the devising of a different approach; and a walk planned for a day which turns out to be grey and miserable can be taken on another of cheering sunshine. Such adjustments to activities are unlikely to incur significant loss of any kind, and any of them can be further developed or varied in all sorts of ways, which may lead to personal growth. The process of shopping, in contrast, though found enjoyable by many, is pretty insensitive to adjustment on those occasions when it does not produce the hoped for result. Mass produced consumer goods which fail to please when they arrive home can at best be returned and replaced, but the only scope there is for a response to unsatisfactory results from shopping is to go through a similar process again. In general, then, the feedback loops inherent in creative and social processes can be far more responsive and adaptive than those involved in the processes of material consumption. People who attach greater importance to doing and being than to having will not only have a richer experience of life, but will also be more flexible and psychologically more resilient to dwindling resources than those with more of a focus on consumption.

Education for a different future

We must all now recognise that the parameters of life are changing. The world economic system is already in a profound state of flux, the outcomes of which nobody can foretell but which will not end in a simple and lasting return to the pre-crisis position. The effects of climate change and the increasing claims of the BRIC and CIVETS[x] countries on the Earth's resources are only going to become more keenly felt as time goes on. It should therefore be a core aim of education to develop each child's inner resources, the personal capacities out of which all other learning – and flourishing – grows. Our education system has overemphasised the cognitive, with employment in the growth economy as its goal. Personal development has been given relatively much less attention. Now that the global framework is shifting irrevocably we must address the demands of "education for the inevitable", in the phrase of educationalist Michael Bassey, whose particular concern is for a future without oil.[614] If flourishing is our aim – and how could it not be? – the balance of emphasis in education must change too. What individuals and society need is education with a therapeutic ethos,[615] that is, education which feeds the soul and awakens thought, is dynamic and empowering, and which will enable people to create a world with healthier values.[616] Of course intellectual learning will always be important, but we need have no fear that it will lose out, for any learner who is intrinsically motivated, curious, reflective and persevering will naturally tend to be successful in this regard. Children should be allowed the freedom to learn by doing, without the constraints of endless assessments. In this way they will discover where their interests, enthusiasms and abilities lie, as well as their limitations,[617] and be able to engage better and take more responsibility for developing their own learning.

Attachment, a Fundamental Factor

The earliest learning

While education in general and individual teachers in particular can exert considerable influence on the shaping of individuals and society (and we have seen references to schooling among the influences cited by the modest consumers), much has happened to children that will colour their future lives long before they start school. So the experience on which I want to focus now is much more intimate than formal education; it is

---

x   BRIC and CIVETS: the fast-growing economies of Brazil, Russia, India and China, and Colombia, Indonesia, Vietnam, Egypt, Turkey, and South Africa

the nature of the attachment relationship that is established between the child and its parent/s or other primary caregiver/s early in life. According to the findings of the seventy-five-year-long Grant Study, "love (or in theoretical terms, attachment)", is "the most important contributor to joy and success in adult life".[618] Contentment among men in their late 70's, the study found, correlated not with early financial privilege or a high salary later on but with the warmth of their childhood environment, to a significant extent, and very significantly with their closeness to their father.[619] Attachment Theory was originated by John Bowlby in England in the late 1960s,[620] based on intensive observations of many young children and their mothers, and was subsequently developed by him and others over many years.

Drawing on evolutionary theory, Bowlby argued that for a species to survive, the young need to be protected from danger and that this gives rise to an instinct which predisposes the human infant to seek attachment to a particular figure, especially when feeling threatened or distressed.[621] The theory that experience of their particular 'attachment figures' has a major impact on individual differences in the mental and behavioural development of children is now supported by a great deal of empirical evidence,[622] and a huge body of data testifies to the importance of the responsiveness of the care-giver in handling the infant in the first year of life for the development of secure attachment.[623] A responsive care-giver is one who is sensitively attuned to the child, understanding his or her individual attributes and accepting his or her behavioural idiosyncrasies, and who is thus capable of managing harmonious interactions with the infant, especially those involving the soothing of distress.[624] The essence of secure attachment lies in its provision of a safe haven at times of anxiety or discomfort and a dependable base for exploration.

Clearly, not all parents (or other attachment figures, who can include grandparents and older siblings, for instance) provide this ideal support. The child adapts its attachment style according to how the adult behaves towards it,[625] and how it can best get its inherent need for attention met. When the main care-giver is warm, available and consistent in their responses, the infant will explore actively, interact positively with the care-giver, and be upset at separation. If, however, the parent does not respond appropriately to the infant's signals of need or distress the attachment style will become insecure. The mark left by the way a baby is handled is deep because its physiological systems are delicate and still in the process of formation, its stress or other arousal responses being set according to its experience when in these states.[626] "When parents respond to the baby's signals, they are participating in many biological processes. They are helping the baby's nervous system to mature in such a way that it does not get overstressed", explains Sue Gerhardt,[627] a psychotherapist who has specialised in the study of early development. Although the degree of sensitivity required by babies for their optimum development may sound demanding of parents it comes naturally to many, and it is reckoned that the majority of people (between 55% and 65%) are securely attached.[628]

Bowlby understood the effect of attachment style as the setting up in the child's mind of a working model of relationships and therefore of what to expect from the social world. He posited that children with sensitive and responsive attachment figures would learn to approach life with confidence or to seek help if they could not manage on their own. Children who could not depend on an available, attuned attachment figure, on the other hand, would come to see the social environment as unreliable, and behave accordingly.[629] This working model construct has now been generally accepted by psychologists and neuroscientists,[630] and its explanation of the way the human mind develops has informed therapeutic approaches taken to a number of psychological difficulties.[631]

Broader effects of attachment

Psychologist Klaus Grossman, who has conducted two longitudinal studies in Germany of twenty and twenty-two years' duration with individuals from birth to adulthood, believes that, "Attachment is *not* one relationship among others; it is the very foundation of healthy individual development. More, it is the pre-condition for developing a coherent mind."[632] In this assertion we see just one of the substantial claims that have been made for how secure attachment favours the development of a wide range of desirable human attributes, attributes which have a crucial bearing on our capacity to enjoy life. True, some children seem to be born with predispositions of remarkable resilience to terrible experience of ill-treatment or brutality;[633] nevertheless, it is generally the case that securely attached individuals have a more stable sense of self-worth and thus feel less need for self-enhancement. They are more compassionate and altruistic, more effective care-givers themselves, have more humane values, are better at communicating, and have greater tolerance of 'outgroup' members.[634] The value of such characteristics is obvious. They will be all the more advantageous for populations of a world in flux.

Attachment and wellbeing

As we have seen, what contributes more than anything to our sense of wellbeing is the quality of our personal relationships; thus the style of attachment established at the beginning of life has profound implications for the level of wellbeing we may be able to attain throughout our lifespan. Indeed the two German studies found that sensitive, supportive, accepting mothers and fathers fostered their children's psychological security throughout their immature years, and that insensitive, rejecting parents were reflected in the disavowal by their young adult children of the value of close relationships, and their inability to communicate openly or seek the help of others at times of distress.[635]

While the secure individual is likely to be inter-personally oriented and to have positive internal models of the self and others as likeable, well-intentioned, good-hearted, dependable and trustworthy, the 'avoidant' individual (whose attachment figures were rigid, rejecting or hostile) tends not to be oriented towards others; they often lack social confidence, and tend to see others as untrustworthy and undependable, to doubt their honesty and integrity, and suspect their motives. The 'ambivalently' attached person (whose attachment figures were intrusive or unpredictable) is also disadvantaged in their potential for making sound relationships, being likely to be wary of others as difficult to understand. They are also likely to see themselves and others as having little control over their own lives.[636] Such people will therefore have scant motivation to try to change in order to adapt to newly challenging conditions.

Taking another angle, Bowlby expected that by enabling the child to explore its environment with confidence, secure attachment would also promote a sense of competence.[637] A personal expectation, gained from experience, that one is generally competent to deal with situations that arise, is a necessary prerequisite for the development of a sense of autonomy, another important aspect of wellbeing, as we have seen. Confidence in one's competence – or potential competence – is likely, too, to encourage an individual to try out new activities and develop new skills; a stance, again, which will favour the proactive engagement that nourishes subjective wellbeing.

Research findings tell volumes about the huge significance of attachment style for personal and, by extension, social wellbeing. One telling study[638] involved two-year-olds being given the task of poking a toy out of a tube with two short sticks which had to be put together somehow to make one long stick. It found that those who were securely attached showed substantially more enthusiasm and persistence, more responsiveness

310

to instructions, and less frustration than the insecure children, and they openly expressed their enjoyment of the challenge. The ambivalent children, in contrast, did not smile or laugh, and nearly half the avoidant children engaged in prominent displays of pouting, whining and hitting; indeed many of the insecure children "fell apart" under the stress of having to solve the problem presented to them. The differences between the secure and the insecure children were so pronounced that they seemed to the observers like two different breeds of children.[639]

Another study found that secure pre-schoolers had more empathy for their peers in distress; indeed there was quite a contrast between them and the ambivalent children who were too preoccupied with their own needs to notice the unhappiness of others, and the avoidant children who sometimes seemed to take pleasure in another child's misery.[640] A further study revealed that secure 4½-5 year-olds were substantially more likely to have high self-esteem, be more independent, be able to enjoy themselves, respond positively to other children and have more friends than insecure children.[641]

All of the qualities fostered by security of attachment facilitate learning and personal development, and a large body of research does indeed show that students do well in school if they arrive having already developed confidence, curiosity, self-control, a sense of effectiveness, the ability to relate well to others, the ability to communicate, and the capacity to co-operate.[642] It seems more than reasonable to suggest from all this empirical evidence of the psychological effects of secure attachment that this start in life contains the best promise for the development of the kinds of personal qualities and capacities that I contend are those that best support our wellbeing and facilitate willingness to change behaviour, and are most likely to come to our aid in the world that's on its way.

Lifelong effects

Adults who were securely attached as children have a better awareness and understanding of their own motives and feelings, and an ability to reflect openly and clearly on their own inner state and that of others.[643] Conversely, attachment difficulties contribute to a large range of functional problems, sometimes to the point of anti-social and/or criminal behaviour.[644] The effect of attachment endures throughout life, and elderly people in one study who remembered supportive attachment figures during their own childhoods reported more active participation and a higher degree of life satisfaction than elderly people with memories of insecure attachment.[645] Corroborating Bowlby's prospective theorising, the Grant Study found retrospectively, from the vantage point of subjects' old age, as well as looking back over the whole course of their lives, that the most loving homes produced the most independent and the most stoical men in the cohort. They had "learnt that they could put their trust in life, which gave them the courage to go out and face it."[646] So the significance of attachment style in babyhood stretches the length of an individual's life span, and has implications far wider than for the individual alone.

Men and fathers

While issues around upbringing and attachment are almost always couched in relation to "the mother or other main care-giver", one important feature of the Grant Study which I mentioned above, albeit in relation to the development of men only and not to women, was that it was able to distinguish between the respective contributions of the mother and the father to lifelong wellbeing. Each parent appears to have their own sphere of influence in this regard. While warm early relationships with mothers emerged as having significance for men's eventual effectiveness at work and mental competence at age 80, warm relationships with fathers seemed to enhance playfulness – a characteristic whose importance we have already seen. The men who had a cordial paternal relationship enjoyed their holidays more, used humour as a coping mechanism and were significantly more satisfied with their lives in retirement. Those with poor fathering, rather than poor mothering, were far more likely to have unhappy marriages, due to an under-developed capacity for intimacy.

Attachment and environmental sustainability

So significant does attachment style appear to be, that one may reasonably suggest that it has relevance to environmental sustainability. But what is the connection? I propose that there are several perspectives from which it is relevant. One is that there is accumulating scientific research connecting successful early attachment with the development of neural networks in the prefrontal cortex of the brain which is the area associated with rational thought, decision-making, social behaviour, and self-control.[647] I also see two other connections. These are based on the different impacts of secure and insecure attachment on overall functioning. One is the effect that insecure attachment could have on personal consumption: amongst anxiously attached individuals there is a need for attention, approval and acceptance and because their relationship skills are less well developed, and because attention, approval and acceptance are commonly believed to be gained by wearing the 'right' clothes and having the 'right' possessions, it seems highly probable that insecurity of attachment will find expression in materialism. Possessions cannot reject you nor fuss over you like people can; they simply return your gaze, reflecting back at you the value with which you invest them. In fact, it has been suggested that a person who grows up feeling unknown and unappreciated as a result of his or her care-giver being unable to respond in an attuned way to his or her complex needs, is likely to develop an attitude of entitlement.[648] A sense of entitlement is, indeed, actively promoted by the kind of advertising which insinuates the idea that the potential customer should cosset and indulge themselves. It is only too easy to assume that because consumer goods are so widely available they are an automatic right. Another conjecture of Bowlby's which suggests a connection with consumption is that the insecurely attached are haunted by a fear of loneliness which they try to deal with by an over-dependence on acquisition – or on other people, work, or achievement.[649] Securely attached individuals, in contrast, will have experienced the freedom to explore and begin to master their environment, a situation which will have tended to foster an internal locus of control or sense of competence. Individuals who lack such a sense of personal control, it has been found, are more likely to become materialistic,[650] oriented outwards more than inwards.

Taking a long term perspective, then, it seems highly likely that the securely attached will be at a distinct advantage over the emotionally insecure when oil no longer gushes from the ground and the upheavals wrought by a changing climate force the all-round adoption of different modes of living, modes that depend less on material goods and more on human conviviality.

A further facet of the connection between attachment theory and sustainability that I propose concerns the wide range of positive psychological effects that have been found to be associated with secure attachment. The connectedness and mutuality which are its likely fruits are clearly advantageous when it comes to being at ease with living in the more localised, shared, co-operative way that supports environmental sustainability and social harmony, as modelled by the Transition movement. Attuned parents' understanding of their children's need to explore is likely to foster openness to experience, an important trait for the capacity to be flexible and responsive to new situations, information and insights – a capacity which will surely be increasingly called upon as the underlying conditions of life change and bring new challenges. A sense of a secure base is essential to the generation of new modes of thinking that are part and parcel of resilience. Returning to the modest consumers, it is interesting to remember that openness to all kinds of experience and their implications for the way life is lived was one of their hallmarks.

Population growth and attachment

It is now generally agreed that one of the greatest threats to ecological sustainability is overpopulation. No longer, then, should it be acceptable for women and men in high-consuming cultures, with free access to contraceptive information, advice and technology to produce children, i.e. yet more consumers, unless they really have a burning desire to raise a family. Procreation is an instinctive impulse in all creatures, and in human society we tend to regard it as an inalienable right. Human beings, however, sometimes override this instinct and there has been an increase in the number of people who have positively taken the decision not to have children. Sometimes, maybe often, though, men and women create new lives without much thought, or indeed any intention, for a variety of social and emotional reasons, or as a result of downright casualness that is nothing to do with the unfortunate failure of contraceptive measures. In light of the importance of secure attachment for life-long wellbeing, it is highly desirable that potential parents ask themselves how willing they really are to attune themselves to any offspring they produce, and to give of themselves accordingly. If they do not, they are likely to find their children to be a burden. No child should have to contend with an unwilling parent, like the mother who finds his or her company so endlessly boring that she far prefers to "ogle luxury goods" in a Knightsbridge store or "have my highlights done" than to take her small child to a pre-school music session, and who begs the nanny to stay late enough to read the bedtime story, as one journalist divulged of herself with apparent pride.[651]

Attachment and mindfulness

An important element of wellbeing, as we have seen, is the ability to respond with appreciation or gratitude. It is, indeed, a quality that shone out of much of the written and spoken testimony of the modest consumers; they noticed and gained pleasure and sustenance from many small details of life. This is a quality that arises out of mindfulness.[652] Mindfulness has been defined as "a receptive attention to and awareness of present events and experience,"[653] which provides, "a clear awareness of one's inner and outer worlds, including thoughts, emotions, sensations, actions, or surroundings as they exist at any given moment".[654] It is an awareness which is thought

314

to facilitate an unbiased insight into reality.[655] Mindfulness is not passive but a kind of participatory observation which allows one to live fully in the present, promoting interest in and concern for life, empathy for others and ecological stewardship.[656] It has been found to support a wide range of benefits: better mental and physical health, better behavioural self-regulation, better academic outcomes, greater relationship satisfaction, more constructive responses to relationship conflict, and less need for defences against threats to the self.[657]

The capacity to approach life mindfully is a clear asset in the process of cultivating the habit of questioning how many and what kinds of products and materials we, as individuals and families, really need. Equally, it aids discernment of those experiences and conditions which genuinely enhance wellbeing. It has been found that anyone who trains in and regularly practises mindfulness meditation is likely to experience enhancement in self-regulation of mood and behaviour, the quality of partner relationships, and empathy for other people generally.[658] It is also suggested that mindfulness nurtures a deeper sense of self and that this enables the individual to feel less threatened by the opinion of others.[659] All in all, then, a developed capacity for mindfulness supports individual wellbeing and will have particular effects that are likely to reduce the desire to consume. Again, secure attachment can give a person a head start, for one more of its effects is the nurture of a disposition towards mindfulness.[660]

Positive interventions

The inability to provide the sensitive interactions that an infant needs should not be taken as a judgement on parents. Mary Ainsworth, who worked with Bowlby and developed his theory further, found that among those she observed whose children were insecurely attached, "Many of the mothers were nice people and well-meaning parents who took pride in their babies and had various means of expressing their love... But what they all had in common was difficulty responding to the baby's attachment needs in a loving, attuned way."[661] An important obstacle to such responding is depression, and the children of mothers who are depressed around the time of their birth later show more behavioural disturbance, poorer cognitive functioning, more insecure attachment, and are at greater risk of developing depression themselves when older.[662] The effects of depression are greatly exacerbated by poverty. Against a background of insecure employment, low pay and public spending cuts, a key finding of recent research is that "poor maternal mental health and low income during babyhood affect children's outcomes negatively and are factors in the creation of future generations of 'Troubled Families'."[663]

There is, in fact, a societal aspect to attachment; it is not only parents' own formative experience which shapes their interactions with their children, current conditions also play a major role. In order to be able to give the sensitive care their baby needs, a parent's own needs for physical and psychological security must be met. Stress arising from within the home or beyond it can compromise a parent's emotional capacity to prioritise the needs of their baby and provide the unconditional love it needs.[664] In Sue Gerhardt's words, "the mother-and-baby system is a delicate one, and can easily be de-railed by a lack of inner or outer resources". "Fortunately," she adds, however, "it can often be put back on track with the right help at the right moment."[665] It is important to think ahead: research has shown that many mental health conditions are preventable if the correct care is given early in life, particularly in the first three years.[666]

So what can be done to improve the chances of secure attachment developing? While attachment style tends to be replicated from one generation to the next,[667] this is not an unalterable state of affairs. A factor which has a significant impact on mother-baby relationships is the presence or absence of social support. When mothers have solid social support, whether from the extended family, friends, neighbours or professionals, the likelihood of secure attachment is enhanced.[668] More specifically, it has been demonstrated that carefully thought out interventions can transform the way that mothers respond to their babies, even if their babies are 'difficult'.

A study which observed mothers and their irritable infants found that giving mothers individual feedback, designed to foster consistent, appropriate responses to both positive and negative infant signals, resulted in their learning to respond to all their babies' social behaviours and to their being attentive to their infants' exploratory behaviour but not interfering in it.[669] Therapeutic work undertaken by Alice Lieberman[670] with mothers in uncomfortable relationships with their babies takes a different approach. It explores how the emotions of the mother which arise out of her own childhood experience may be getting in the way of responsive care. This has been found to have the power to make a great difference in the development of secure attachment. Thus a parent who grew up as an insecurely attached child can be helped to engender secure attachment in their own child with appropriate intervention. The increase in security of attachment can be startlingly fast to bring about as babies are so responsive and adaptable, their mental growth so rapid.[671] Governments' social and economic policies should take very serious account of what has been established by well-conducted research over many years on what impacts for better or worse on family life and relationships, and on the potential for nurturing good or impaired mental health in the long term.

A New Culture from Birth

A key word which we can usefully take from attachment theory is attunement. Not only do infants need their parents to be sensitively attuned to their needs, parents also need society to be attuned to theirs. On the macro scale the Earth needs all of us to develop a keen sense of our relationship with it and to behave with proactive and responsive attunement to the possibilities it offers and the limitations it imposes on human activity.

"You must be the change you want to see in the world," are some of the wise words that Mahatma Gandhi bequeathed humanity.[672] The insight they encapsulate could not be more relevant in pointing to how the changes that are necessary for the avoidance of extreme environmental change depend on individual human action, possibly to the point of personal transformation. How much better it would be for the next generation to set out along a different path from the very beginning of life. It is time for a fresh approach to the now rather ridiculed Victorian notion of 'character building'. Cold showers and long hikes may not be the desired prescription today, but they are not so far off the mark in terms of the physical exercise in natural surroundings which makes us feel good, and the reduced expectations we need to cultivate, in place of the trend towards ever more comfort and luxury. We need to pay much more attention to the character we help to nurture in children, both at home and at school. There is a similar need, of course, for adults to change their thinking. We all need to do what we can to cultivate in ourselves and each other the personal qualities and capacities I have outlined.

We have seen how secure attachment at the beginning of life is likely to favour the development of a plethora of advantageous human attributes. We therefore need to create a culture which actively cherishes the young and their care-givers, and invests seriously in three related spheres:

- ensuring that every new parent (or other primary care-giver) has the opportunity to learn how to develop secure attachment in his/her child if this does not come readily to him or her

317

- protection of the social and economic conditions in which all young families live, in order to minimise familial stress
- swift and effective help for mothers to overcome depression in pregnancy and the postnatal period

These measures would reap untold personal and societal rewards not only in terms of enhanced mental health and wellbeing for a significant proportion of the population, but also in helping in the longer term to fortify us to deal constructively with the major challenges ahead. I do not mean to suggest that secure attachment would be a universal panacea and cure of all ills. For all its benefits, secure attachment does not guarantee a problem-free life. Even those who have this advantage are not immune to troubles, anxieties, self-doubts, depression and so on.[673] Moreover, consumption statistics would suggest that far fewer than the more-than-fifty-per-cent who are thought to enjoy secure attachment are particularly modest in material consumption. Neither can it be claimed that less than perfect early attachment automatically condemns the individual to a joyless existence or necessarily results in marked material profligacy, as testified by many lives. Nevertheless, there is strong reason to claim that secure attachment gives the individual the best chance of a happy, balanced life. Proper recognition of its significance and the need to give the development of secure attachment active,practical support, combined with other fresh thinking about and promotion of the factors that *really* matter in life, and how to ensure their pre-eminence, would together have a transformative effect on personal wellbeing and our collective future.

Promoting intrinsic values
Another highly favourable change of orientation would be to concentrate efforts on creating a norm in which everyone enjoyed plenty of intrinsically valuable experiences at all stages of life. If people don't have the opportunity to enjoy enough inherently worthwhile, personally nourishing experiences, they simply don't come fully to realise that such possibilities exist and are unlikely to pursue them. They thus remain unable to develop the intrinsic motivation that contributes to wellbeing. Instead, they are likely to fall prey to the extrinsic motivation that fuels material consumption. A change in culture which properly recognised the personal importance of intrinsically valuable activities and their wider significance would benefit everyone. Such a change would find expression through, for example, public spaces ceasing to be dominated by shops and becoming instead sites of public goods such

as libraries, parks or gardens, performance areas and forums for discussion and exchange, communality and culture. Commerce would take up only such space and attention as necessary for addressing real material needs.

Education and intrinsically valuable experience
Schooling would cease to be dominated by *outcomes* in the form of test results and exam grades, and would instead attend to the provision of learning *processes* which cultivate rounded, self-motivated, fully functional individuals. Such learning would be the vehicle for what Michael Bassey calls the "life-directing ethos of conviviality",[674] "the joy which comes from being in harmony with one's environment, one's fellows and oneself", embracing ideas of ecological sustainability, social justice, elimination of poverty at home and worldwide, peace, community and democracy,[675] which he advocates as the right aim of education. This ethos is a far cry from our current approach to education. Official discourse continues to frame schooling principally in terms of exam grades. Pupils are urged to go on to higher education chiefly in order to improve their future earning prospects, rather than to advance their knowledge or critical skills or capacity to contribute to the betterment of society. This is not the way to foster young people's enjoyment of learning.

Policy-makers who believe that minute-by-minute lesson planning by teachers, frequent testing and the publication of school league tables is the way to 'drive up standards' may blench at the notion of enhancing learning through fostering autonomy, but promoting genuine enjoyment is not indulgence, for it is students who are self-motivated who attain high grades, relish challenge, and display creativity.[676] Autonomous motivation is, to a significant extent, the result of teachers who are responsive, flexible and supportive rather than controlling and critical;[677] individually attuned to their students much like the mothers of securely attached infants.

One means which has been recommended towards achieving this end in school is the development of 'learning goals' which have meaning for the child, rather than 'achievement goals' which are dependent on the judgement of others.[678] Another approach is taken by the early education provided in Montessori schools. Here, time is not divided up into different lessons, so that the child is allowed the freedom to choose his or her own activity from a given range, and his or her deep concentration on their chosen activity is not interrupted.[679] Because autonomously motivated children learn more effectively and practise the exercise of judgment when making choices, rather than simply doing what they are told (or not!), they are likely to become more discerning, critical, responsible and proactive adults, and thus become properly prepared to perform well in anything they do, paid or unpaid, and contribute both to their own wellbeing and to that of society. It follows, then, that we need to build a public culture in general and an education system in particular which gives due regard to intrinsically valuable pursuits, and to the provision of engaging, hands-on, eyes-, ears- and mind-opening learning experiences, intellectual, practical and social.

Transforming Culture, De-gilding the Lily

I talked in Chapter 5 of toppling wealth as the marker and measure of status. Complementary to this would be a thorough recognition that a secure start to life with loving and sensitive parents actually constitutes the most fundamental privilege of all. Unlike money, it is a privilege of which there can be a potentially unlimited supply, distributed more or less equally. In terms of happiness, the personal lack of such a springboard is a different but no less real and significant form of deprivation and disadvantage than economic poverty.

In order to flourish – or bloom – human beings require certain physical and social conditions and certain personal attributes. A beautiful, freely growing wild flower can be imagined as a metaphorical representation of a human being in their optimal state. The culture of consumption, exploiting the now dangerously outdated evolutionary human leaning towards material things, fools most of us into believing that we can get closer to the ideal state by an exaggerated focus on money and material possession. For those whose basic material needs are met and who are socially, emotionally, spiritually and intellectually well provided for, the level of consumption typical of our society simply gilds the lily, adding a superfluous and dangerous layer. For those who lack the non-material foundations of wellbeing, no amount of purchasing will substitute for what they actually need to enable them to thrive.

Until recently the layer of gilt which our society regards as a normal aspiration has come to mean an insatiable desire for expenditure and acquisition. Now, however, it is possible to see that the gilt entails guilt, guilt for the despoliation and degradation of the bio-physical world in which we live and on which we and other species are entirely dependent. It is time to de-gild the lily, to act on the realisation that true wellbeing is nourished and nurtured in other ways than unnecessary material consumption. We may well enjoy buying things, and consumption in the form of travel or unthinking, extravagant use of energy may genuinely enhance our immediate experience of life. But we have to come to terms with the fact that many of the kinds or levels of consumption we have come to take for granted in recent decades can no longer be justified now that we know that they are irreversibly heating up and eating up the Earth. Even if the impossible were to happen and the means of energy generation were somehow miraculously globally decarbonised overnight, thus slowing climate change, other environmental pressures would remain; spaceship Earth will always be a finite entity.

Conclusion: Humanity Needs to Take a New Direction

We have to realise that in order to escape the fast-sinking ship of combined economic growth and ecosystem destruction we must replace our materialistic impulses with the understanding that sustainable, equitable human thriving is to be found in modest material conditions and rich social, emotional, cultural and spiritual ones. But it will not be easy. In order to implement this understanding on a societal scale we need to change our cultural values.

What is necessary is no less than the redirection of the trajectory of human development. If we don't overcome our age-old focus on material acquisition, drastic changes will be forced upon us. It is far better that we determine the shape of those changes as much as we can while there is still time to have some say in them. Radical intervention of our own devising is self-evidently preferable to allowing our material demands to run away with us entirely, destroying life as we know it. Social justice, too, requires that we ensure that what the Earth can provide is shared equitably amongst its people so that all have access to the basic requirements of a decent life. The time has come to recognise once and for all that living beyond a certain modest yet perfectly workable level of material consumption makes each of us who does so responsible for a fragment of the ruination. This includes not only out-and-out materialists but everyone who takes more than their fair share of what the Earth can provide for each of us without jeopardising its carefully balanced systems.

The number of answerable people worldwide is rising fast. But the number of happy people is not. The creeping destruction that comes in the wake of the lifestyles that so many hold dear is clearly an uncomfortable realisation to have to confront. Unwelcome as it may seem, those of us who have become accustomed to expecting a level of material acquisition, comfort and convenience more than the planet can bear must learn to live within its means. This will be immensely easier if we come fully to understand what generates and nourishes real wellbeing, and cultivate our non-material assets accordingly. That understanding is the key to happier lives in a more sustainable world. It will enable us to alter the trajectory of human development towards a more promising future.

We must devise ways of exchanging today's grasping, competitive, fearful individualism and social fragmentation for collaborative pursuit of those aspects of life which really matter for our wellbeing: cordial relationships and supportive human ties, creativity, local vitality, contact with the natural world, the feeling of belonging, and of making a positive contribution. The priceless prize to be won in return for this radical redirection of human sights, will be happier, more satisfying and fulfilled human lives on an Earth that is better able to sustain healthy life of all kinds. The minutely personal is globally ecological. The choice of direction is there for us all to take.

Endnotes and References

Chapter 1 Line Drawing: A Sketch of the Contemporary Landscape

1. Botsman, R. and Anderson, L. (2011, 2-8 May) Share Options. *The Big Issue*, p12-14
2. Kay, K. (2013, 6 Jan) Modern-day dandies rediscover the art of dressing – at £1,000 a month. *The Observer*, p.16-17
3. In the four decades of most rapid economic growth the average UK income rose from £9,770 to £20,497. These figures are derived from World Bank statistics and were provided to me in a personal communication [17 Jan 2012] by Charles Kenny, a senior fellow at the US Center for Global Development
4. Ibid.
5. http://www.creditaction.org.uk/assets/PDF/statistics/2007/august-2007.pdf (viewed 16 Jan 2012)
6. According to Survival International, a charity which acts as advocate for tribal peoples, there are about 150 million tribal individuals in the world today, living on all inhabited continents, in about 60 countries. They constitute about 40% of the wider category of indigenous people, which includes many who have now been deprived of their lands and self-sufficiency. http://www.survivalinternational.org/info (viewed 21 Feb 2011)
7. Douglas, M. (1996) "The Consumer's Revolt" in Douglas, M. *Thought Styles: Critical essays on good taste.* p.106-125. London: Sage
8. Clarke, D., Doel, M. and Housiaux, K. (Eds.) (2003) *The Consumption Reader.* London: Routledge, p.27
9. Levy, S. (2010, 10 April) We shop too much. We don't save up. But it's not our fault. *Saturday Guardian Money*, p.5
10. nVision (2007) *Consumer Kids: An insight into the everyday lives of children and 'tweens' in Europe and their role in consumption.* London: The Future Foundation, p.6
11. Ibid. Introduction
12. Kinnes, S. (2006) Flying off the Shelves at...Hamleys. *The Guardian* (Wed 11 Oct 2006) http://www.guardian.co.uk/lifeandstyle/2006/oct/11/consumerpages?INTCMP=ILCNETTXT3487#history-link-box (viewed 10 July 2012)
13. www.http://barbiegirls.com/home.html
14. Carrington, V. and Hodgetts, K. (2010) Literacy-lite in *BarbieGirl*TM. *British Journal of the Sociology of Education* 31(6), pp.671-682
15. Ibid.
16. Gordon, O. (2008, 15 June) Salons boom as girls yearn to grow up fast. *The Observer.* http://www.guardian.co.uk/lifeandstyle/2008/jun/15/healthandwellbeing.uk (viewed 10 July 2012)
17. Harkin, J. and Huber, J. (2004) *Eternal Youths.* London: Demos

18. Ibid.

19. Ibid.

20. http://www.nspcc.org.uk/news-and-views/media-centre/press-releases/2012/12-06-11-neglect-theme-launch/child-neglect-crisis_wdn89914.html (viewed 16 July 2012)

21. *The Independent on Sunday* (2011,18 Sept) http://www.independent.co.uk/news/uk/politics/jobcentres-to-send-poor-and-hungry-to-charity-food-banks-2356578.html (viewed 19 June 2012)

22. The Resolution Foundation (2013) *Squeezed Britain 2013*. London: The Resolution Foundation

23. Hill, A. (2009, 27 Dec) Stampeding shoppers cause chaos at sales. *The Observer*, p.4

24. Insley, J. (2010, 19 Dec) Want to improve your finances? It's the way the cookie crumbles. *The Observer*, p.49

25. Siegle, L. (2010, 6 June) Ethical Living *The Observer*, p.35

26. http://bookofrubbishideas.wordpress.com/2010/01/06/from-the-lovely-john-naish-on-the-landfill-prize/ (viewed 16 July 2012)

27. Lodziak, C. (2002) *The Myth of Consumerism*. London: Pluto Press

28. http://www.bbc.co.uk/news/business-11618429 (viewed 21 June 2012)

29. It is not only the carbon emissions from the transport of cut flowers and the green houses where they may be grown, that is cause for concern with regard to the cut flower industry, but also the under-regulated use of pesticides and fertilisers, the extraction of water from lakes and rivers to irrigate them, and the working conditions and wages of the growers in developing countries, Thomas, P. (2009 18 August) Behind the Label: Cut Flowers *The Ecologist* http://www.theecologist.org/green_green_living/behind_the_label/302429/behind_the_label cut_flowers.html (viewed 21 June 2012)

30. Clarke, L. (2007, 11 April) Ministers' latest bright idea for curbing classroom thugs: Don't punish, reward. Disrupt School and Win an Ipod! *Daily Mail*, p.1-2

31. http://www.caci.co.uk/492.aspx

32. *The Independent* (2012,18 April), Escape. The Ten Best In-flight Essentials p.39

33. Ibid.

34. Kohn, M. (2010) *Turned Out Nice: How the British Isles will Change as the World Heats Up*. London: Faber and Faber, p.6

35. http://www.clickgreen.org.uk/analysis/general-analysis/121582-emissions-from-consumption-far-outstrip-efficiency-savings.html (viewed 9 July 2012)

36. de Almeida, P. and Silva, P. D. (2011) Timing and future consequences of the peak of oil production. Futures 42, 1044-1055.

37. Final Draft of the Intergovernmental Panel on Climate Change Working Group Assessment Report No.5, Summary for Policymakers, published 31 March 2014.

38. Brundtland, G.H., Ehrlich, P., Goldenberg, J., Hansen, J., Lovins, A., Likens, G., Lovelock, J., Manabe, S., May, B., Mooney, H., Robert, K-H., Salim, E., Sato, G., Solomon, S., Stern, N., Swaminathan, M.S., Watson, B., Barefoot college. Conservation International. International Institute of Environment and Development, and International Union for the Conservation of Nature (2012) *Environment and Development Challenges: The imperative to act*. A synthesis of the key messages from the individual papers written by the Blue Planet Laureates. Tyndall Centre for Climate Change, University of East Anglia, Norwich, UK. All the

authors had been individually awarded the Blue Planet Prize, an award presented since 1992 to individuals or organisations worldwide in recognition of outstanding achievements in scientific research and its application that have helped provide solutions to global environmental problems.

39. Hansen, J., Ruedy, R., Sato, M. and Lo, K. (2010) *Global Surface Temperature Change*. New York: NASA Goddard Institute for Space Studies.

40. The National Snow and Ice Data Center (NSIDC), Cooperative Institute for Research in Environmental Sciences, University of Colorado, Boulder. 19 September 2012. Press Release: *Arctic sea ice reaches lowest extent for the year and the satellite record* http://nsidc.org/news/press/2012_seaiceminimum.html

41. Brundtland, G. H. et al (2012) Environment and Development Challenges: The imperative to act. A synthesis of the key messages from the individual papers written by the Blue Planet Laureates. Tyndall Centre for Climate Change

42. Meinshausen, M., Meinshausen, N., Hare, W., Raper, S.C.B, Frieler, K., Knutti, R., Frame, D.J & Allen, M.R (2009) Greenhouse-gas emission targets for limiting global warming to 2°C. (April 2009) *Nature* 458 (7242). 1158-1162. Letter http://www.nature.com/nature/journal/v458/n7242/full/nature08017.html

43. http://ncadac.globalchange.gov/download/NCAJan11-2013-publicreviewdraft-chap1-execsum.pdf (viewed 14 Jan 2013)

44. Ibid. p5-6

45. Kohn, M. (2010) *Turned Out Nice: How the British Isles will Change as the World Heats Up*. London: Faber and Faber, p6

46. Grant, H., Randerson, J. And Vidal, J. (2009, 5 Dec) UK should open up its borders to climate refugees, says Bangladeshi minister. *The Guardian*, p.1

47. Foresight: *Migration and Global Environmental Change* (2011) Final Project Report. London: The Government Office for Science

48. Lovelock, J. (2009) *The Vanishing Face of Gaia; a final warning*. London: Allen Lane

49. Sanderson, M. (2010) *Changes in the frequency of extreme rainfall events for selected towns and cities*. Exeter: Met Office

50. http://www.environment-agency.gov.uk/homeandleisure/floods/default.aspx

51. Urwin, K. (2005) *Adapting to Climate Change in the UK: Policy Fit and Misfit* (Unpublished PhD thesis). University of East Anglia, Norwich UK

52. Ibid.

53. Kohn, M. (2010) *Turned Out Nice: How the British Isles will Change as the World Heats Up*. London: Faber and Faber, p6

54. Ibid. p12

55. http://www.nature.com/news/2011/110824/full/news.2011.501.html?s=news_rss (viewed 9 July 2012)

56. *Water Resources Strategy* (2009) Bristol: Environment Agency

57. Ibid.

58. http://www.virtual-water.co.uk (viewed 21 Sept 2012). Precise calculations are difficult and vary to some degree from one source to another

59. de Almeida, P. and Silva, P. D. (2011) Timing and future consequences of the peak of oil production. *Futures* 42 1044-1055

60. Jackson, R. (2012) *Occupy World Street: a global roadmap for radical economic and political reform*. Totnes, UK: Green Books

61. de Almeida, P. and Silva, P. D. (2011) Timing and future consequences of the peak of

oil production. *Futures* 42, 1044-1055, Ann. N.Y. Acad. Sci. 1219: 52-72

62. Ibid.

63. Jackson, R. (2012) *Occupy World Street: a global roadmap for radical economic and political reform*. Totnes, UK: Green Books

64. Murphy, D.J. and Hall, C.A.S. (2011) Energy return on investment, peak oil, and the end of economic growth. In R. Costanza, K. Limburg and I. Kubiszewski (Eds.) *Ecological Economics Reviews*.

65. de Almeida, P. and Silva, P. D. (2011) Timing and future consequences of the peak of oil production. *Futures* 42 1044-1055, Ann. N.Y. Acad. Sci. 1219: 52-72

66. Ibid.

67. Murphy, D.J. and Hall, C.A.S. (2011) Energy return on investment, peak oil, and the end of economic growth. In R. Costanza, K. Limburg and I. Kubiszewski (Eds.) *Ecological Economics Reviews*. New York Academy of Sciences

68. Mason, L., Prior, T., Mudd, G. and Giurco, D. (2011) Availability, addiction, and alternatives: three criteria for assessing the impact of peak minerals on society. *Journal of Cleaner Production* 19, 958-966

69. Ibid.

70. Valero, Al. And Valero, A. (2011) A prediction of the exergy loss of the world's mineral reserves in the 21st century. *Energy*, 36, 1848 -1854

71. (2012) *Unsustainable consumption – the mother of all environmental issues?* European Environment Agency http://www.eea.europa.eu/highlights/unsustainable-consumption-2013-the-mother (viewed 2 August 2012)

72. Full crisis starts to bite. (2000, 13th September) *The Guardian* http://news.bbc.co.uk/1/hi/uk/923543.stm (viewed 6 July 2012)

73. Davies, C. (2008, 24 August) Cable thieves bring trains to a £10m halt. *The Observer*

74. http://plasticpollutioncoalition.org/learn/basic-concepts/

75. Hosking, R. (2007, 18th November) Bag Lady. *The Mail on Sunday*, p64-5

76. http://www.niehs.nih.gov/health/assets/docs_a_e/bisphenol_a_bpa_508.pdf

77. http://www.chemtrust.org.uk/documents/CHEM%20Trust%20Obesity%20&%20Diabetes%20Summary%20Report.pdf

78. Rockström, J. (2009) A Safe Operating Space for Humanity. *Nature*, Vol. 4, 472-475

79. Ibid. p.472

80. By 2012 greenhouse gas emissions had risen to 445 ppm carbon dioxide equivalent. Brundtland, G. H. et al (2012) Environment and Development Challenges: The imperative to act. A synthesis of the key messages from the individual papers written by the Blue Planet Laureates. Tyndall Centre for Climate Change, University of East Anglia, Norwich, UK

81. Rockström, J. (2009) A Safe Operating Space for Humanity. *Nature*, Vol. 46, 472-475

82. UNFPA *State of Population 2011: People and possibilities in a world of 7 billion*. New York: UNFPA

83. Ibid.

84. "Improving human well-being on a resource-limited planet: can we do it?" Lecture given by Professor Sir David King at the University of East Anglia (2013, 7 October). Other sources give the UK average annual per capita figure as higher or lower – it is difficult to estimate more precisely.

85. Goodall, C. (2010) *How to Live a Low Carbon Life: The individual's guide to tackling climate change* (second edition). London and Washington: Earthscan.

86. Ibid.
87. Data seen by Goodall at www.apple.com/environment/reports in April 2010
88. Randall, R. (2009) *Carbon Conversations: Six meetings about climate change and carbon reduction.* Cambridge UK: Cambridge Carbon Footprint.
89. In fact life-cycle energy inputs and greenhouse gas emissions contribute an additional 63% for road vehicles, 155% for trains and 31% for flying, in addition to those produced by the burning of fuel for propulsion. Chester, M.V and Horvath, A. (2009) Environmental assessment of passenger transportation should include infrastructure and supply chains. *Environ. Research Letters* 4 (2)
90. *European Happy Planet Index* (2006) London: nef and Friends of the Earth
91. Druckman, A. and Jackson, T. (2009) *Mapping our Carbon Responsibilities: More key results from the Surrey Environmental Lifestyle Mapping (SELMA) Framework.* Resolve Working Paper 02-09. University of Surrey. Printable version: (www.guardian.co.uk/environment/2011/nov/09/fossil-fuel-infrastructure-climate-change/print). This information is shocking because it reflects the level of our collective personal consumption. It also reflects the level of energy (in)efficiency in our homes, something over which it is possible to have some personal control – eg, in terms of the insulation we have in our houses, whether we have installed solar panels, etc – and the source of the energy used to make the things we buy, over which the only control individuals have is limited to their purchasing energy from a green energy supplier.
92. Brundtland, G. H. et al (2012) Environment and Development Challenges: The imperative to act. A synthesis of the key messages from the individual papers written by the Blue Planet Laureates. Tyndall Centre for Climate Change, University of East Anglia, Norwich, UK
93. http://www.opendemocracy.net/rupert-read/last-refuge-of-prejudice
94. Christopher, A.N., Saliba, L. and Deadmarsh, E.J. (2009) Materialism and wellbeing: the mediating effect of locus of control. *Personality and Individual Differences.* 46, 682-686
95. Layard, R. (2005) *Happiness: Lessons form a New Science.* London: Penguin
96. *Happy Planet Index* 2.0. (2009) London: nef
97. Ibid. p6
98. *European Happy Planet Index* (2006) London: nef and Friends of the Earth
99. Willsher, K. (2011, 10 Dec.) Violence, abuse, vomit: a night with the 'booze-bus' medics at Christmas. *The Guardian.* http://www.guardian.co.uk/society/2011/dec/10/violence-booze-bus-christmas (viewed 1 Aug. 2012)
100. http://www.britishlivertrust.org.uk/home/about-us/media-centre/facts-about-liver-disease.aspx
101. http://www.emcdda.europa.eu/stats11/gpstab2b http://www.emcdda.europa.eu/stats11/gpstab2a (viewed 29th June 2012)
102. http://www.addictiontoday.org/addictiontoday/2009/02/gps-nta-drug-deaths-numbers-game.html (viewed 29 June 2012)
103. *Sinking and Swimming: Understanding Britain's Unmet Needs* (2009) London: The Young Foundation
104. Layard, R. (2005) *Happiness: Lessons from a New Science.* London, Penguin
105. *The State of the Nation Report: Fractured Families* (2006) London: Social Policy Justice Group

106. Wilkinson, R. and Pickett, K., (2009) *The Spirit Level*. London: Allen Lane

107. Hutton, W. and Porter, H. (2011, 14th August) Unfairness and inequality are corroding the social ties that bind us. *The Observer* http://www.guardian.co.uk/commentisfree/2011/aug/14/henry-porter-will-hutton-uk-riots-responsibility (viewed 1 Aug. 2012)

108. Chang, L. and Arkin, R. (2002) Materialism as an Attempt to Cope with Uncertainty. *Psychology and Marketing* 19 (5) 389-406

109. *Child Poverty in Perspective: an overview of child well-being in rich countries. A comprehensive assessment of the lives and well-being of children and adolescents in the economically advanced nations.* (2007) Unicef

110. Brandon, M., Sidebotham, P., Bailey, S., Belderson, P., Hawley, C., Ellis, C. and Megson, M. (2012) *New Learning from Serious Case Reviews*. London: Department for Education. DFE-RR226

111. http://cebmh.warne.ox.ac.uk/csr/profile.html (viewed 19 July 2012)

112. The Truth about Self-harm (2013, February) *Talk Back*. London: Mental Health Foundation

113. Doward, J. (2014, 18th May) Child mental health care in meltdown. *The Observer*, p12

114. *The State of the Nation Report: Fractured Families* (2006) London: Centre for Social Justice

115. Ibid.

116. Ibid.

117. Layard, R. and Dunn, J. (2009) *A Good Childhood: Searching for Values in ad Competitive Age*. London: Penguin, commissioned by the Children's Society

118. *The State of the Nation Report: Fractured Families* (2006) London: Centre for Social Justice

119. Layard, R. and Dunn, J. (2009) *A Good Childhood: Searching for Values in ad Competitive Age*. London: Penguin

120. *Sinking and Swimming: Understanding Britian's Unmet Needs* (2009) London: The Young Foundation

121. Nairn, A. and Ipsos MORI (2011) *Child well-being in the UK, Spain and Sweden: the role of inequality and materialism*. Unicef, p2

122. Gordon, R.J. (2012) Is U.S. *Economic Growth Over? Faltering innovation confronts the six headwinds.* Working papers 18315. Cambridge, Mass: National Bureau of Economic Research

123. Jackson, R. (2012) *Occupy World Street: a global roadmap for radical economic and political reform.* Totnes, UK: Green Books

124. Day, E. (2013, 29 Dec.) Interview with Robert Peston *The Observer New Review*, p5.

125. Boyle, D. And Simms, A. (2009) *The New Economics: A bigger picture. London and Stering VA: Earthscan*

126. Daly, H.E. (1973) Introduction to Daly, H.E. (Ed.) *Toward a Steady State Economy*. San Francisco: W.H. Freeman and Co.

127. Daly, H.E. (1980, 1973) The Steady State Economy : toward a political economy of biophysical equilibrium and moral growth. In Daly, H.E. (Ed.) *Economics, Ecology and Ethics*, in part a revision of Toward a Steady State Economy. San Francisco: W.H. Freeman and Co. p324-372

128. Mill, J.S. (1857) *Principles of Political Economy*, Vol. II, London: John W. Parker and Son,

320-326, quoted omissions in Daly, H.E. (Ed.) (1973) *Toward a Steady State Economy.* San Francisco: W.H. Freeman and Co

129. Oswald, A. (2006) The Hippies were Right All Along about Happiness. *Financial Times*

130. Bassey, M. (2011) *Education for the Inevitable: schooling when the oil runs out.* Brighton: Book Guild Publishing

131. *Towards a Circular Economy: Economics and business rationale for an accelerated transition.* Isle of Wight, UK: Ellen MacArthur Foundation – Rethink the future.

132. Ibid.

133. Hutton, W. (2013, 29 Sept.) Socialism failed. Neoliberalism has failed. But Ed's new deal might work. *The Observer,* p36

134. Porritt, J. (2005) *Capitalism as if the World Matters.* Earthscan: London, Sterling VA

135. Helm, D. and Hepburn, C. (2012) The Economic Analysis of Biodiversity: an assessment. *Oxford Review of Economic Policy,* 28 (1), p1-21

136. Frey, B. S. (2008) *Happiness: A revolution in economics.* Cambridge, Mass and London: MIT Press

137. Jackson, T. (2009) *Prosperity without Growth: Economics for a Finite Planet.* London and Washington: Earthscan

138. Ibid. p193

139. Boyle, D. and Simms, A. (2009) *The New Economics: A bigger picture.* London and Sterling VA: Earthscan

140. Jackson, R. (2012) *Occupy World Street: a global roadmap for radical economic and political reform.* Totnes, UK: Green Books

141. Ibid. pxvii

142. Ibid. pxviii

143. Ibid. p194

144. Ibid. p243

145. Rockström, J. (2009) A Safe Operating Space for Humanity. *Nature,* 46, 472-475

146. Brundtland, G. H. et al (2012) Environment and Development Challenges: The imperative to act. A synthesis of the key messages from the individual papers written by the Blue Planet Laureates. Tyndall

147. Ibid.

148. World Resources Institute (2005) *Millennium Ecosystem Assessment. Ecosystems and Human Well-being: Synthesis.* Washington: Island Press

149. Ibid. p1

150. *Towards a Circular Economy: Economics and business rationale for an accelerated transition.* Isle of Wight, UK: Ellen MacArthur Foundation – Rethink the future.

151. Zhijun, F. and Nailing, Y. (2007) Putting a circular economy into practice in China. *Sust Sci* 2. 95-101

152. *Towards a Circular Economy: Economics and business rationale for an accelerated transition.* Isle of Wight, UK: Ellen MacArthur Foundation – Rethink the future.

153. Brundtland, G. H. et al (2012) Environment and Development Challenges: The imperative to act. A synthesis of the key messages from the individual papers written by the Blue Planet Laureates. Tyndall Centre for Climate Change. University of East Anglia, Norwich, UK.

154. Holzer, S. (2004) *The Rebel Farmer.* Graz-Stuttgart: Leopold Stocker, and Lawton, G. *Greening the Desert;* cited in Jackson, R. (2012) *Occupy World Street: a global roadmap for*

radical economic and political reform. Totnes, UK: Green Books. See Lawton's video at: permaculture.org.au/2009/12/11/greening-the-desert-ii-final

155. Jackson, R. (2012) *Occupy World Street: a global roadmap for radical economic and political reform*. Totnes, UK: Green Books

156. Ray, P.H. and Anderson, S.R. (2000) *The Cultural Creatives*. New York: Harmony Books

157. Crompton, T. (2010) *Common Cause: the case for working with our cultural values*. WWF. With Friends of the Earth (FoE), Campaign for the Protection of Rural England (CPRE), WWF-UK (Worldwide Wildlife Fund – UK), Climate Outreach and Information (COIN), and Oxfam. Online only. assets.wwf.org.uk/downloads/common_cause_report.pdf

158. Boyle, D. and Simms, A. (2009) *The New Economics: A bigger picture*. London and Sterling VA: Earthscan

159. Clare Melford: Talk at the Royal Society for the Encouragement of Arts, Manufacture and Commerce, Broadcast 2nd May 2012 BBC Radio 4 Four Thought Series www.bbc.co.uk/iplayer/episode/b01gvryj/Four_Thought_Series_3_Clare_Melford/

160. www.buynothingday.org/buynothing.html

161. *Happy Planet Index* 2.0. (2009) London: nef and Friends of the Earth

162. Boyle, D. And Simms, S. (2009) *The New Economics: a bigger picture*. London and Sterling VA: Earthscan

Chapter 2 Investigating Happily Modest Consumers

163. Appleby, J. (1993) "Consumption in Early Modern Social Thought" in Brewer, J. and Porter, R. (Eds.) *Consumption and the World of Goods*. Abingdon: Routledge pp162-173

164. http://news.bbc.co.uk/1/hi/england/london/4252421.stm

165. eg, Layard, R. (2005) *Happiness: Lessons from a New Science*. London: Allen Lane

166. McKendrick, N. (1982) "The Consumer Revolution in Eighteenth-century England" in McKendrick, N., Brewer, J. and Plumb, J.H. *The Birth of a Consumer Society: The Commodification of eighteenth-century England*. pp9-11. London: Europa Publications

167. Schivelbusch, W. (1988) "Night Life" in Schivelbusch, W. Disenchanted *Night: the industrialisation of light in the nineteenth century* pp137 -154. Republished in Clarke, D., Doel, M. and Housiaux, K. (Eds.) (2003) *The Consumption Reader*. London and New York: Routledge

168. Abelson, E. (1989) *When Ladies go a-thieving: Middle-class Shoplifters in the Victorian Department Store*. Oxford: Oxford University Press.

169. Fine, B. and Leopold, E. (1990) "Consumerism and the Industrial Revolution" *Social History* 15 (2) pp165-173. Reprinted in Clarke, D.B., Doel, M.A. and Housiaux, K.M.L. (Eds.) *The Consumption Reader*. London and New York; Routledge

170. Miller, R. (1983) "The Hoover® in the Garden: Middle-class Women and Suburbanisation, 1850-1920". *Environment and Planning D: Society and Space 1.* pp82-87. Reprinted in Clarke, D.B., Doel, M.A. and Housiaux, K.M.L. (Eds.) *The Consumption Reader*. London and New York: Routledge

171. Bowlby, R. (1985) "Commerce and Femininity" in Dreiser, Gissing and Zola *Just Looking: Consumer Culture* pp, 18-24, 29-34, 157-158 Reprinted in Clarke, D.B.,

Doel, M.A. and Housiaux, K.M.L. (eds.) *The Consumption Reader*. London and New York: Routledge

172. Lury, C. (1996/2003) Consumer Culture. Cambridge: Polity Press

173. http://www.creditaction.org.uk/assets/PDF/statistics/2007/march-2007.pdf (viewed 16 Jan 2012)

174. Boyle, M. (2009, 9 Nov.) My Year of Living without Money, *The Guardian*

175. Hibbert, K. (2010 2 Jan.) My Free and Easy Life, *The Guardian*

176. Weinberg, S. (2008, 19 Oct.) "I gritted my teeth and hid my credit card", *The Observer Magazine*

177. according to 2008 figures. Tofield, B (2013) Making homes better for the climate, your wallet and health. *The Conversation*. http://theconversation.com/making-homes-better-for-the-climate-your-wallet-and-health-15829

178. It is difficult to calculate a precise figure. It is fourteen tonnes per annum according to Goodall, C. (2010 2nd edn.) *How to Live a Low-carbon Life*. London and Washington: Earthscan

179. Randall, R. (2009) *Carbon Conversations: six meetings about climate change and carbon reduction* www.cambridgecarbonfootprint.org

Chapter 4 No Wonder they were Living Happily!

180. Huppert, F., Baylis, N. And Keverne, B. (Eds) (2005) *The Science of Wellbeing*. Oxford: Oxford University Press. Preface.

181. Jackson, T. (2009) *Prosperity without Growth*. London: Earthscan

182. Huppert, F.A. and So, T.C. (2009) *What Percentage of People in Europe are Flourishing and What Characterises Them?* Paper prepared for the OECD/ISQOLS meeting "Measuring subjective wellbeing: an opportunity for NSOs?", Florence 23-24 July 2009. The study (carried out in 2006/7) which this paper reported found that 19% of the population of the UK were flourishing, compared with 33% in Denmark at the top end of the scale and 6% in the Russian Federation. The UK came ninth out of twenty-three European countries.

183. Huppert, F.A (2005) Positive Mental Health in Individuals and Populations in Huppert, F., Baylis, N. and Keverne, B. (Eds) (2005) *The Science of Wellbeing*. Oxford: Oxford University Press, pp307-340

184. One of these is Richard Layard, the Labour government's 'Happiness Tsar', who points out in his book *Happiness: Lessons from a New Science* (2005) London and New York: Penguin Books, that elementary economics operates on the theory that perfect markets lead to the greatest happiness by providing for all our wants, and that as people's wants are taken as given, national income has become a proxy for national happiness, and that an alternative to this thinking which dominates Western governments is to look at what actually makes people happy. Another economist of this stripe is Bruno Frey, who has gone as far as to declare that, "Economic happiness research is revolutionary" Frey, B.S. (2008) *Happiness: A Revolution in Economics*. Cambridge, Mass and London: MIT Press. p.xii

185. Stiglitz, J.E., Sen, A., Fitoussi, J-P. (2009) *Report by the Commission on the Measurement of Economic Performance and Social Progress*. Executive summary. www.stiglitz-sen-fitoussi.fr

186. The ONS decided to add these subjective questions to its next annual Integrated Household Survey.

Overall, how satisfied are you with your life nowadays?

Overall, how happy did you feel yesterday?

Overall, to what extent do you feel the things you do in your life are worthwhile?

There are also broader questions which are designed to try to explain people's feelings.

David Cameron, Conservative prime minister of the 2010 Conservative-Liberal Democrat Coalition government was not the first British premier to take an interest in wellbeing; Labour PM Tony Blair's Strategy Unit had already in 2002 commissioned a review of the policy implications of psychological research on life satisfaction. Marks, N. and Shah, H. (2005) "A Wellbeing Manifesto for a Flourishing Society" in Huppert, F. (2005) "Positive mental health in individuals and populations" in Huppert, F., Baylis, N. and Keverne, B. (Eds.) (2005) The Science of Wellbeing. Oxford: Oxford University Press. 504-53. Earlier, in 1998, the king of Bhutan, a small kingdom in the Himalayas, declared that henceforth his nation's objective would be Gross National Happiness.

187. http://www.ons.gov.uk/ons/dcp171766_287415.pdf

188. http://www.actionforhappiness.org

189. Seligman, Martin E.P. and Csikszentmihalyi, M. (2000). "Positive Psychology: An Introduction". *American Psychologist* 55 (1), 5–14

190. Linley, P.A. and Joseph, S. (Eds.) (2004) *Positive Psychology in Practice.* John Wiley and Sons: Hoboken NJ

191. E.L.Deci and R.M. Ryan (Eds.) (2002) Handbook of Self-determination Research. University of Rochester Press

192. Griffin, J. and Tyrrell, I. (2003) *Human Givens: A new approach to emotional health and clear thinking.* Chalvington, UK: Human Givens Publishing

193. new economics foundation (2008) *Five Ways to Wellbeing* commissioned by the UK Government as part of its Foresight Project on Mental Capital and Wellbeing

194. Sen, A. (1999) *Development as Freedom* Oxford: Oxford University Press, p18

195. Sen, A. (1999, reprinted 2007) *Commodities and Capabilities.* Oxford: Oxford University Press, p3

196. Sen, A. (1999) *Development as Freedom* Oxford: Oxford University Press

197. Ricard, M (2007) *Happiness: a guide to developing life's most important skill.* (Jesse Browner, trans). London: Atlantic Books

198. Ibid. p31

199. Ibid. p56

200. Kahneman, D. and Krueger, A.B. (2006) Developments in the Measurement of Subjective Wellbeing. *Journal of Economic Perspectives* 20 (1), 3-24

201. This is the 2009 UK figure. World Database of Happiness http://worlddatabaseofhappiness.eur.nl/hap_nat/nat_fp.php?mode=1

202. Layard, R. (2005) *Happiness: Lessons from a New Science.* London and New York: Penguin Books

203. Kahneman, D. and Krueger, A.B. (2006) Developments in the Measurement of Subjective Wellbeing. *Journal of Economic Perspectives* 20 (1) p3-24

204. A common finding is that subjective wellbeing is best predicted by the breadth and depth of individuals' social connections, and people themselves report that good relationships with family members, friends or romantic partners – far more than

money or fame – are pre-requisites for their happiness. Helliwell, J.F. and Putnam, R.D. (2005) "The Social Context of Wellbeing" in Huppert, F., Baylis, N. and Keverne, B. (Eds) *The Science of Wellbeing*. Oxford: Oxford University Press 436-459

People who are married or living together are on average happier, and in better mental and physical health, than those who live alone, never married or are widowed, divorced or separated; but friendships and other relationships also influence happiness and physical and mental health, by providing companionship, emotional support and instrumental help. Argyle, M (2003) "Causes and Correlates of Happiness" in Davidson, R.J., Scherer, K.R. and Hill Goldsmith, H. (eds.) *Handbook of Affective Sciences* Oxford and New York, Oxford: Oxford University Press p354-373

205. Myers, D.G. (2003) "Close Relationships and Quality of Life" in Davidson, R.J., Scherer, K.R. and Hill Goldsmith, H. (eds.) *Handbook of Affective Sciences*. Oxford and New York: Oxford University Press. p374-391

206. Vaillant, G.E (2012) *Triumphs of Experience: The Men of the Harvard Grant Study*. Cambridge Mass and London: The Belknap Press

207. Physical exercise increases the sense of wellbeing, whether it is regular or one-off. Biddle, S.J.H. and Ekkekakis, P. (2005) "Physically Active Lifestyles and Walking" in Huppert, F., Baylis, N. and Keverne, B. (Eds) (2005) *The Science of Wellbeing*. Oxford: Oxford University Press, p141-168

208. Layard, R. (2005) *Happiness: Lessons from a New Science*. London: Penguin Books, p19

209. Communities and Local Government (2010). 2008-09 Citizenship Survey Volunteering and Charitable Giving Topic Report. Communities and Local Government: London. cited in Green Paper on Giving (2010) London; Cabinet Office http://www.cabinetoffice.gov.uk/resource-library/giving-green-paper

210. eg., Seligman, M.E.P., Parks, A,C., and Steen, T. (2005) *A Balanced Psychology and a Full Life* Huppert, F., Baylis, N. and Keverne, B. (Eds) The Science of Wellbeing. Oxford: Oxford University Press

211. unltd.org.uk

212. Heaversedge, J. and Halliwell, E. (2010) *The Mindful Manifesto: How doing less and noticing more can help us thrive in a stressed-out world* Hay House http://themindfulmanifesto.com/about-mindfulness.html

213. Emmons, R.A. and McCullough, M.E. (2003) "Counting blessings versus burdens: an experimental investigation of gratitude and subjective wellbeing in everyday life" *Journal of Personality and Social Psychology* 84 (2) p377-389

214. Using data supplied by the Broadcasters' Audience Research Board (BARB), Thinkbox, a marketing body, found that the average TV viewer watched 4 hours 2 minutes a day in the first three months of 2010, (8% more than in the first quarter of 2009). http://www.guardian.co.uk/media/2010/may/04/thinkbox-television-viewing viewed 13th Feb 2011

215. Sheldon, K.M. and Lyubomirsky, S. (2004) "Achieving Sustainable New Happiness: prospects, practices and prescriptions" in Linley, P.A. and Joseph, S. (Eds.) *Positive Psychology in Practice*. Hoboken NJ: John Wiley and Sons. 217-145

216. Only 10% of happiness is reckoned to be accounted for by life circumstances, and 50% by personality – personality itself being the outcome of the interaction of genes and environment. Marks, N. And Shah, H. (2005) "A Wellbeing Manifesto for a Flourishing Society" in Huppert, F., Baylis, N. and Keverne, B. (Eds.) (2005) *The Science of Wellbeing*. Oxford: Oxford University Press

217. Sheldon, K.M. and Lyubomirsky, S. (2004) "Achieving Sustainable New Happiness: prospects, practices and prescriptions" in Linley, P.A. and Joseph, S (eds.) *Positive Psychology in Practice.* Hoboken NJ: John Wiley and Sons. p217-145

218. Frijda, N. H. (2003) "Emotions and Hedonic Experience" in Davidson, R.J., Scherer, K.R. and Hill Goldsmith, H. (Eds.) *Handbook of Affective Sciences* Oxford and New York, Oxford University Press. p190-210

219. "Flow" is the term coined by Hungarian-American psychologist Mihalyhi Csikszent-mihalyi to describe the feeling of complete immersion in and focus on an activity

220. Csikszentmihalyi, M. (1975, 2000 25th anniversary edition) *Beyond Boredom and Anxiety.* San Francisco: Jossey-Bass

221. Chang, L.C. and Arkin, R. (2002) Materialism as an Attempt to Cope with Uncertainty. *Psychology and Marketing* 19 (5) p389-406

222. Richins, M. and Dawson, S. (1992) *A Consumer Values Orientation for Materialism and Its Measurement: Scale Development and Validation,* 19, p303-316

223. Richins, M. (1991) *Possessions in the lives of materialists: an analysis of consumption-related affect and expectations.* Paper presented at the Joint Conference of the Society for the Advancement of Socio-Economics and the International Association for Research in Economic Psychology on 'Interdisciplinary Approaches to Economic Problems. p16-19 June, Stockholm, Sweden. Cited in Dittmar, H. (1992) *The Social Psychology of Material Possessions: To have is to be.* Hemel Hempstead: Harvester Wheatsheaf

224. Ibid. p8

225. Christopher, A.N., Saliba, L. and Deadmarsh, E.J. (2009) Materialism and Wellbeing: The mediating effect of locus of control. *Personality and Individual Differences* 46, p682-686

226. Ibid.

227. Kasser, T., Ryan, R.M., Zax, M. and Sameroff, A.J. (1995) The Relations of Maternal and Social Environments to Late Adolescents' Materialistic and Prosocial Values. *Developmental Psychology,* 31 (6) p907-914

228. Kasser, T. (2002) *The High Price of Materialism.* Cambridge Mass and London: MIT Press The main reason that the research looked at mothers only was that it is nearly impossible to get fathers to go into a lab to take part in such studies. Fathers also tend to be absent from the child's life more, especially in the kind of high-risk sample that was used. (Personal communication from Tim Kasser).

229. Kasser, T., Ryan, R.M., Zax, M. and Sameroff, A.J. (1992) The Relations of Maternal and Social Environments to Late Adolescents' Materialistic and Prosocial Values. *Developmental Psychology* 31 (6) p907-914. The adolescents in question were born in the late 1970's

230. Csikszentmihalyi, M. and Rochberg-Halton, E. (1981) *The Meaning of Things: Domestic symbols and the self.* Cambridge and New York: Cambridge University Press

231. Christopher, A.N., Saliba, L. and Deadmarsh, E.J. (2009) Materialism and Wellbeing. *Personality and Individual Differences* 46, p682-686

232. "Voluntary simplifiers" is the term used by Duane Elgin in a book which was first published in 1981 in America and which instigated the Voluntary Simplicity movement there. Elgin, D. (2010) *Voluntary Simplicity: toward a way of life that is outwardly simple, inwardly rich.* London, HarperCollins [1st edn.1981, revised 1993]

233. Rindfleisch, A., Burroughs, J.E. and Denton, F. (1997) Family Structure, Materialism and Compulsive Consumption. *Journal of Consumer Research*, 23. 312-325

234. Christopher, A.N., Saliba, L. And Deadmarsh, E. J. (2009) Materialism and Well-being: the mediating effect of locus of control. *Personality and Individual Differences*, 46, p682-686

235. Martin, P. (2005) *Making Happy People: The nature of happiness and its origins in childhood*. London and New York: Fourth Estate

236. Frederickson, B. (2005) "The Broaden-and-Build Theory of Positive Emotions" in Huppert, F., Baylis, N. and Keverne, B. (Eds.) *The Science of Well-being*. Oxford: Oxford University Press. p218-238

237. Baylis, N. (2005) "Relationship with Reality and its Role in the Well-being of Young Adults" in Huppert, F., Baylis, N. and Keverne, B. *The Science of Well-being*. Oxford: Oxford University Press. p241-272

238. Martin, P. (2005) *Making Happy People: The nature of happiness and its origins in childhood*. London and New York: Fourth Estate

239. Lyubomirsky, S., Schkade, D. and Sheldon, K.M. (2005) Pursuing Happiness: The Architecture of Sustainable Change. *Review of General Psychology* 9 (2) p111-131

240. Dittmar, H. (1992) *The Social Psychology of Material Possessions: to have is to be*. Hemel Hempstead, UK: Harvester Wheatsheaf

241. Ibid.

242. Ibid.

243. James Thickett, Ofcom's director of research quoted in McVeigh, T. (2012, 2 Dec.) *Text Messaging Turns 20. The Observer*, p34

244. Csikszentmihalyi, M. and Rochberg-Halton, E. (1981) *The Meaning of Things: Domestic Symbols and the Self.* Cambridge and New York: Cambridge University Press

245. Hurdley, R. (2012, 22nd November) *Thinking through Things: the craftiness of organising materials.* Paper given at 'Researching Material Culture' Morgan Centre Interdisciplinary Dialogue, Manchester

246. Miller, D. (2010) *Stuff.* Cambridge: Polity

247. Ibid.

248. Csikszentmihalyi, M. and Rochberg-Halton, E. (1981) *The Meaning of Things: Domestic Symbols and the Self.* Cambridge and New York: Cambridge University Press

249. Dittmar, H. (1992) *The Social Psychology of Material Possessions: to have is to be*. Hemel Hempstead, UK: Harvester Wheatsheaf

250. eg, Hurdley, R. (2006) Dismantling Mantelpieces: Narrating Identities and Materializing Culture in the Home. *Sociology* 40 (4) p717-733

251. Dittmar, H. (1992) *The Social Psychology of Material Possessions: to have is to be*. Hemel Hempstead, UK: Harvester Wheatsheaf

252. Lury, C. (2003) *Consumer Culture* (first publ. 1996) Cambridge: Polity Press

253. Dittmar, H. (1992) *The Social Psychology of Material Possessions: to have is to be*. Hemel Hempstead, UK: Harvester Wheatsheaf

254. Ibid.

255. Siegle, L. (2007, 22 July) "How ethical are our high streets?" *Observer Magazine*

256. Gray, L. (2009, 20 Feb.) 'Primark effect' prompts government drive to cut clothes sent to landfill, *Daily Telegraph,* http://www.telegraph.co.uk/earth/ earthnews/4734946/Primark-effect-prompts-government-drive-to-cut-clothes-

sent-to-landfill.html (viewed 4th May 2012)

257. Leiss, W. (1976) *the Limits of Satisfaction*. Toronto: Toronto University Press, in Lury, C. (2003) *Consumer Culture* (first publ. 1996) Cambridge: Polity Press

258. Lury, C. (2003) *Consumer Culture* (first publ. 1996) Cambridge, Polity Press

259. Spencer, M. (2007, December) The Year Our Handbag Habit Got Out of Control. *Observer Woman*, p36–44

260. Ibid.

261. Ibid.

262. Giddens, A. (1991) *Modernity and Self-Identity: self and society in the late modern age*. Cambridge: Polity, p198, quoted in Lodziak, C. (2002) *The Myth of Consumerism*. London: Pluto Press.

263. Bauman, Z. (1989) *Legislators and Interpreters*. Cambridge: Polity Press, p189, quoted in Giddens, A. (1991) *Modernity and Self-Identity: Self and society in the late modern age*. Cambridge: Polity, p198 and Lodziak, C. (2002) *The Myth of Consumerism*. London: Pluto Press, p65

264. Hirsch, F. (1977) *Social Limits to Growth*. London: Routledge and Kegan Paul

265. Ibid. p6

266. Archer, L., Hollingworth, S. and Halsall, A. (2008) 'University's not for Me – I'm a Nike Person': Urban, Working-class Young People's negotiations of 'Style', Identity and Educational Engagement. *Sociology* 41 (2) p219–237

267. Wilkinson, R. and Pickett, K. (2009) *The Spirit Level: Why more equal societies almost always do better*. Allen Lane: London.

268. Ibid. p25

269. *The Independent on Sunday* (2007, 29th April) p24

270. Veblen, T. (1925) *Theory of the Leisure Class: an economic study of institutions*. London: George Allen and Unwin

271. Ibid. p73

272. Duffy, C A (1999) *The World's Wife*. London: Picador. p23

273. eg., nef (2009) *Happy Planet Index 2.0*. London: nef www.happyplanetindex.org

274. Marmot, M. (2004) *Status Syndrome: how your social standing directly affects your health and life expectancy*. London: Bloomsbury

275. Ward-Perkins, B. (2010) We'll Cope, Mankind always has: the fall of Rome and the cost of crisis. In Levene, M., Johnson, R. and Roberts, P. (Eds.) *History, Climate Change and the Possibility of Closure*. Penrith: Humanities – Ebooks, LLP 46-52

276. Barratt, D. (2010) *Supernormal Stimuli: How primal urges overran their evolutionary purpose*. New York: W.W. Norton and Co.

277. Ibid; Tinbergen, N. (1951) *The Study of Instinct*. Oxford: Clarendon Press

278. Marx, K. (1890) *Das Kapital. Book One, Der Produktionsprozess des Kapital's*. Translated (1928) from the fourth German edition by Eden and Cedar Paul as *Capital: a Critique of Political Economy*. The Process of Capitalist Production. London: George Allen and Unwin

279. This phrase was originally used in a quite different context, that of the damaging effect of the human appetite for too much, too intrusive reporting of tittle tattle by the news media. Rutledge, P. (2012, 16-22 Jan.) Does the News Make you Sick? *The Big Issue*. 18-21

280. Cottey, A. (2012) *Asset and Income Limits* http://www.uea.ac.uk/~c013/v2/ail/ail.xhtml

281. Miller, D. (2012) *Consumption and its Consequences*. London: Polity

282. Traits are internal dispositions toward certain behaviours which are stable over a considerable period of time and show reliable individual differences. Brown, R.T. (1989) Creativity: what are we to measure? In Glover, A.J., Ronning, R.R., and Reynolds, C.R. (Eds.) *Handbook of Creativity: Perspectives on individual differences.* New York: Plenum Press, 3-32

283. Zuckerman, M. (2nd edn. 2005) *Psychobiology of Personality* New York: Cambridge University Press

284. *eg* the American pair of identical twins who were raised respectively in Trinidad by a Jewish father and in Germany by a Catholic grandmother, and who when they met were both wearing rectangular wire-framed glasses, short moustaches, and blue two-pocket shirts with epaulettes, and found that they both liked reading magazines back to front and startling people in elevators by sneezing: Rich Harris, J. (1998) *The Nurture Assumption: why children turn out the way they do.* London: Bloomsbury, p.33

285. Zuckerman, M. (1991) Psychobiology of Personality. Cambridge: Cambridge University Press

286. Bouchard, T. J. (2004) Genetic Influence on Human Psychological Traits. *Current Directions in Psychological Science* 13 (4) 148-151

287. Zuckerman, M. (1991) Psychobiology of Personality. Cambridge: Cambridge University Press

288. Jablonka, E. and Lamb, M.J. (2005) *Evolution in Four Dimensions: Genetic, Epigenetic, Behavioural, and Symbolic Variation in the History of Life* Cambridge MA and London: MIT Press

289. Oakley, B. (2007) *Evil Genes: Why Rome Fell, Hitler Rose, Enron Failed, and My Sister Stole My Mother's Boyfriend.* New York: Prometheus Books

290. Greenfield, S. (2008) *The Quest for Identity in the 21st Century.* London: Sceptre

291. Jablonka, E. and Lamb, M.J., (2005) *Evolution in Four Dimensions: Genetic, Epigenetic, Behavioural, and Symbolic Variation in the History of Life* Cambridge MA and London: MIT Press, p.59-60

292. http://biology.about.com/od/geneticsglossary/g/alleles.htm

293. Jablonka, E. and Lamb, M.J. (2005) p.59-60

294. Ridley, M, (2003, 2nd June) What Makes You Who You Are. *Time*

295. Greenfield, S. (2008) *The Quest for Identity in the 21st Century.* London: Sceptre, p20-21

296. Kim-Cohen, J., Caspi, A. Taylor, A., Williams, B., Newcombe, R., Craig, I.W. and Moffitt, T.E., (2006) MAOA, maltreatment and gene-environment interaction predicting children's mental health: new evidence and a meta-analysis. *Molecular Psychiatry* 11, 903-913

297. Bateson, P. and Gluckman, P. (2011) "Clarifications" in *Plasticity, Robustness, Development and Evolution.* Cambridge: Cambridge University Press, p8

298. Ibid.

299. eg, Karen, R. (1998) *Becoming Attached: first relationships and how they shape our capacity to love.* Oxford: Oxford University Press

300. Joussemet, M., Vitaro, F. Barker, F.D., Cote, S., Nagin, D.S., Zoccolillo, M., and Tremblay, R.E., (2008) Controlling parenting and physical aggression during elementary school. *Child Development* 79 (2) 411-425

301. Soenes, B., Duirez, B. Vansteekiste, M. and Goossens, L. The intergenerational transmission of empathy-related responding in adolescence: the role of maternal

support. *Personality and Social Psychology Bulletin*, 33, 1-13.

302. Kagan, J. and Snidman, N. (2004) *The Long Shadow of Temperament* Cambridge MA and London: The Belknap Press

303. Christopher, H.N., Saliba, L. and Deadmarsh, E.J. (2009), "Materialism and well-being: The mediating effect of locus of control", *Personality and Individual Differences* 46, 682-686

304. Clarke, A. and Clarke, A. (2000) *Early Experience and the Life Path*. London and Philadelphia: Jessica Kingsley

305. *Looked After Children and Offending: Reducing Risk and Promoting Resilience* (2012) Schofield, G., Ward, E., Biggart, L., Scaife, V., Dodsworth, J., Larsson, B., Haynes, A. and Stone, N. Norwich, Centre for Research on the Child and Family, University of East Anglia, and The Adolescent and Children's Trust

306. http://www.bbc.co.uk/news/uk-england-london-14509902 12 August 2011 (viewed 12 Aug. 2011)

307. James, O. (2010) *How Not to F*** Them Up*. London: Vermillion

308. Wallis Simons, J. (2010, 30 May) Interview: It's all about You *The New Review, Independent on Sunday*, p121

309. Kellaway, K. (2010, 21 March) People Agenda Naomie Harris *The Observer New Review*, p5

310. Parks, L. and Guay, R.P. (2009) Personality, Values and Motivation. *Personality and Individual Differences* 47 pp675-684 cite Goldberg, L.R. (1993) The Structure of Phenotypic Personality Traits. *American Psychologist*, 48, 26-34 and Olver, J.M. and Mooradian, T.A. (2003) Personality Traits and Personal Values: A conceptual and empirical integration. *Personality and Individual Differences*, 35, 109-125

311. Rich Harris, J. (1998) *The Nurture Assumption: why children turn out the way they do*. Bloomsbury: London.

312. Ibid. p48

313. eg, The home visiting provided by the Sure Start programme which was set up to help disadvantaged young families and improve outcomes for their children, intended to promote maternal wellbeing and/or "sensitive mothering" has been found to have a positive impact, reducing household chaos and negative parenting such as slapping, scolding and physical restraint, and increasing acceptance of three-year-olds' behaviour. *National Evaluation Report, Early Impacts of Sure Start Local Programmes on Children and Families* (2005, Nov.) Report 13, Birkbeck University of London

314. eg, Eysenk, H. (1990) Genetic and Environmental Contributions to Individual Differences: The three major dimensions of personality. *Journal of Personality* 58 (1) 245-261; and Loehlin, J.C. (1992) *Genes and Environment in Personality Development, Individual Differences and Development Series*, Vol 2. London: Sage

315. Zuckerman, M. (1991, 2nd Edn. 2005) *Psychobiology of Personality*. New York: Cambridge University Press

316. Wiseman, E. (2011, 4th September) This Much I Know, *The Observer Magazine*

317. Rich Harris, J., (1998) *The Nurture Assumption: why children turn out the way they do*. London: Bloomsbury

318. incl. Ballantine, R. (1975) *Richard's Bicycle Book*. London: Pan; Schumacher, E.F., (1974 2nd edn.) *Small is Beautiful: A* study of economics as if people mattered. London: Abacus; Von Weizsäcker, U. *(1998) Factor Four: doubling wealth, halving resource use* – a report to the Club of Rome. London: Earthscan; *An Inconvenient Truth:* the

2006 documentary film on Al Gore's campaign to make the issue of global warming a recognised problem worldwide; directed by Davis Guggenheim Writers: John Seymour, John Humphreys, James Lovelock

319. Norberg-Hodge, H. (1991) *Ancient Futures: Learning from Ladakh*. Delhi, Oxford: Oxford University Press

320. Macy, J. (1999) *Coming Back to Life: Practices to reconnect our lives, our world*. Gabriola BC: New Society Publishers

321. Permaculture is a system of working with nature, according to principles which are observable in the natural world, which Mollison originated and others have developed further. The Permaculture Association website explains that, "Permaculture design uses these principles to develop integrated systems that provide for our needs of food, shelter, energy and community in ways that are healthy and efficient. We can use permaculture design methods to improve the quality and productivity of our individual lives, our society and our environment. http://www.permaculture.org.uk/ (viewed 7 April 2011)

322. Hillman, J. (1997) *The Soul's Code: In search of character and calling*. Toronto: Bantam Books, p.6

323. Ibid. p7

324. Donovan (2011, Feb 14-20) "If I'd known then what I know now" in *The Big Issue*, p5

325. Hillman, J. (1997) *The Soul's Code: In search of character and calling*. Toronto: Bantam Books, p8

326. Bateson, P and Martin, P. (1999) *Design for a Life: how behaviour develops*. London: Jonathan Cape

327. Ibid. p239

328. Olver, J.M., and Mooradian, T.A. (2003) Personality Traits and Personal Values: a conceptual and empirical integration. Personality and Individual Differences, 35, 109-125

329. Chamorro-Premuzic, T. (2007) Personality and Individual Differences: BPS Textbooks in Psychology. Malden MA, Oxford, Victoria: Blackwell Publishing

330.

Domain	Some high end trait descriptions	Some low end trait descriptions
Extroversion	outgoing, talkative, energetic, sociable, confident, emotionally expressive, adventurous	reserved, quiet, shy
Neuroticism	anxious, pessimistic, fearful, self-pitying, temperamental, touchy	self-confident, calm, optimistic, undemanding, resilient
Agreeableness	considerate, kind, nurturing, altruistic, compliant, modest, tolerant, cooperative	unfriendly, cold, unsympathetic, quarrelsome, rude
Conscientiousness	proactive, self-disciplined, efficient, organised, competent, determined, productive, deliberate	irresponsible, frivolous, sloppy, inefficient

331. Hirsh, J. and Dolderman, D. (2007) Personality Predictors of Consumerism and Environmentalism: a preliminary study. *Personality and Individual Differences*, 43, 1583-1593

332. Chamorro-Premuzic, T. (2007) *Personality and Individual Differences: BPS Textbooks in*

Psychology. Blackwell Publishing: Malden MA, Oxford, UK., Victoria, Australia

333. Cain, S. (2012) *Quiet: The Power of Introverts in a World that Can't Stop Talking.* London: Viking

334. Kasser, T. (2002) *The High Price of Materialism.* Cambridge, Mass and London: MIT Press

335. Olver, J.M. and Mooradian, T.A. (2003) Personality Traits and Personal Values: a conceptual and empirical integration. Personality and Individual Differences, 35, 109-125

336. Vaillant, G.E. (2012) *Triumphs of Experience: The Men of the Harvard Grant Study.* Cambridge Mass and London: The Belknap Press

337. Ibid. p352

338. Oakley, B. (2007) *Evil Genes: Why Rome Fell, Hitler Rose, Enron Failed, and My Sister Stole My Mother's Boyfriend,* New York: Prometheus Books

339. Fellowes, J. (2010, 3 Sept.) "Once Upon a Life", *The Observer Magazine,* p12-13

340. Giddens, J.L., Aitken Schmerer, J., Vernon, P.A. (2009) Material Values are Largely in the Family: a twin study of genetic and environmental contributions to materialism *Personality and Individual Differences* 46, 482-431

341. Ibid.

Chapter 7 The Vital Role of Values

342. Shalom Schwartz organised ten universal human value domains in Schwartz, S. (1994) Are there universal aspects in the structure and contents of human values? *Journal of Social Issues,* 50 (4), 19-45. He did not set them out in tabular form; the column heading of "consequent orientation" is my own, not Schwartz's. Schwartz structured these values along two axes: Openness to change – Conservation, and Self-enhancement – Self-transcendence.

Value	Motivational goals	Consequent orientation
Achievement	personal success through demonstrating competence according to social standards	ambitious, capable, successful, influential, self-respecting, intelligent
Benevolence	preservation and enhancement of the welfare of people with whom one is in frequent personal contact	helpful, honest, forgiving, loyal, a spiritual life, meaning in life, true friendship
Conformity	restraint of actions, inclinations and impulses likely to upset or harm others and violate social expectations or norms	honouring parents and elders, obedient, polite
Hedonism	pleasure and sensuous gratification for oneself	enjoying life, pleasure
Power	social status and privilege, control or dominance over people and resources	authority, social power, wealth, social recognition, preserving one's public image
Self-direction	independent thought and action, creating, exploring, choosing	creativity, curiosity, freedom, choosing own goals, independence
Stimulation	excitement, novelty, challenge in life	an exciting life, a varied life, daring

Tradition	respect, commitment, and acceptance of the customs and ideas that traditional culture or religion provide	accepting my portion in life, detachment, devoutness, humility, moderation, respect for tradition
Universalism	understanding, appreciation, tolerance, and protection of the welfare of all people and for nature	social justice, protecting the environment, broad-mindedness, a world of beauty, unity with nature, wisdom.

343. Parks, L. and Guay, R.P. (2009) Personality,Values and Motivation, Personality and Individual Differences47, 675-684

344. Ibid.

345. Kasser,T. and Ryan, R.M. (1996) Further examining the American dream: Differential correlates of intrinsic and extrinsic goals. *Personality and Social Psychology Bulletin* 22, 280-287

346. Wiseman, E. (2011, 6 Mar.) "This Much I Know", *The Observer Magazine*

347. John, E. (2012, 19 Feb.) "This Much I Know", *The Observer Magazine*

348. Lewis, Z. (2009, May11-17) "Fashion Debate: Are we what we wear?", *The Big Issue*, p.5

349. Kappala-Ramsay (2011, 23 Oct.) "This Much I Know", *The Observer Magazine*

350. Greenfield, S. (2008) The Quest for Identity in the 21st Century. London: Sceptre

351. Crompton,T. (2010) Common Cause:Working with our CulturalValues. Godalming, Surrey:WWF-UK http://assets.wwf.org.uk/downloads/common_cause_report.pdf

352. Meyer, J.H.F. and Land, R. (Eds.) (2006) *Overcoming Barriers to Student Learning: threshold concepts and troublesome knowledge*; Editors' Preface. London and New York: Routledge

353. Perkins D. (2006) Constructivism and troublesome knowledge, in *Overcoming Barriers to Student Learning: threshold concepts and troublesome knowledge*. London and New York: Routledge. 33-47

354. Cousin, G. (2006) Threshold concepts, troublesome knowledge and emotional capital: an exploration into learning about others in Meyer, J.H.F. and Land, R. (Eds) (2006) *Overcoming Barriers to Student Learning: threshold concepts and troublesome knowledge*. London and New York: Routledge. 134-147

355. Meyer, J.H.F. and Land, R. (Eds) (2006) *Overcoming Barriers to Student Learning: threshold concepts and troublesome knowledge*; Editors' preface. London and New York: Routledge. p3

356. Perkins, D. (1999, November) The Many Faces of Constructivism. *Educational Leadership* 57 (3)

357. Cousin, G. (2006) Threshold Concepts,Troublesome Knowledge and Emotional Capital: an exploration into learning about others in Meyer, J.H.F. and Land, R. (Eds) (2006) *Overcoming Barriers to Student Learning: threshold concepts and troublesome knowledge*. London and New York: Routledge. 134-147

358. Ibid.

359. Ibid.

360. Bourdieu, P. (1986) The Forms of Capital originally in "Ökonomisches Kapital, kulturelles Kapital, soziales Kapital." in Soziale Ungleichheiten (Soziale Welt,

Sonderheft 2), by Reinhard Kreckel (Ed.). Goettingen: Otto Schartz & Co. 1983. pp. 183-98. First published in English (Richard Nice, trans) in Bourdieu, P. (1986) The forms of capital. In J. Richardson (Ed.) *Handbook of Theory and Research for the Sociology of Education* (New York, Greenwood), 241-258.

361. Parks, L. and Guay, R.P. (2009) Personality, values and motivation. *Personality and Individual Differences*, 47, 675-684

362. Thomas Nagel, Professor of Law and Professor of Philosophy in the Department of Philosophy at New York University, wrote these lines in Who is Happy and When, a review of two books on happiness in *The New York Review of Books* 04 December 2011. The books were, Bok, S. (2010) *Exploring Happiness: from Aristotle to Brain Science*. Yale University Press, and Bok, D. (2010) *The Politics of Happiness: what government can learn from the new research on well-being*. Princeton University Press

363. McKibben, B. *The End of Nature: humanity, climate change and the natural world* (1989, revised edn. 2003) (Random House) Bloomsbury: London

364. Levene, M., Johnson, R. and Roberts, P. (2010) *History at the End of the World? History, climate change and the possibility of closure*, Penrith, HEB

365. Ware, B. (2009, Nov 14) *Top Five Regrets of the Dying* http://ezinearticles.com/?Top-Five-Regrets-of-the-Dying&id=3268063 http://myadvice-captbokkhari.blogspot.com/2010/09/five-regrets-of-dying-by-bronnie-ware.html (viewed 19 April 2011)

Chapter 8 The Place of Spirituality

366. http://www.medizin-ethik.ch/publik/spirituality_definition_health.htm

367. Department of Health (2004) *Standards for Better Health*. London: Department for Health

368. Culliford, L. (2011) *The Psychology of Spirituality*. London: Jessica Kingsley

369. Collins, M. (2012). Spiritual and transpersonal developments within occupational therapy education. In C.S., Hong, C.S.D, Harrison (eds.), *Tools for Continuing Professional Development*, pp. 137-56. London: Quay Books

370. Watson, J. (2012) Spiritual Development: A Summary of the History, Key Themes, Problems and Questions. 2B15 *Spirituality, Education and the Child Handbook*. Norwich, UK: School of Education and Lifelong Learning, University of East Anglia

371. Bell, D. (2004) *Change and Continuity: Reflections on the Butler Act*. Speech to commemorate the 60th anniversary of the 1944 Education Act, given by the chief inspector of schools. http://www.guardian.co.uk/education/2004/apr/21/ofsted. schools (viewed 18 Jan. 2013)

372. Bloom, A. (2012, 14th December) Life, the Universe and Everything. *TES Propedagogy*, 4-7

373. Bell. D. (2004) *Change and Continuity: Reflections on the Butler Act*. Speech to commemorate the 60th anniversary of the 1944 Education Act, given by the chief inspector of schools. http://www.guardian.co.uk/education/2004/apr/21/ofsted. schools (viewed 18 Jan. 2013)

374. Watson, J. (2012) Spiritual Development: A Summary of the History, Key Themes, Problems and Questions. 2B15 *Spirituality, Education and the Child Handbook*. Norwich, UK: School of Education and Lifelong Learning, University of East Anglia

375. Watson, J. (2001) OFSTED's Spiritual Dimension: an analytical audit of inspection

reports. *Cambridge Journal of Education*, 31 (2), 205-219

376. Bloom, A. (2012,14th December) Life, the Universe and Everything. *TES Propedagogy*, 4-7

377. Sheldrake, P. (2012) *Spirituality: A very short introduction*. Oxford: Oxford University Press

378. Jenkins, J. (1995/2005 third edn.) *The Humanure Handbook: a guide to composting human manure*. Grove City, PA: Joseph Jenkins Inc.

379. King, U. (2009) *The Search for Spirituality: Our global quest for meaning and fulfilment*. Norwich: Canterbury Press, p13-14

380. Froggatt, and Moffitt, (1997) Spiritual needs and religious practice in dementia care. In M. Marshall (Ed.) *State of the Art in Dementia Care*. London: Centre for Policy on Ageing, p225, cited in Killick, J. "Becoming a Friend of Time: A Consideration of how we may Approach persons with Dementia through Spiritual Sharing in the Moment". In Jewell, A. (Ed.) *Spirituality and Personhood in Dementia*. London and Philadelphia: Jessica Kingsley Publishers, 52-63, p60

381. Sheldrake, P. (2012) *Spirituality: A very short introduction*. Oxford: Oxford University Press

382. eg. Watson, J. (2012) Spiritual Development: A Summary of the History, Key Themes, Problems and Questions. 2B15 *Spirituality, Education and the Child Handbook*. Norwich, UK: School of Education and Lifelong Learning, University of East Anglia

383. King, U. (2009) *The Search for Spirituality: Our global quest for meaning and fulfilment*. Norwich: Canterbury Press

384. Ibid.

385. Ibid.

386. in Britain and America. Wuthnow, R., (1976) *The Consciousness Reformation*. Berkeley: University of California Press. Cited in Hay, D. with Nye, R. (2006 revised edition. First published 1998) *The Spirit of the Child*. London and Philadelphia: Jessica Kingsley

387. Collins, M. (2012). p146-7

388. *Spiritual Strategy Consultation Report* (2012, Dec.). Norfolk and Suffolk NHS Foundation Trust

389. Hitler, A. (1925) *Mein Kampf*. Verlag Frz. eher Nachf. GMBH., reissued 2002 Boston: Houghton Mifflin. (Manheim, R., trans).

390. 390 Hay, D. with Nye, R. (2006 revised edition. First published 1998) *The Spirit of the Child*. London and Philadelphia: Jessica Kingsley

391. Ibid. p29

392. Ibid.

393. Nye, R (2006) Chapter 6 Listening to Children Talking 92-107 and Chapter 7 Identifying the Core of Children's Spirituality 108-128 in Hay, D. with Nye, R. (2006 revised edition. First published 1998) *The Spirit of the Child*. London and Philadelphia: Jessica Kingsley

394. Culliford, L. (2011) *The Psychology of Spirituality*. London: Jessica Kingsley

395. Mithen, S. (1998) Introduction: The archaeological study of human creativity. In Mithen S. (Ed.) *Creativity in Human Evolution and History*. London and New York: Routledge. 1-15

396. eg., Russ, S.W. and Fiorelli, J.A. (2010) Developmental Approaches to Creativity. In Kaufman, J.C. and Sternberg, R.J. (Eds.) *The Cambridge Handbook of Creativity*. New

York: Cambridge University Press. 233-249

397. Personal interview with Professor Susan Greenfield, the neuroscientist well known for her work on consciousness, about boredom and creativity 24th September 2012, together with Esther Priyadharshini

398. Craft, A. (2008) Tensions in Creativity and Education: Enter Wisdom and Trusteeship. In Craft, A., Gardner, H. and Claxton, G. (Eds.) *Creativity, Wisdom and Trusteeship: Exploring the Role of Education.* Thousand Oaks, CA: Corwin Press

399. National Advisory Committee on Creative and Cultural Education (1999) *All our Futures: creativity, culture and education.* London: Department for Education and Employment. In 2012, there was no publication on the UK Department for Education's website dated later than 2007

400. Craft, A. (2008) Tensions in Creativity and Education: Enter Wisdom and Trusteeship. In Craft, A., Gardner, H. and Claxton, G. (Eds.) *Creativity, Wisdom and Trusteeship: Exploring the Role of Education.* Thousand Oaks, CA: Corwin Press

401. In 2007 the Scottish Executive was renamed Scottish Government

402. Craft, A. (2008) Tensions in Creativity and Education: Enter Wisdom and Trusteeship. In Craft, A., Gardner, H. and Claxton, G. (Eds.) *Creativity, Wisdom and Trusteeship: Exploring the Role of Education.* Thousand Oaks, CA: Corwin Press

403. Ibid.

404. Ibid.

405. Gordon, R.J. (2012) *Is U.S. Economic Growth Over? Faltering innovation confronts the six headwinds.* Working paper 18315. Cambridge, Mass: National Bureau of Economic Research

406. Feldman, D.H. (2008) Creativity and Wisdom: are they compatible? In Craft, A., Gardner, H. and Claxton, g. (Eds) *Creativity, Wisdom and Trusteeship: Exploring the Role of Education.* Thousand Oaks, CA: Corwin Press, 77-83

407. Rogers, D.E. (2001) Embracing the Range. in Pfenninger and Shubik (Eds.) *The Origins of Creativity.* Oxford: Oxford University Press. 47-57

408. Levy, B. and Langer, E. (2011) Aging. In Runco, M.A. and Pritzker, S.R. (Eds.) *Encyclopedia of Creativity.* Vol.1 London: Academic Press. 45-52

409. Dewey, J. (1934. Reissued 2005) *Art as Experience.* New York: Penguin

410. Crompton, T. (2013) Art, Hope and the Market, in *The Art of Life: understanding how participation in Arts and Culture can affect our values.* Mission, Models, Money and Common Cause. missionmodelsmoney.org.uk/rethink. p 22-24

411. Kasser, T. (2013) The Potential of Engagement in the Arts and Culture to Encourage Values that Support Wellbeing, Social Justice, and Ecological Sustainability, in *The Art of Life: understanding how participation in Arts and Culture can affect our values.* Mission Models Money and Common Cause. missionmodelsmoney.org.uk/rethink. p8-12

412. Hart, J. (2012) *Life Saving: Why We Need Poetry.* London: Virago

413. Claudius, C. (2010, 11th December) Music for Healing: from magic to medicine. *The Lancet,* 376 (9757) 1980-81

414. Sacks, O. (2008) *Musicophilia: Tales of Music and the Brain.* New York and Toronto: Alfred A. Knopf

415. Claudius, C. (2010, 11th December) Music for Healing: from magic to medicine. *The Lancet,* 376 (9757) 1980-81

416. Ibid.

417. Staricoff, R.L. (2010) *A Study of the Effects of Visual and Performing Arts in Health Care.*

http://www.music-in-hospitals.org.uk/documents/263_study_visual_performing_arts.pdf (viewed 6th Dev 2012)

418. Sacks, O. (2008) *Musicophilia: Tales of Music and the Brain*. New York and Toronto: Alfred A. Knopf

419. Altenmüller, E. and Schlaug, G. (2012) Music, Brain, and Health: Exploring Biological Foundations of Music's Health Effects. In Macdonald, R., Kreutz, G. and Mitchell, L. *Music, Health and Wellbeing*. Oxford: Oxford University Press. 12-24

420. Singing exercises major muscles in the upper body and the face, increasing lung capacity and bringing more oxygen into the bloodstream, which can in turn increase mental alertness. Singing boosts the immune system, and even increases life expectancy, according to a joint Harvard and Yale study. http://www.heartresearch.org.uk/hearthealth/singinggood (viewed 6th Dec 2012)

421. Research with over 1,000 singers in three countries has shown this. Clift, S. (1021) Singing, Wellbeing and Health. In Macdonald, R., Kreutz, G. and Mitchell, L. *Music, Health and Wellbeing*. Oxford: Oxford University Press 113-124

422. Majno, M. (2012) From the model of El Sistema in Venzuela to current applications: learning and integration through collective music education. *Annals of the New York Academy of Sciences* 1252. 56-64

423. Carroll, V. The Power of Music. (2012, 25 June -1 July) *Big Issue*, pp15-19

424. Archer, R. (2010, 18 Feb.) *Science, Society and Resilience in the Arts*. After-dinner talk at the Australia21 conference, shaping Australia's Resilience: policy development for uncertain futures. Canberra.

425. http://www.creative-partnerships.com/about-creative-partnerships/

426. Age 11-14. Creative Partnerships

427. Brice Heath, S. and Wolf, S. (2004) *Art is all about Looking: drawing and detail*. London: Creative Partnerships

428. Daykin, N. (2012) Developing Social Models for Research and Practice in Music, Arts, and Health: A Case Study of Research in a Mental Health Setting. In Macdonald, R., Kreutz, G. and Mitchell, L. *Music, Health and Wellbeing*. Oxford: Oxford University Press. 65-75

429. http://www.education.gov.uk/schools/teachingandlearning/qualifications/englishbac/a0075975/theenglishbaccalaureate. Plans for the Ebacc, proposed in September 2012, in what would have been the biggest shake-up of the school exam system in a generation, were in fact later withdrawn by Secretary of State for Education, Michael Gove, in February 2013, due to vigorous opposition from the Liberal Democrats and exam boards.

430. http://oecdpisaletter.org/ (viewed 2 June 2014)

431. Sarason, S. B. (1990) *The Challenge of Art to Psychology*. New Haven and London: Yale University Press, p5

432. eg, Peffer, J. (2009) *Art and the End of Apartheid*. University of Minnesota Press; Reed, T.V. (2005) *The Art of Protest*. Minneapolis: University of Minnesota Press

433. Hooper, J, Tremlett, G, and Willsher, K. (2012, 24 Aug.) Theatre flourishes in austerity Europe. *The Guardian Weekly*. p34-5

434. Cloughton, R. (2012, 24 Aug.) Athens art scene rise to challenge of financial crisis. *The Guardian Weekly*, p34-5

435. Skinner, B.F. (1976) *Walden Two*. New York: Macmillan; London : Collier Macmillan, pxiii. Cited in Sarason, S. B. (1990) *The Challenge of Art to Psychology*. New Haven and

London:Yale University Press

436. Elbaek, U. (2013) Foreword, *The Art of Life: understanding how participation in Arts and Culture can affect our values.* Mission Models Money and Common Cause. missionmodelsmoney.org.uk/rethink, p7

437. Smith, D. (2013) Imagine That, in *The Art of Life: understanding how participation in Arts and Culture can affect our values.* Mission Models Money and Common Cause. missionmodelsmoney.org.uk/rethink. p28-29

438. Archer, R. (2010, 18th February) *Science, Society and Resilience in the Arts.* After-dinner talk at the Australia21 conference, shaping Australia's Resilience: policy development for uncertain futures. Canberra.

439. Belton, T. (1998) *An Investigation of the Influence of Television and Videos on 10-12 Year-old Children's Storymaking* (Unpublished doctoral thesis). University of East Anglia, Norwich, UK

440. Konlaan, B.B., Bygren, L.O. and Johansson, S-E. (2000) Visiting the cinema, concerts, museums or art exhibitions as determinant of survival: a Swedish fourteen-year cohort follow-up. *Scandinavian Journal of Public Health*; 28: 174-178. There may, of course, be confounding factors, eg, that those suffering serious chronic conditions or disabilities are less likely than fully fit individuals to find it easy, possible or even pleasurable to attend cultural events.

441. Richards, R. (2010) Everyday Creativity: process and way of life – four key issues. In Kaufman, J.C. and Sternberg, R.J. (Eds.) *The Cambridge Handbook of Creativity.* New York: Cambridge University Press. pp189-125

442. Ibid.

443. Studies over the last 40 years show that, in America at least, adults, including teachers, do not value creativity very highly. Moran, S. (2010) The Roles of Creativity in Society. In Kaufman, J.C. and Sternberg, R.J. (Eds.) *The Cambridge Handbook of Creativity.* New York: Cambridge University Press. 74-90

444. Richards, R. (2010) Everyday Creativity: process and way of life – four key issues. In Kaufman, J.C. and Sternberg, R.J. (Eds.) *The Cambridge Handbook of Creativity.* New York: Cambridge University Press. pp189-125

445. Egan, K. (1992) *Imagination in Teaching and Learning 8-15.* London: Routledge

446. Hughes, T. (1977) Myth and Education. In *Times Educational Supplement.* 11-13

447. Lamont, T. (2012, 16 Dec.) Graphic Visions from the Dark Magician of The Midlands. *The Observer Review.* p14-17

448. Duncan, A. (22 Dec 2012 – 4 Jan 2013,) Let it Snow. *Radio Times* pp14-17

449. Guilford, J. P. (1956). Structure of intellect. *Psychological Bulletin*, 53, 267-293. Cited in Bateson, P. and Martin, P. (2013) *Play, Playfulness, Creativity and Innovation.* Cambridge: Cambridge University Press.

450. Guilford, J.P. (1950) Creativity. *American Psychologist*, 5, 444-454. p446

451. Torrance, E.P. (1964) *Education and the Creative Potential.* Minneapolis: University of Minnesota. p46-47

452. Ibid.

453. Vygotsky, L.S. (2004) Imagination and Creativity in Childhood (M.E. Sharpe, Inc. Trans.). *Journal of Russian and East European Psychology*, 42, 7-97. (Original work published 1967). Quoted in Beghetto, R.A., Creativity in the Classroom. In Kaufman, J.C. and Sternberg, R.J. (Eds.) *Cambridge Handbook of Creativity* 447-466, p447

454. Torrance, E.P. (1964) *Education and the Creative Potential*. Minneapolis: University of Minnesota

455. Claxton, G., Craft. A. and Gardner, H. (2008). *Concluding thoughts: Good thinking – education for wise creativity*, 168-176, p168

456. Rowson, J. (2008) How are we Disposed to be Creative? In Craft, A., Gardner, H. and Claxton, G. (Eds) *Creativity, Wisdom and Trusteeship: Exploring the Role of Education*. Thousand Oaks, CA: Corwin Press. 84-96

457. Beghetto, R.A. (2010) Creativity in the Classroom. In Kaufman, J.C. and Sternberg, R.J. (Eds.) *The Cambridge Handbook of Creativity*. New York: Cambridge University Press. p447-463

458. Winnicott, D. (2005) *Playing and Reality*. Abingdon: Routledge (first published 1971, London: Tavistock)

459. Ibid. p87

460. Torrance, E.P (1964) *Education and the Creative Potential*. Minneapolis: University of Minnesota

461. Guilford, J.P. (1950) Creativity. *American Psychologist*, 5, 444-454

462. Claxton, G., Craft. A. and Gardner, H. (2008) *Concluding thoughts: Good thinking – education for wise creativity*. In Craft, A., Gardner, H. and Claxton, G. (Eds.) *Creativity, Wisdom and Trusteeship: Exploring the Role of Education*. Thousand Oaks, CA: Corwin Press. 168-176.

Chapter 10 Nurturing Playfulness

463. Bateson, P. and Martin, P. (2013) *Play, Playfulness, Creativity and Innovation*. Cambridge: Cambridge University Press.

464. Ibid.

465. Fagen, R., & Fagen, J. (2009). Play behaviour and multi-year juvenile survival in free-ranging brown bears, Ursus arctos. *Evolutionary Ecology Research*, 11, 1-15

466. Bateson, P. and Martin, P. (2013) *Play, Playfulness, Creativity and Innovation*. Cambridge: Cambridge University Press.

467. Russ, S.W. and Fiorelli, J.A. (2010) Developmental Approaches to Creativity. In Kaufman, J.C. and Sternberg, R.J. (Eds.) *The Cambridge Handbook of Creativity*. New York: Cambridge University Press. 233-249

468. Vygotsky, L.S. (1976) Play and its Role in the Mental Development of the Child. In Bruner, J.S., Jolly, A. and Sylva, K. (Eds.) *Play: Its role in development and evolution*. Harmondsworth: Penguin. 537-554. p544. First published in Soviet Psychology, Vol. 12, No.6, 1966, pp.62-76, based on a lecture given in 1933 at the Hertzen Pedagogical Institute, Leningrad.

469. Ibid.

470. Godwin, S. (1994, Winter) Pot Pourri of Play Memories from group reminiscence session. Norwich: *Play for Life Magazine* No.33

471. Singer, D. J. and Singer, J.L. (1990) *The House of Make-Believe: Children's Play and the Developing Imagination*. Cambridge MA and London: Harvard University Press

472. Singer, D.J. (1999) Imaginative Play and Television: factors in a child's development. In Singer, J.A. and Salovey, P. (Eds.) *At Play in the Fields of Consciousness: Essays in Honor of Jerome L. Singer*. Mahwah and London: Lawrence Erlbaum Associates. 303-326

473. Singer, D.G. and Singer, J.L. (2005) *Imagination and Play in the Electronic Age*. Cambridge, MA: Harvard University Press

474. Wenner, M. (2009) The Serious Need for Play. *Scientific American*, 20 (1), 22-29

475. Kahn, P. Jr. (1999) *The Human Relationship with Nature*. Cambridge MA:MIT Press

476. Louv, R. (2005, revised and updated 2009) *Last Child in the Woods: Saving our Children from Nature Deficit Disorder*. London: Atlantic Books

477. ibid.

478. Ibid. p120

479. Ibid.

480. Nicholson, S. (1971) How not to Cheat Children: The Theory of Loose Parts. *Landscape Architecture* 62 (1) 30-34. Quoted in Louv, R. (2005, revised and updated 2009) *Last Child in the Woods: Saving our Children from Nature Deficit Disorder*. London: Atlantic Books

481. Singer, D.G. and Singer, J.L (2005) *Imagination and Play in the Electronic Age*. Cambridge, MA: Harvard University Press

482. Ibid.

483. Bruce, T. (1991) *Time to Play in Early Childhood Education*. London: Hodder and Stoughton, p40

484. Ibid.

485. Garvey, C. (1977) Play. *The Developing Child* series. Bruner, J., Cole, M. and Lloyd, B. (Eds.) London: Collins/Fontana Open Books. Cited in Bruce, T. (1991) Time to Play in Early Childhood Education. London: Hodder and Stoughton

486. Singer, D.G (1999) Imaginative Play and Television: Factors in a Child's Development. In Singer, J.A. and Salovey, P. *At Play in the Fields of Consciousness: Essays in Honour of Jerome L. Singer*. Mahwah and London: Lawrence Erlbaum Associates. 303-326

487. Bruner, J. S. and Sherwood, V. (1976) Peekaboo and the Learning of Rule Structures. In Bruner, J.S. Jolly, A. and Sylva, K. *Play – Its Role in Development and Evolution*. New York: Basic Books. 2 277-285

488. Winnicott, D. (2005) (first publ. 1971 Tavistock Publishers) London and New York: Routledge p136-7

489. Singer, D.G. and Singer, J.L. (2005) *Imagination and Play in the Electronic Age*. Cambridge, Mass: Harvard University Press

490. Greenfield, S. (2012, 27th October) *The Young Mind of the 21st Century: Realising Its True Potential*. Keynote address, Unhurried Pathways – Towards a New Paradigm for Early Childhood Conference, University of Winchester

491. Verran, L. (1994, Spring) Garden Dens – yet more! *Play for Life Magazine*. No 32. p2-3

492. Sigman, A. (2011) Does not Compute, Revisited: Screen Technology in Early years Education. In House, R. *Too Much, Too Soon? Early Learning and the Erosion of Childhood*. Stroud, UK: Hawthorn Press, p269

493. Crawford, M. (2011) *The Case for Working with your Hands or why office work is bad for us and fixing things feels good*. London: Penguin Books. First published (2009) as *Shop Class as Soulcraft* in the USA by Penguin Press and in the UK by Penguin Books). p7

494. Bruner, J. (1980) "The Conditions of Creativity". In *On Knowing: Essays for the Left Hand*. London and Cambridgm Mass: Belknap Press of Harvard University. p18

495. Belton, T. (2001) 'Television and Imagination: The Influence of the Media on Children's Storymaking', *Media, Culture and Society* 23; pp799 -820

496. Greenfield, S. (2008) *The Quest for Identity in the 21st Century*. London: Sceptre

497. Ibid. p59

498. CHILDWISE Monitor Pre-school Report 2012 http://www.childwise.co.uk (viewed 6th November 2012)

499. Haddon, L. and Livingstone, S. and the EU Kids Online network (2012) *EU Kids Online: national perspectives.* www.eukidsonline.net (viewed 6th November 2012)

500. Gutnic, A.L., Robb, M., Takeuchi, L. and Kotler, J. (March 2011) *Always connected: The new digital media habits of young children.* New York: The Joan Ganz Cooney Centre, Sesame Workshop. OTX Research http://www.joanganzcooneycenter.org/publication/always-connected-the-new-digital-media-habits-of-young-children/

501. Sigman, A. (2011) Does not Compute, Revisited: Screen Technology in Early years Education. In House, R. *Too Much, Too Soon? Early Learning and the Erosion of Childhood.* Stroud, UK: Hawthorn Press, p269

502. Greenfield, S. (2008) *The Quest for Identity in the 21st Century.* London: Sceptre

503. Ibid.

504. Sigman, A. (2011) Does not Compute, Revisited: Screen Technology in Early years Education. In House, R. *Too Much, Too Soon? Early Learning and the Erosion of Childhood.* Stroud, UK: Hawthorn Press, p269

505. Department of Children, Schools and Families (DCSF) (2007) *Early Years Foundation Stage from Birth to Five.* London

506. Department of Children, Schools and Families (DCSF) (2007) *Early Years Foundation Stage from Birth to Five.* London: Section 4.4, Learning and development: ICT quoted in Sigman, A. (2011) Does not Compute, Revisited: Screen Technology in Early years Education. In House, R. *Too Much, Too Soon? Early Learning and the Erosion of Childhood.* Stroud, UK: Hawthorn Press

507. http://www.childrenscentres.org.uk/media/file/ey/EYFS%20downloads%20from%20 2008/GPG%204.01%20ICT%20(WEB).pdf (viewed 5th November 2012)

508. Ball, D. (2010) *Play and Risk – in search of new ground.* Proceedings of United in Play conference, Fremantle, November 2012. Available from David Ball at http://www.davidjball.com/

509. Children's Society and the Children's Play Council (2002); cited in Ball. D (2010) *Play and Risk – in search of new ground.* Proceedings of United in Play conference, Fremantle, November 2012. Available from David Ball at http://www.davidjball.com/

510. Cited in Singer, D.G. and Singer, J.L (2005) *Imagination and Play in the Electronic Age.* Cambridge, Mass: Harvard University Press

511. Russ, S.W. and Fiorelli, J.A. (2010) Developmental Approaches to Creativity. In Kaufman, J.C. and Sternberg, R.J. (Eds.) *The Cambridge Handbook of Creativity.* New York: Cambridge University Press. 233-249

512. Millar, S. (1968) *The Psychology of Play.* Harmondsworth: Penguin

513. Wilson, F.R. (1998) *The Hand: how its use shapes the brain, language, and human culture.* New York: Vintage Books

514. Wilson, F.R. (1999, July) The Real Meaning of Hands-on Education. Paper presented at the Institute for Development of Education Activities (IDEA) Los Angeles, Atlanta, Appleton, Denver. Revised for publication by the *Waldorf Research Bulletin,* October 1999, p9

515. Sennett, R. (2008) *The Craftsman.* New Haven and London: Yale University Press, p12

516. Beghetto, R.A. (2010) Creativity in the Classroom. In Kaufman, J.C. and Sternberg, R.J. (Eds.) *The Cambridge Handbook of Creativity.* New York: Cambridge University

Press. 447-463

517. Greenfield, S. (2012, 27 October) *The Young Mind of the 21st Century: Realising Its True Potential*. Keynote address, Unhurried Pathways – Towards a New Paradigm for Early Childhood Conference, University of Winchester

518. Webster, J. D. and McCall, M. E. (1999) Reminiscence Functions across Adulthood: a Replication and Extension. *Journal of Adult Development* 6 (1). p73

519. Belton, T. (1992, Summer) I Remember… Memories of Play. *Play for Life Magazine*. No 26. p16

520. Fowler, F. (1949, August) The Day we Flew the Kites. Reader's Digest. Reprinted in Britz-Crecelius, H. (1979) *Children at Play: Preparation for Life*. Edinburgh: Floris Books (trans. C. and I. von Arnim from 2nd edition 1972)

521. Crowe, B. (1983) *Play is a Feeling*. London: George Allen and Unwin

522. Ibid.

523. Personal communication 19 October 1991

524. Crowe, B. (1983), p.21

525. Ibid. p13

Chapter 11 Bonding with Nature

526. Moreton, C. (2008, 28 September) What Tickles the Fancy *The Independent on Sunday*, p.26

527. Wilson, E.O. (1984) *Biophilia*. Harvard University Press, Cambridge MA and London. Prologue

528. Ibid. Prologue

529. eg, Pretty, J., Barton, J., Colbeck, I., Hine, R., Mourato, S., MacKerron, G. And Wood, C. (2011) "Health Values from Ecosystems" Chapter 23 of *UK National Eco-system Assessment*. UNEP-WCMC, Cambridge. UK National Ecosystem Assessment (2011); The UK National Ecosystem Assessment: Synthesis of the Key

530. BTCV Position Paper *Health and Wellbeing*. Doncaster: BTCV

531. Orsega-Smith, E., Mowen, A.J., Payne, L.L., Godbey, G. (2004, 2nd quarter) The Interaction of Stress and Park Use on Psycho-physiological Health in Older Adults. *Journal of Leisure Research*, 36 (2). pp232-256; Velarde, M.D., Fry. G. and Tveit, M. (2007) Health Effects of Viewing Landscapes – landscape types in environmental psychology. *Urban Forestry and Urban Greening* 6 (4). pp.199-212

532. Kaplan, R. and Kaplan, S. (1989) *The Experience of Nature: a psychological perspective* New York and Cambridge: Cambridge University Press

533. Ibid.

534. Velarde, M.D., Fry. G. and Tveit, M. (2007) Health Effects of Viewing Landscapes – landscape types in environmental psychology. *Urban Forestry and Urban Greening* 6 (4). pp199-212.

535. Kaplan, R. and Kaplan, S. (1989) *The Experience of Nature: a psychological perspective* New York and Cambridge: Cambridge University Press

536. Ibid.

537. Kahn, P. Jr. (1999) *The Human Relationship with Nature: development and culture*. Cambridge Mass and London: The MIT Press.

538. Cimprich, B. (1992) Attentional Fatigue Following Breast Cancer Surgery. *Research in Nursing and Health*, 15, 199-207, and Cimprich, B (1993) Development of an intervention to restore attention in cancer patients. *Cancer Nursing*, 16, 83-92, cited in

Kaplan S (1995) The Restorative Benefits of Nature: toward an integrative framework. *Journal of Environmental Psychology*, 15. pp.169-182

539. May, R. (2007, 18th March) "The Mad Doctor", *The Independent on Sunday Magazine*, pp-12-15

540. Sacks, O (1984) A Leg To Stand On. Simon and Schuster, United States and Canada, and (large print version) John Farquharson Ltd, UK p.202

541. MIND (2007) *Ecotherapy: The Green Agenda for Mental Health*. MIND, London

542. Kahn, P. Jr. (1999) *The Human Relationship with Nature: development and culture*. Cambridge Mass and London: The MIT Press

543. Shipman, P. (2011) *The Animal Connection: new hypothesis for human evolution and human nature*. London: WW Norton and Co.

544. McKie, R. (2011, 2 Oct.) Love of animals led to language and man's domination of Earth. *The Observer*.

545. Ibid.

546. Stutz, E. (1987) *Growing Up to Love Nature*. Norwich: Play for Life. p1

547. Cobb, E., (1959, summer) the Ecology of Imagination in Childhood – work in Progress. *Daedalus* 1/4 No 3. 537-548 http://bloge.miwako-kurosaka.com/?eid=943678 (viewed 29th January 2012)

548. England Marketing. (2009) Report to Natural England. *Childhood and Nature: a survey on changing relationships with nature across generations*. Sheffield: Natural England

549. There are now approximately 7,000 Forest School trained practitioners and 150 individuals providing Forest School programmes in England. Source: email correspondence with Learning Outside the Classroom.

550. O'Brien, Elizabeth A. and Murray, R. *A marvellous opportunity for children to learn: a participatory evaluation of Forest School in England and Wales* (2006) Forest Research, Farnham, Surrey. Evaluation carried out jointly by the Forestry Commission and the New Economics Foundation. http://www.forestry.gov.uk/pdf/fr0112forestschoolsreport.pdf/$FILE/fr0112forestschoolsreport.pdf

551. Ibid. p8

552. (2008, March 14th) *Norwich Advertiser*, p24

553. Rockliff, S. and Chinnery, P. (2007) Report of Wellie Wednesday, A Six Week Pilot Project. Unpublished evaluation

554. I learned this in conversation with the Tackle Learning Director, Mark Scott

555. Ringsfield Hall Trust http://www.ringsfield-hall.co.uk/home.htm

556. Institute of Earth Education http://www.eartheducation.org/

557. Van Matre, S. (1990) *Earth Education: A New Beginning*. Greenville, West Virginia; Institute of Earth Education. p129

558. I learned this in a conversation with Chris Walton the Ringsfield Hall Outreach Director, who provided examples of his observations and children's work.

559. Bixler, R.D, Carlisle, C.L., Hammitt, W.E. and Floyd, M.F. (1994) Observed fears and discomforts among urban students on school field trips to wildland areas. *Journal of Environmental Education* 26 (1). p24–33

560. Kahn, P. H. Jr. (1999) *The Human Relationship with Nature: Development and Culture*. Cambridge, Mass and London: MIT Press

561. Riccio, V. and Slocum, B. (1962) All the Way Down: The Violent Underworld of Street Gangs. New York: Simon and Schuster pp.100-101, cited in Yi-Fu Tuan (1978) Children and the Natural Environment in Altman, I. and Wohlwill, J. (Eds.)

Children and the Environment; Human Behaviour and Environment: Advances in theory and knowledge Vol 3. New York and London: Plenum Press

562. Wilson, E.O. (1984) *Biophilia*. Cambridge MA and London: Harvard University Press. Prologue

563. Pyle, R.M. (1993) *The Thunder Tree: Lessons for an Urban Wildland*. Corvallis: Oregon State University Press

564. Pilgrim, S., Smith, D. and Pretty, J. (2007) A Cross-regional Assessment of the Factors Affecting Ecoliteracy: implications for policy and practice. *Ecological Applications* 17 (6). pp1742-1751

565. Capra, F. (2008) Adapted from a lecture "Linking Food, Health, and the Environment" hosted by the Centre for Ecoliteracy and Teachers College Columbia University. http://www.ecoliteracy.org/essays/new-facts-life

566. Ibid.

567. Louv, R. (2005, revised and updated 2009) *Last Child in the Woods: Saving our Children from Nature Deficit Disorder*. London: Atlantic Books

568. Severin, W.T. and Tankard, J.W. (1992) Communication theories: origins, methods and uses in the mass media. 3rd edition. London: Longman

569. Tarring, B. (2011, 18 Dec) "Betjeman's beloved Kennet runs dry and raises fears for England's rivers" *The Observer*

570. Walton, C. (2008) *The Dancing of the Shaping of the Earth-plain Members in the Community of Life; Humans and the more-then-human community: Earth Education and therapeutic conditions*. Paper at Conference for Person-Centred Counselling, University of East Anglia, Norwich, UK

571. Orr, D. (1992) *Ecological Literacy; Education as transition to a postmodern world*. New York: State of New York Press; Orr, D. (2004) *On Education, Environment and the Human Prospect*. Washington and London: Island Press. (A collection of essays written 1990-93).

572. Orr, D. (2004) *On Education, Environment and the Human Prospect*. Washington and London: Island Press. p2

573. Ibid. p11

574. Beekeeping takes flight in primary school (2011, 30th August) *The Guardian Mortarboard Blog*. http://www.guardian.co.uk/education/mortarboard (viewed 15 Feb. 2013). There are now four hives at the school, and the impact on the children is "fantastic". They also keep chickens and grow fruit and vegetables on the school site, and there is a teaching kitchen. The school tries to teach the children the curriculum in a practical, hands-on way, and develop skills for life. Personal correspondence with head teacher Tim Baker.

575. Palmer, J. (1999) Research Matters: a call for the application of empirical evidence to the task of improving the quality and impact of environmental education. *Cambridge Journal of Education* 29 (3). Pp.379-395 Special Issue – Environmental Education and the Transformation of Schooling.
Palmer, J., Suggate, J., Robottom, I. and Hart, P. (1999) Significant Life Experiences and Formative Influences on the Development of Adults' Environmental Awareness in the UK, Australia and Canada. *Environmental Education Research* 5 (2). pp.181-200

576. Ibid. p388

577. Pilgrim, S., Smith, D. and Pretty, J. (2007) A Cross-regional Assessment of the Factors Affecting Ecoliteracy: Implications for Policy and Practice. *Ecological Applications* 17 (6). pp1742-1751

578. Ibid.
579. Orr, D. (2004) *Earth in Mind: On Education, Environment and the Human Prospect.* Washington and London: Island Press. p45
580. Pretty, J. (2007) *The Earth only Endures: On reconnecting with nature and our place in it.* London and Stirling VA: Earthscan. p215
581. Barnes, S. (2007) *How to be Wild.* London: Short Books. p55-6
582. Blezard, P. (2010) Face to Face. *The Independent on Sunday.* p28
583. Juniper, T. (2013) *What has Nature Ever Done for Us?* London: Profile Books
584. Juniper, T. (2007) *How Many Light Bulbs does it Take to Change a Planet? 95 Ways to Save Planet Earth.* London: Quercus
585. Ibid. p5
586. My Week (2008 24 Aug) *The Observer.* p.43
587. Taylor, G. (1986) *Planting Acorns; an adventure story and guide book: How to give your city child a country childhood.* London: Impact Books
588. Wondering Walks were suggested by Geraldine Taylor at a workshop on 'Finding the Countryside' as a means of stimulating children's interest in nature, and an antidote to the tendency to look up information. Play for Life Day of Workshops, London, 1992.
589. Louv, R. (2005, revised and updated 2009) *Last Child in the Woods: Saving our Children from Nature Deficit Disorder.* London: Atlantic Books
590. Ibid. p.8
591. Carson, R. (1962) *Silent Spring.* Boston: Houghton Mifflin
592. Carson, R. (1998; previous edition 1965; text 1956) *The Sense of Wonder.* New York: Harper Collins, p.56
593. Ibid. p.66
594. Barrows, A. (1995) "The Eco-psychology of Child Development" in Roszac, T., Gomes, E.M. and Kanner. A.D. (Eds.) *Ecopsychology: Restoring the Earth, Healing the Mind.* San Francisco: Siearra Club Books. pp.101-110
595. Kahn, P.H. Jr. And Kellert, S. R. (Eds) *Children and Nature: Psychological, Sociocultural and Evolutionary Investigations.* Cambridge Mass and London: MIT Press. Introduction
596. Natural England (2010) *'Nature Nearby': Accessible Natural Greenspace Standard.* Sheffield: Natural England

Chapter 12 Personal Qualities and Capacities for Building a Better Future

597. Sen, A. *Development as Freedom.* Oxford: Oxford University Press. p87
598. Jackson, M. (2008) *Distraction: The Erosion of Attention and the Coming Dark Age.* New York: Prometheus Books
599. Ibid.
600. Schmidt, M.E., Pempek, T., Kirkorian, H. L., Lund, A. F., and Anderson, D. R. (2008). The effects of background television on the toy play behaviour of very young children. *Child Development.* 79 (4) pp.1137-51
601. Palmer, S. (2009) What is Toxic Childhood? House, R. and Loewenthal, D. (Eds.) (2009) *Childhood, Well-being and a Therapeutic Ethos.* London: Karnac. p37-54
602. NICE (2007) *Behaviour Change at Population, Community and Individual Levels* London: National Institute for Clinical Excellence
603. Friedli, L. (2009) *Mental Health, Resilience and Inequalities Executive Summary* WHO, European Regional Office, and The Mental Health Foundation, London
604. Kohn, M. (2010) *Turned out Nice: How the British Isles will Change as the World Heats*

Up. London: Faber and Faber

605. Wilson, S. and Ferch, S. (2005, Winter) Enhancing Resilience in the Workplace Through the Practice of Caring Relationships. *Organisation Development Journal.*

606. Martin, P. (2005) *Making Happy People: The nature of happiness and its origins in childhood.* London and New York: Fourth Estate

607. Isen, A.M., Daubman, K.A. and Nowicki, G.P. (1987) Positive Affect Facilitates Creative Problem Solving. *Journal of Personality and Social Psychology* 52 (6) p1122-1131

608. Grothmann, T. and Patt, A. (2005) Adaptive Capacity and Human Cognition: The process of individual adaptation to climate change. *Global Environmental Change* 15 (3) pp.199-213

609. http://www.transitionnetwork.org/

610. Hopkins, R. (2008) *The Transition Town Handbook: From oil dependency to local resilience.* Totnes, Devon: Green Books

611. Ibid.p134

612. Hopkins, R. (2011) *The Transition Companion: making your community more resilient in uncertain times.* Totnes, Devon: Green Books

613. eg, Levin, S.A. (1999) *Fragile Dominion.* New York: Perseus Books Group

614. This is the title of a book which argues for the complete overhaul of schools at all levels so as to produce an education system which prepares children for a very different future. Bassey, M. (2011) *Education for the Inevitable: Schooling when the oil runs out.* Brighton: The Book Guild

615. House, R. and Loewenthal, D. (Eds) (2009) *Childhood, Well-being and a Therapeutic Ethos.* London: Karnac.

616. House, R. and Loewenthal, D. (2009) "'Therapeutic Ethos' in therapeutic, educational and cultural perspectives". Editorial introduction; and Loewenthal, D. (2009) "Childhood, Well-being and a Therapeutic Ethos: a case for therapeutic education" in House, R. and Loewenthal, D. (eds) *Childhood, Well-being and a Therapeutic Ethos.* London: Karnac. pp 1-16 and 19-36

617. Crowe, B. (2008) *People Don't Grow by Being Measured: recollections and reflections of a dyslexic grandmother.* Leicester: Matador

618. Vaillant, G.E. (2012) *The Triumphs of Experience: The Men of the Harvard Grant Study.* Cmabridge Mass and London. The Belknap Press. p370

619. Ibid.

620. Bowlby, J. (1969) *Attachment and Loss* Vol 1 *Attachment.* London: Hogarth Press; Bowlby, J. (1973) *Attachment and Loss: anxiety and anger. Vol 2 Separation.* London: Hogarth Press ; Bowlby, J. (1980) *Attachment and Loss: sadness and depression. Vol 3: Loss.* London: Hogarth Press

621. Baim, C. and Morrison, T. (2011) *Attachment-based Practice with Adults: understanding strategies and promoting positive change. A new practice model and interactive source for assessment, intervention and supervision.* Brighton: Pavilion

622. Grossman, K., Grossman, K.E. and Kindler, H. (2005) "Early Care and the Roots of Attachment and Partnership Representations" in Grossman, K.E., Grossman, K, and Waters, E. (Eds) *Attachment from Infancy to Adulthood: the major longitudinal studies.* New York and London: Guilford Press p98-136

623. Belsky, J., Rosenberger, K., and Crnic, K. (1995) "The Origins of Attachment Security: 'Classical' and contextual determinants" in Goldberg, S., Muir, R. and Kerr, J. (Eds.) *Attachment Theory: Social, developmental and clinical perspectives.* Hillsdale and

London: The Analytic Press pp153-183

624. Ainsworth, M.D. (1973) "The Development of Infant-mother Attachment" in B.M Caldovell and HN Ricciuti (eds) *Review of Child Development Research* Vol 3. Chicago: University of Chicago Press. 1-94

625. Grossman, K.E. (1995) "The Evolution and History of Attachment: research and theory" in Goldberg, S., Muir, R. and Kerr, J. (Eds) *Attachment Theory: Social, developmental and clinical perspectives.* Hillsdale and London: The Analytic Press pp85-121

626. Gerhardt, S. (2004) *Why Love Matters: how affection shapes a baby's brain.* London and New York: Routledge.

627. Ibid. p210

628. This figure was derived in the US. Goldberg, S., Introduction. in Goldberg, S., Muir, R. and Kerr, J. (eds) *Attachment Theory: Social, developmental and clinical perspectives.* Hillsdale and London: The Analytic Press. Appendix 2, p11.

629. Bowlby, J. (1969) *Attachment and Loss* Vol 1 *Attachment.* London: Hogarth Press

630. Bretherton, I. (2005) "In Pursuit of the Internal Working Model" in Grossman, K.E., Grossman, K, and Waters, E. (eds) *Attachment from Infancy to Adulthood: the major longitudinal studies.* New York and London: Guilford Press. p13-47

631. Baim, C. and Morrison, T. (2011) *Attachment-based Practice with Adults: understanding strategies and promoting positive change. A new practice model and interactive source for assessment, intervention and supervision.* Brighton: Pavilion

632. Grossman, K.E. (1995) "The Evolution and History of Attachment: research and theory" in Goldberg, S., Muir, R. and Kerr, J. (eds) *Attachment Theory: Social, developmental and clinical perspectives.* Hillsdale and London: The Analytic Press p85-121

633. Bateson, P. and Martin, P. (1999) *Design for a Life: How behaviour develops.* London: Jonathan Cape

634. Brown, K.W., Ryan, R.M. and Creswell, J.D. (2007) Mindfulness: theoretical foundations and evidence for its salutary effects. *Psychological Inquiry* 18 (4) 211-237

635. Ibid.

636. Feeney, J. And Noller, P. (1996) *Adult Attachment.* Thousand Oaks, London, New Delhi: Sage

637. Bowlby, J (1982) *Attachment and Loss: Vol 1, Attachment* (2nd rev.ed.) New York: Basic Books cited in Grossman, K, Grossman, K.E., and Kindler, H. (2005) "Early Care and the Roots of Attachment and Partnership Representations" in Grossman, K.E., Grossman, K., and Waters, E. (eds) *Attachment from Infancy to Adulthood: the major longitudinal studies.* New York and London: Guilford Press. Pp 98-136

638. Karen, R. (1998) *Becoming Attached: first relationships – how they shape our capacity to love.* New York and Oxford: Oxford University Press

639. Ibid.

640. Karen, R. (1998) *Becoming Attached: first relationships – how they shape our capacity to love.* New York and Oxford: Oxford University Press

641. Ibid.

642. Ibid.

643. Ibid.

644. Rich, P. (2006) From Theory to Practice: the application of attachment theory to assessment and treatment in forensic mental health services. *Criminal Behaviour and Mental Health.* 16. Editorial 211-216.

645. Grossman, K.E. (1995) The Evolution and History of Attachment: research and theory.

In Goldberg, S., Muir, R. and Kerr, J. (eds) *Attachment Theory: social, developmental and clinical perspectives.* Hillsdale and London: The Analytic Press. 85-121

646. Ibid. p118

647. Palmer, S. (2009) "What is Toxic Childhood?" House, R. and Loewenthal, D. (Eds) (2009) *Childhood, Well-being and a Therapeutic Ethos.* London: Karnac. p37-54

648. Karen, R. (1998) *Becoming Attached: first relationships – how they shape our capacity to love.* New York and Oxford: Oxford University Press

649. Ibid.

650. Christopher, A. N., Sabila, L, and Deadmarsh, E.J. (2009) Materialism and Wellbeing: the mediating effect of locus of control. *Personality and Individual Differences,* 46, p682-686

651. Kerwan-Taylor, H. (2006) Sorry but my children bore me to death. *Mailonline 26th July.* http://www.dailymail.co.uk/femail/article-397672/Sorry-children-bore-death.html (viewed 18th Jan 2013)

652. Brown, K.W. Ryan, R. M. and Creswell, J. D. Mindfulness: theoretical foundations and evidence for its salutary effects. *Psychological Inquiry* 18 (4) 211-237

653. Ibid. p212

654. Ibid. p213

655. Ibid.

656. Brown, K.W. Ryan, R. M. and Creswell, J. D. Mindfulness: theoretical foundations and evidence for its salutary effects. *Psychological Inquiry* 18 (4) p211-237

657. Shaver, P.R., Lavy, S., Saron, C.D. and Mikulincer, M. (2007) Social Foundations of the Capacity for Mindfulness: An Attachment Perspective. *Psychological Inquiry.* 18 (4). 264-271

658. Brown, K.W., Ryan, R.M. and Creswell, J.D. (2007) Mindfulness: theoretical foundations and evidence for its salutary effects. *Psychological Inquiry* 18 (4) p211-237

659. Ibid.

660. Shaver, P., R., Lavy, S., Saron, C., D. And Mikulincer, M. (2007) Social Foundations for the Capacity for Mindfulness: an attachment perspective. *Psychological Inquiry* 18 (4) 264-271

661. Karen, R. (1998) *Becoming Attached: first relationships –how they shape our capacity to love.* New York and Oxford, Oxford University Press

662. Foreman, D. (1998) Maternal Mental Illness and Mother-child Relations. *Advances in Psychiatric Treatment,* 4, 135-143

663. Family Action (2012) *Against All Odds: Mind the Gap Report. Creating services and welfare to tackle perinatal depression.* London: Family Action

664. Grossman, K.E. (1995) The Evolution and History of Attachment: research and theory. In Goldberg, S., Muir, R. and Kerr, J. (eds) *Attachment Theory: Social, developmental and clinical perspectives.* Hillsdale and London: The Analytic Press, 85-121.

665. Gerhardt, S. (2004) Why Love Matters: how affection shapes a baby's brain. London and New York, Routledge. p39

666. http://www.mentalhealth.org.uk/our-work/research/sutton-early-intervention-project/?view=Standard

667. Karen, R. (1998) *Becoming Attached: first relationships –how they shape our capacity to love.* New York and Oxford: Oxford University Press

668. Ibid.

669. van den Boom (1990) Preventive intervention and the quality of mother-infant

interaction and infant exploration in irritable infants. In Koops, W. et al (Eds.) *Developmental Psychology Behind the Dike.* Amsterdam, Eburou pp 249-270. Cited in Belsky, J., Rosenberger, K., and Crnic, K. (1995) The Origins of Attachment Security: "Classical" and contextual determinants in Goldberg, S., Muir, R. and Kerr, J. (eds) *Attachment Theory: Social, developmental and clinical perspectives.* Hillsdale and London, The Analytic Press pp153-183

670. Karen, R. (1998) *Becoming Attached: first relationships —how they shape our capacity to love.* New York and Oxford, Oxford University Press

671. Gerhardt, S. (2004) Why Love Matters: how affection shapes a baby's brain. London and New York, Routledge

672. http://www.sfheart.com/Gandhi.html

673. Karen, R. (1998) *Becoming Attached: first relationships —how they shape our capacity to love.* New York and Oxford: Oxford University Press p156

674. Bassey, M. (2011) Education for the Inevitable: Schooling when the oil runs out. Brighton, The Book Guild

675. Ibid. p115

676. Reeve, J. (2002) "Self-Determination Theory Applied to Educational Settings" in E.L Deci and R. M. Ryan (eds) *Handbook of Self-Determination Research.* Rochester, NY: University of Rochester Press. 184-203

677. Ibid.

678. Dweck, C. and Leggett, E. (1988) A social-cognitive approach to motivation and personality, *Psychological Review*, 95(2), 256–273.

679. Isaacs, B. (2010) *Bringing the Montessori Approach to your Early Years Practice* (2nd edn.) London and New York: Routledge

About the Author

Dr. Teresa Belton studied Art History at the University of East Anglia 1971-74, and during her undergraduate years was a founder member of the UEA Eco-action Group. After taking a diploma in Arts Administration at City University, she worked for two years as foyer manager at the Everyman Theatre, Liverpool, mounting exhibitions to accompany stage productions, and organising other cultural events.

While her three sons were young she was involved in developing the charity Play for Life which aimed to stimulate fresh public thinking about the kinds of free-time activities which nurture children's social, emotional, cultural and spiritual development. This led to doctoral research into the influence of television on children's story-making. Since then she worked for four years as the education officer for a rural regeneration partnership, and during the last fifteen years as a researcher in the School of Education and Lifelong Learning at the University of East Anglia, where she is now a visiting fellow.

Teresa has employed her professional social science research skills to work on this book which brings together her long-standing personal concern for the environment and her interests in individual wellbeing and the origins of attitudes, values and behaviours.

For further thoughts about the roots of and routes to wellbeing and to willingly modest material consumption, and to contribute to the discussion initiated in this book, visit www.happierpeoplehealthierplanet.com

Index

Lightning Source UK Ltd.
Milton Keynes UK
UKOW04f1901240715

255802UK00001B/45/P